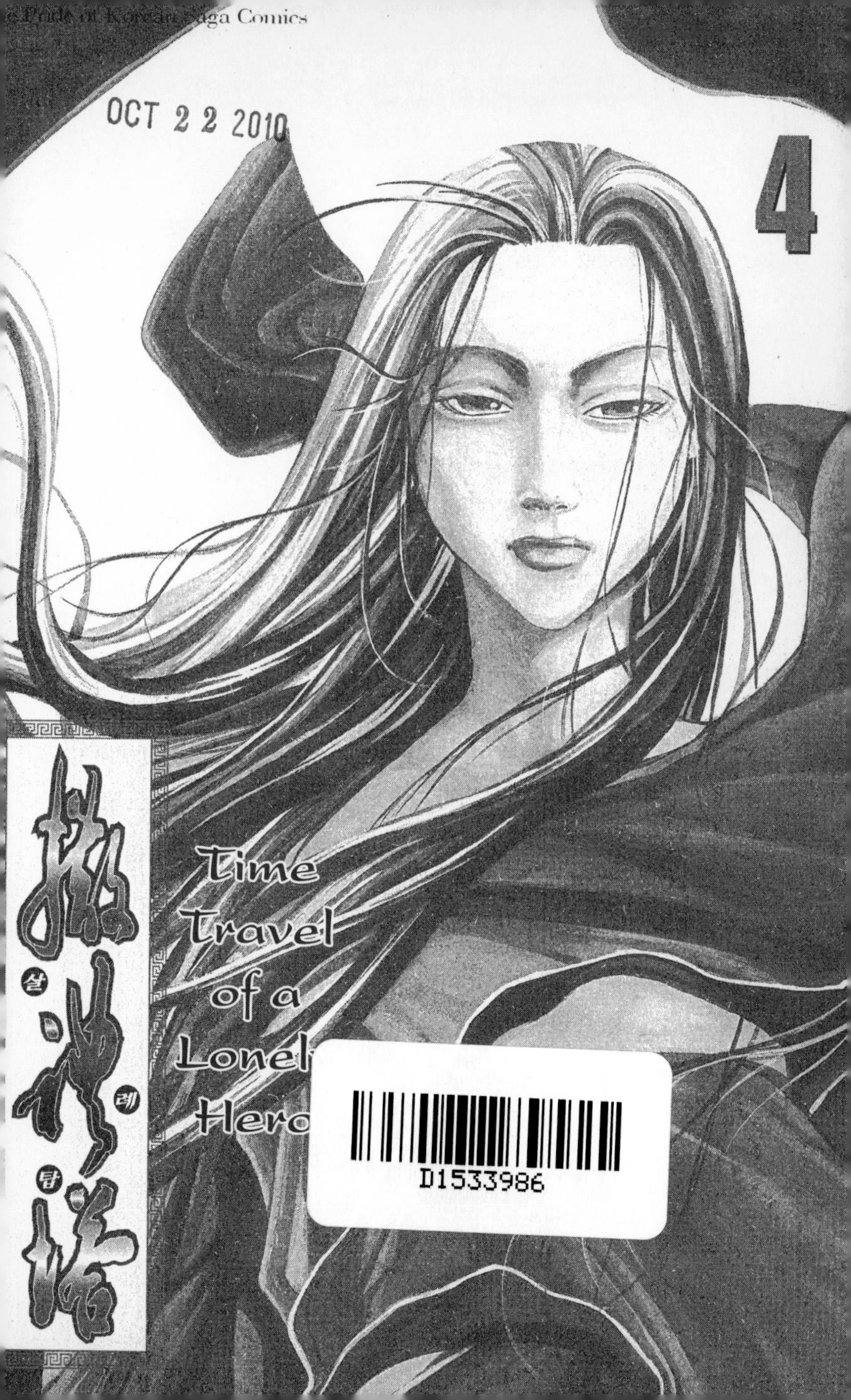
e Pride of Korean Saga Comics
4
살 레 탑
Time Travel of a Lonel Hero

# *Threads of Time Vol. 4*
## created by Mi Young Noh

Translation - Jihae Hong
English Adaptation - Brandon Montclare
Retouch and Lettering - Deron Bennet
Production Artist - James Lee
Cover Design - Kyle Plummer

Editor - Luis Reyes
Digital Imaging Manager - Chris Buford
Pre-Press Manager - Antonio DePietro
Production Managers - Jennifer Miller and Mutsumi Miyazaki
Art Director - Matt Alford
Managing Editor - Jill Freshney
VP of Production - Ron Klamert
Editor-in-Chief - Mike Kiley
President and C.O.O. - John Parker
Publisher and C.E.O. - Stuart Levy

A  Manga

TOKYOPOP Inc.
5900 Wilshire Blvd. Suite 2000
Los Angeles, CA 90036

E-mail: info@TOKYOPOP.com
Come visit us online at www.TOKYOPOP.com

ISBN: 1-59532-035-0

First TOKYOPOP printing: March 2005
10 9 8 7 6 5 4 3 2 1
Printed in the USA

# Threads of Time

撤神塔

## Volume 4

## By
## Mi Young Noh

TOKYOPOP®

HAMBURG // LONDON // LOS ANGELES // TOKYO

Threads of Time Vol. 1

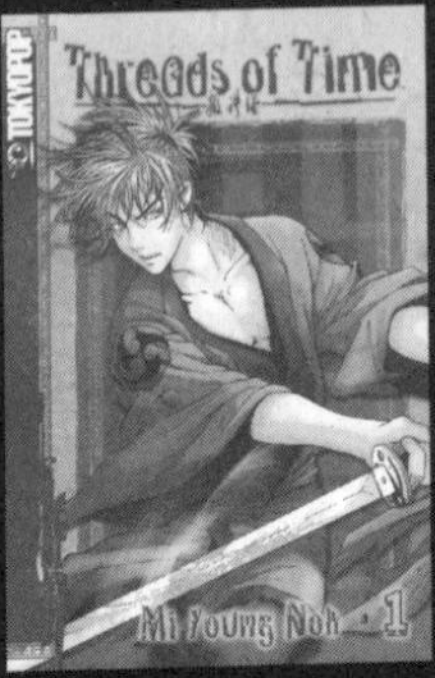
Threads of Time
TOKYOPOP
Mi Young Noh 1

High school kendo champion Moon Bin Kim suffers from a recurring nightmare in which he lives as Sa Kyung Kim, the son of a prominent warrior family in 13th Century Korea (Koryo). After a freak accident at the school swimming pool Moon Bin falls into a coma, but his modern-day personality resurfaces in the distant past as Sa Kyung revives miraculously after years of unconsciousness. As if being displaced in medieval Koryo isn't enough, Moon Bin finds himself at the very brink of war. From his deathbed Genghis Kahn decreed that Koryo should be conquered. Sali Tayi, the most brutal and feared general of the Mongol army, is appointed to lead the invasion into the peninsula. Opposing him is Moon Bin's 13th Century father, the legendary warlord Kim Kyung-Sohn.

Threads of Time Vol. 2

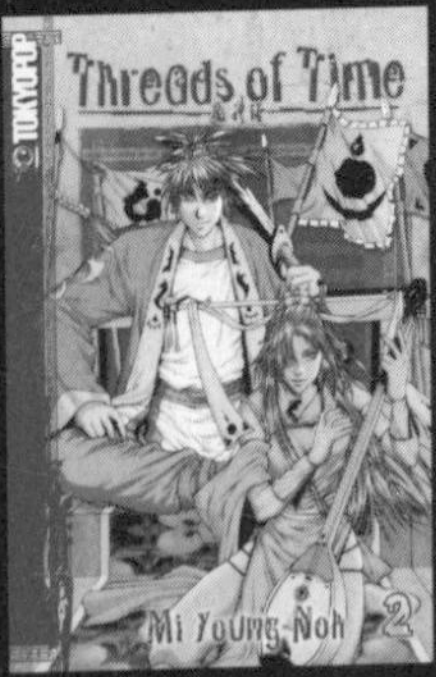
Threads of Time
TOKYOPOP
Mi Young Noh 2

Using her clever wiles and substantial might, the stunning granddaughter of Genghis Kahn, Atan Hadas, is made second-in-command to the ruthless Sali Tayi. Her first mission is to be sent into the heart of Koryo to gather intelligence on the defensive forces. In the woods near Ghu-Zhu Palace, Moon Bin happens upon the princess while she is bathing in a waterfall, and is smitten immediately by her beauty. At the same time, Kim Kyung-Sohn discovers the true identity of Atan Hadas, and orders her arrest. Unaware that she is a princess and a spy of the enemy, the impetuous Moon Bin helps her escape capture. Returning to Sali Tayi, Atan Hadas learns that a full-scale invasion of Koryo has begun.

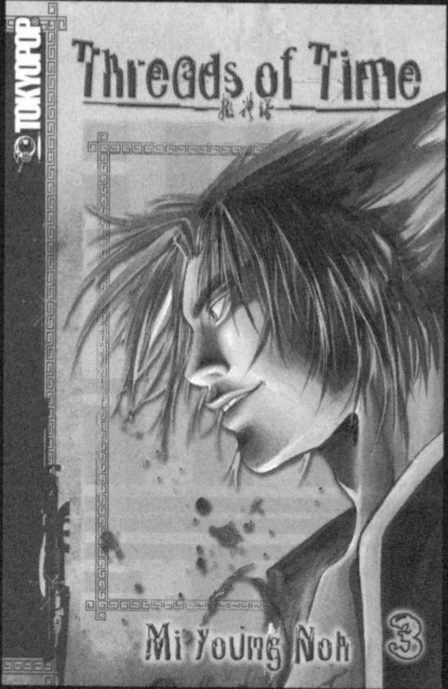
TOKYOPOP
Threads of Time
Mi Young Noh
3

Threads of Time Vol. 3

As the Mongol hordes prepare for war, Moon Bin continues to adapt to his new existence in medieval Koryo. He recognizes that many of the people around him are different versions of his friends and acquaintances from the 20th Century. The mystery of Moon Bin's displacement in time deepens as puzzling visions from the modern world bleed into the past.

Meanwhile, the Mongol army ravages the northern towns and outposts of the land. With their howling warcries, the invaders cut a bloody swath toward Ghu-Zhu Palace, the stronghold of Koryo's defense. General Sali Tayi offers Koryo an ultimatum: surrender to the devastating ferocity of the Mongol army of go to war with it. With his valor unmoved by the Mongol's threats, Kim Kyung-Sohn upholds a remarkable resistance. Despite facing overwhelming enemy forces, the Koryo palace weathers the storm of a vicious Mongol siege. In a climactic battle, Kim Kyung-Sohn leads a battered collection of twelve soldiers on a desperate mission against Sali Tayi and a force of over a hundred Mongol warriors. On the field of battle, the two commanders engage one another in personal combat, and Kim Kyung-Sohn astonishingly perseveres—keeping the hopes of a successful resistance alive for one more day. Having had both himself and his pride injured, Sali Tayi vows to deliver death to not only Kim Kyung-Sohn, but to his entire family as well...

# contents

Threads of Time

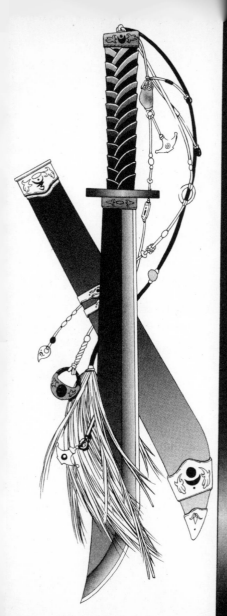

# Chapter 14
## Pillage

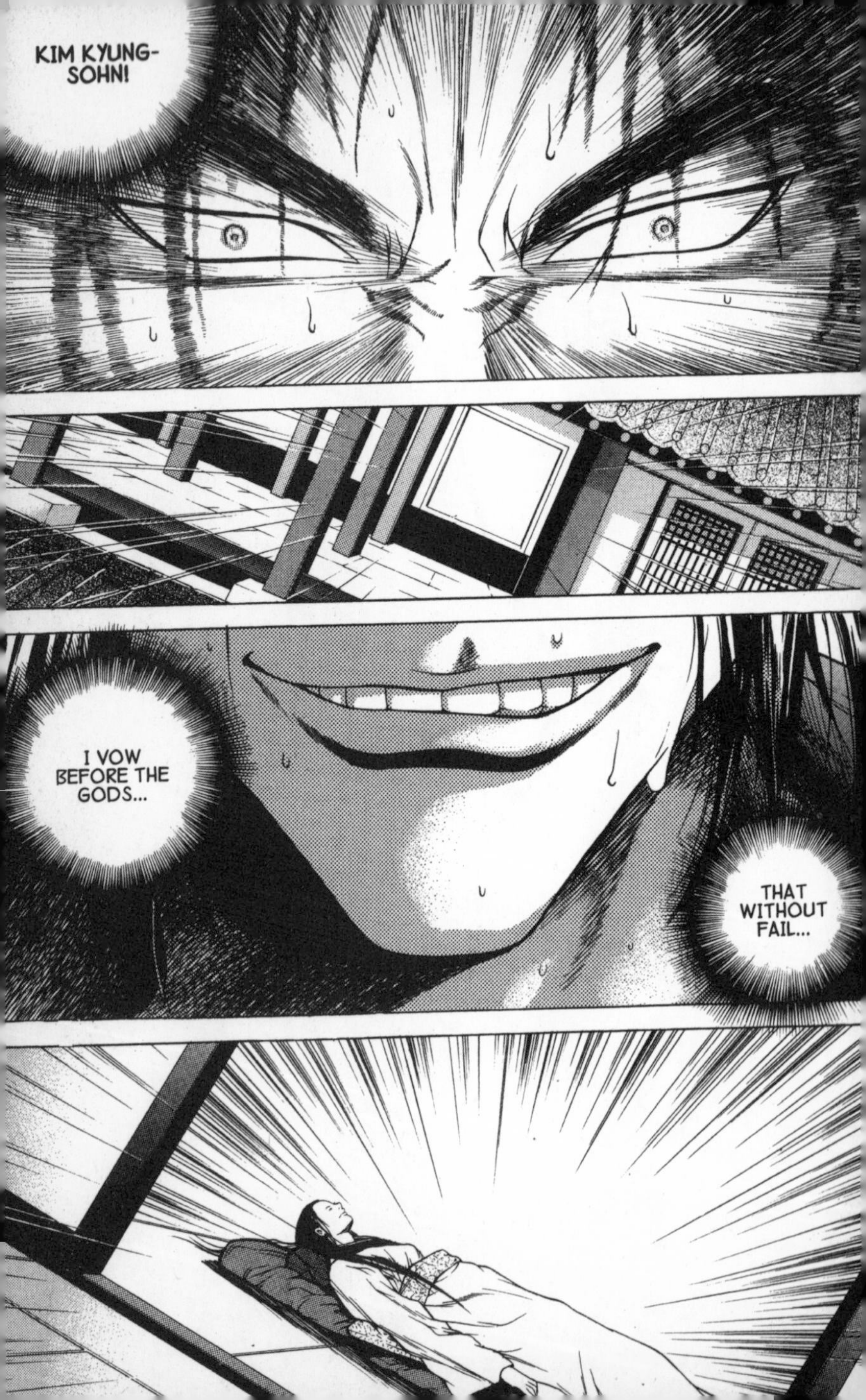
KIM KYUNG-SOHN!
I VOW BEFORE THE GODS...
THAT WITHOUT FAIL...

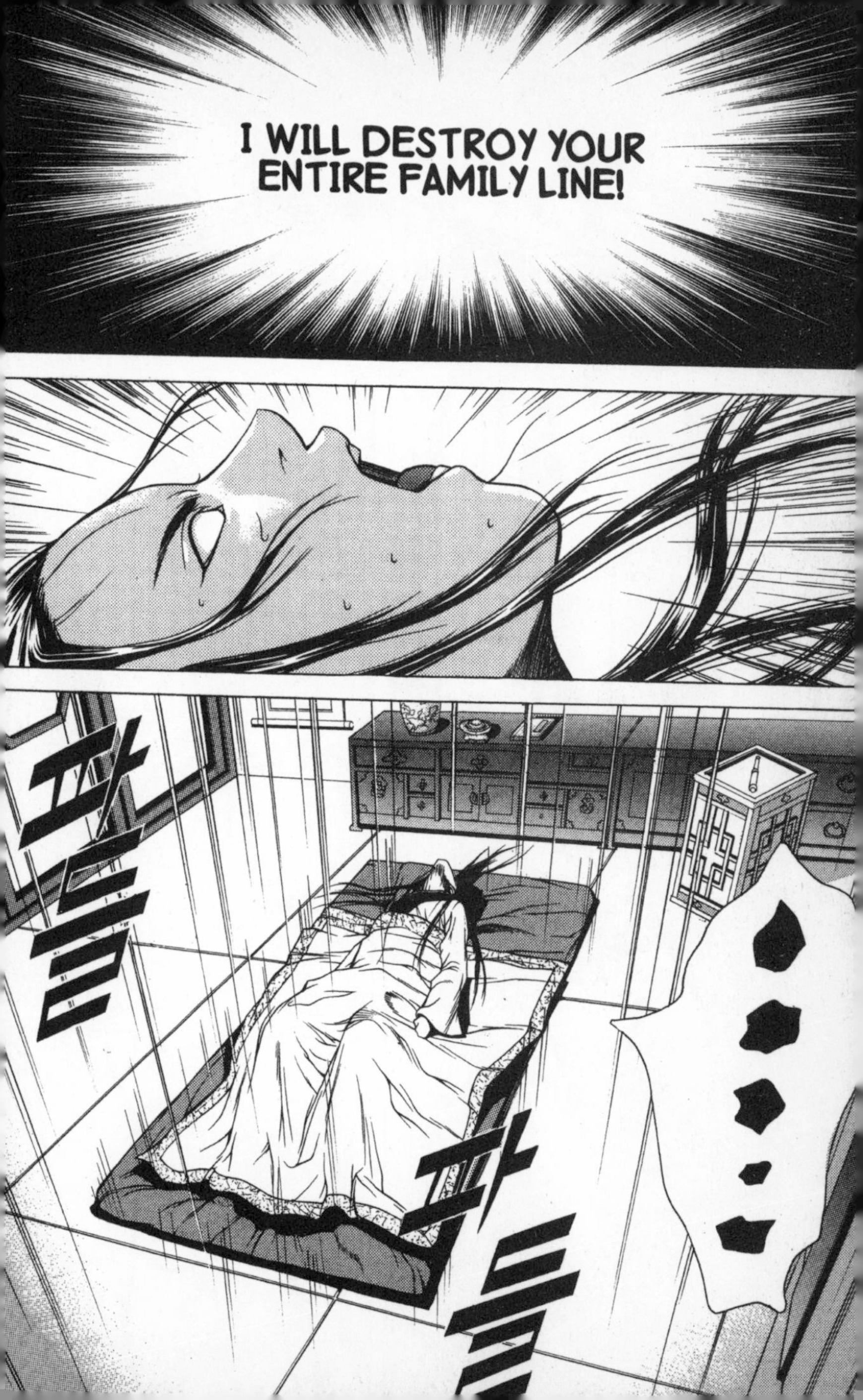
I WILL DESTROY YOUR ENTIRE FAMILY LINE!

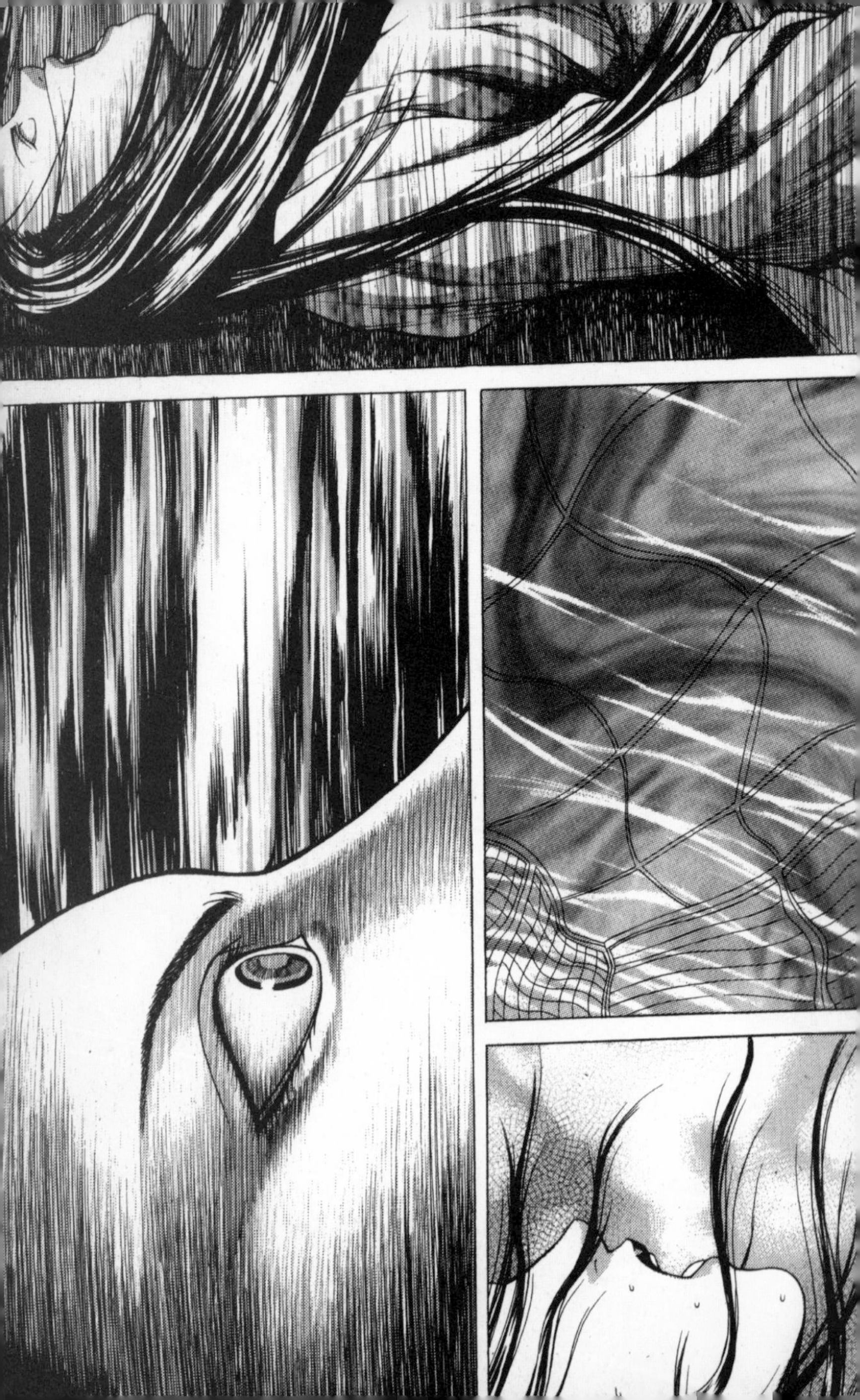

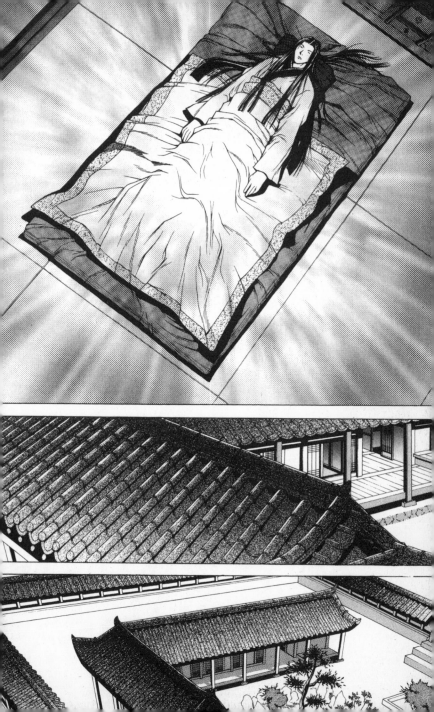

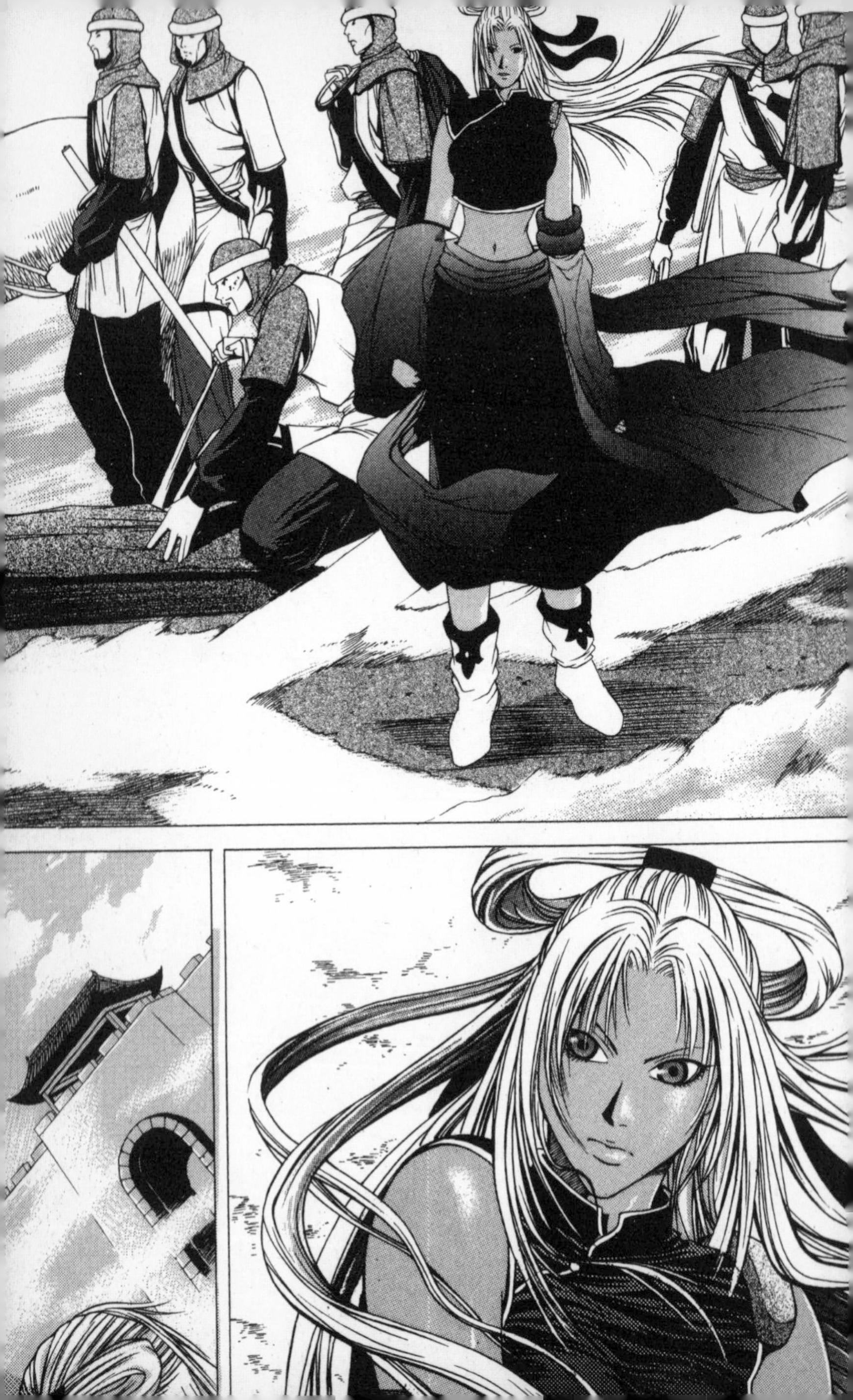

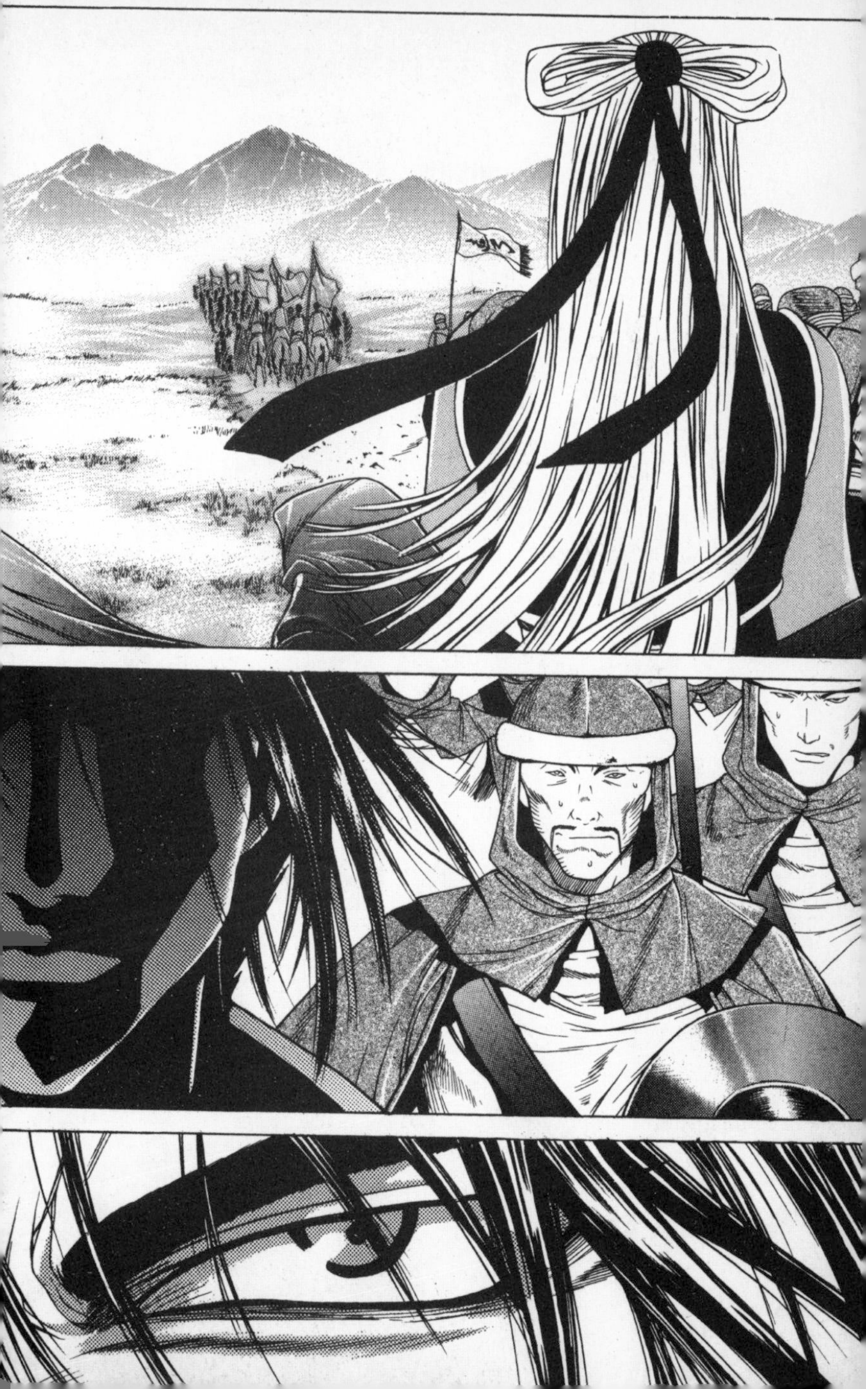

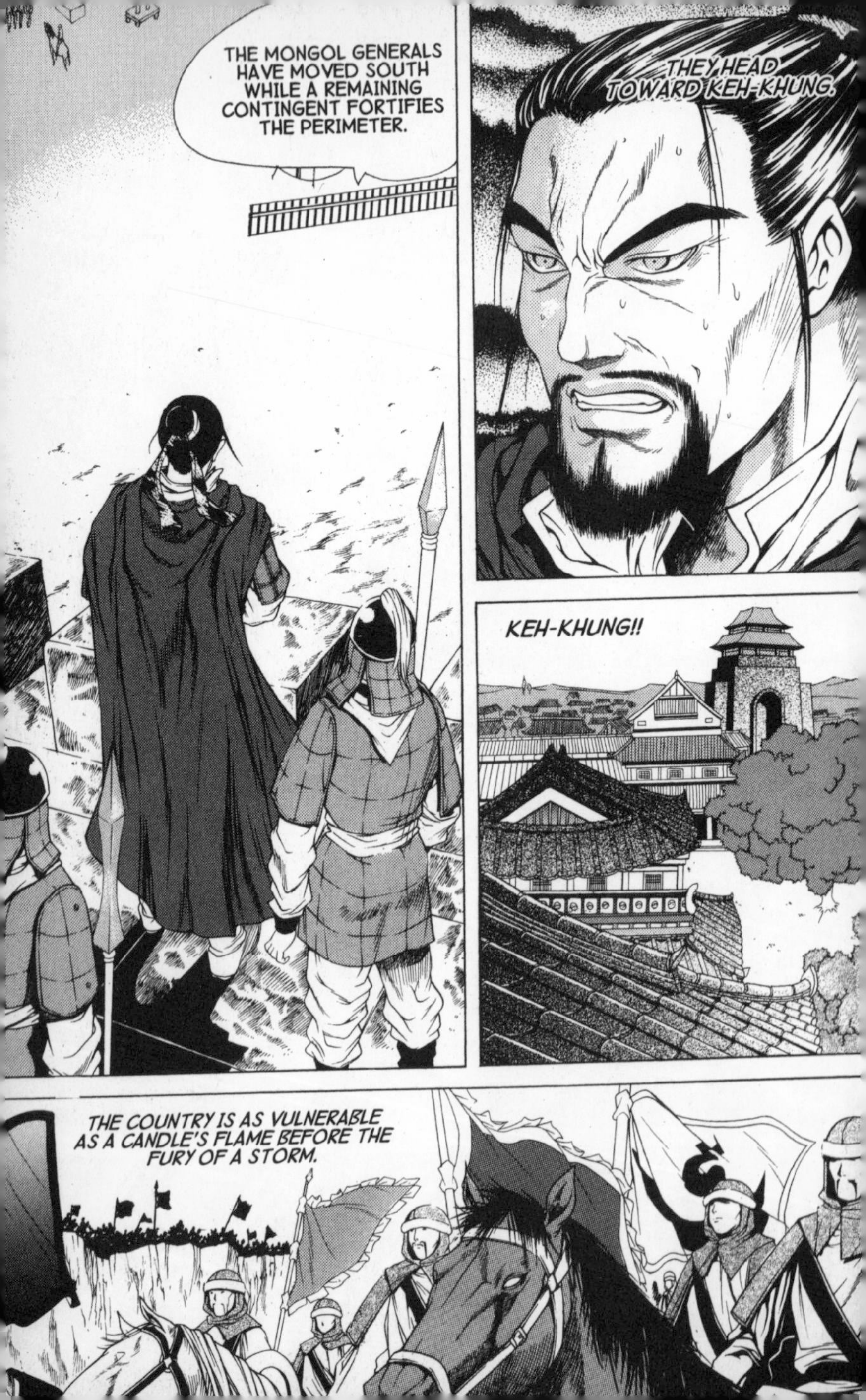
THE MONGOL GENERALS HAVE MOVED SOUTH WHILE A REMAINING CONTINGENT FORTIFIES THE PERIMETER.
THEY HEAD TOWARD KEH-KHUNG.
KEH-KHUNG!!
THE COUNTRY IS AS VULNERABLE AS A CANDLE'S FLAME BEFORE THE FURY OF A STORM.

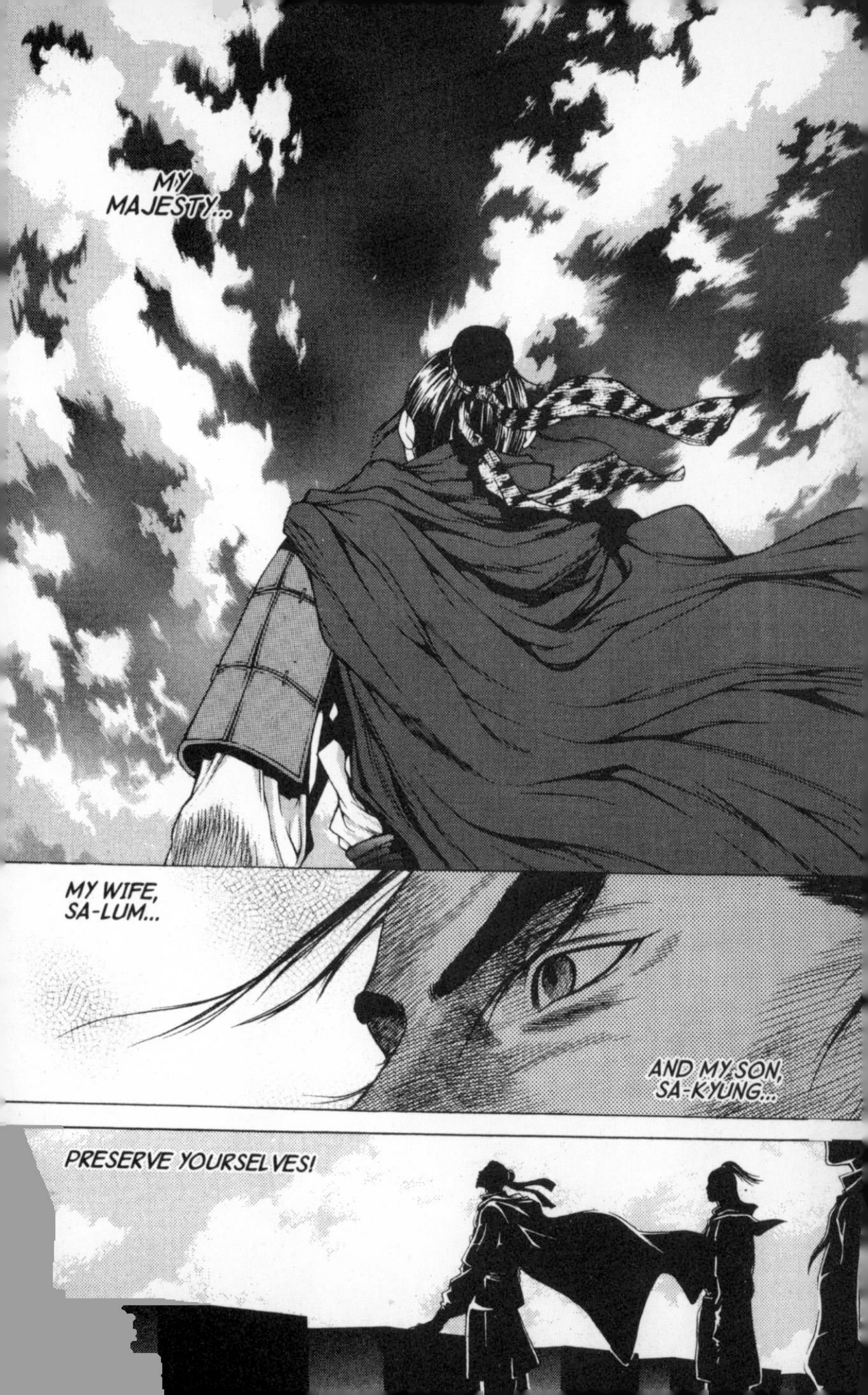
MY MAJESTY...
MY WIFE, SA-LUM...
AND MY SON, SA-KYUNG...
PRESERVE YOURSELVES!

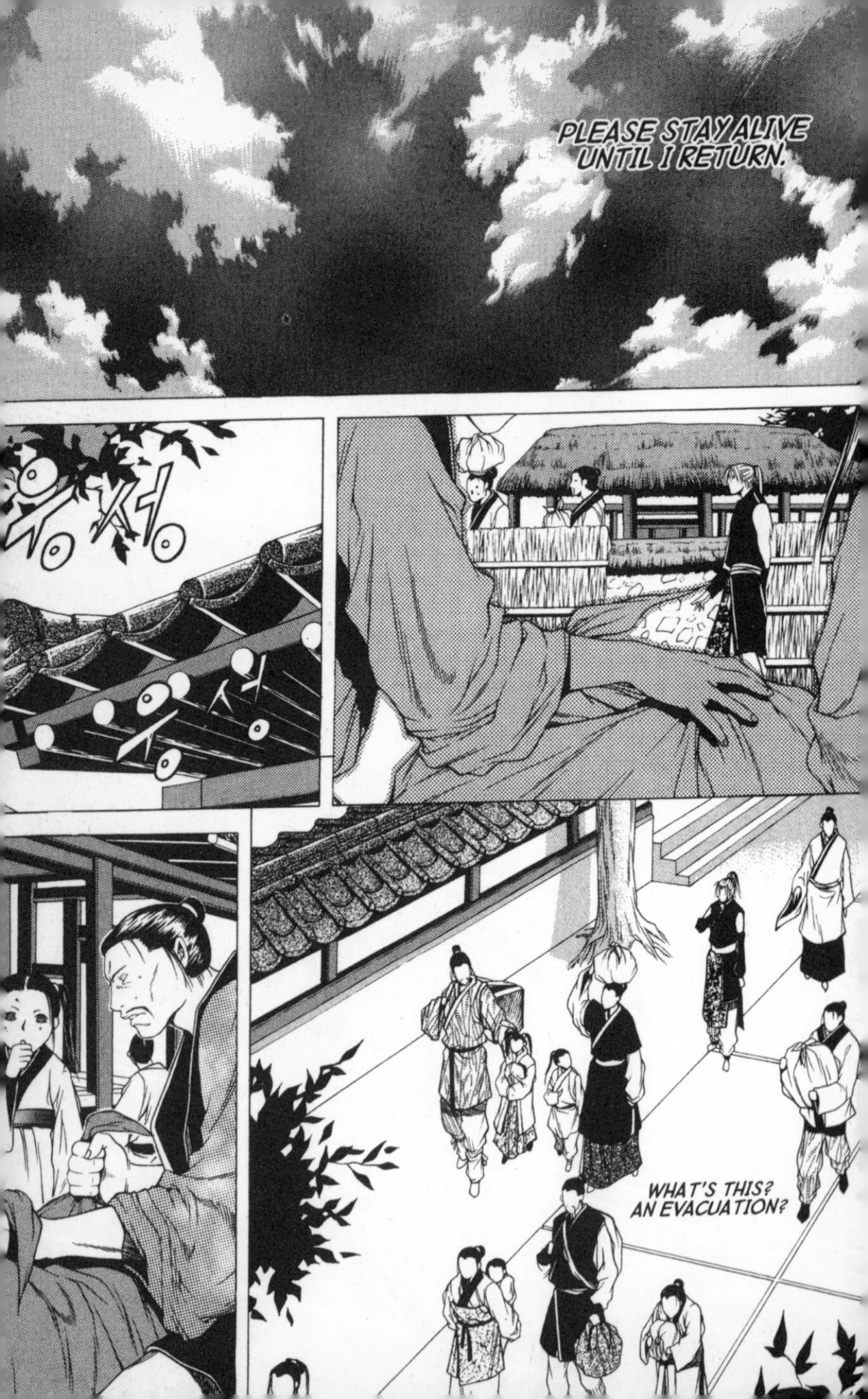
PLEASE STAY ALIVE UNTIL I RETURN.
WHAT'S THIS? AN EVACUATION?

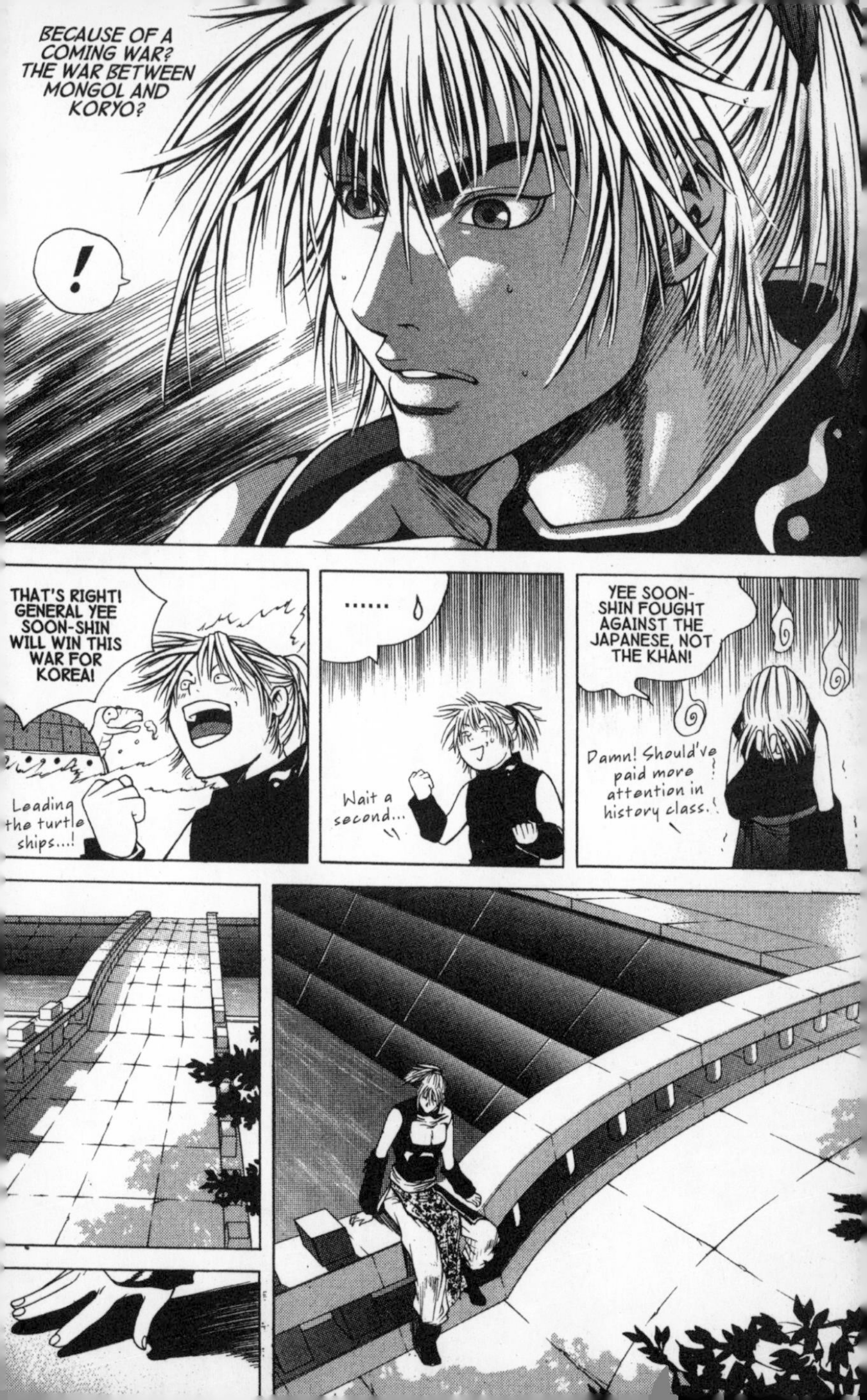
BECAUSE OF A COMING WAR? THE WAR BETWEEN MONGOL AND KORYO?
!
THAT'S RIGHT! GENERAL YEE SOON-SHIN WILL WIN THIS WAR FOR KOREA!
Leading the turtle ships...!
......
Wait a second...
YEE SOON-SHIN FOUGHT AGAINST THE JAPANESE, NOT THE KHAN!
Damn! Should've paid more attention in history class.

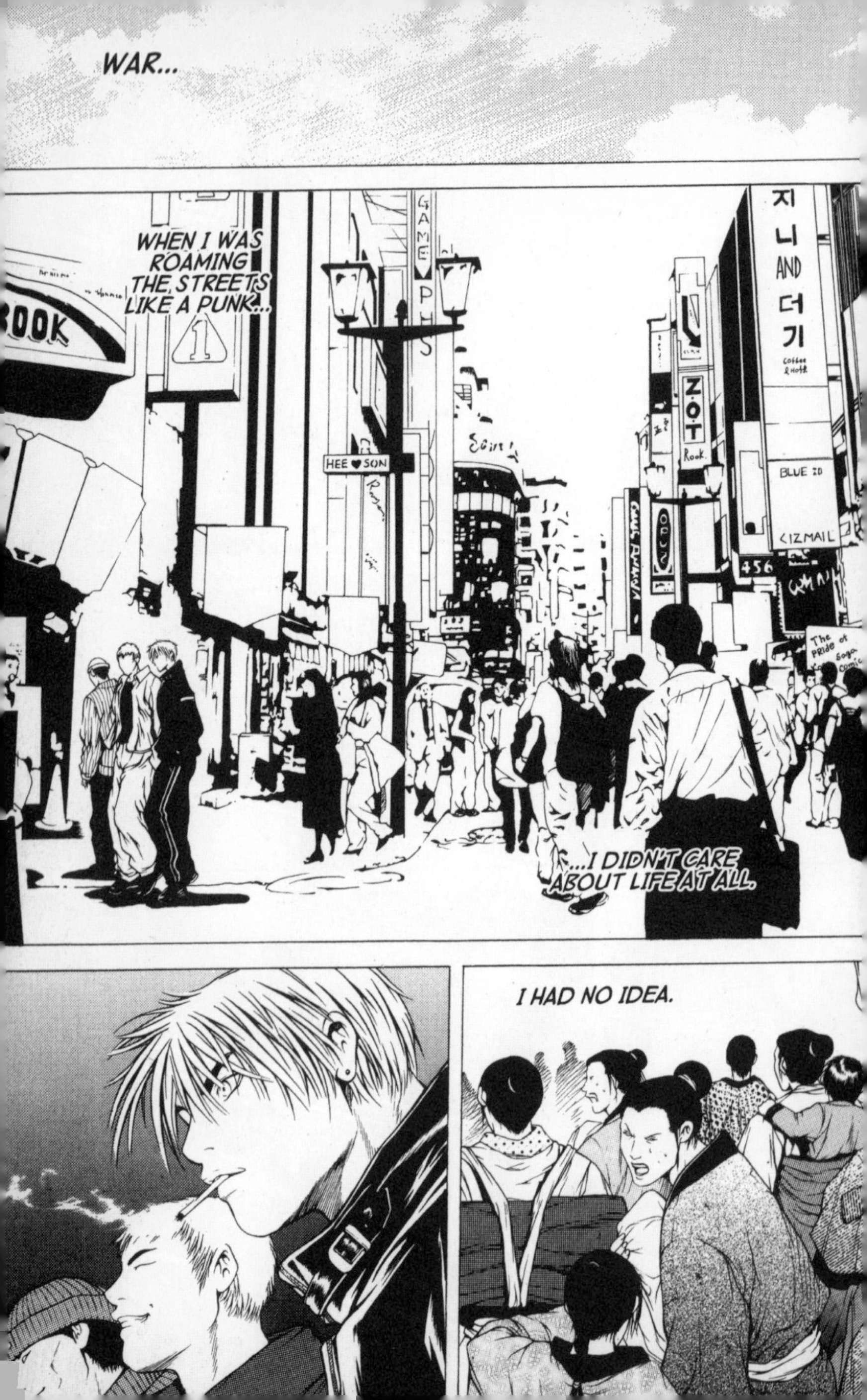
WAR...
WHEN I WAS ROAMING THE STREETS LIKE A PUNK...
BOOK
1
GAME PHS
HEE SON
지니 AND 더기
ZOT
BLUE
456
...I DIDN'T CARE ABOUT LIFE AT ALL.
I HAD NO IDEA.

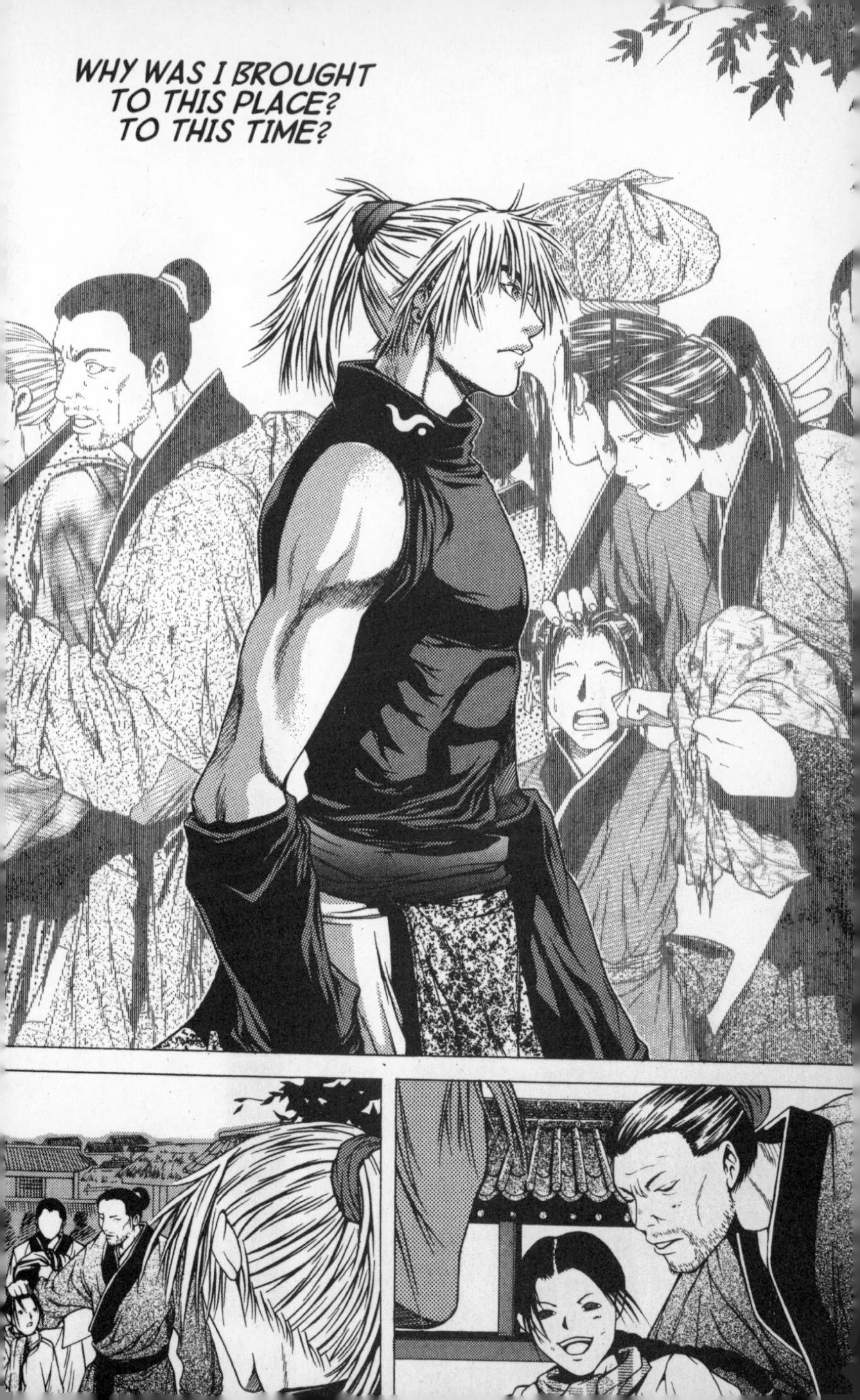
WHY WAS I BROUGHT
TO THIS PLACE?
TO THIS TIME?

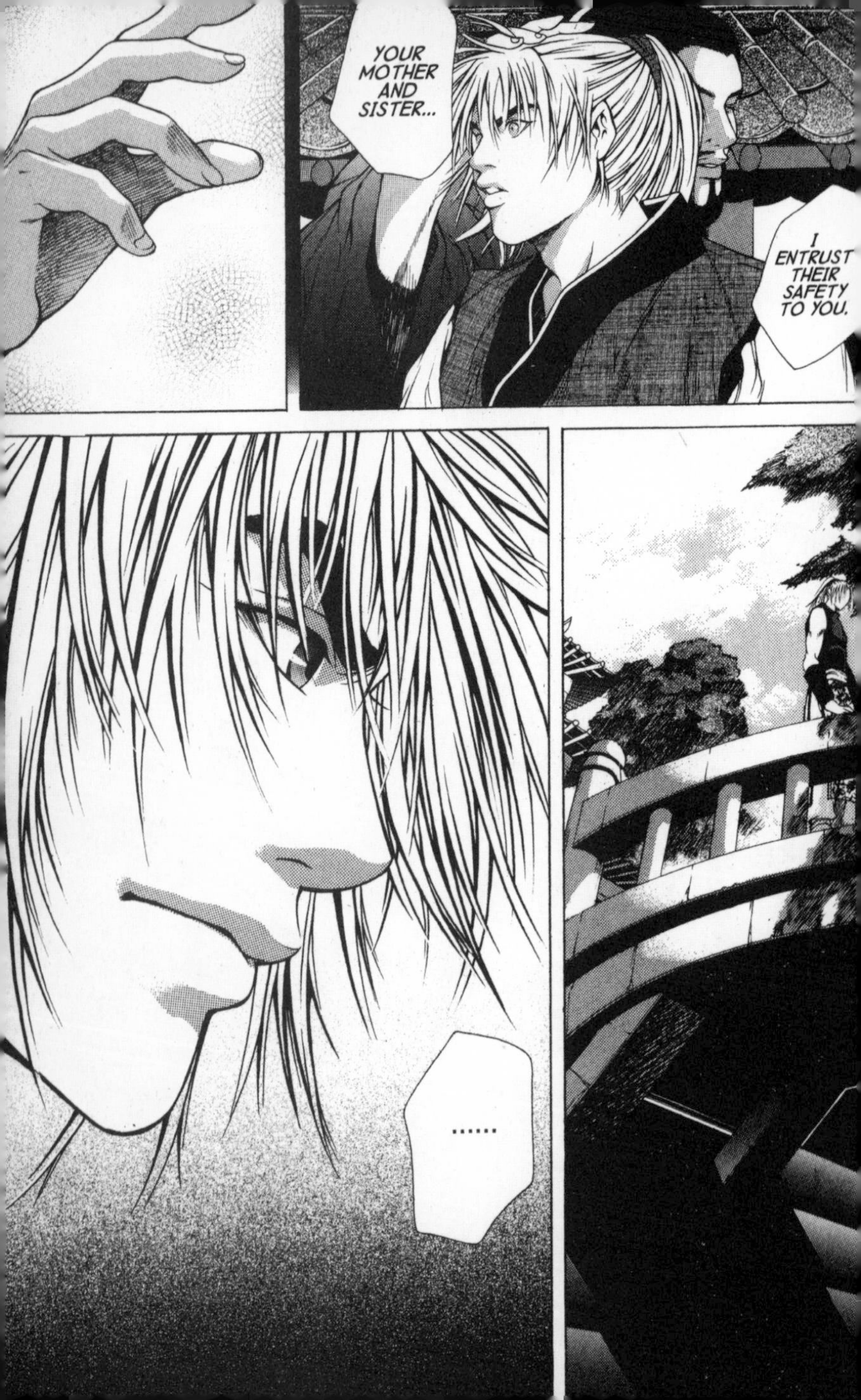
YOUR MOTHER AND SISTER...
I ENTRUST THEIR SAFETY TO YOU.
......

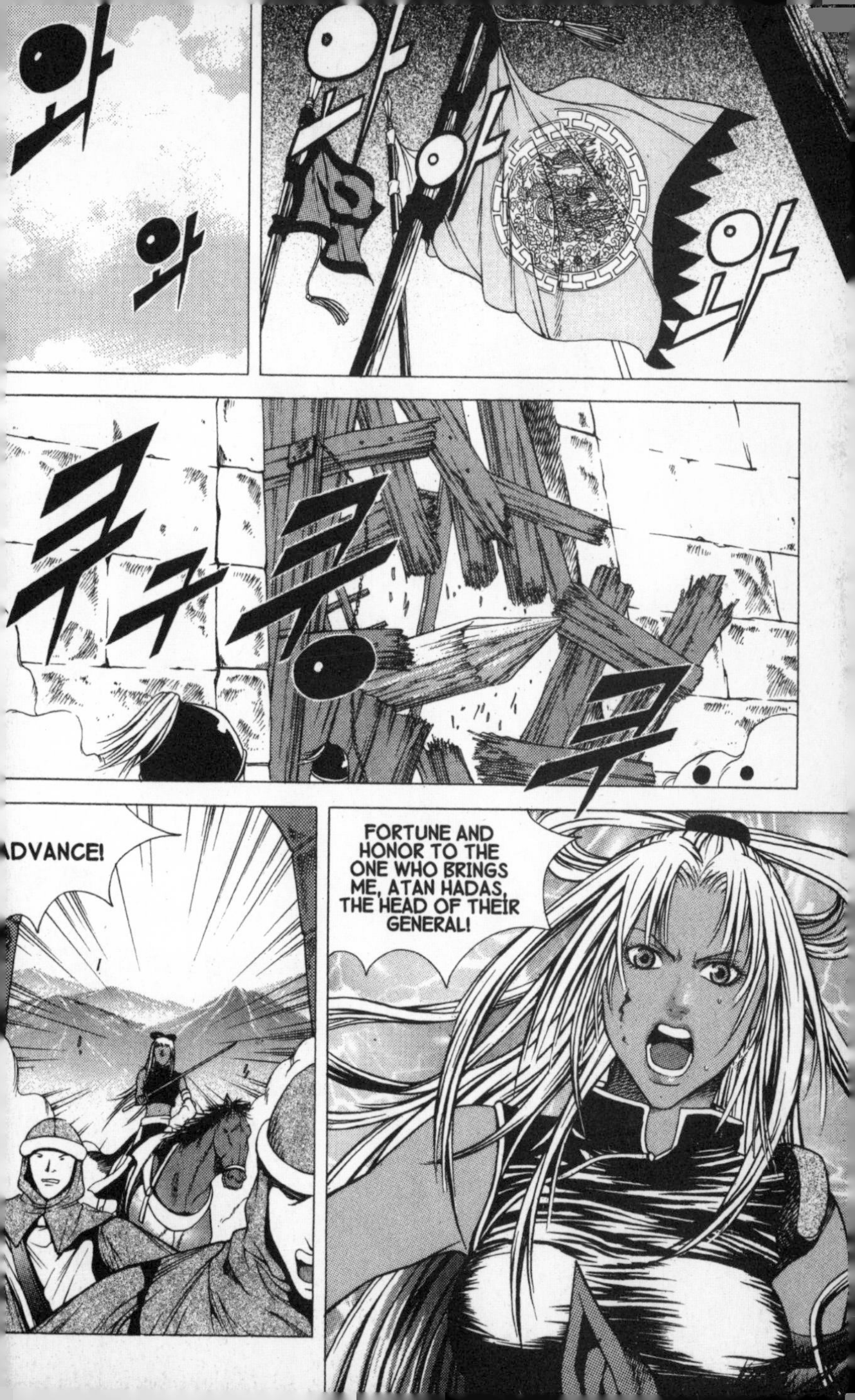
와
와
ADVANCE!
FORTUNE AND HONOR TO THE ONE WHO BRINGS ME, ATAN HADAS, THE HEAD OF THEIR GENERAL!

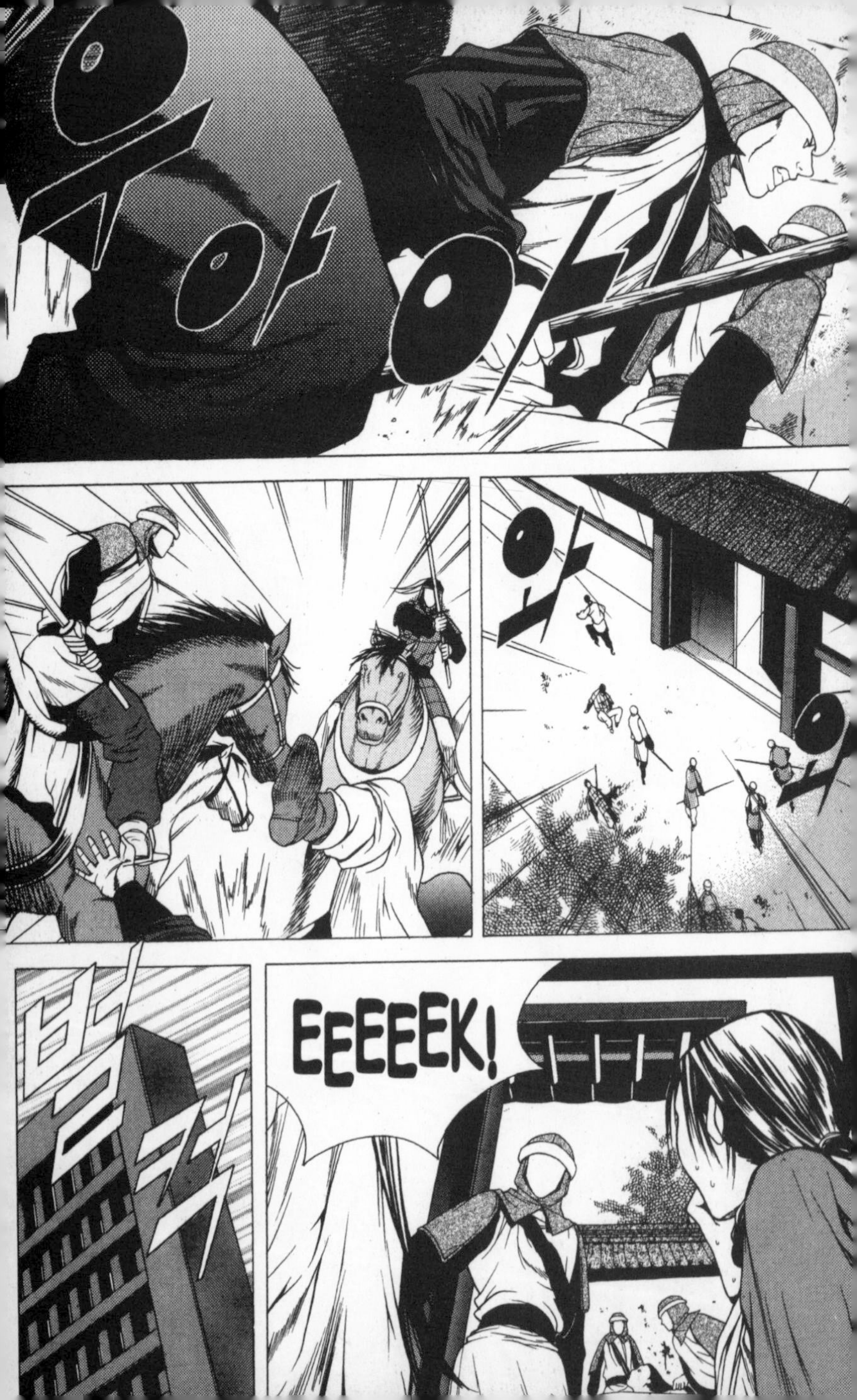
EEEEEK!

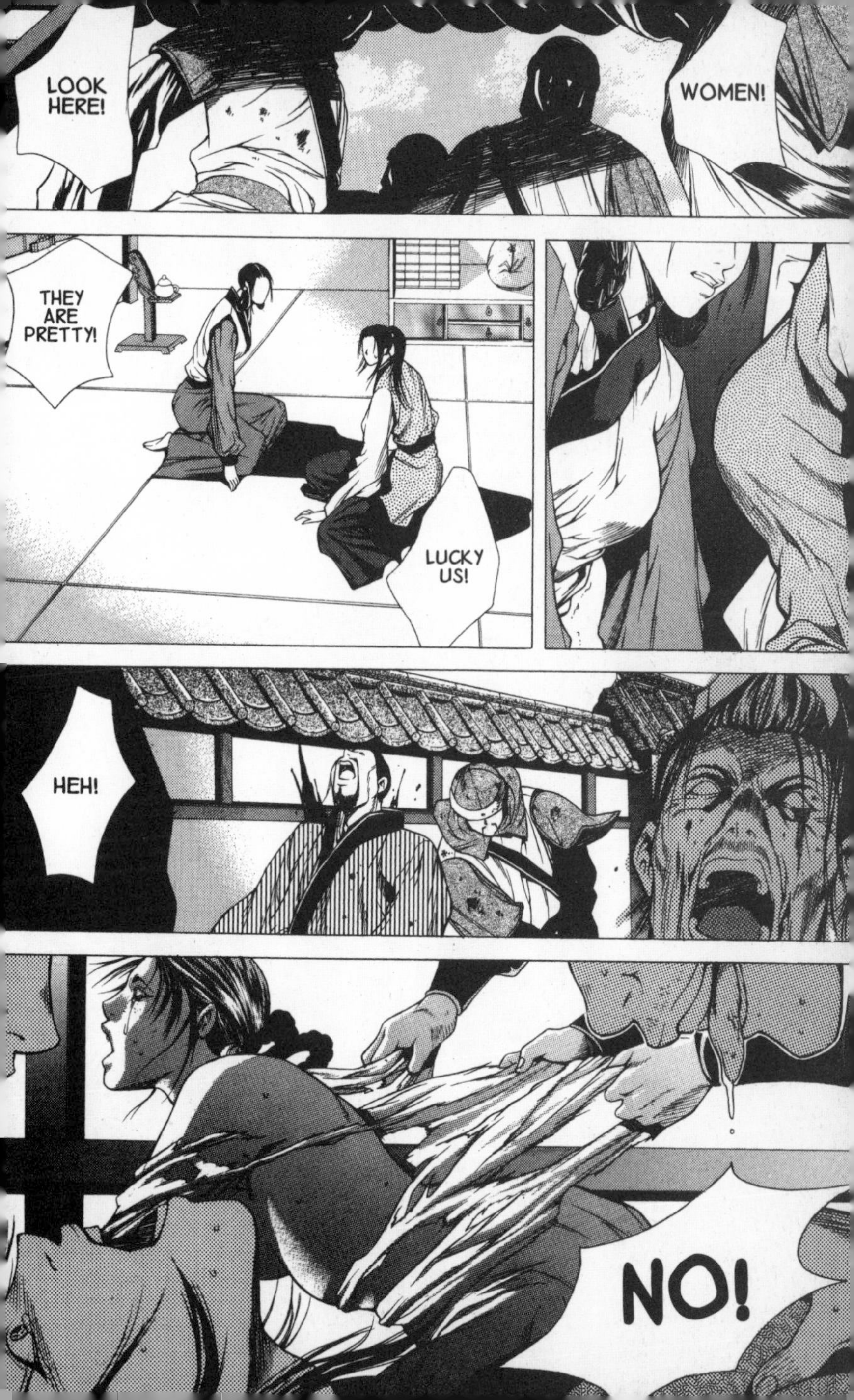
LOOK HERE!
WOMEN!
THEY ARE PRETTY!
LUCKY US!
HEH!
NO!

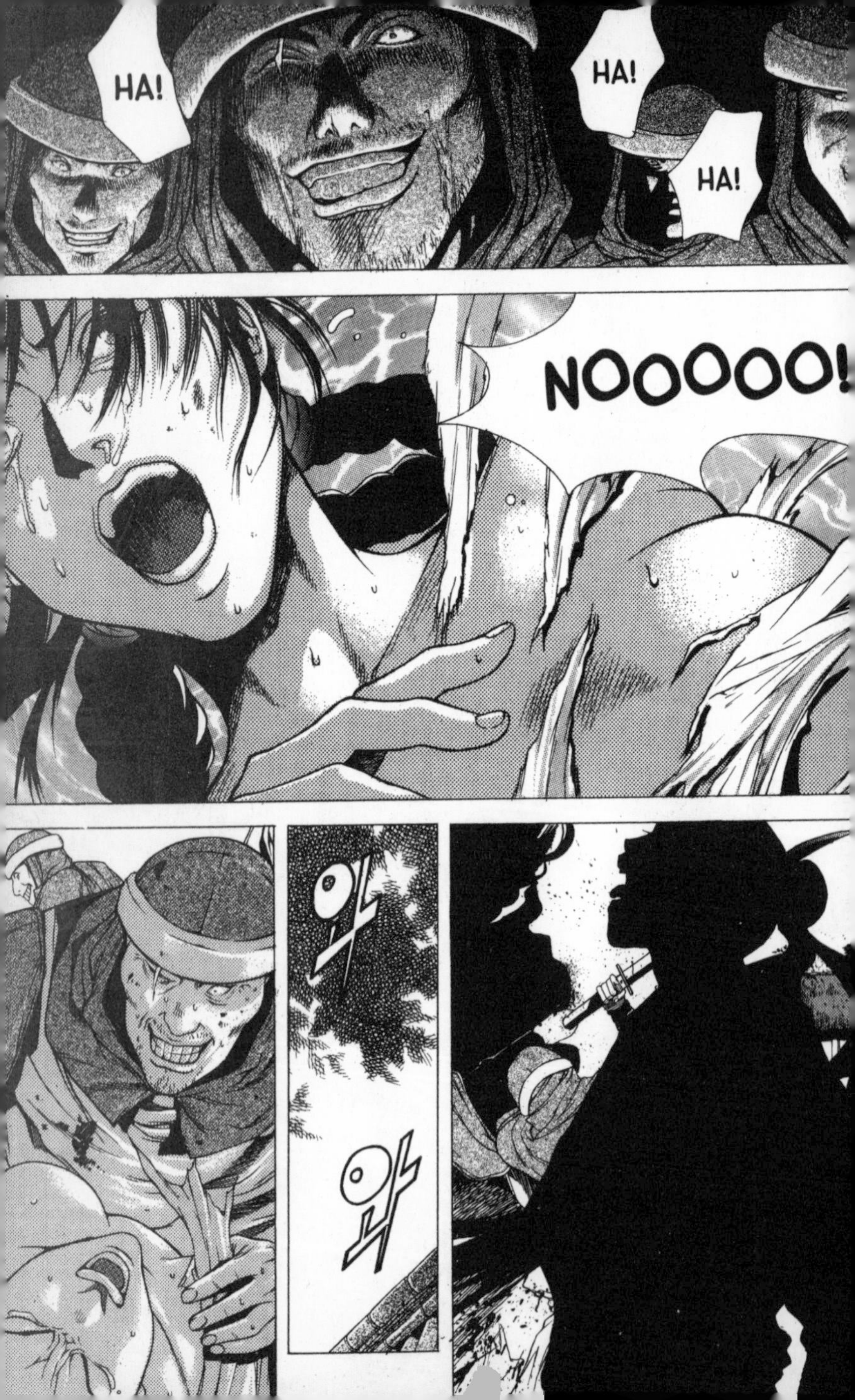
HA!
HA!
HA!
NOOOOO!

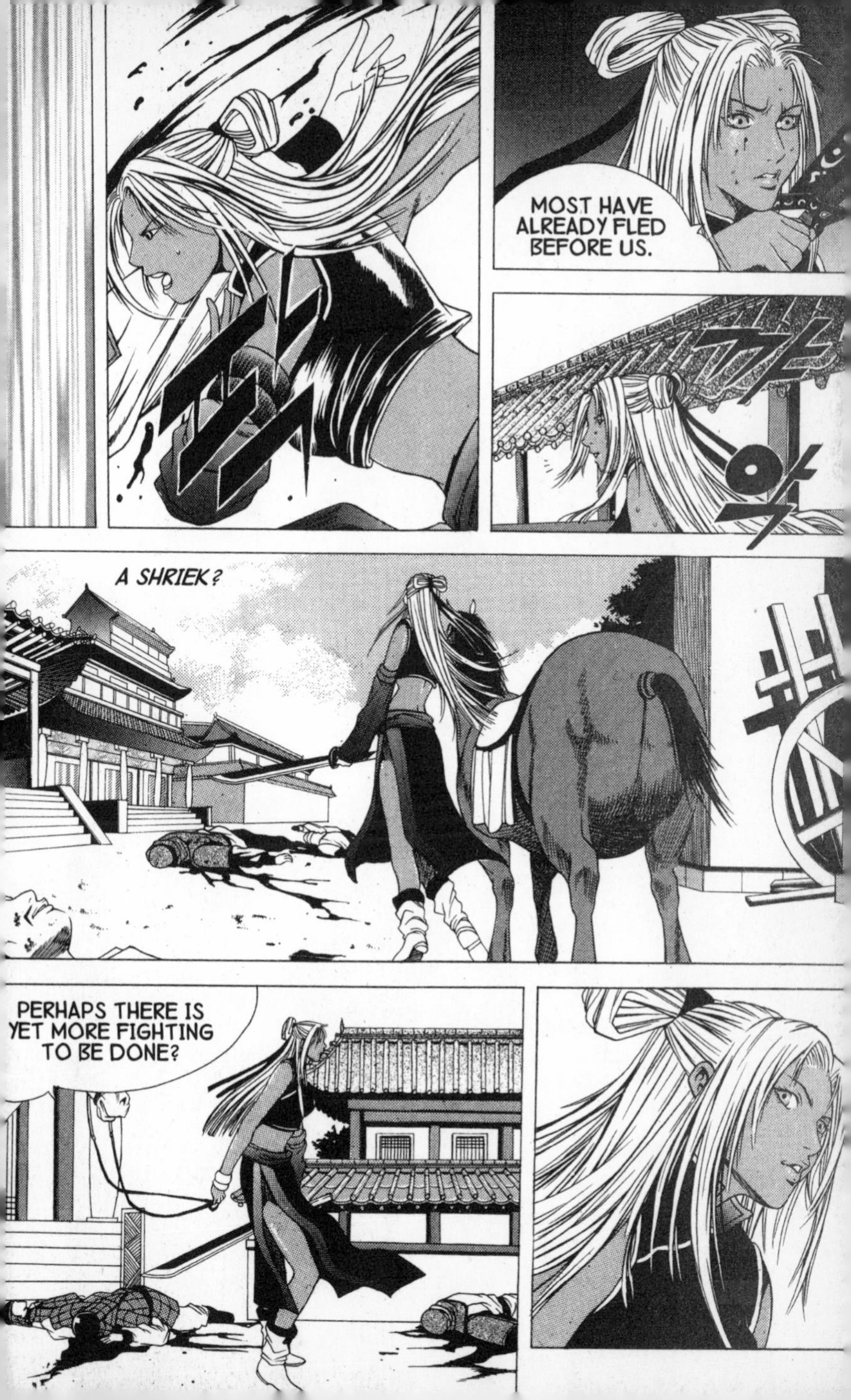
MOST HAVE ALREADY FLED BEFORE US.
A SHRIEK?
PERHAPS THERE IS YET MORE FIGHTING TO BE DONE?

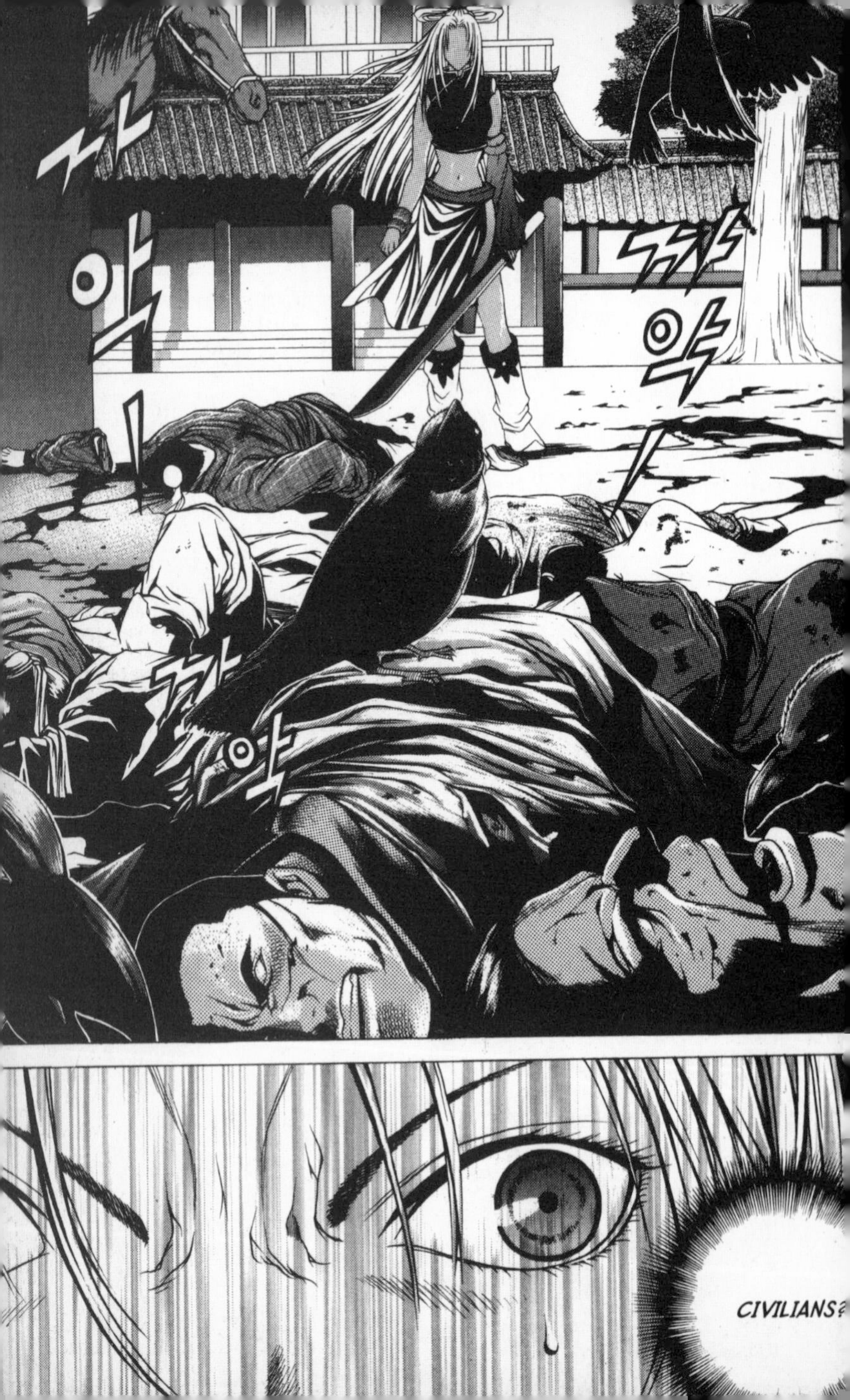
CIVILIANS?

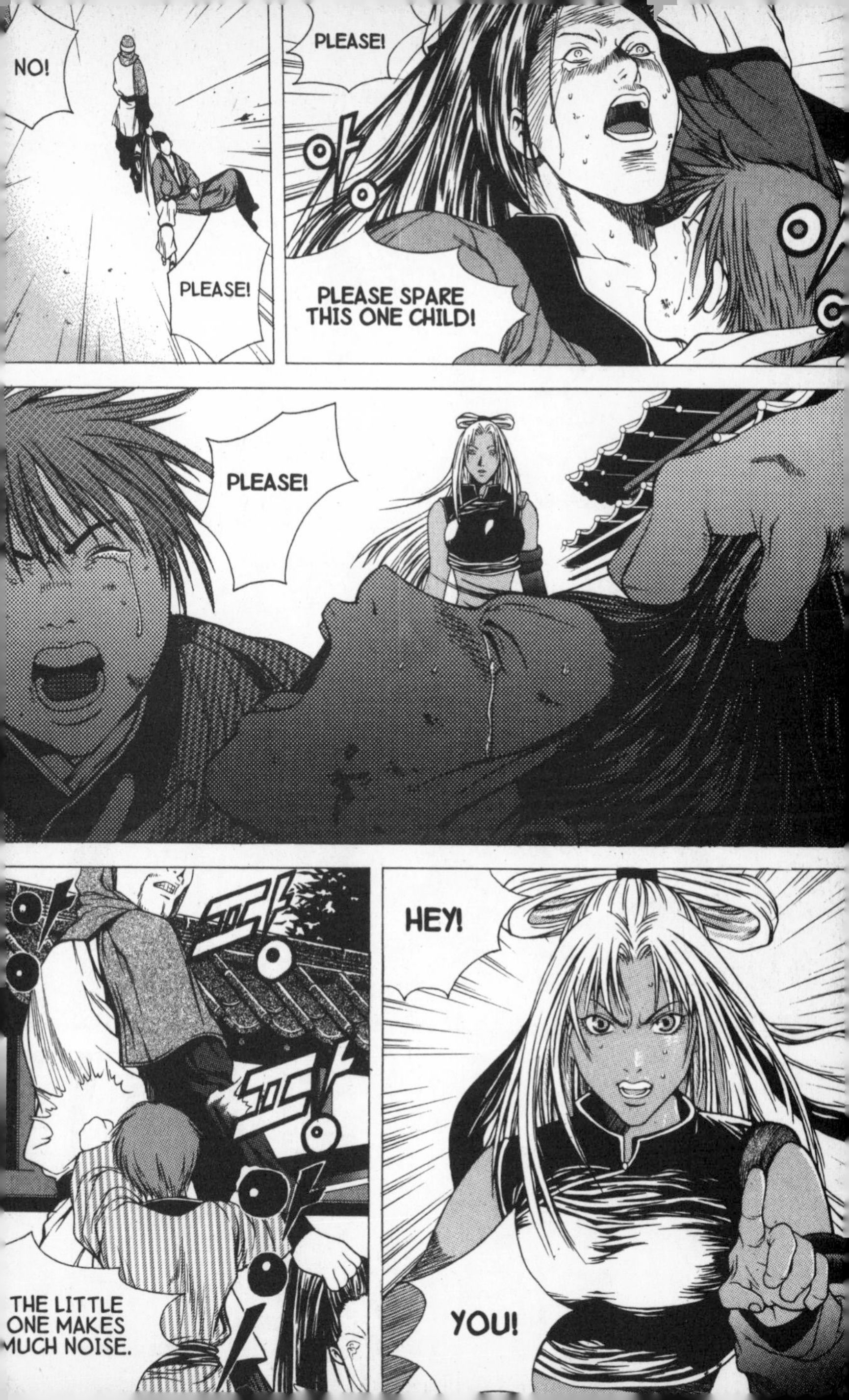
NO!
PLEASE!
PLEASE!
PLEASE SPARE THIS ONE CHILD!
PLEASE!
THE LITTLE ONE MAKES MUCH NOISE.
HEY!
YOU!

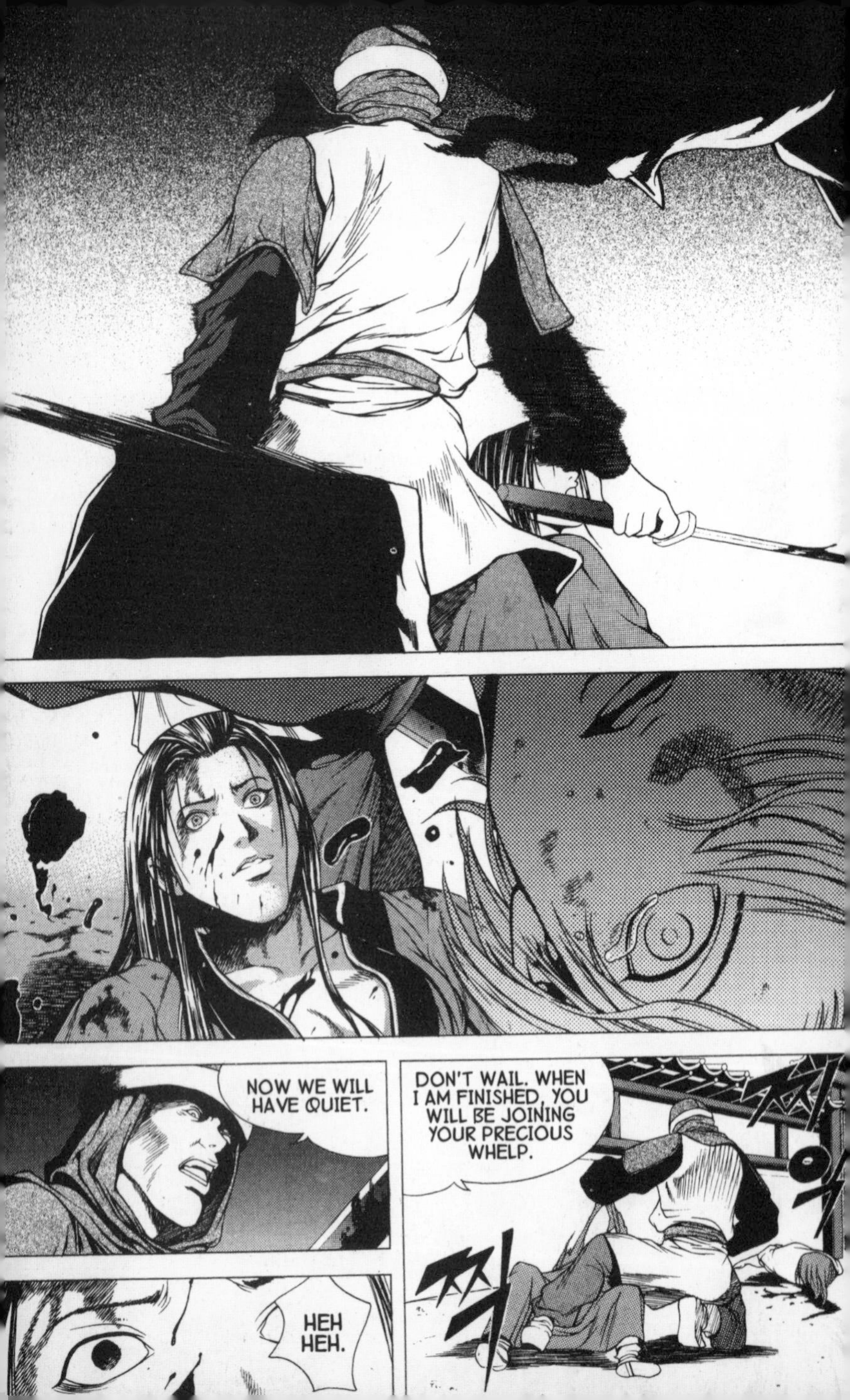
NOW WE WILL HAVE QUIET.
HEH HEH.
DON'T WAIL. WHEN I AM FINISHED, YOU WILL BE JOINING YOUR PRECIOUS WHELP.

pant...

pant...

pant

pant...

pant...

pant

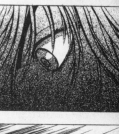

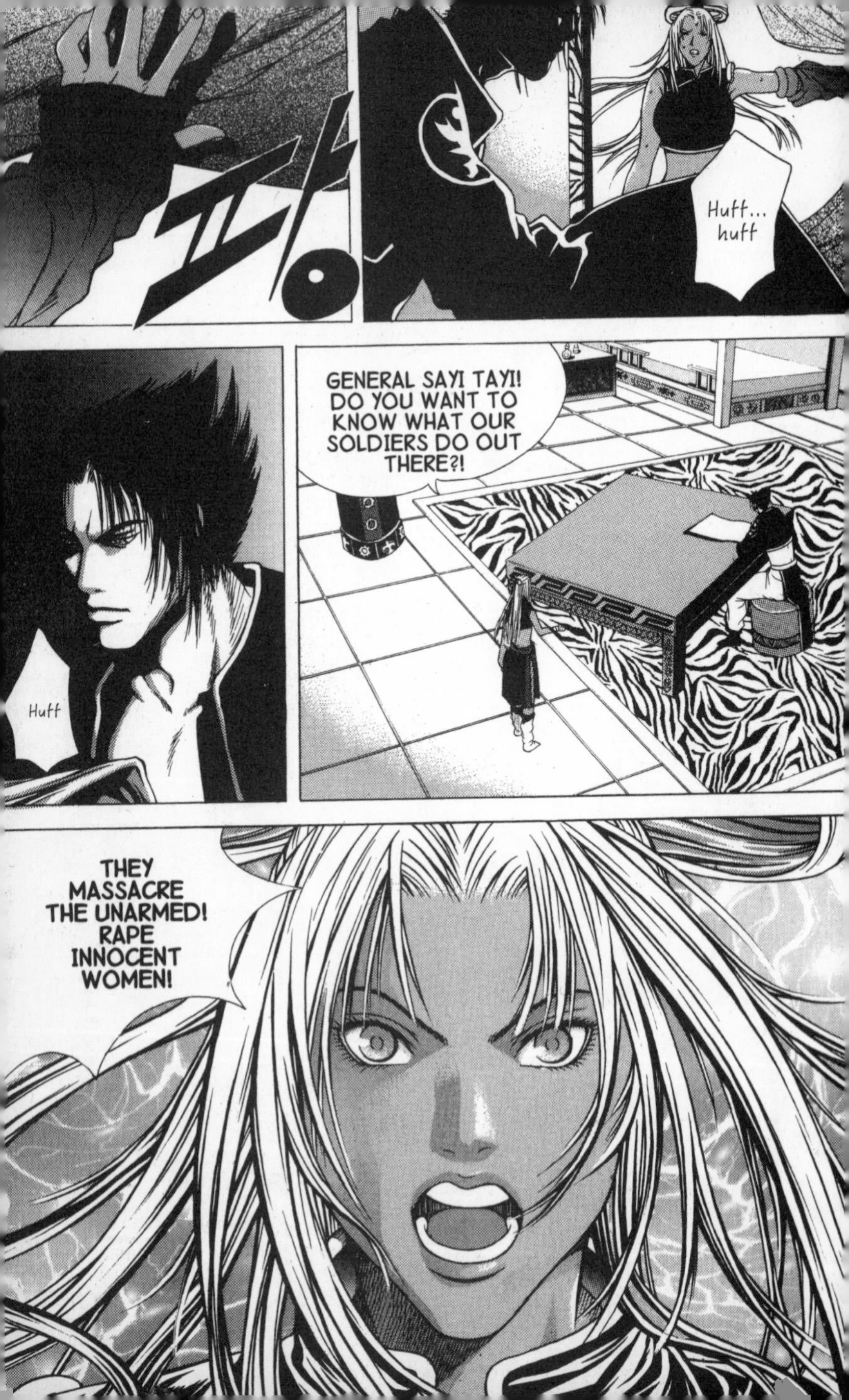
Huff...
huff
Huff
GENERAL SAYI TAYI! DO YOU WANT TO KNOW WHAT OUR SOLDIERS DO OUT THERE?!
THEY MASSACRE THE UNARMED! RAPE INNOCENT WOMEN!

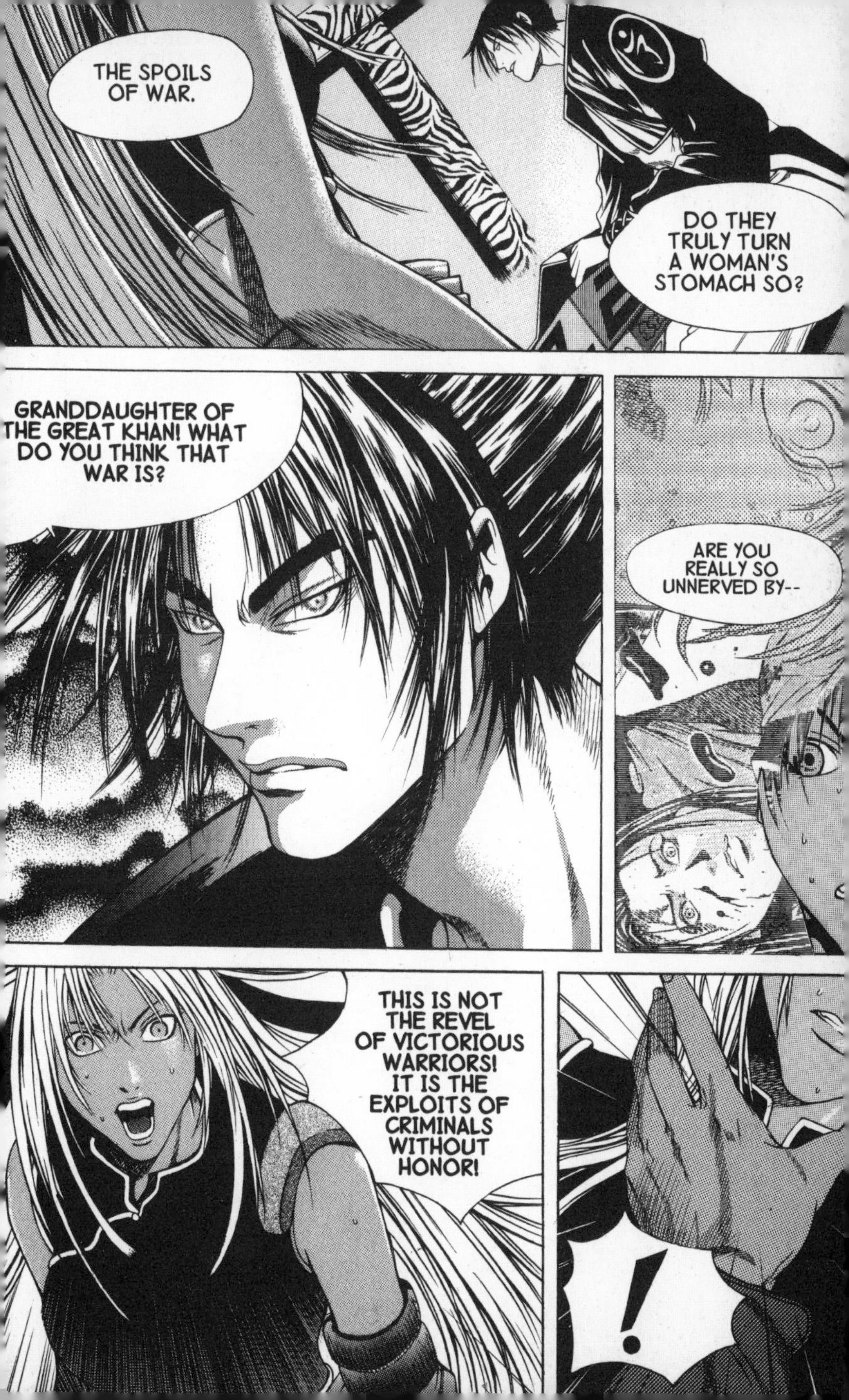
THE SPOILS OF WAR.
DO THEY TRULY TURN A WOMAN'S STOMACH SO?
GRANDDAUGHTER OF THE GREAT KHAN! WHAT DO YOU THINK THAT WAR IS?
ARE YOU REALLY SO UNNERVED BY--
THIS IS NOT THE REVEL OF VICTORIOUS WARRIORS! IT IS THE EXPLOITS OF CRIMINALS WITHOUT HONOR!
!

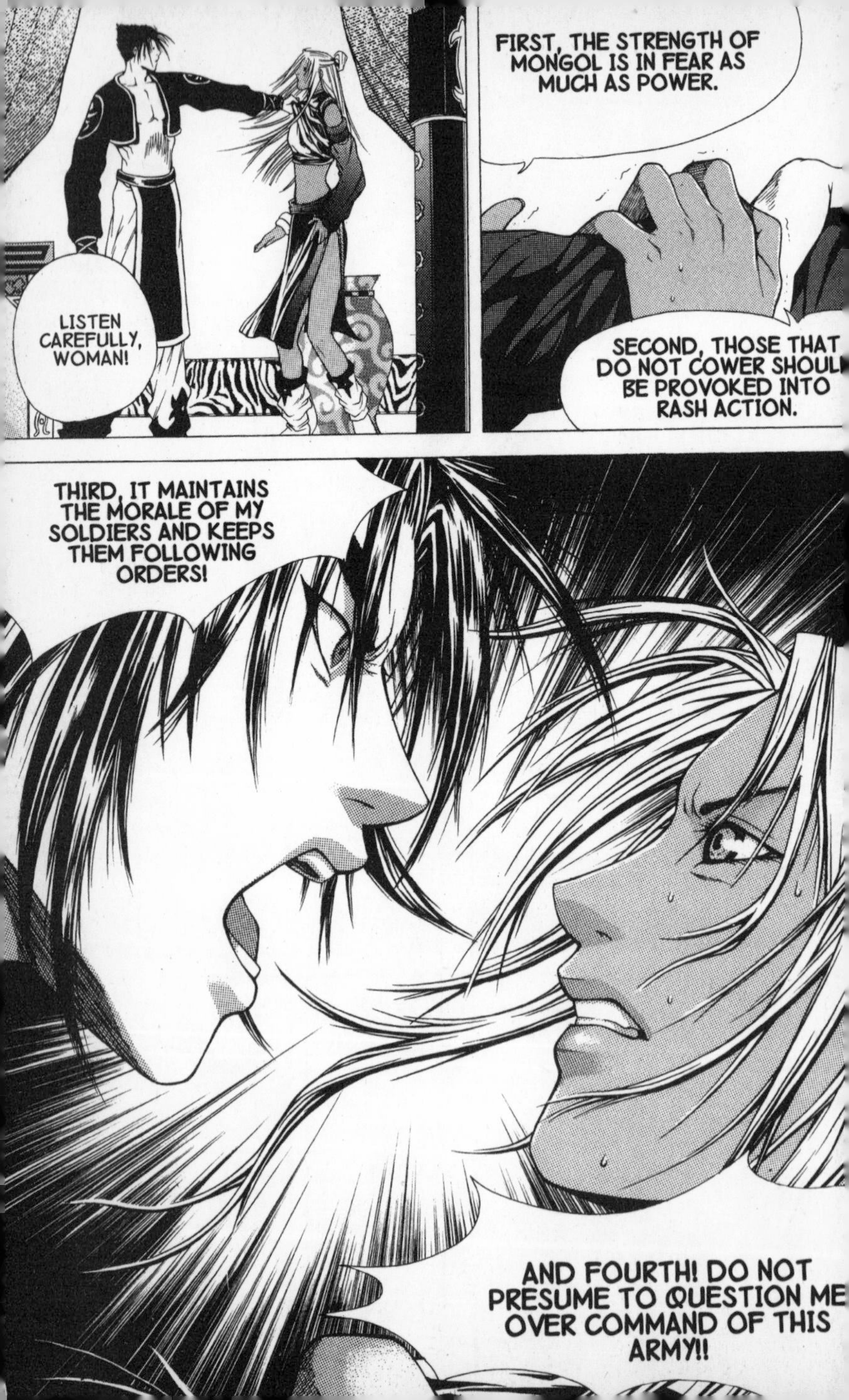
LISTEN CAREFULLY, WOMAN!
FIRST, THE STRENGTH OF MONGOL IS IN FEAR AS MUCH AS POWER.
SECOND, THOSE THAT DO NOT COWER SHOUL BE PROVOKED INTO RASH ACTION.
THIRD, IT MAINTAINS THE MORALE OF MY SOLDIERS AND KEEPS THEM FOLLOWING ORDERS!
AND FOURTH! DO NOT PRESUME TO QUESTION ME OVER COMMAND OF THIS ARMY!!

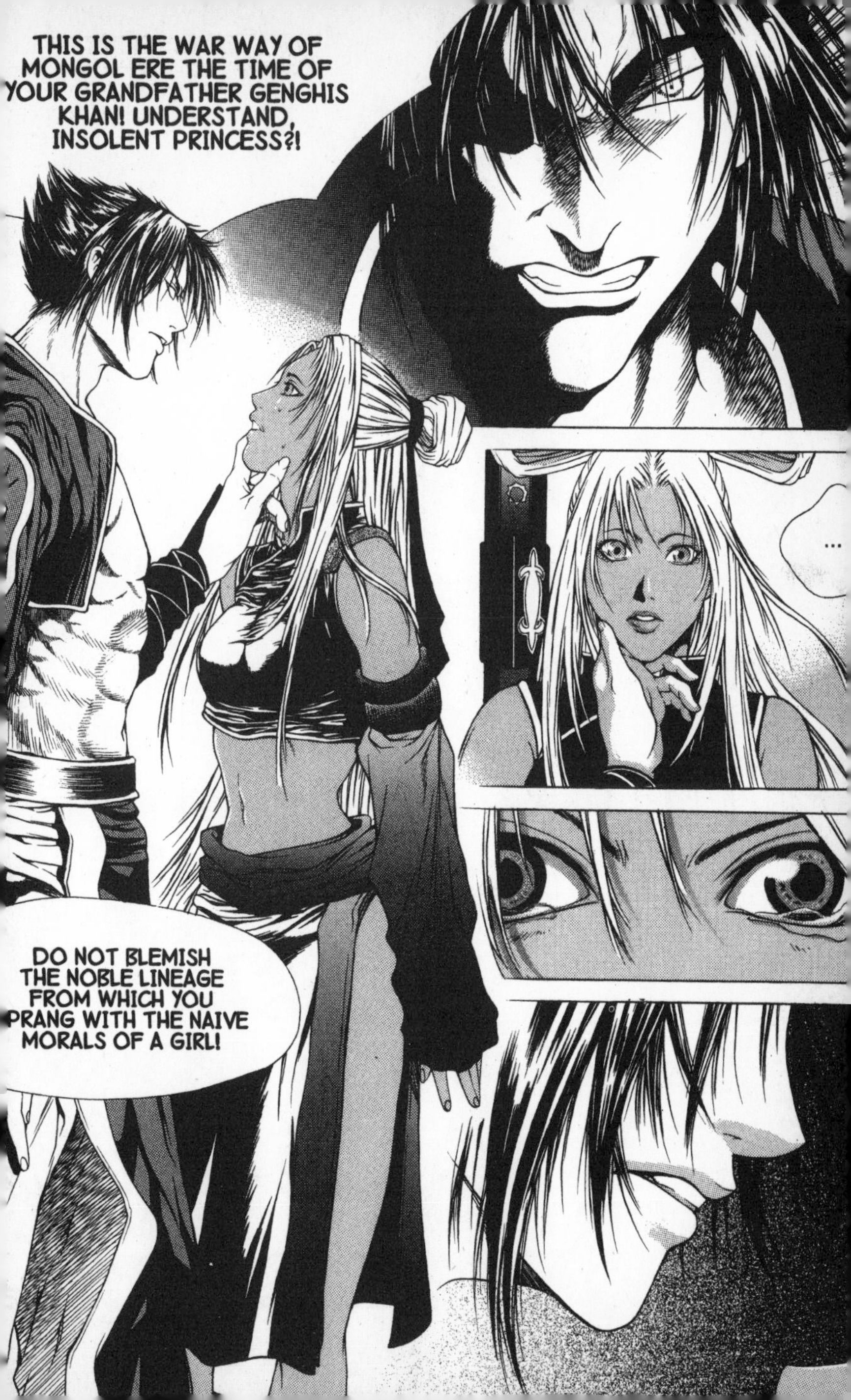
THIS IS THE WAR WAY OF MONGOL ERE THE TIME OF YOUR GRANDFATHER GENGHIS KHAN! UNDERSTAND, INSOLENT PRINCESS?!
...
DO NOT BLEMISH THE NOBLE LINEAGE FROM WHICH YOU PRANG WITH THE NAIVE MORALS OF A GIRL!

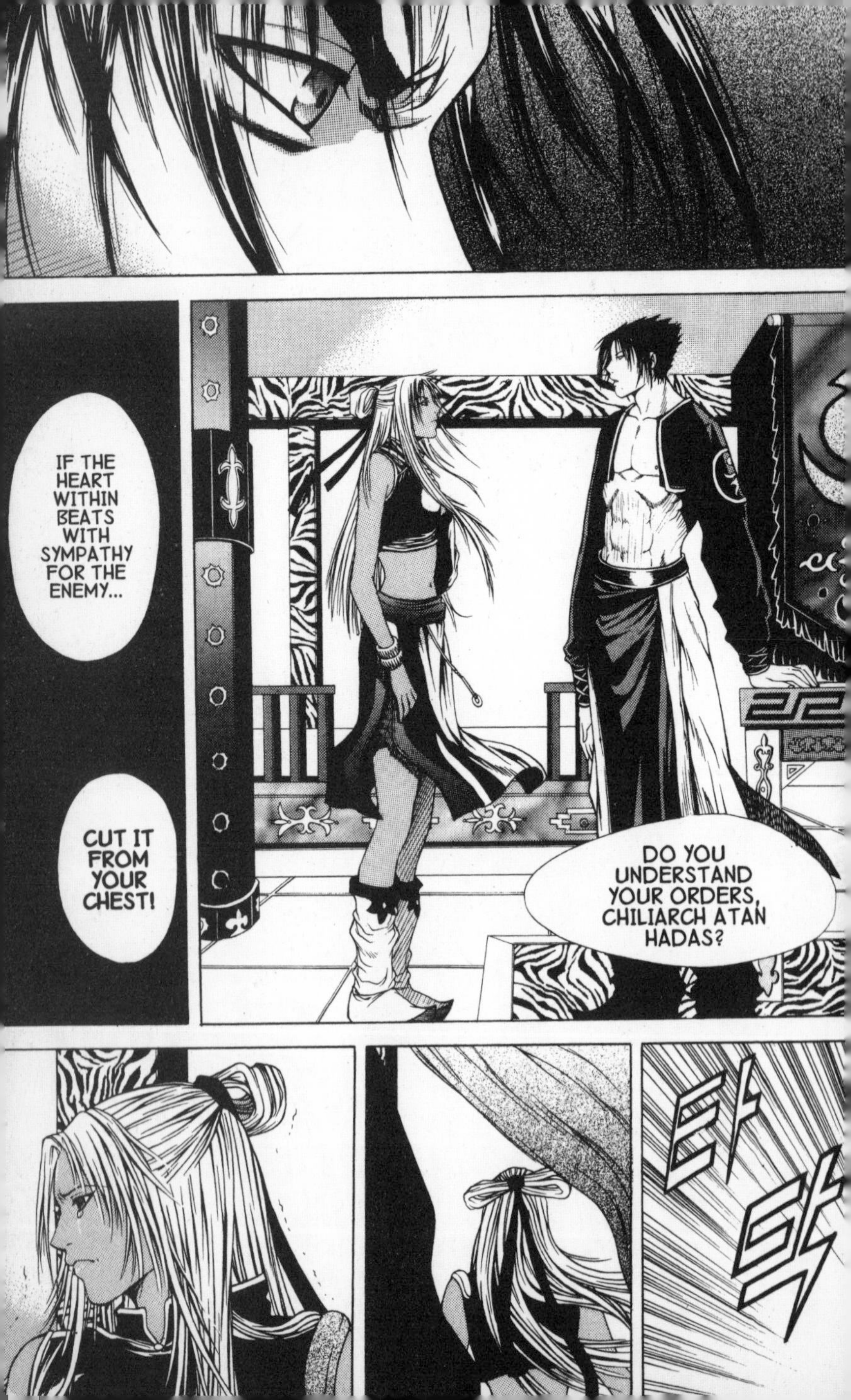
IF THE HEART WITHIN BEATS WITH SYMPATHY FOR THE ENEMY...
CUT IT FROM YOUR CHEST!
DO YOU UNDERSTAND YOUR ORDERS, CHILIARCH ATAN HADAS?

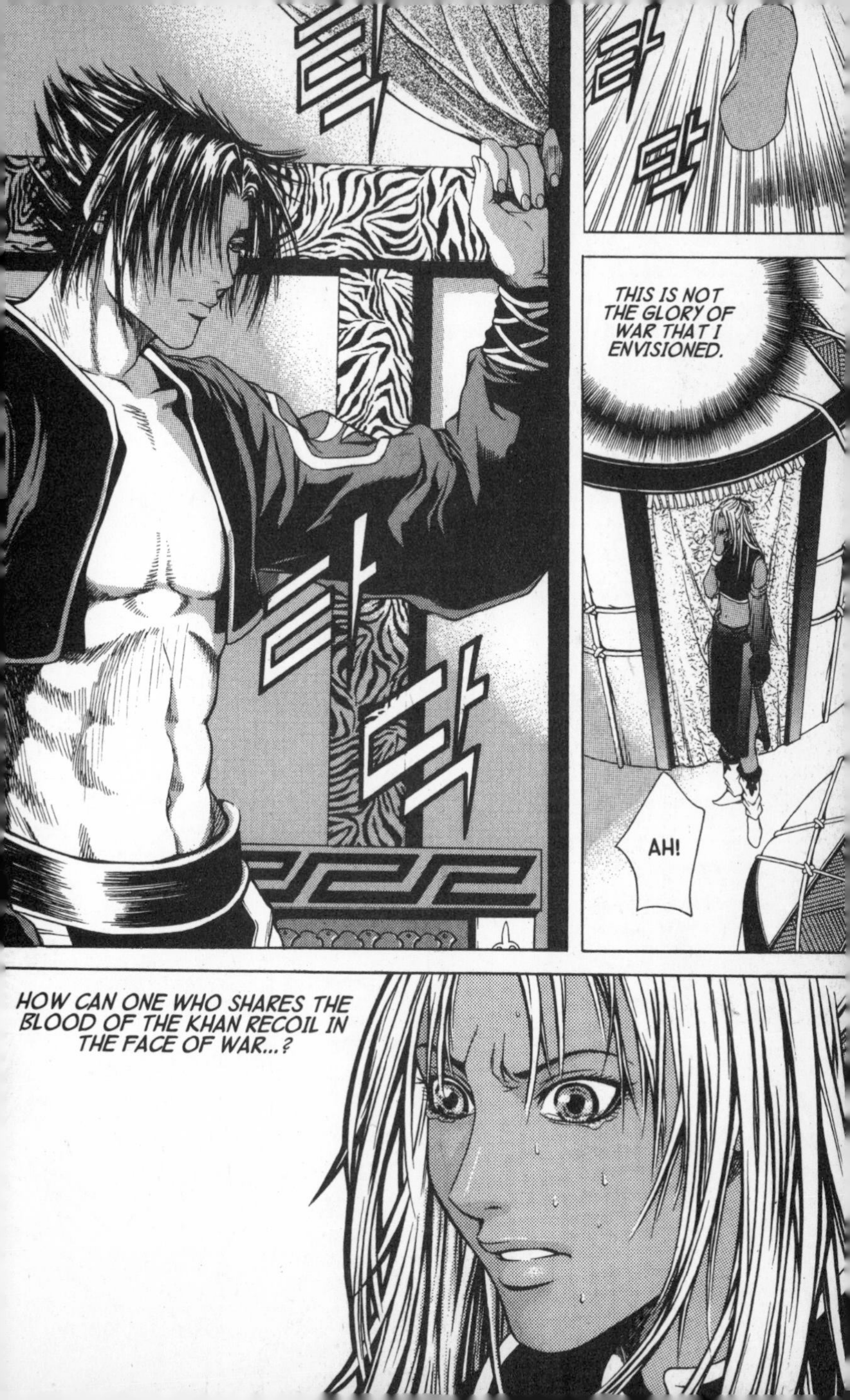
THIS IS NOT THE GLORY OF WAR THAT I ENVISIONED.
AH!
HOW CAN ONE WHO SHARES THE BLOOD OF THE KHAN RECOIL IN THE FACE OF WAR...?

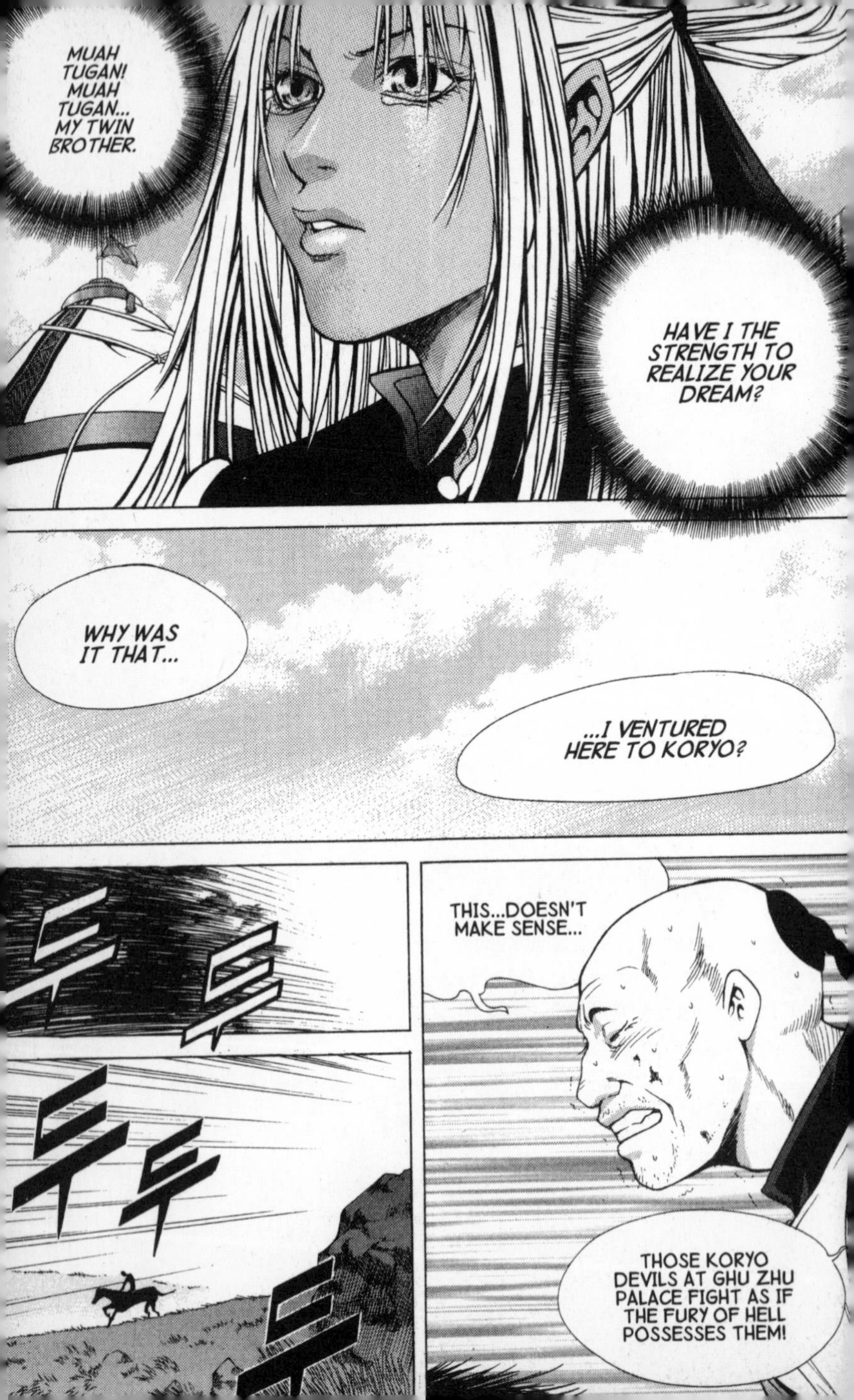

MUAH TUGAN! MUAH TUGAN... MY TWIN BROTHER.
HAVE I THE STRENGTH TO REALIZE YOUR DREAM?
WHY WAS IT THAT...
...I VENTURED HERE TO KORYO?
THIS...DOESN'T MAKE SENSE...
THOSE KORYO DEVILS AT GHU ZHU PALACE FIGHT AS IF THE FURY OF HELL POSSESSES THEM!

ARE THE REPORTS ACCURATE, MESSENGER?

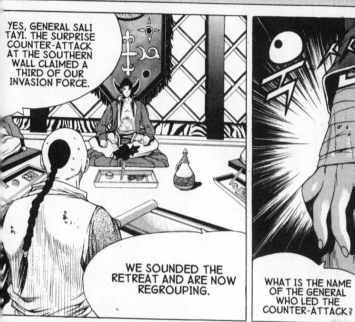

YES, GENERAL SALI TAYI. THE SURPRISE COUNTER-ATTACK AT THE SOUTHERN WALL CLAIMED A THIRD OF OUR INVASION FORCE.

WE SOUNDED THE RETREAT AND ARE NOW REGROUPING.

WHAT IS THE NAME OF THE GENERAL WHO LED THE COUNTER-ATTACK?

THEY SAY IT IS KIM KYUNG-SOHN.

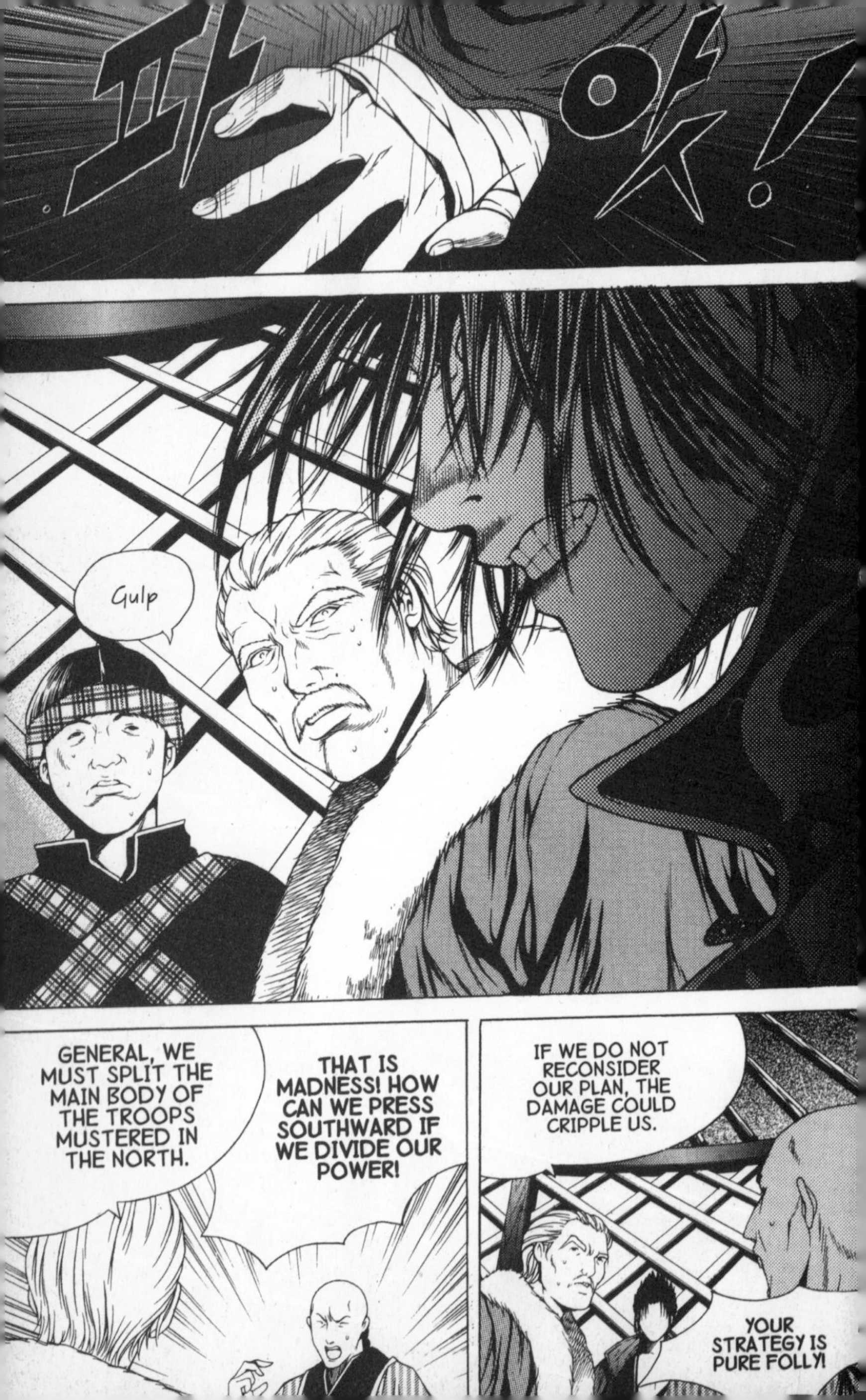
Gulp
GENERAL, WE MUST SPLIT THE MAIN BODY OF THE TROOPS MUSTERED IN THE NORTH.
THAT IS MADNESS! HOW CAN WE PRESS SOUTHWARD IF WE DIVIDE OUR POWER!
IF WE DO NOT RECONSIDER OUR PLAN, THE DAMAGE COULD CRIPPLE US.
YOUR STRATEGY IS PURE FOLLY!

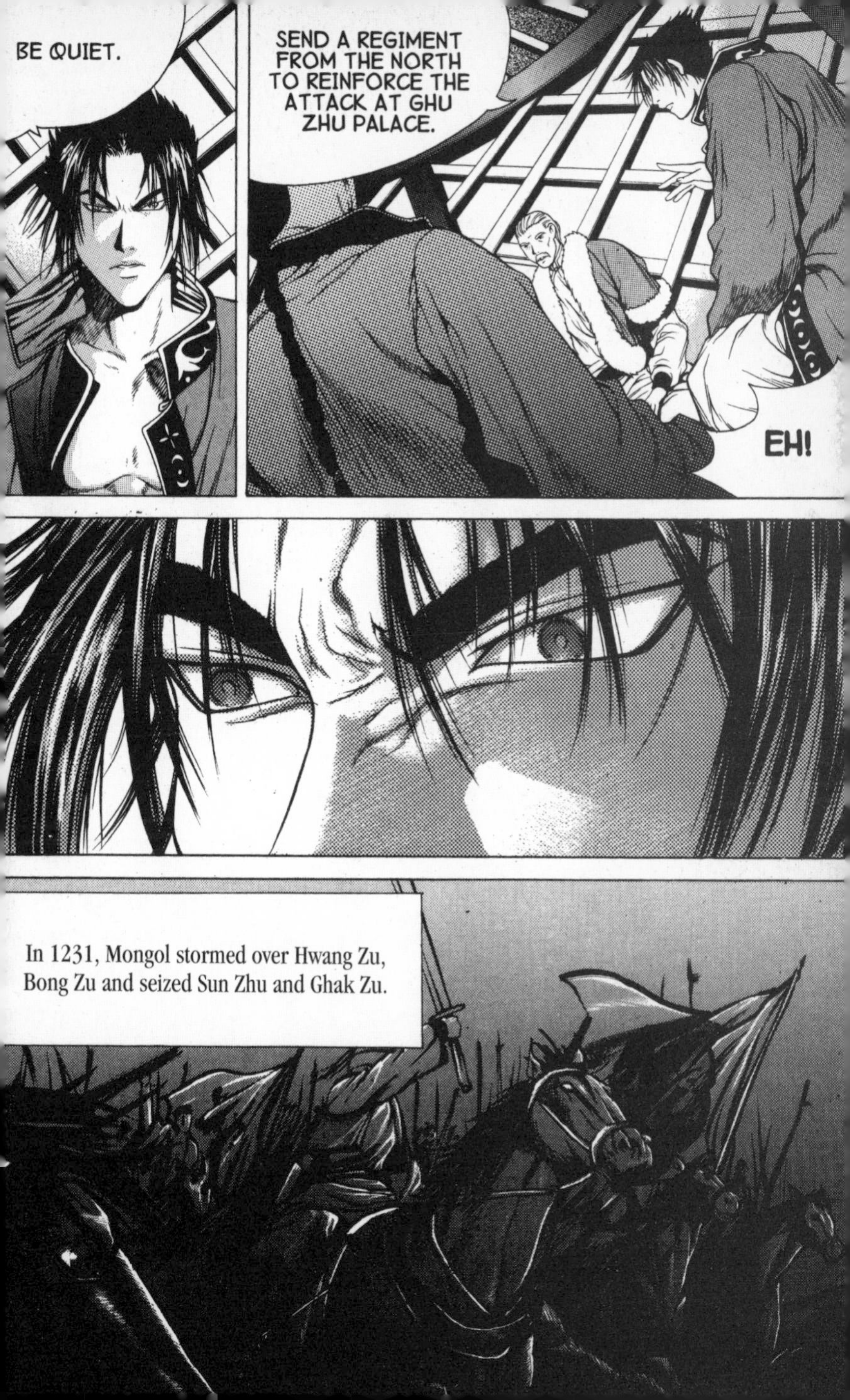
BE QUIET.
SEND A REGIMENT FROM THE NORTH TO REINFORCE THE ATTACK AT GHU ZHU PALACE.
EH!
In 1231, Mongol stormed over Hwang Zu, Bong Zu and seized Sun Zhu and Ghak Zu.

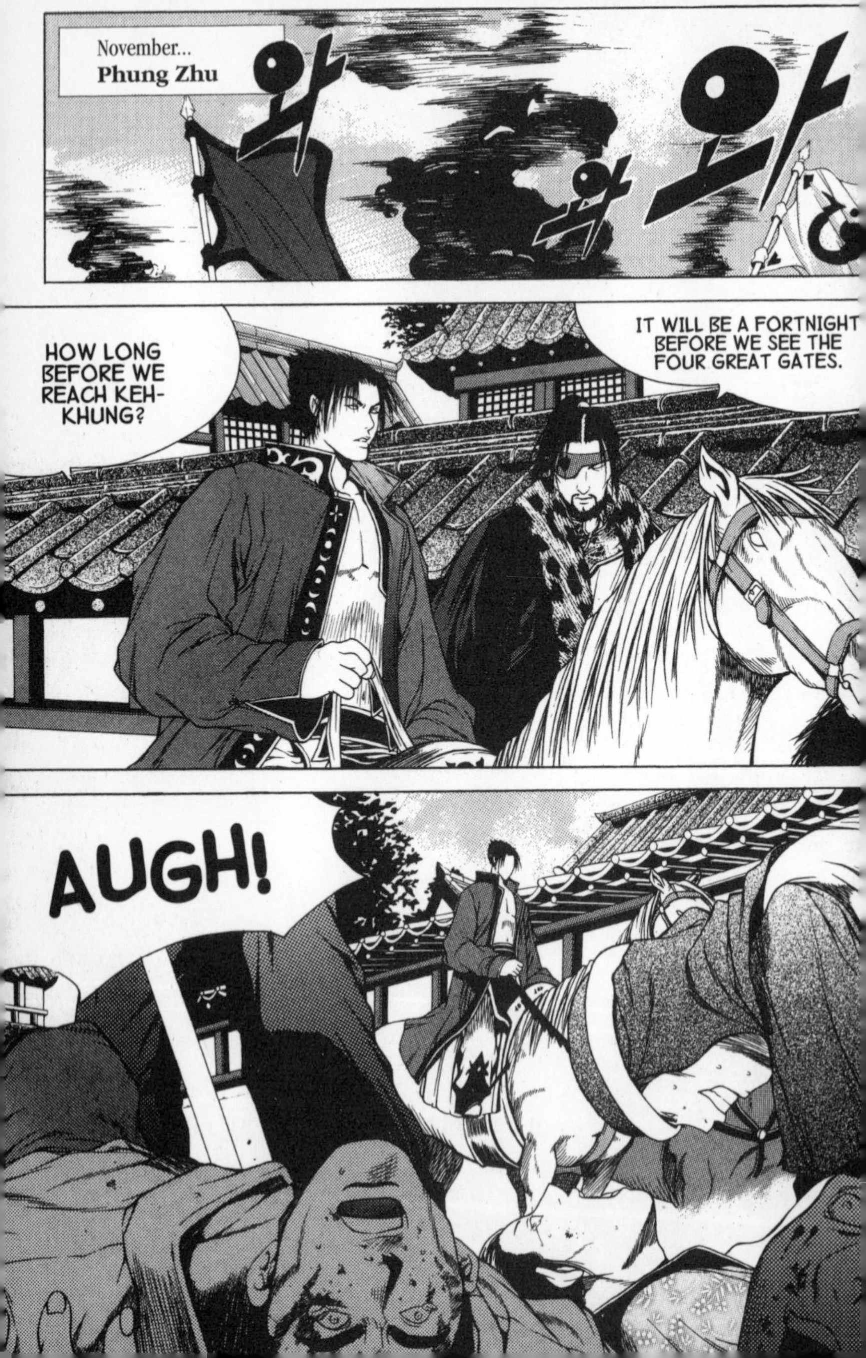
November...
Phung Zhu
와
와
와
HOW LONG BEFORE WE REACH KEH-KHUNG?
IT WILL BE A FORTNIGHT BEFORE WE SEE THE FOUR GREAT GATES.
AUGH!

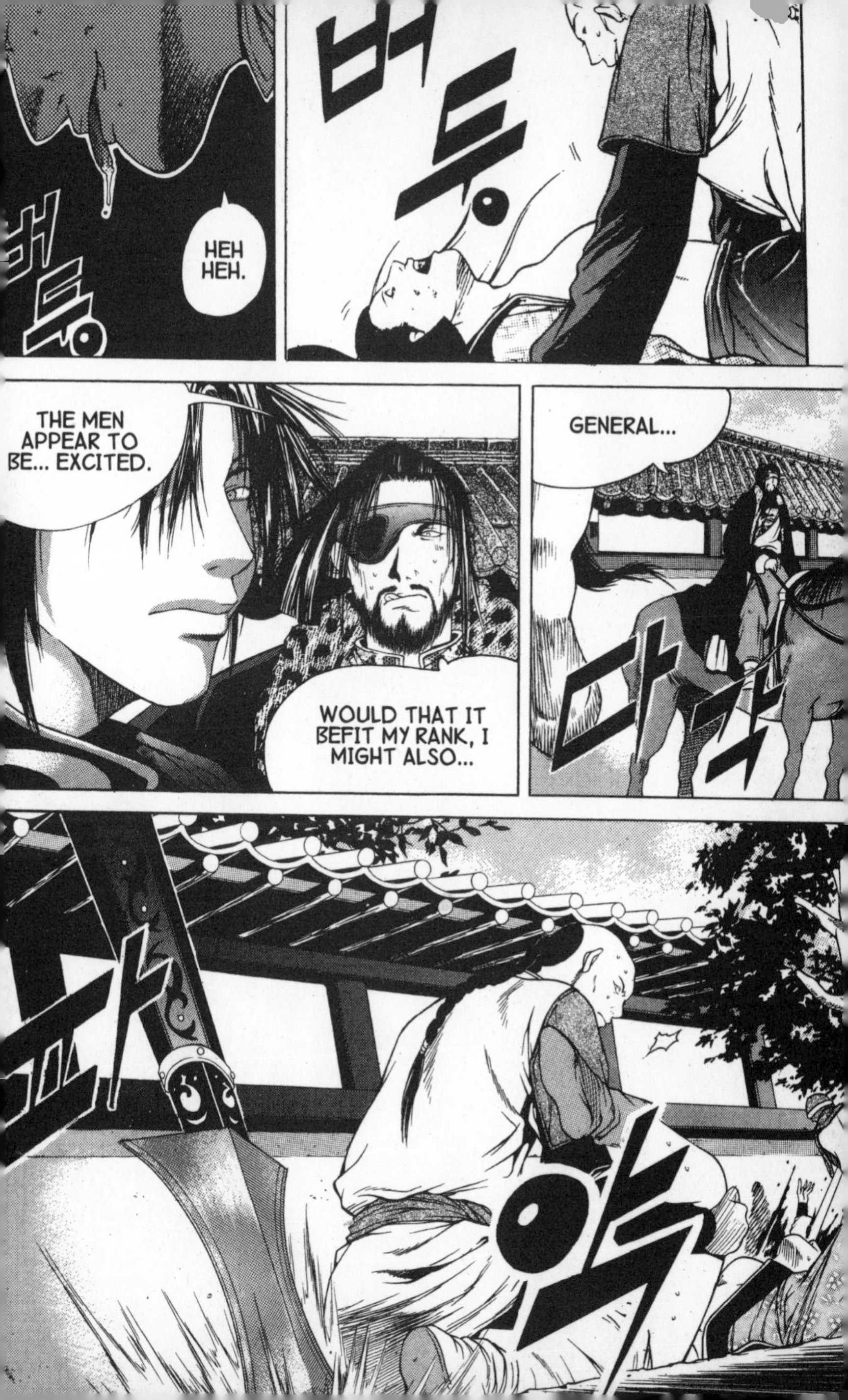
HEH HEH.
THE MEN APPEAR TO BE... EXCITED.
WOULD THAT IT BEFIT MY RANK, I MIGHT ALSO...
GENERAL...

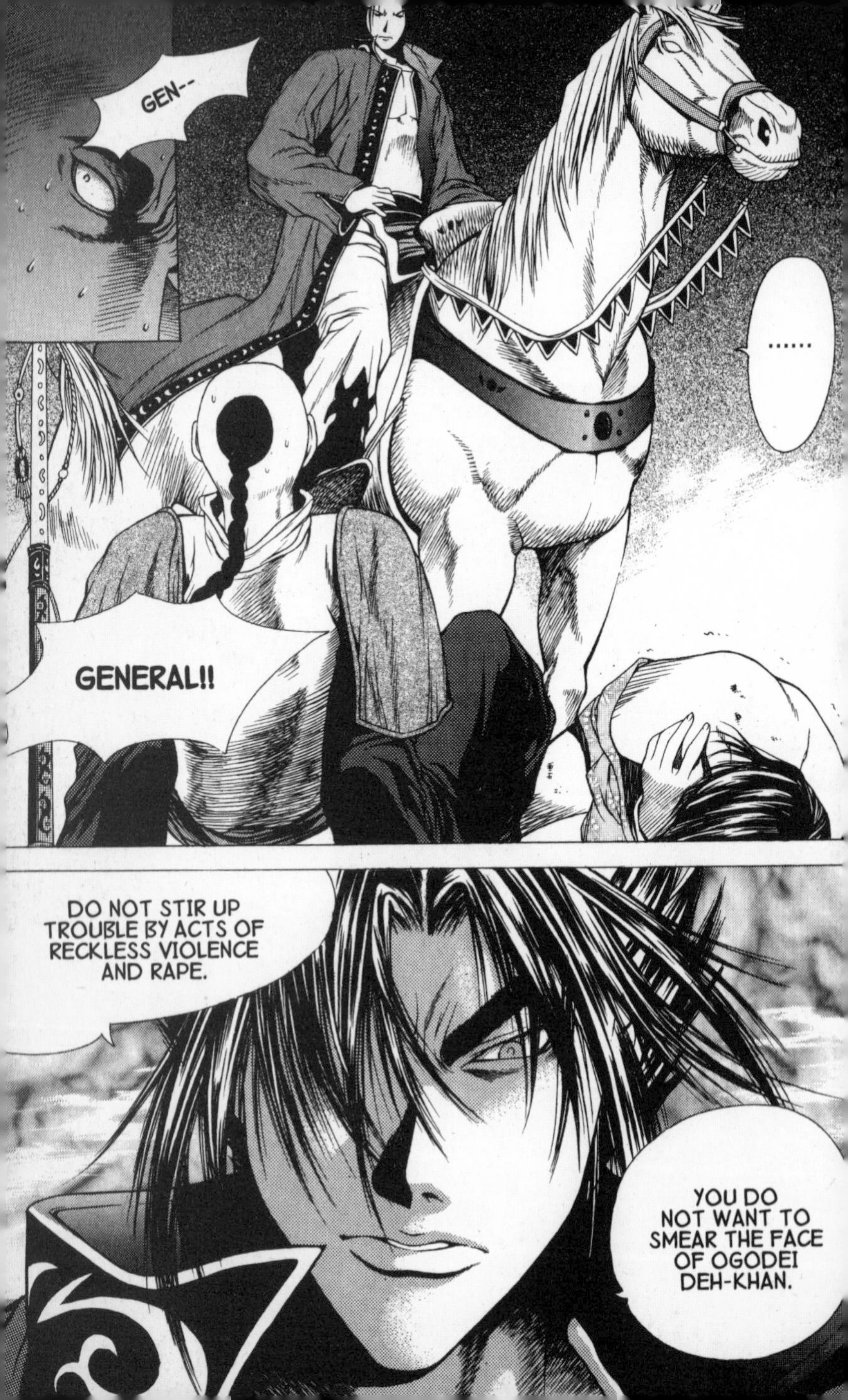
GEN--
......
GENERAL!!
DO NOT STIR UP TROUBLE BY ACTS OF RECKLESS VIOLENCE AND RAPE.
YOU DO NOT WANT TO SMEAR THE FACE OF OGODEI DEH-KHAN.

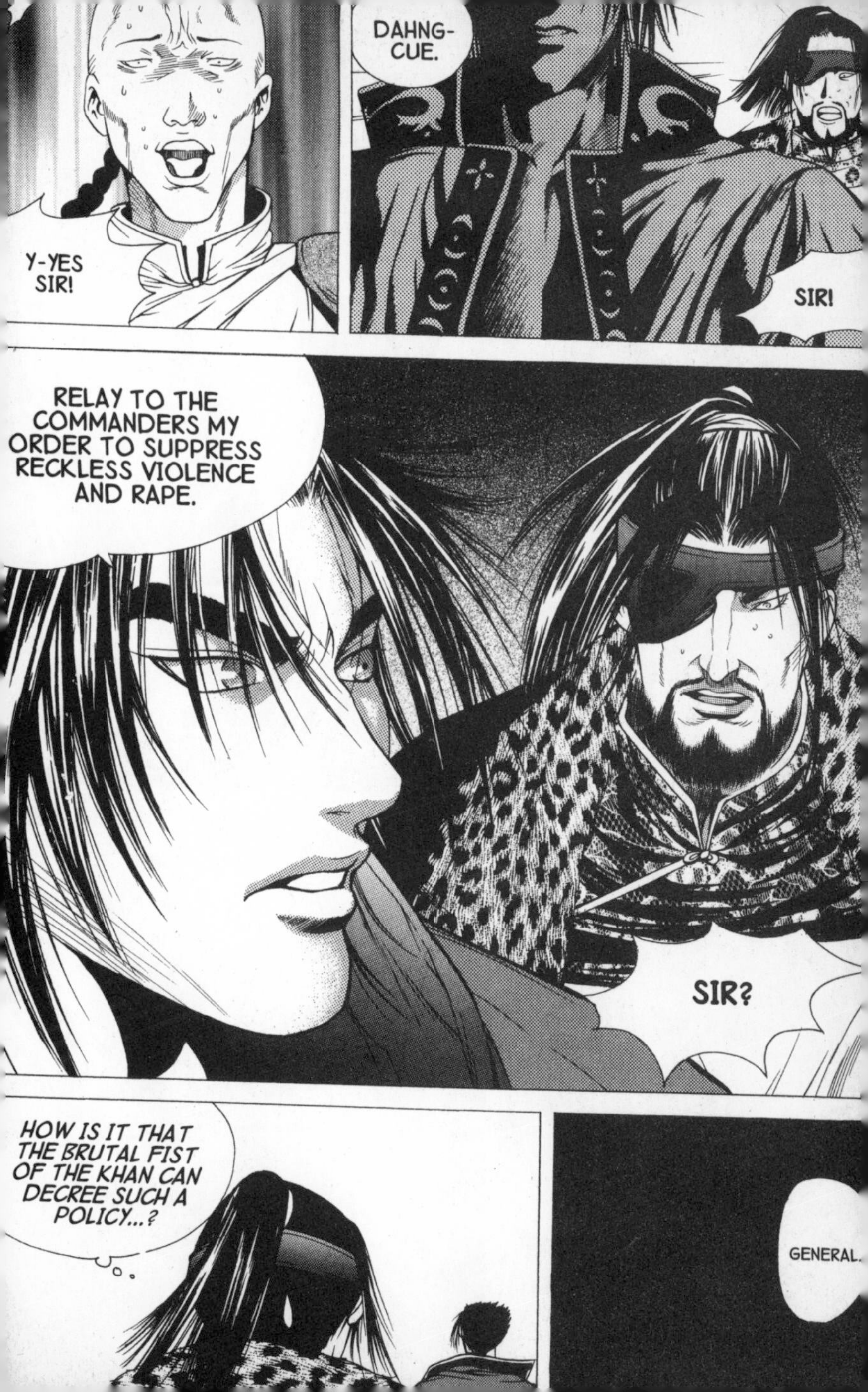
Y-YES SIR!
DAHNG-CUE.
SIR!
RELAY TO THE COMMANDERS MY ORDER TO SUPPRESS RECKLESS VIOLENCE AND RAPE.
SIR?
HOW IS IT THAT THE BRUTAL FIST OF THE KHAN CAN DECREE SUCH A POLICY...?
GENERAL.

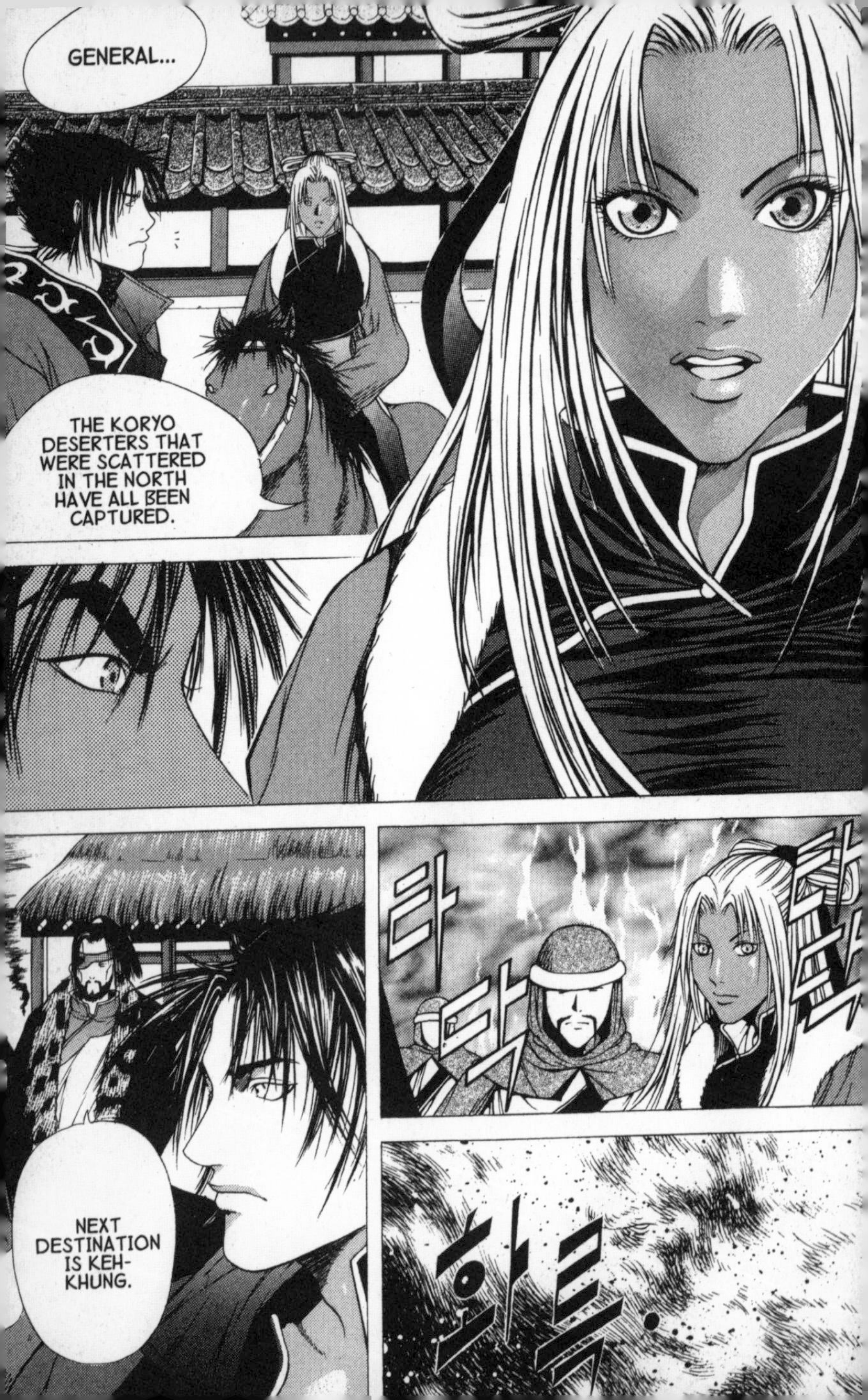
GENERAL...
THE KORYO DESERTERS THAT WERE SCATTERED IN THE NORTH HAVE ALL BEEN CAPTURED.
NEXT DESTINATION IS KEH-KHUNG.
타닥
화륵.

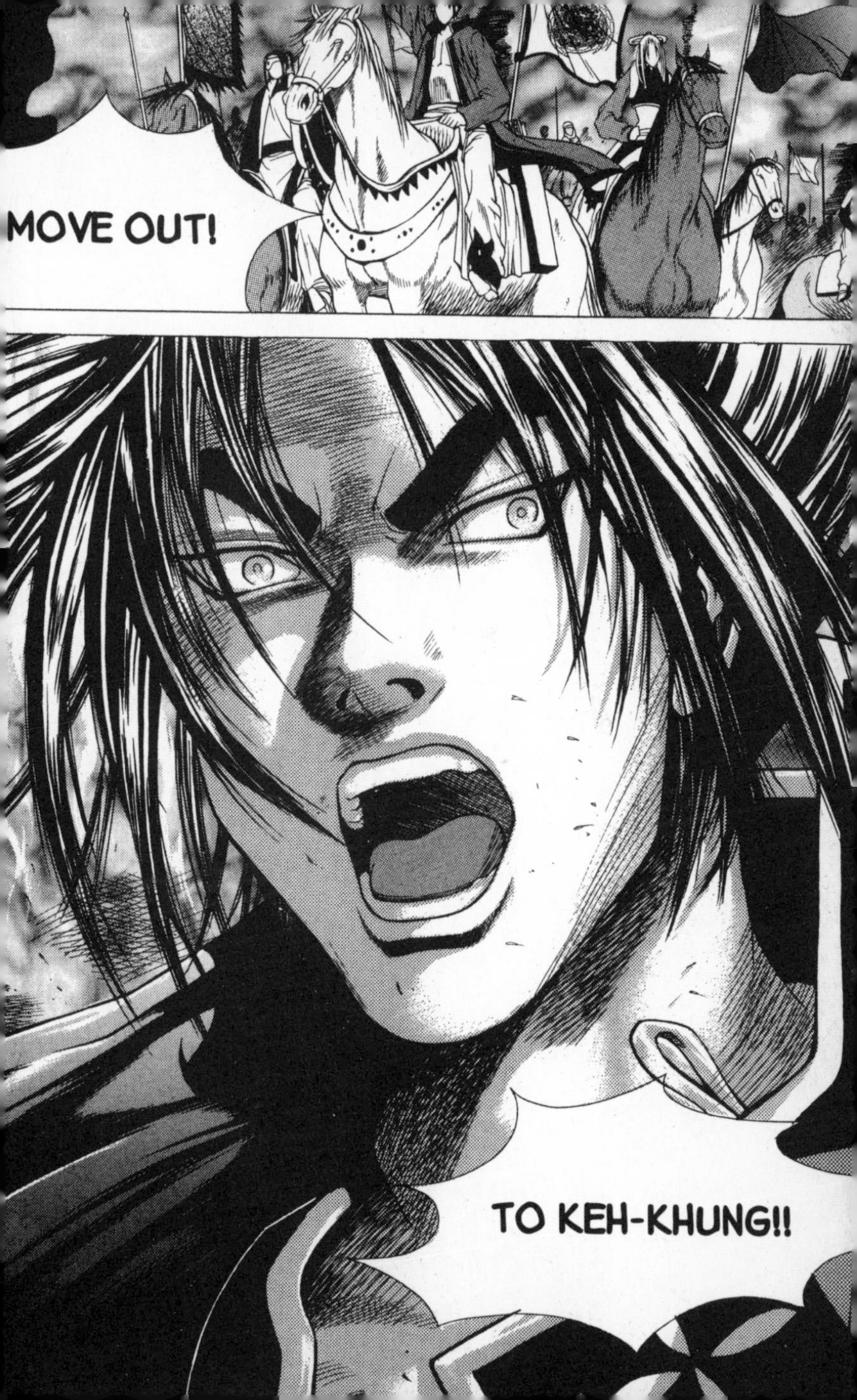
MOVE OUT!
TO KEH-KHUNG!!

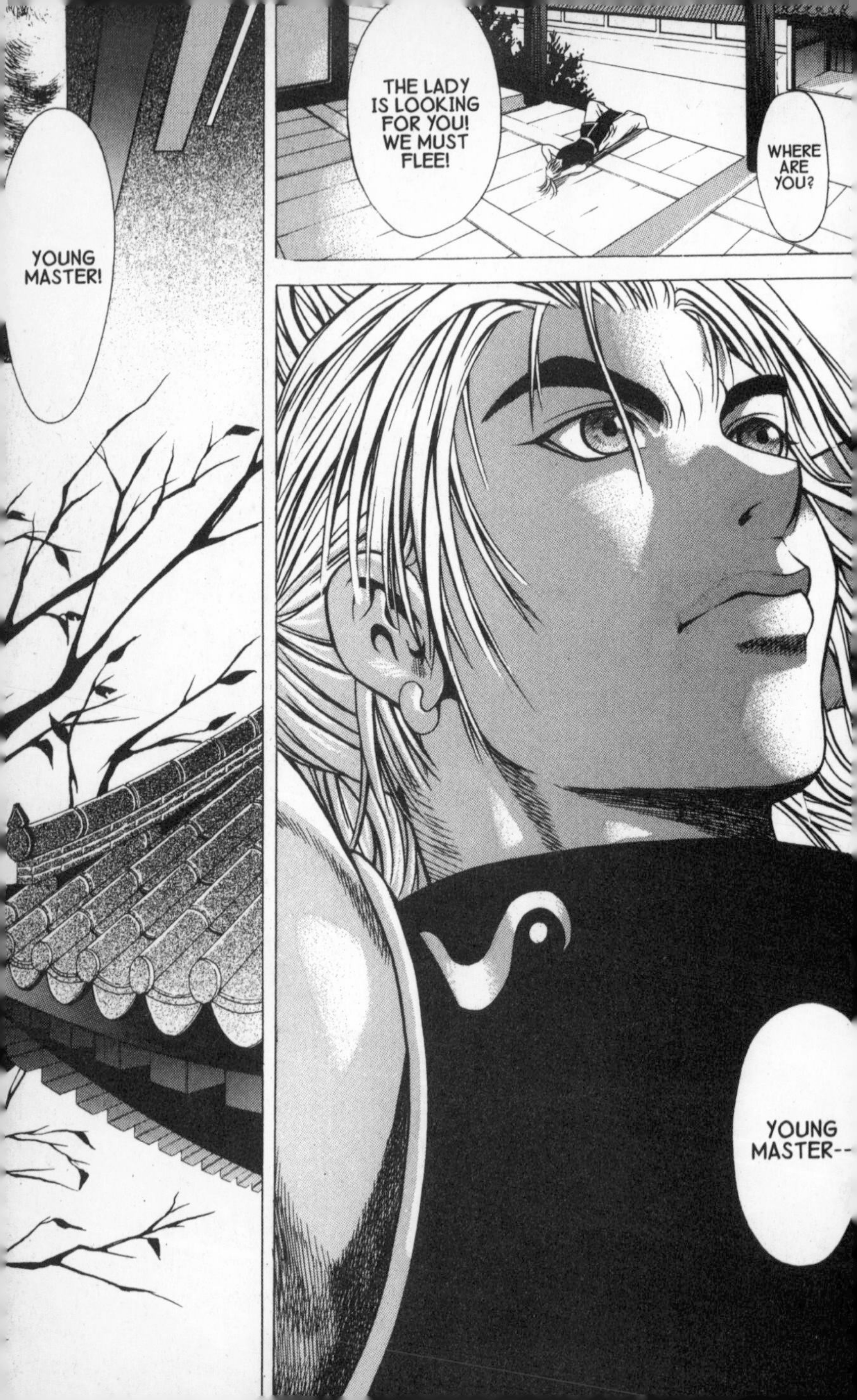
YOUNG MASTER!
THE LADY IS LOOKING FOR YOU! WE MUST FLEE!
WHERE ARE YOU?
YOUNG MASTER--

# Chapter 15
# An Omen

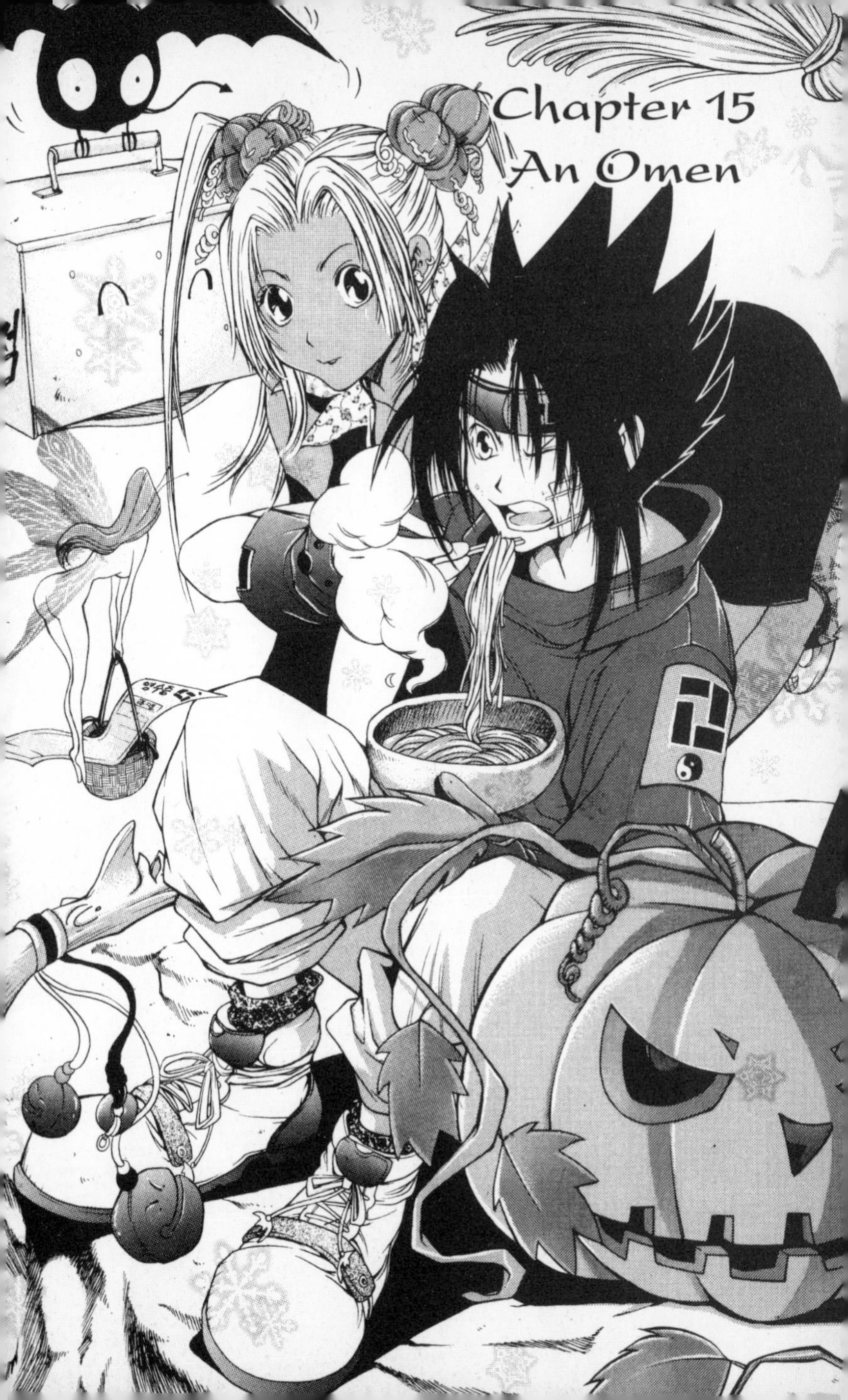

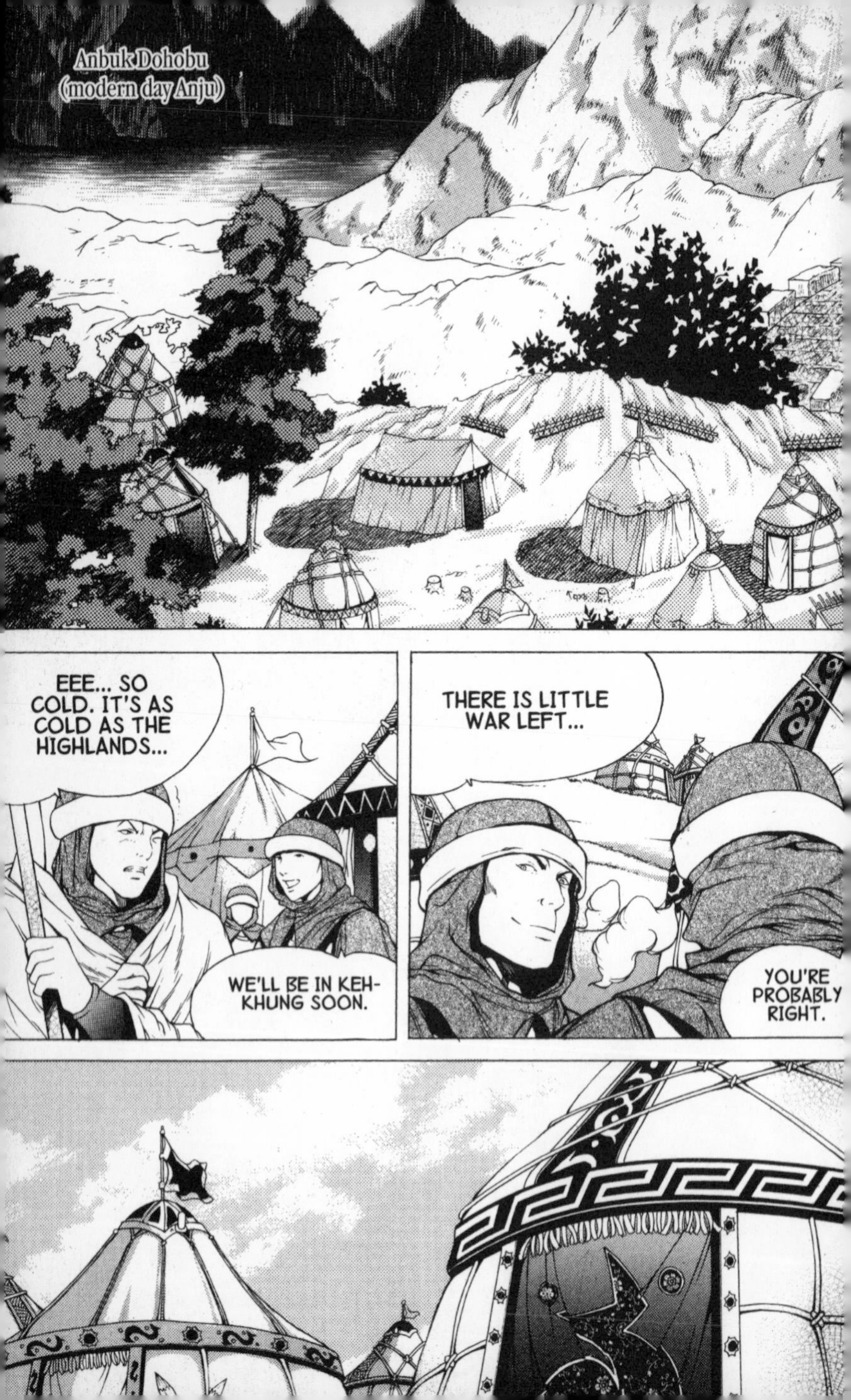
Anbuk Dohobu (modern day Anju)
EEE... SO COLD. IT'S AS COLD AS THE HIGHLANDS...
WE'LL BE IN KEH-KHUNG SOON.
THERE IS LITTLE WAR LEFT...
YOU'RE PROBABLY RIGHT.

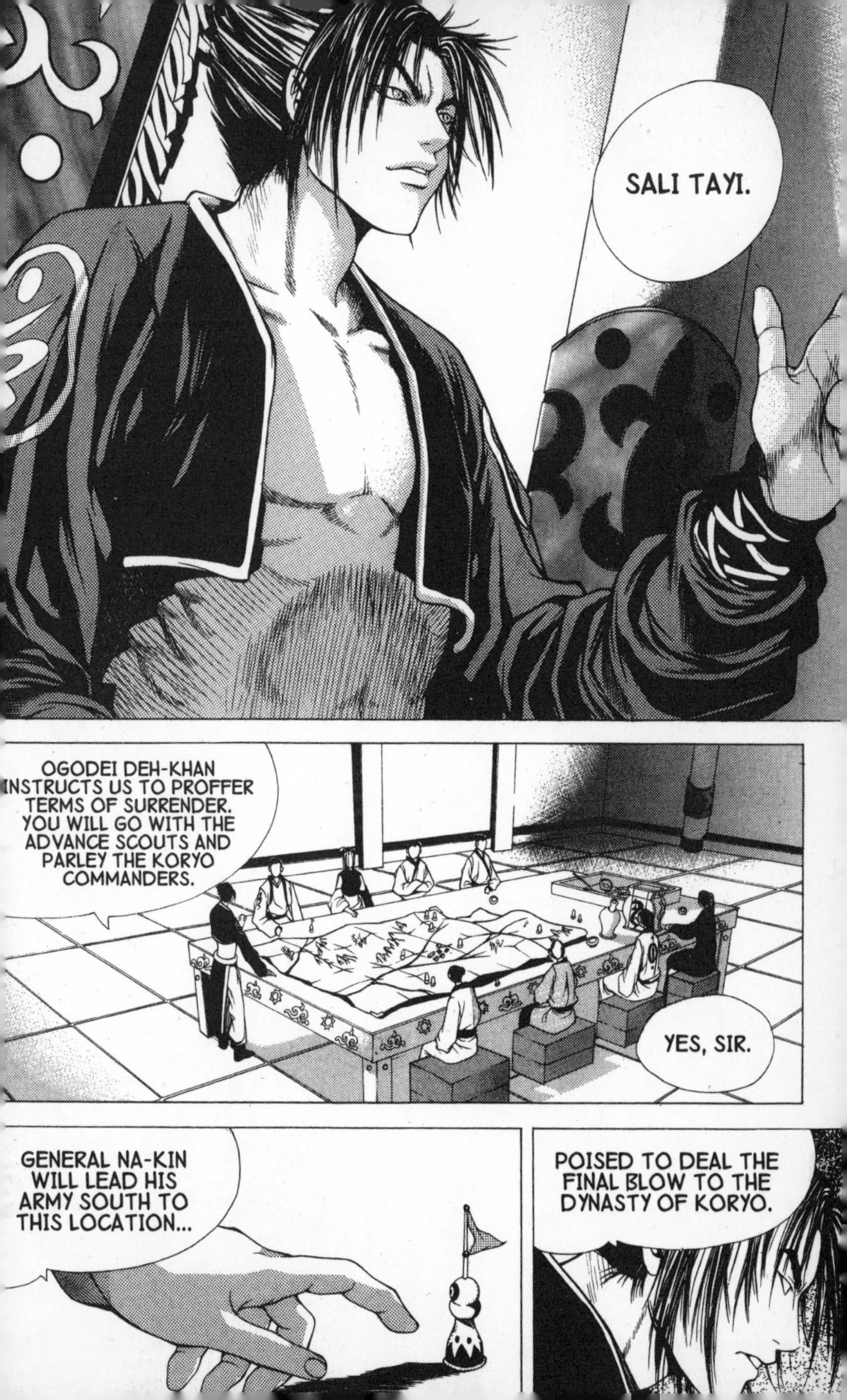
SALI TAYI.
OGODEI DEH-KHAN INSTRUCTS US TO PROFFER TERMS OF SURRENDER. YOU WILL GO WITH THE ADVANCE SCOUTS AND PARLEY THE KORYO COMMANDERS.
YES, SIR.
GENERAL NA-KIN WILL LEAD HIS ARMY SOUTH TO THIS LOCATION...
POISED TO DEAL THE FINAL BLOW TO THE DYNASTY OF KORYO.

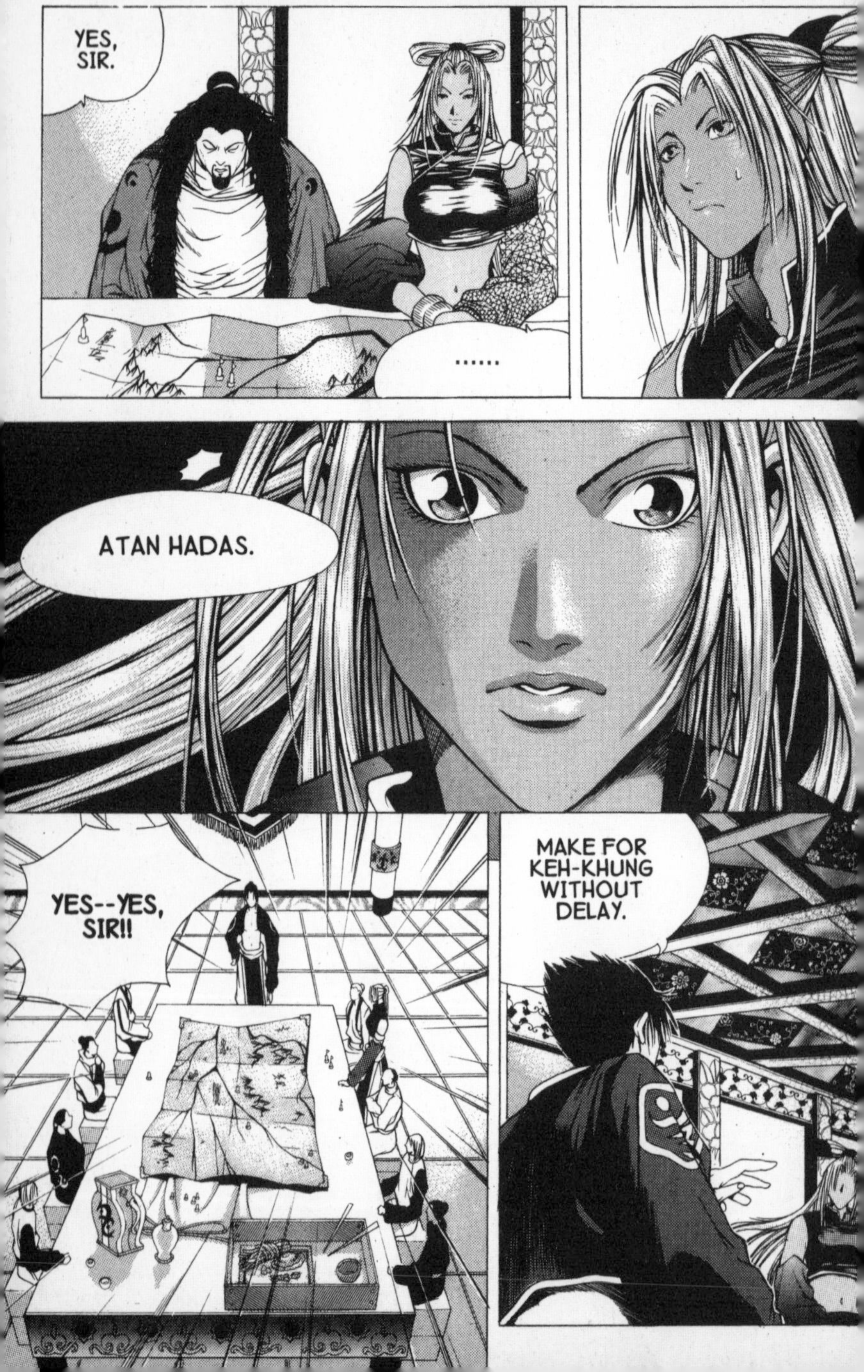
YES, SIR.
......
ATAN HADAS.
YES--YES, SIR!!
MAKE FOR KEH-KHUNG WITHOUT DELAY.

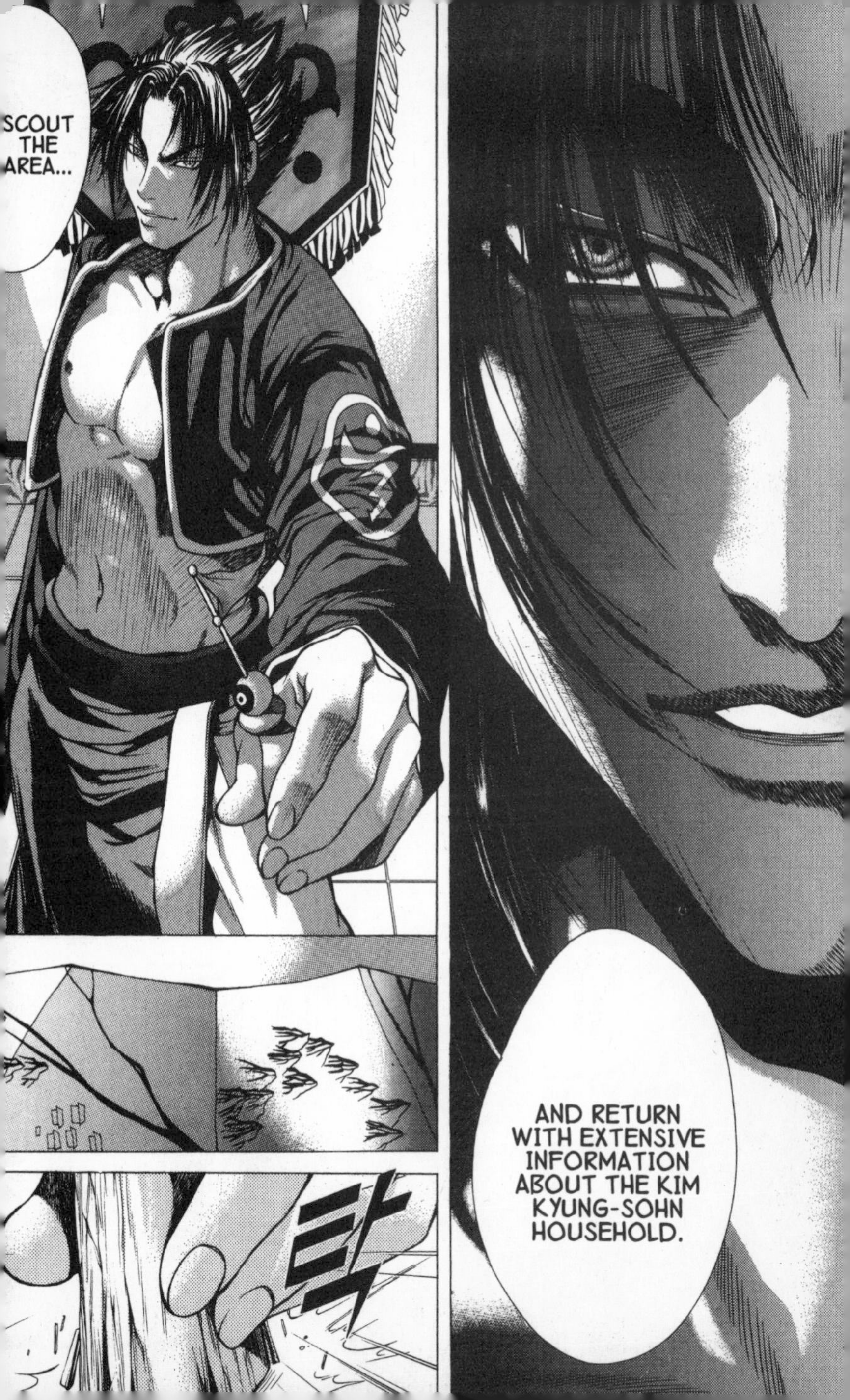
SCOUT THE AREA...
AND RETURN WITH EXTENSIVE INFORMATION ABOUT THE KIM KYUNG-SOHN HOUSEHOLD.

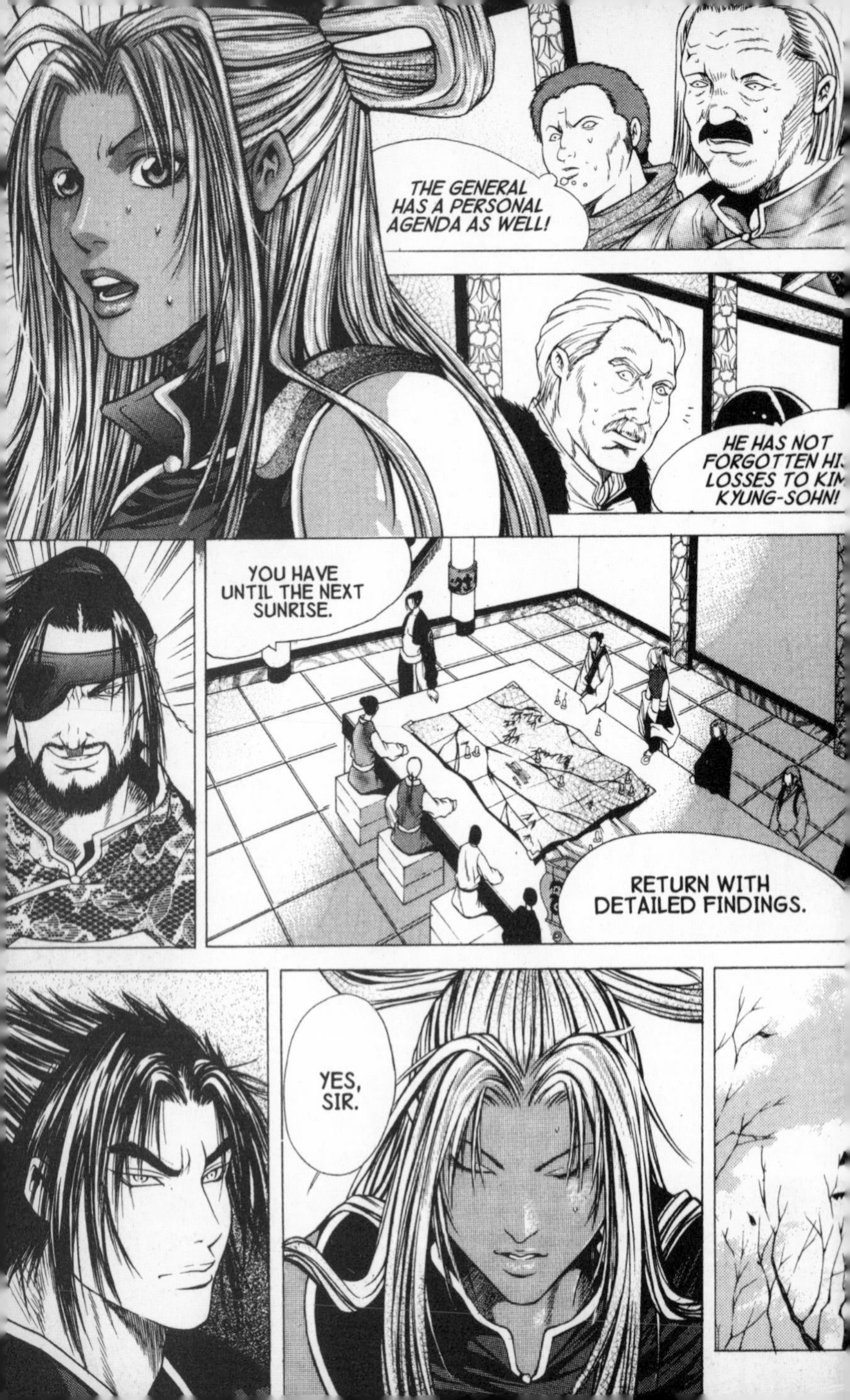
THE GENERAL HAS A PERSONAL AGENDA AS WELL!
HE HAS NOT FORGOTTEN HIS LOSSES TO KIM KYUNG-SOHN!
YOU HAVE UNTIL THE NEXT SUNRISE.
RETURN WITH DETAILED FINDINGS.
YES, SIR.

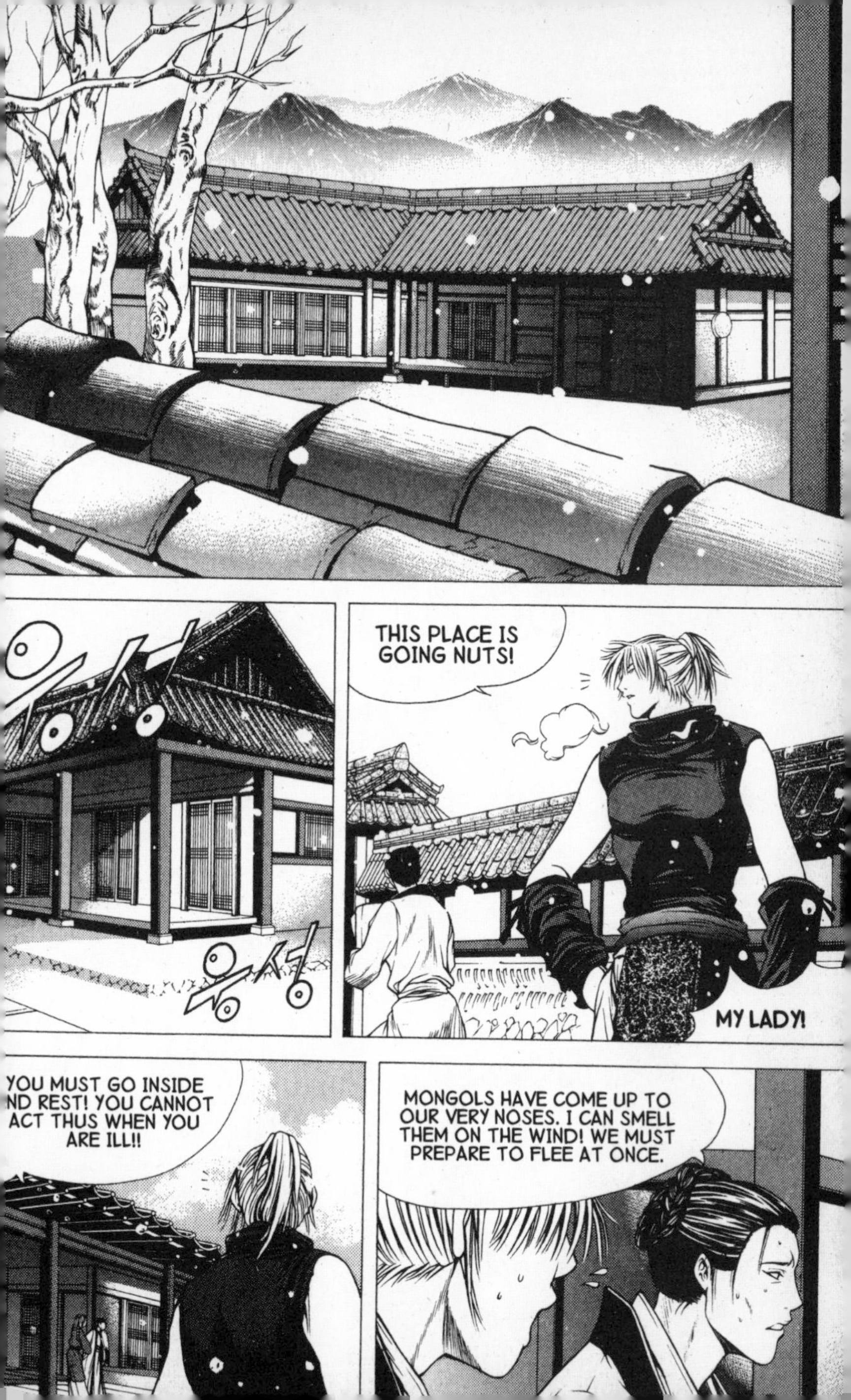
THIS PLACE IS GOING NUTS!
MY LADY!
YOU MUST GO INSIDE ND REST! YOU CANNOT ACT THUS WHEN YOU ARE ILL!!
MONGOLS HAVE COME UP TO OUR VERY NOSES. I CAN SMELL THEM ON THE WIND! WE MUST PREPARE TO FLEE AT ONCE.

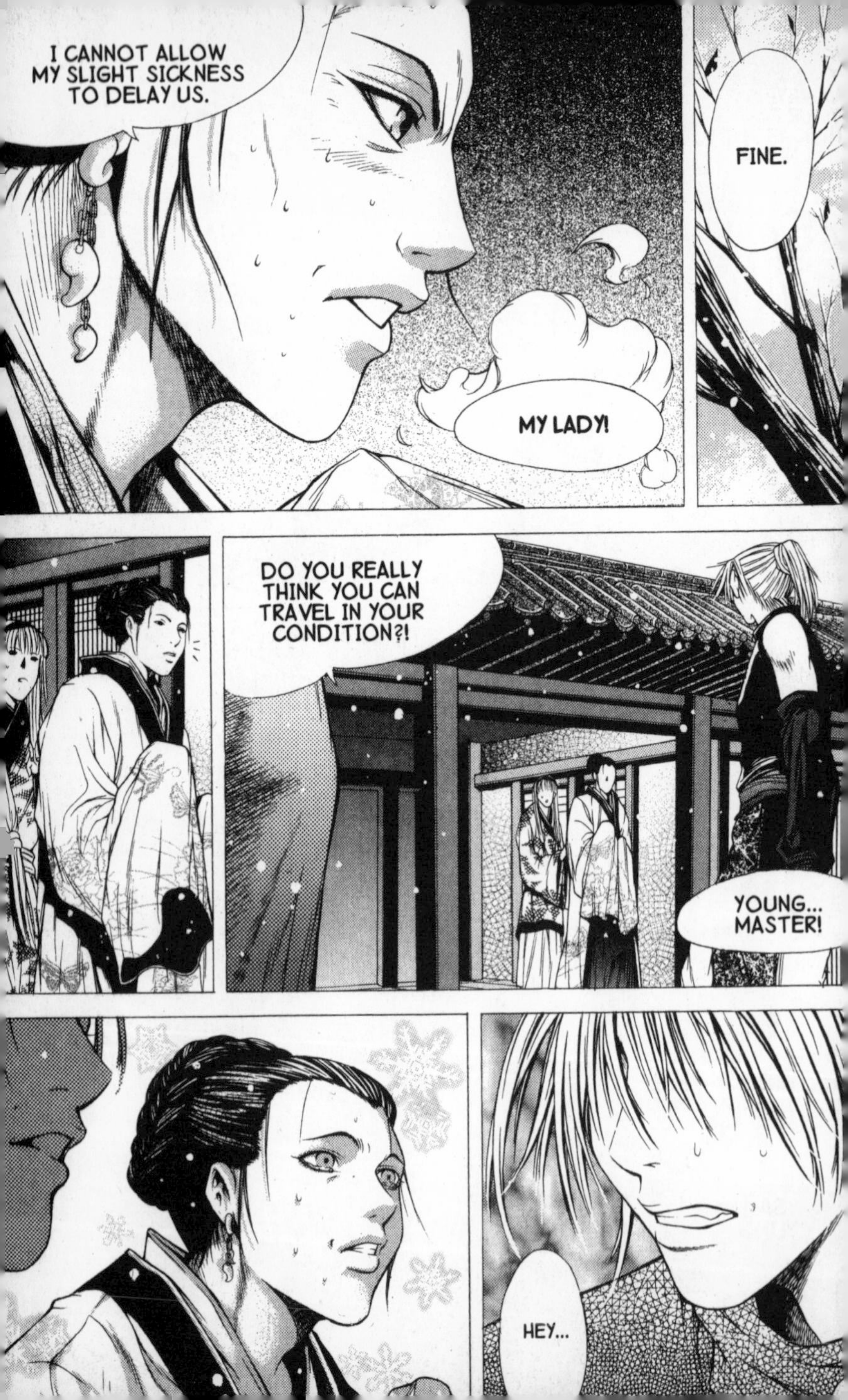
I CANNOT ALLOW MY SLIGHT SICKNESS TO DELAY US.
MY LADY!
FINE.
DO YOU REALLY THINK YOU CAN TRAVEL IN YOUR CONDITION?!
YOUNG... MASTER!
HEY...

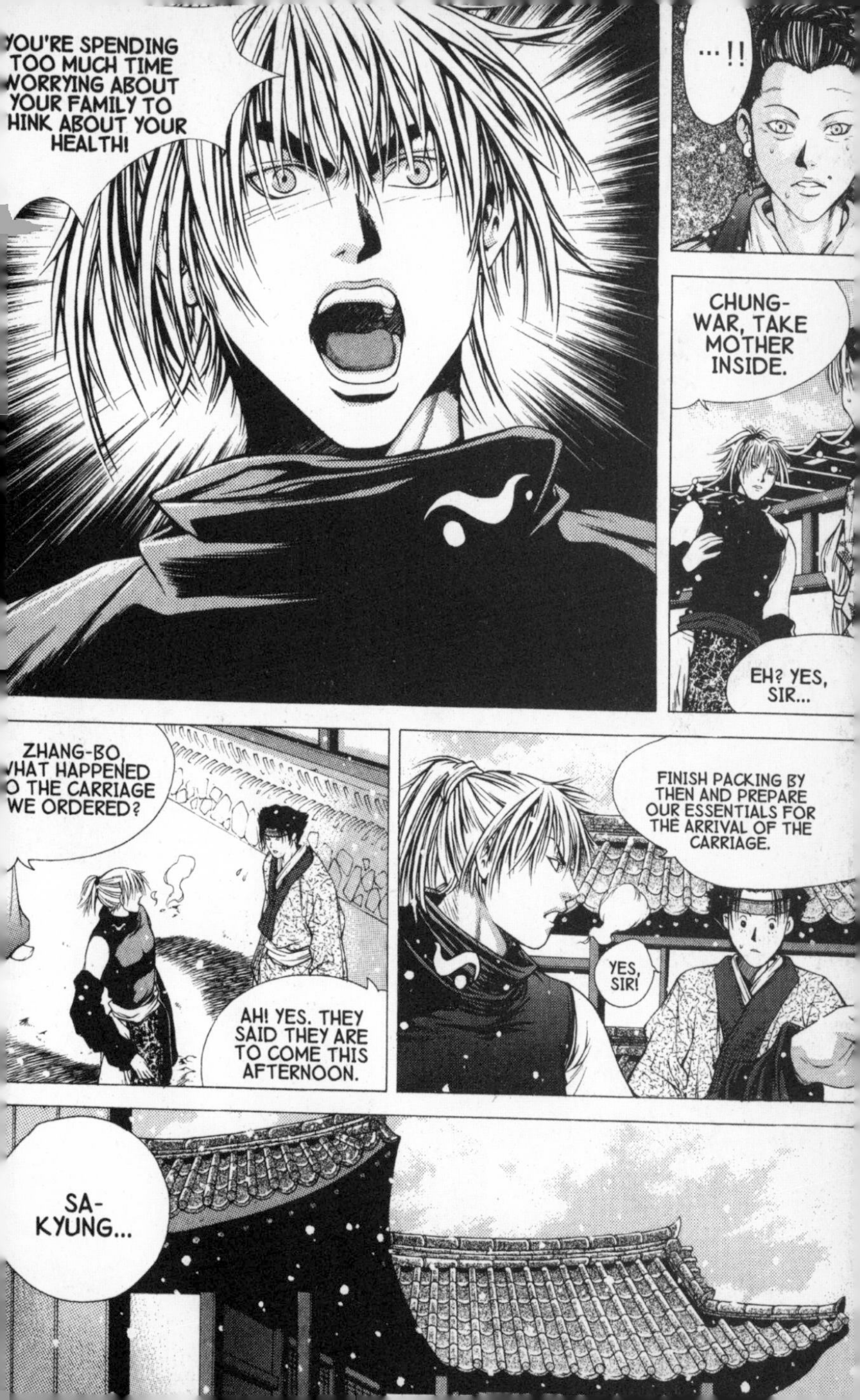
YOU'RE SPENDING TOO MUCH TIME WORRYING ABOUT YOUR FAMILY TO HINK ABOUT YOUR HEALTH!
...!!
CHUNG-WAR, TAKE MOTHER INSIDE.
EH? YES, SIR...
ZHANG-BO, WHAT HAPPENED O THE CARRIAGE WE ORDERED?
AH! YES. THEY SAID THEY ARE TO COME THIS AFTERNOON.
FINISH PACKING BY THEN AND PREPARE OUR ESSENTIALS FOR THE ARRIVAL OF THE CARRIAGE.
YES, SIR!
SA-KYUNG...

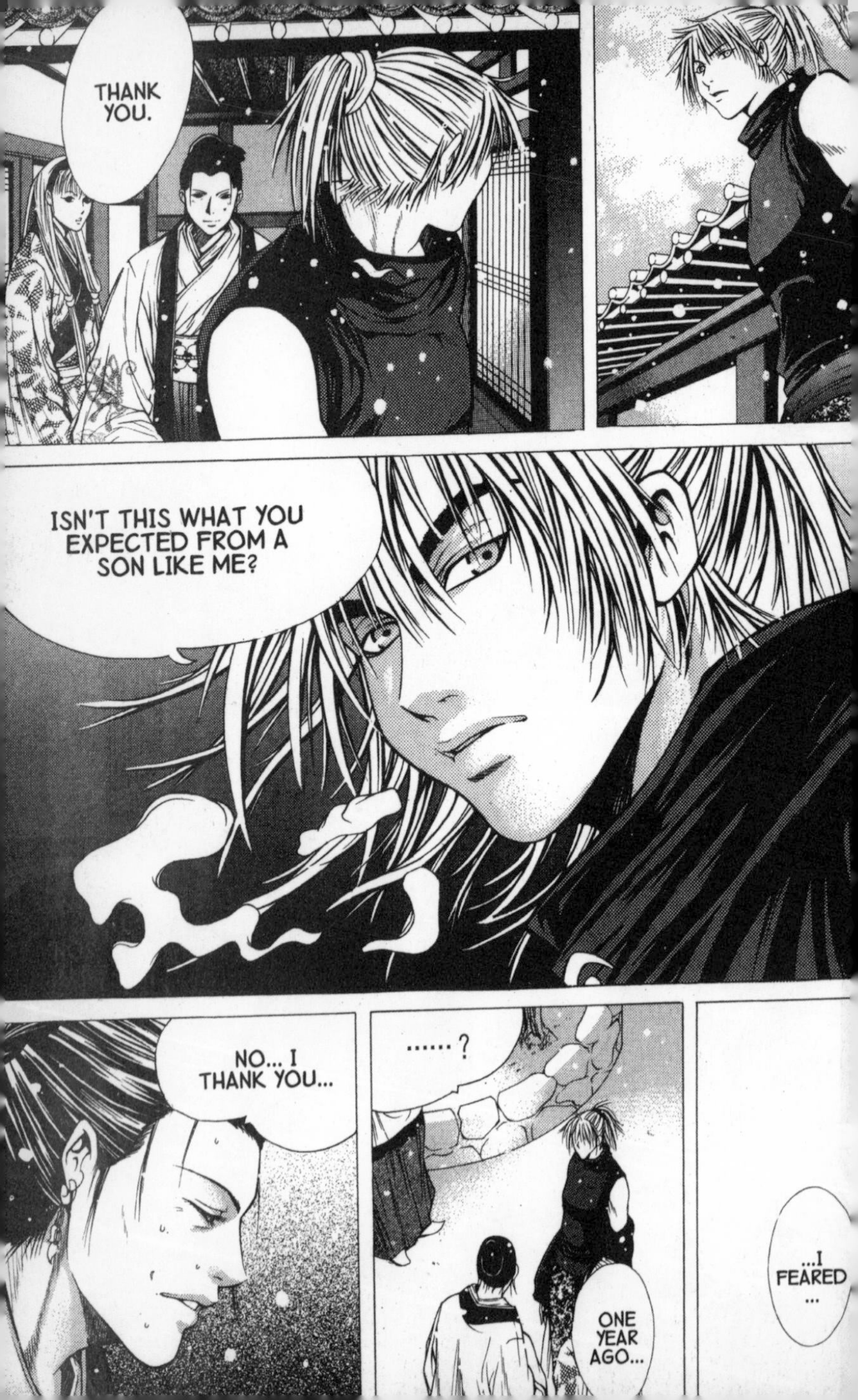
THANK YOU.
ISN'T THIS WHAT YOU EXPECTED FROM A SON LIKE ME?
NO... I THANK YOU...
......?
ONE YEAR AGO...
...I FEARED ...

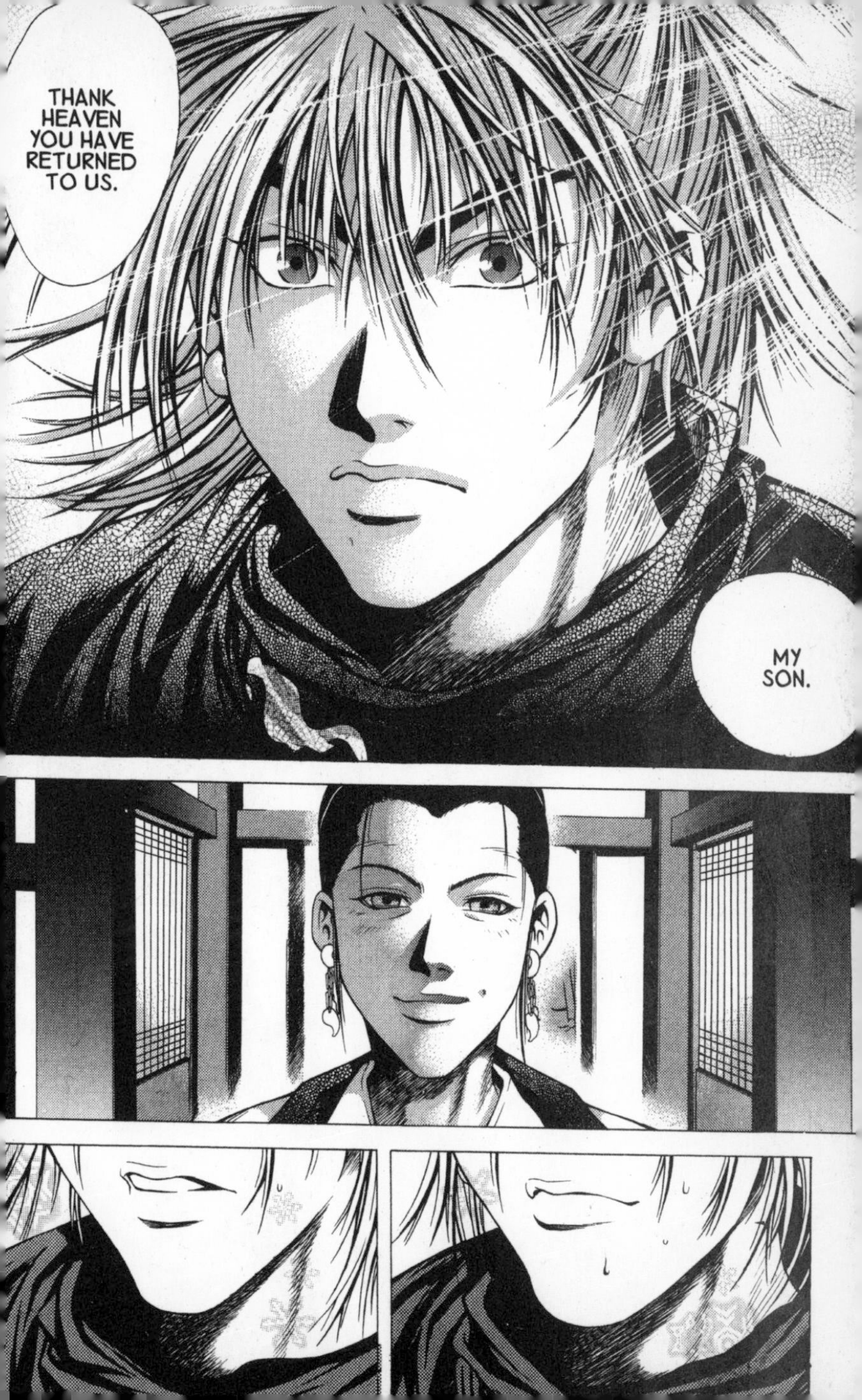
THANK HEAVEN YOU HAVE RETURNED TO US.
MY SON.

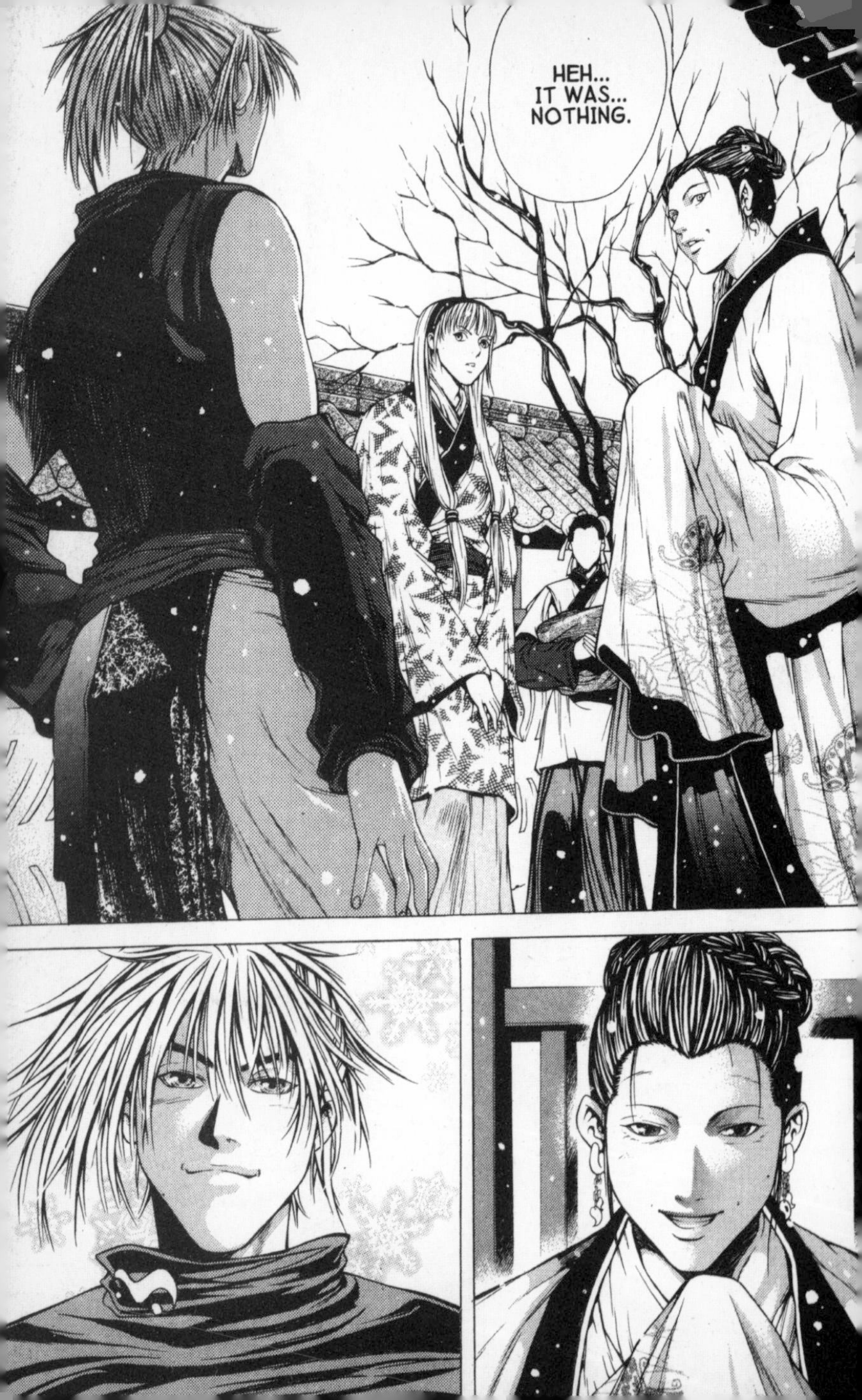
HEH...
IT WAS...
NOTHING.

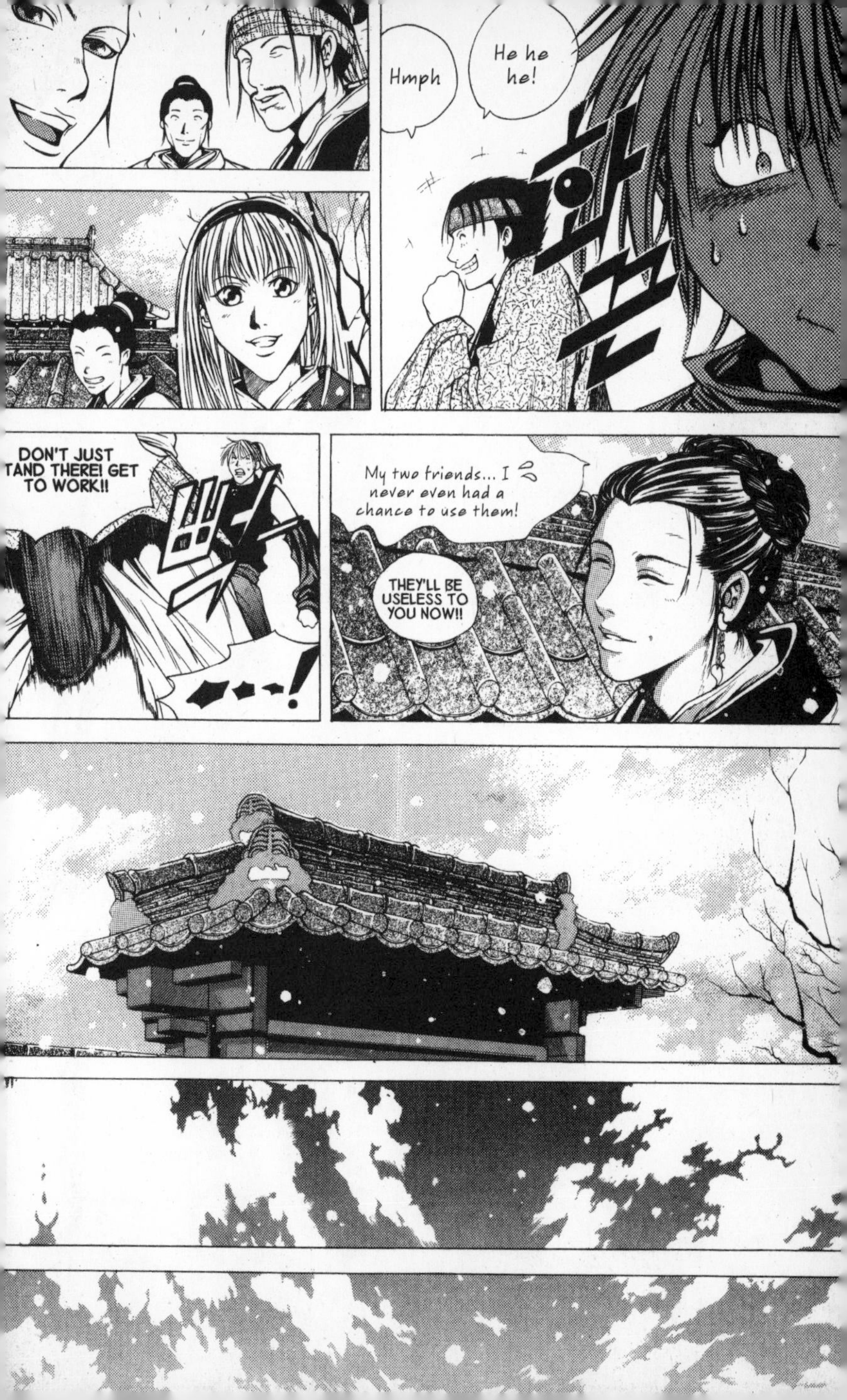
Hmph
He he he!
DON'T JUST TAND THERE! GET TO WORK!!
My two friends... I never even had a chance to use them!
THEY'LL BE USELESS TO YOU NOW!!

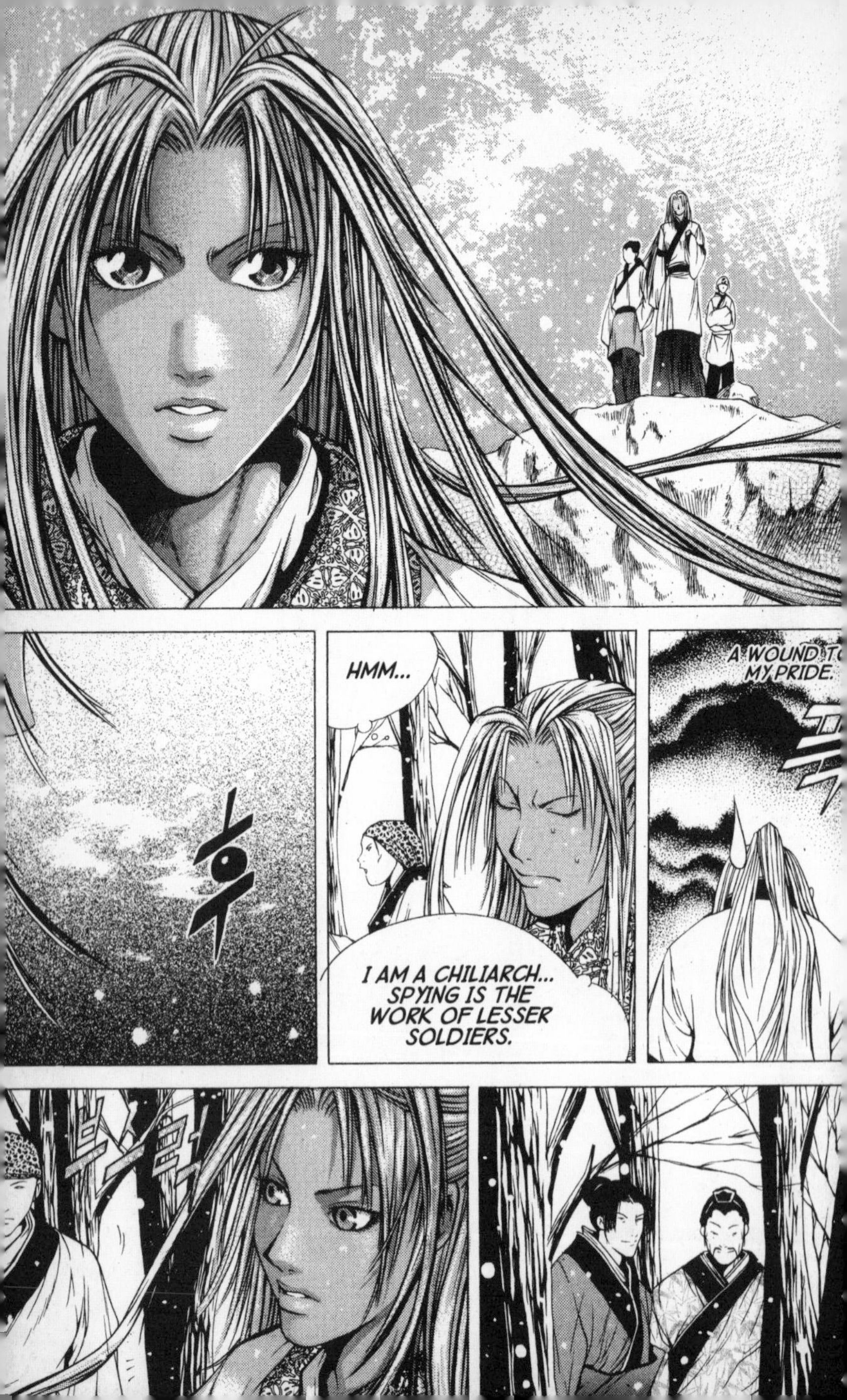
HMM...
I AM A CHILIARCH... SPYING IS THE WORK OF LESSER SOLDIERS.
A WOUND TO MY PRIDE.

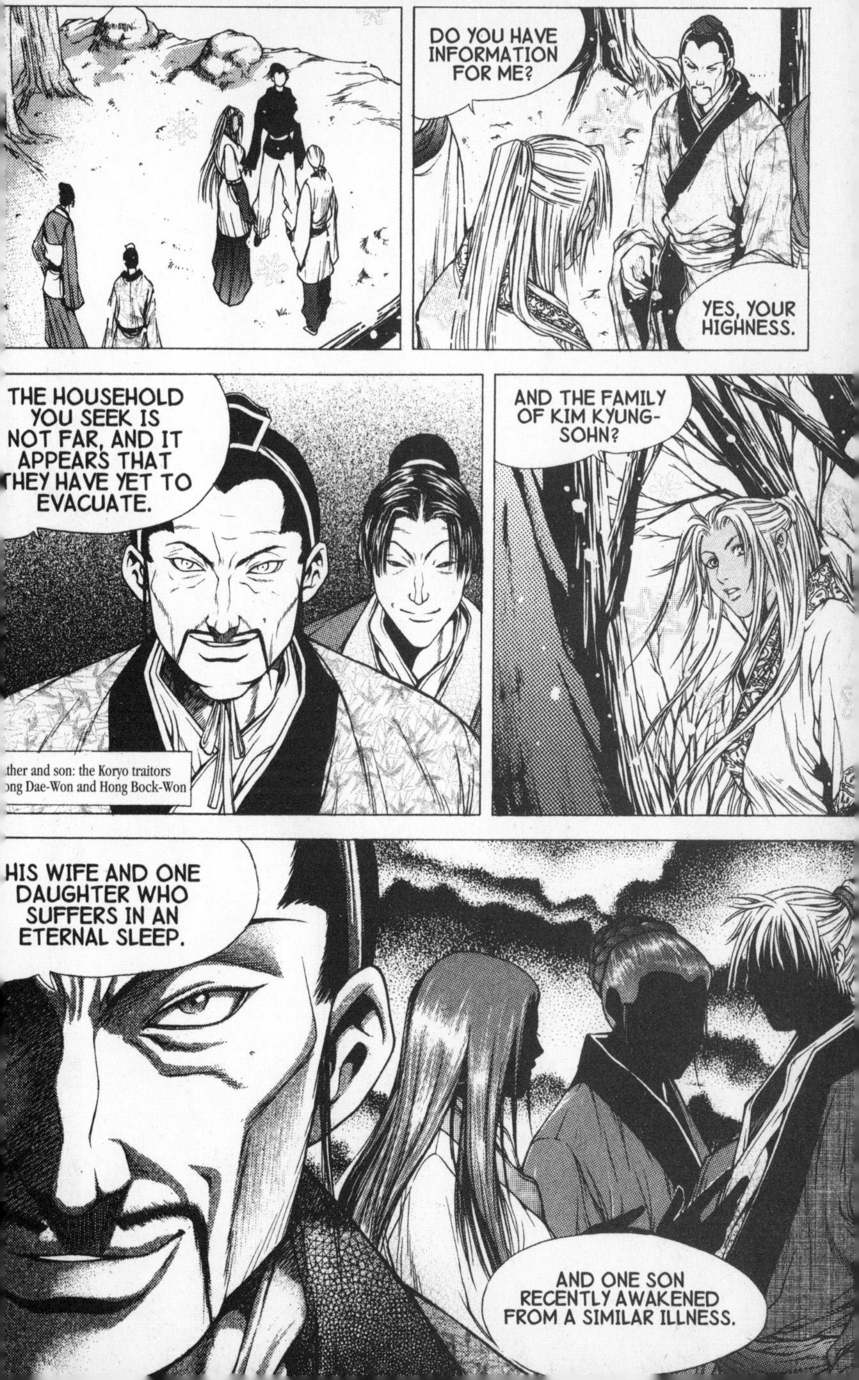

DO YOU HAVE INFORMATION FOR ME?
YES, YOUR HIGHNESS.
THE HOUSEHOLD YOU SEEK IS NOT FAR, AND IT APPEARS THAT THEY HAVE YET TO EVACUATE.
ather and son: the Koryo traitors
ong Dae-Won and Hong Bock-Won
AND THE FAMILY OF KIM KYUNG-SOHN?
HIS WIFE AND ONE DAUGHTER WHO SUFFERS IN AN ETERNAL SLEEP.
AND ONE SON RECENTLY AWAKENED FROM A SIMILAR ILLNESS.

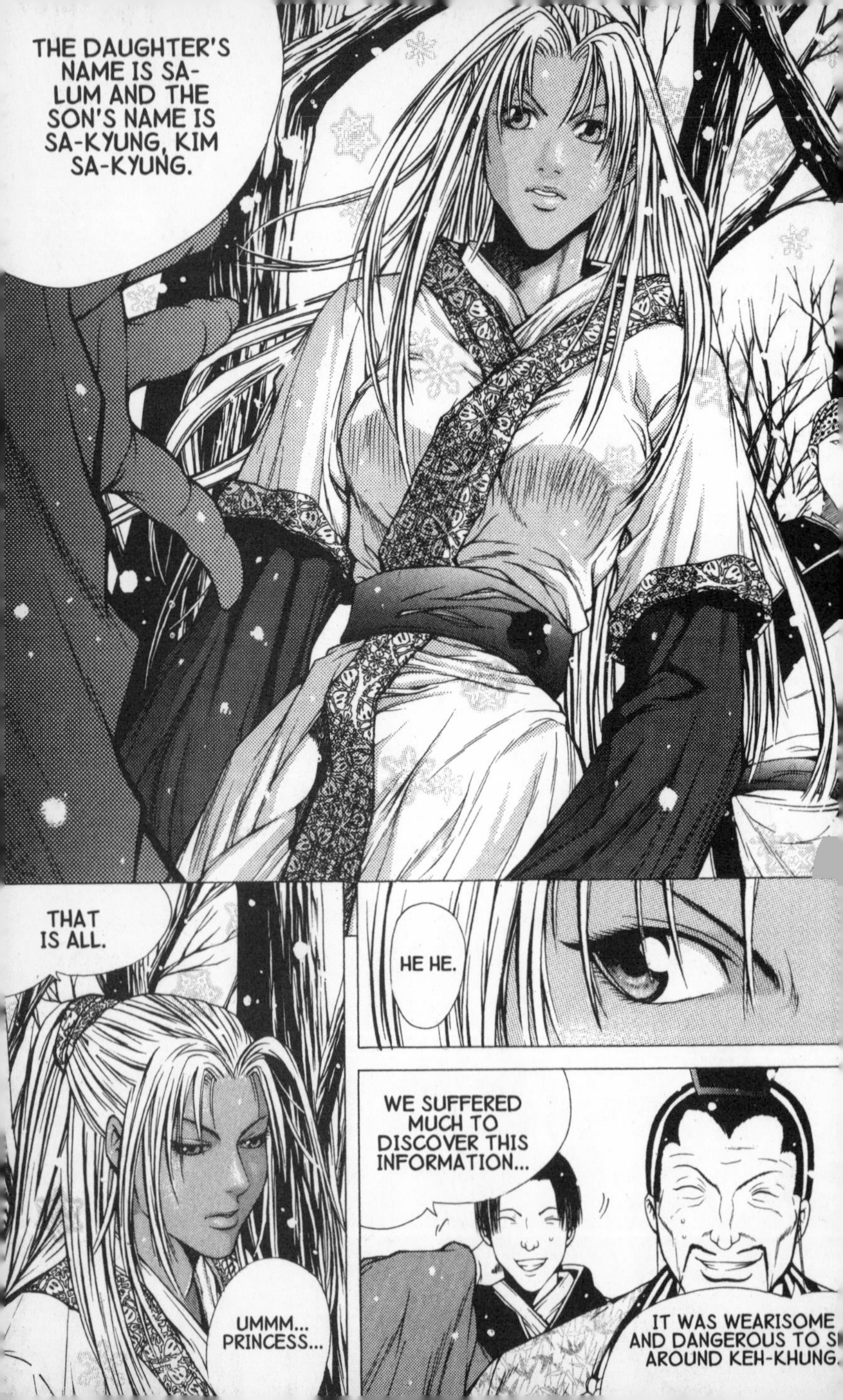
THE DAUGHTER'S NAME IS SA-LUM AND THE SON'S NAME IS SA-KYUNG, KIM SA-KYUNG.
THAT IS ALL.
UMMM... PRINCESS...
HE HE.
WE SUFFERED MUCH TO DISCOVER THIS INFORMATION...
IT WAS WEARISOME AND DANGEROUS TO S AROUND KEH-KHUNG.

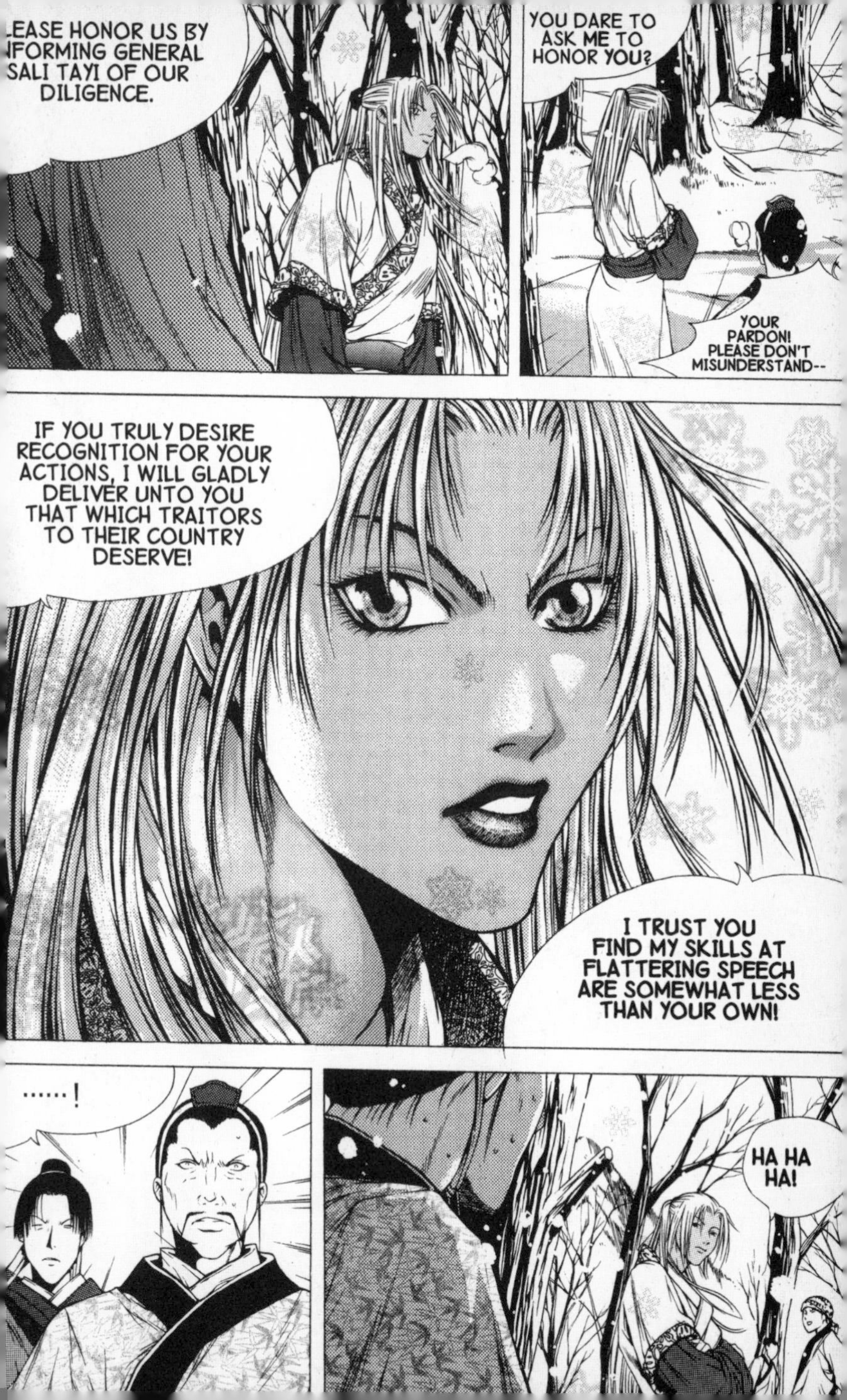
LEASE HONOR US BY
NFORMING GENERAL SALI TAYI OF OUR DILIGENCE.
YOU DARE TO ASK ME TO HONOR YOU?
YOUR PARDON! PLEASE DON'T MISUNDERSTAND--
IF YOU TRULY DESIRE RECOGNITION FOR YOUR ACTIONS, I WILL GLADLY DELIVER UNTO YOU THAT WHICH TRAITORS TO THEIR COUNTRY DESERVE!
I TRUST YOU FIND MY SKILLS AT FLATTERING SPEECH ARE SOMEWHAT LESS THAN YOUR OWN!
......!
HA HA HA!

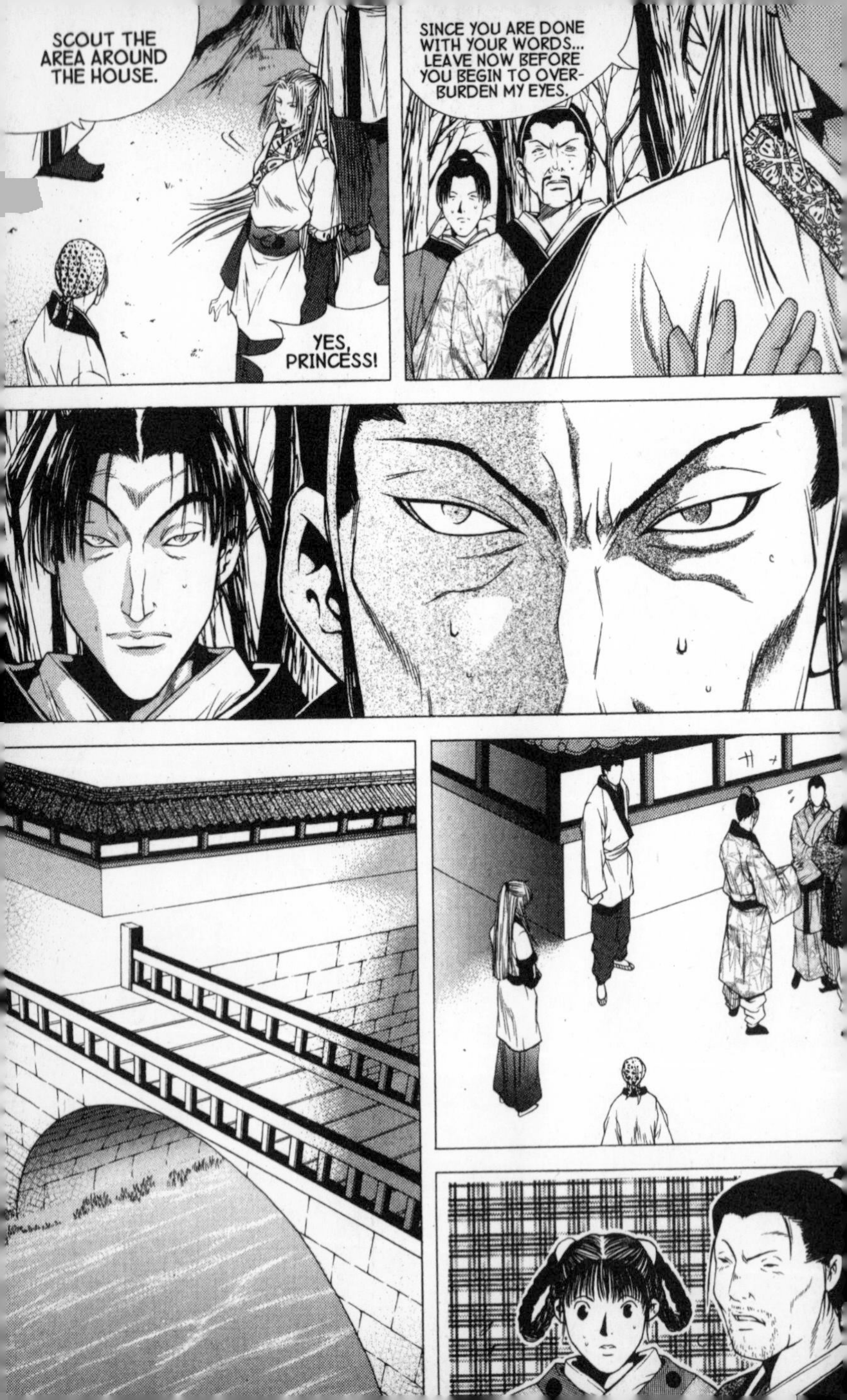
SCOUT THE AREA AROUND THE HOUSE.
YES, PRINCESS!
SINCE YOU ARE DONE WITH YOUR WORDS... LEAVE NOW BEFORE YOU BEGIN TO OVER-BURDEN MY EYES.

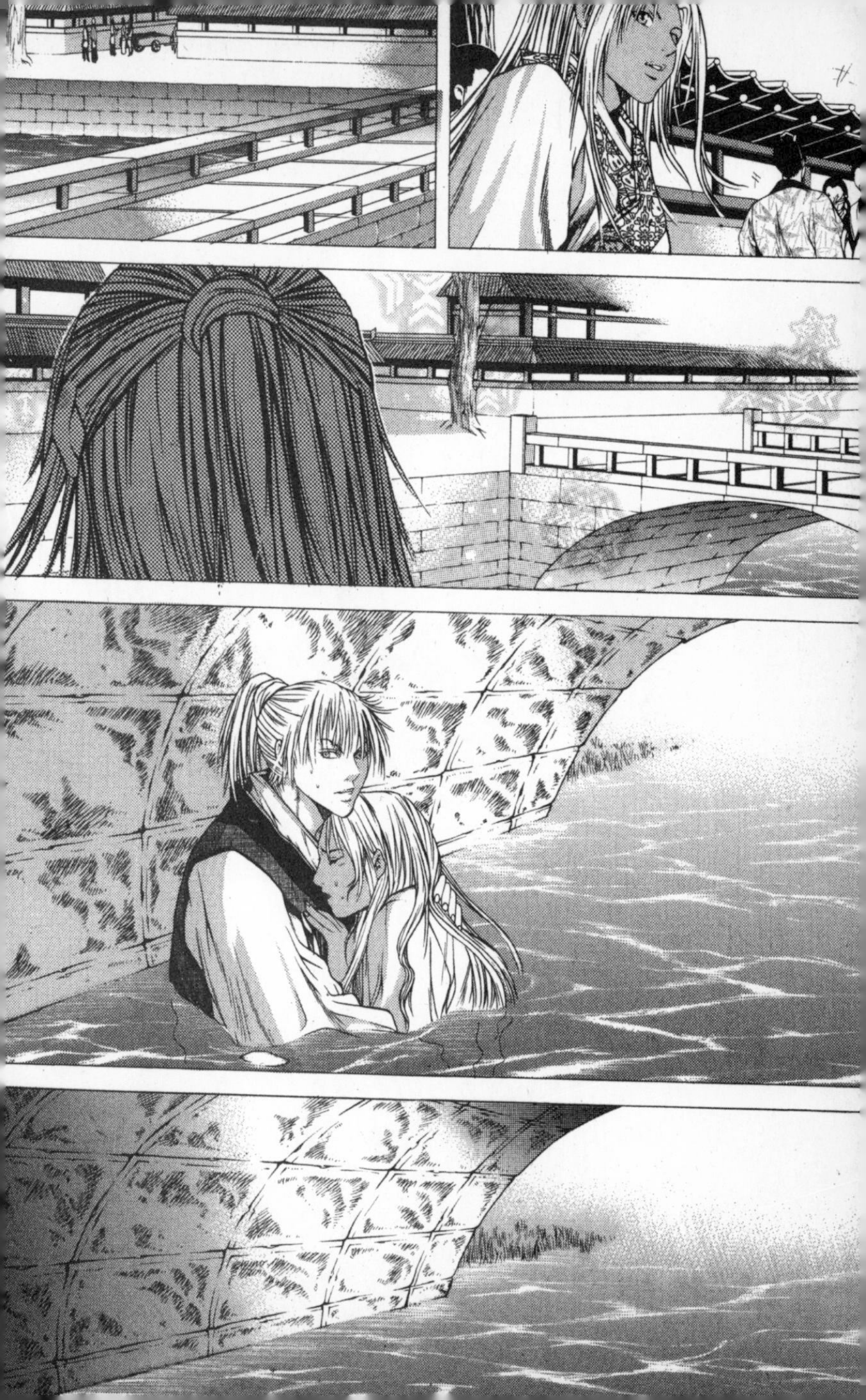
ザ-

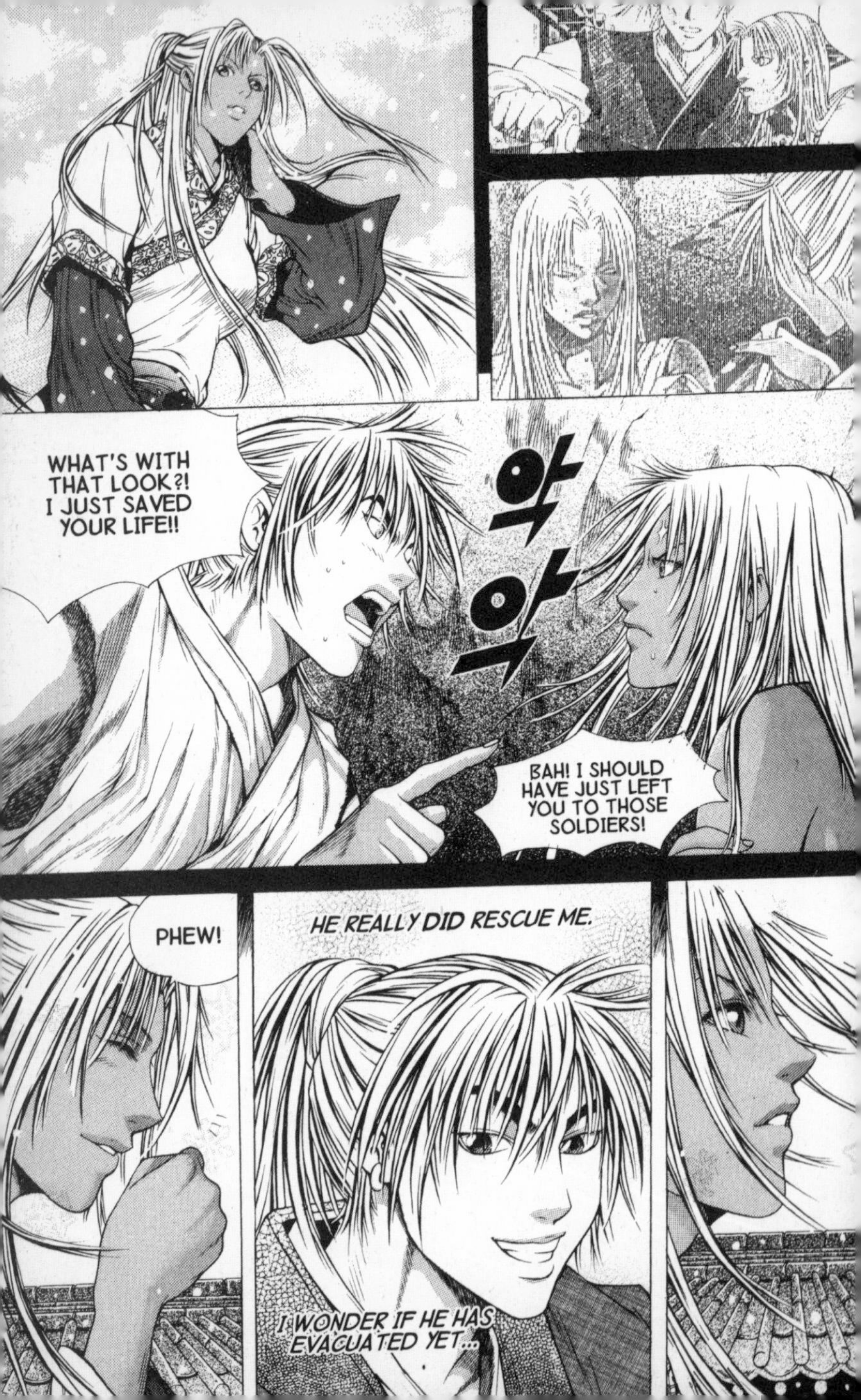
WHAT'S WITH THAT LOOK?! I JUST SAVED YOUR LIFE!!
악아악
BAH! I SHOULD HAVE JUST LEFT YOU TO THOSE SOLDIERS!
PHEW!
HE REALLY DID RESCUE ME.
I WONDER IF HE HAS EVACUATED YET...

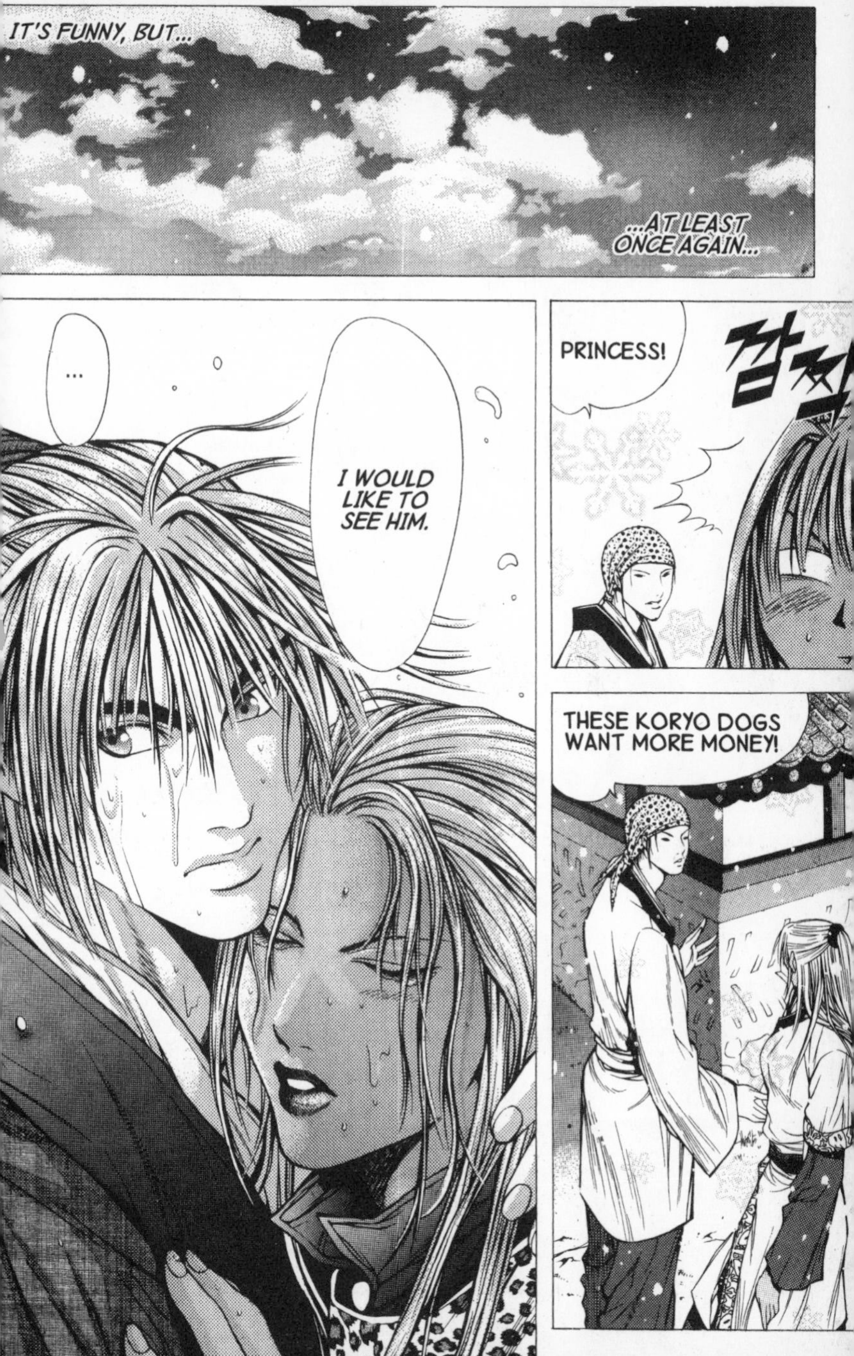
IT'S FUNNY, BUT...
...AT LEAST ONCE AGAIN...
...
I WOULD LIKE TO SEE HIM.
PRINCESS!
깜짝
THESE KORYO DOGS WANT MORE MONEY!

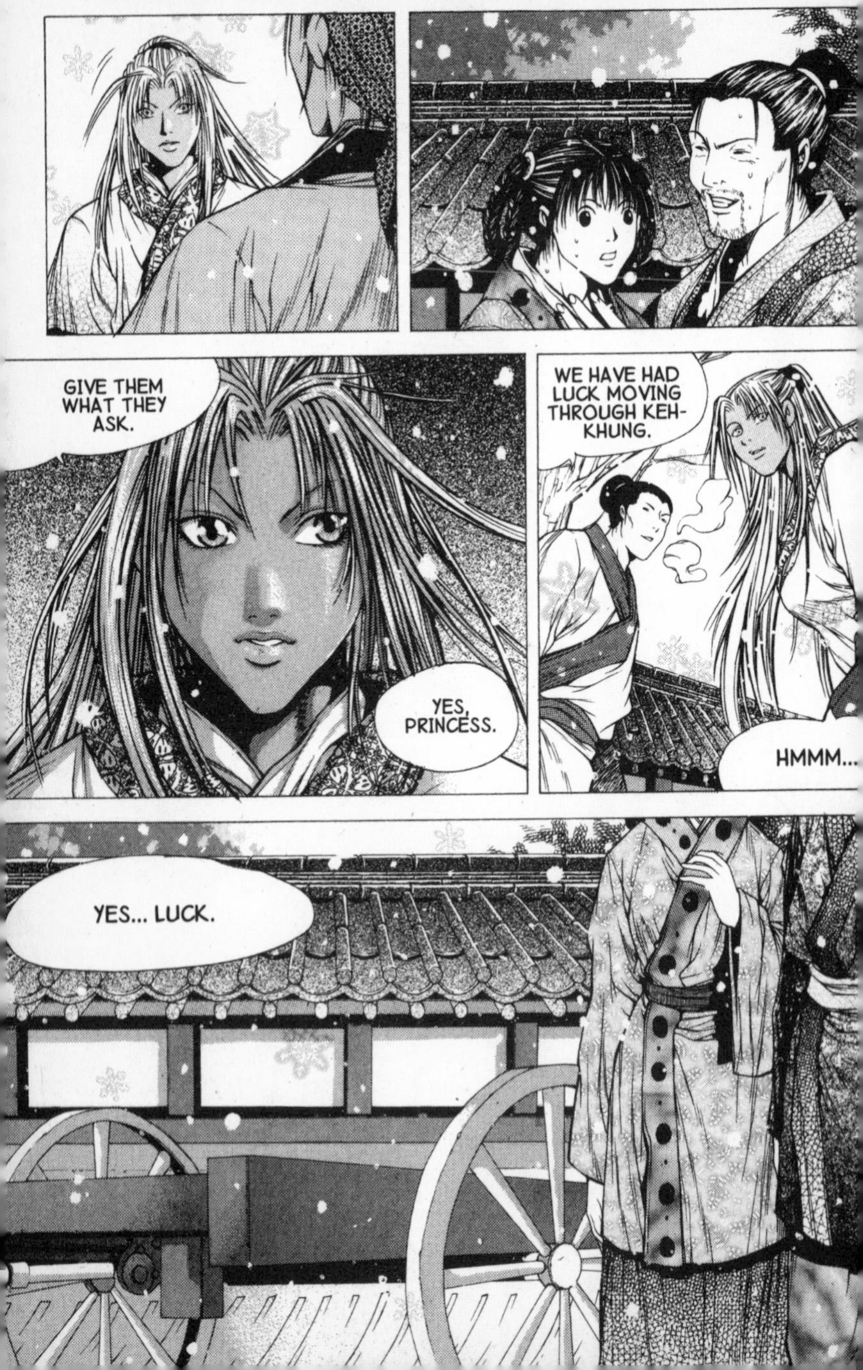
GIVE THEM WHAT THEY ASK.
YES, PRINCESS.
WE HAVE HAD LUCK MOVING THROUGH KEH-KHUNG.
HMMM...
YES... LUCK.

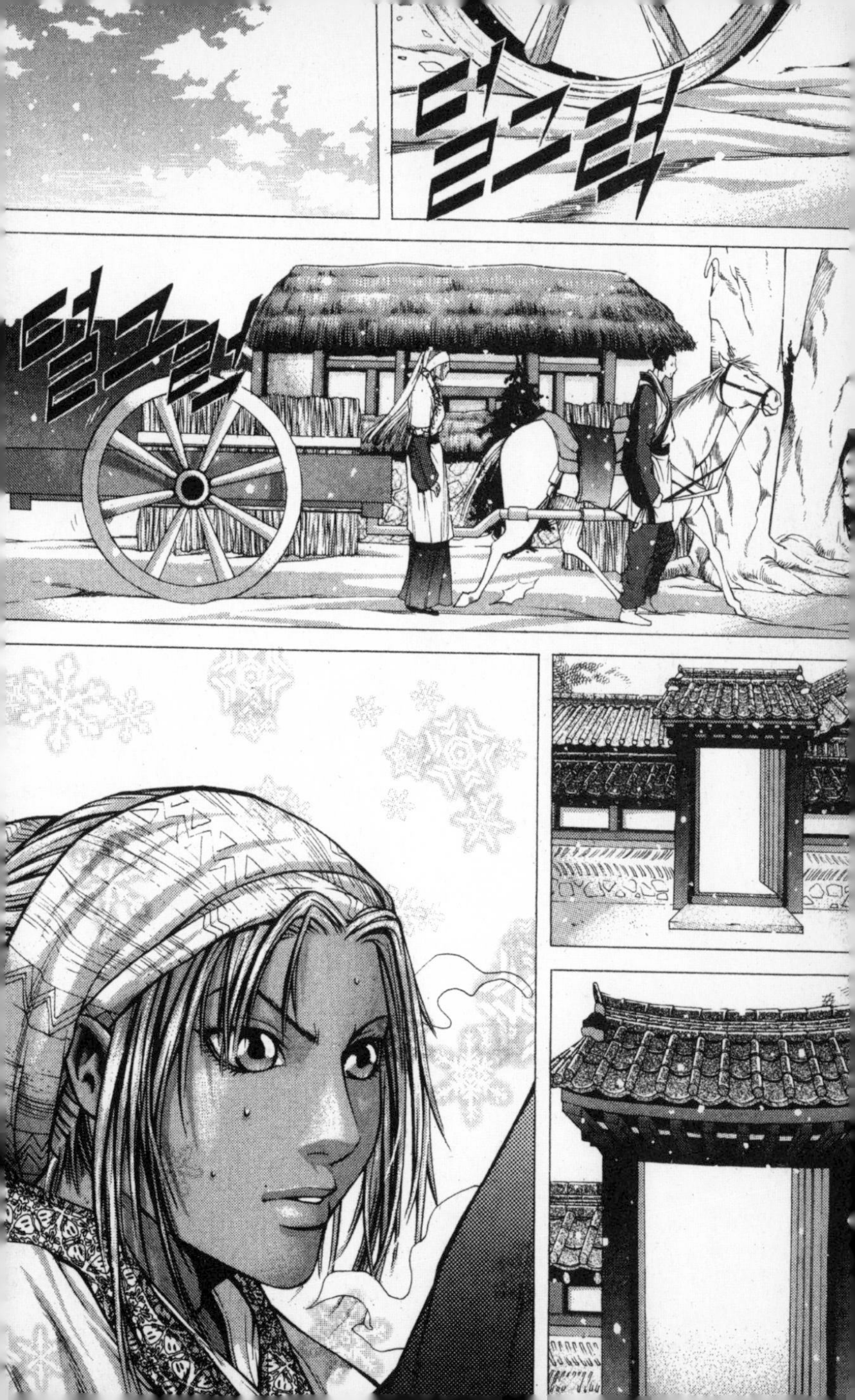
덜그럭
덜그럭

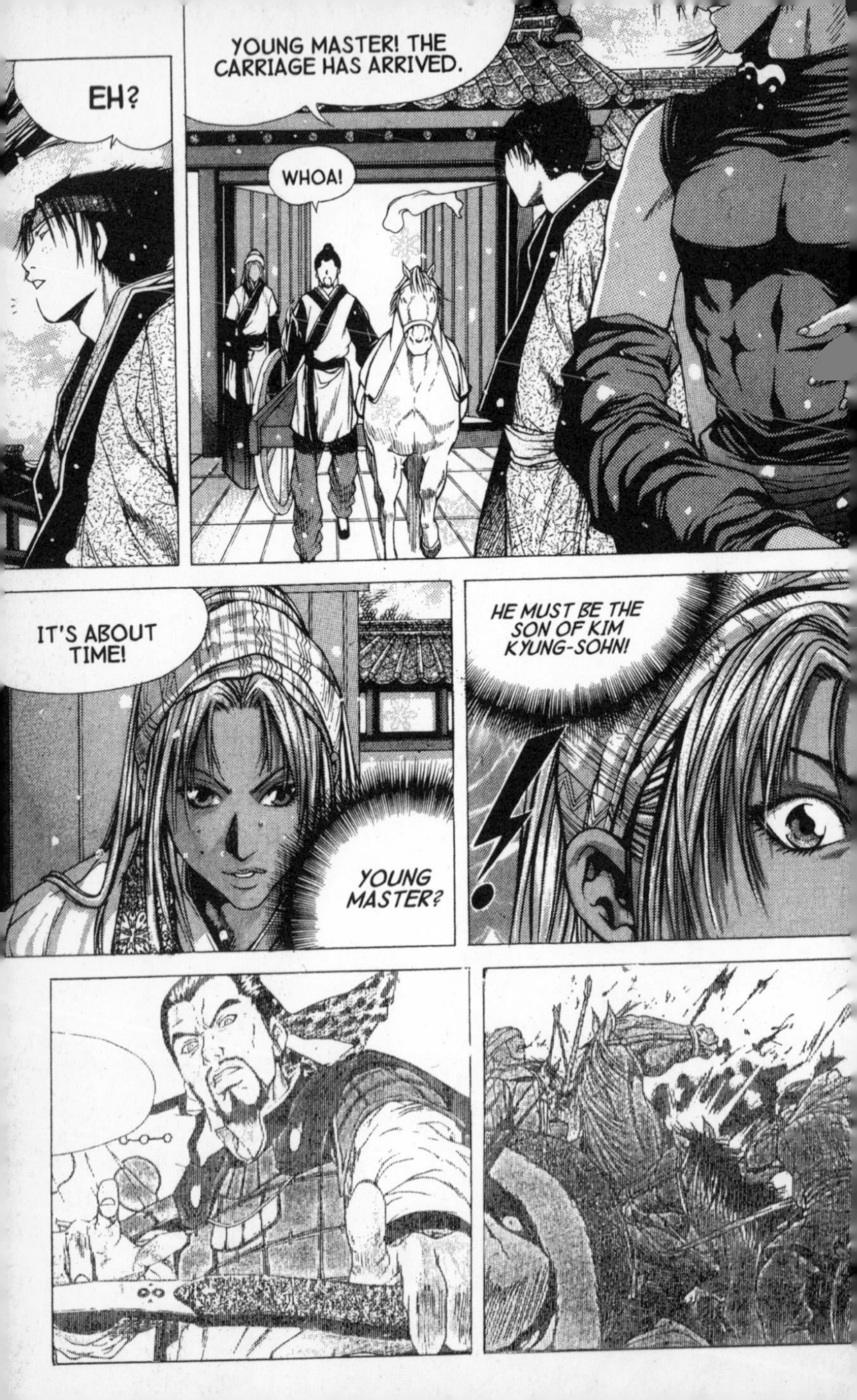
EH?
YOUNG MASTER! THE CARRIAGE HAS ARRIVED.
WHOA!
IT'S ABOUT TIME!
YOUNG MASTER?
HE MUST BE THE SON OF KIM KYUNG-SOHN!

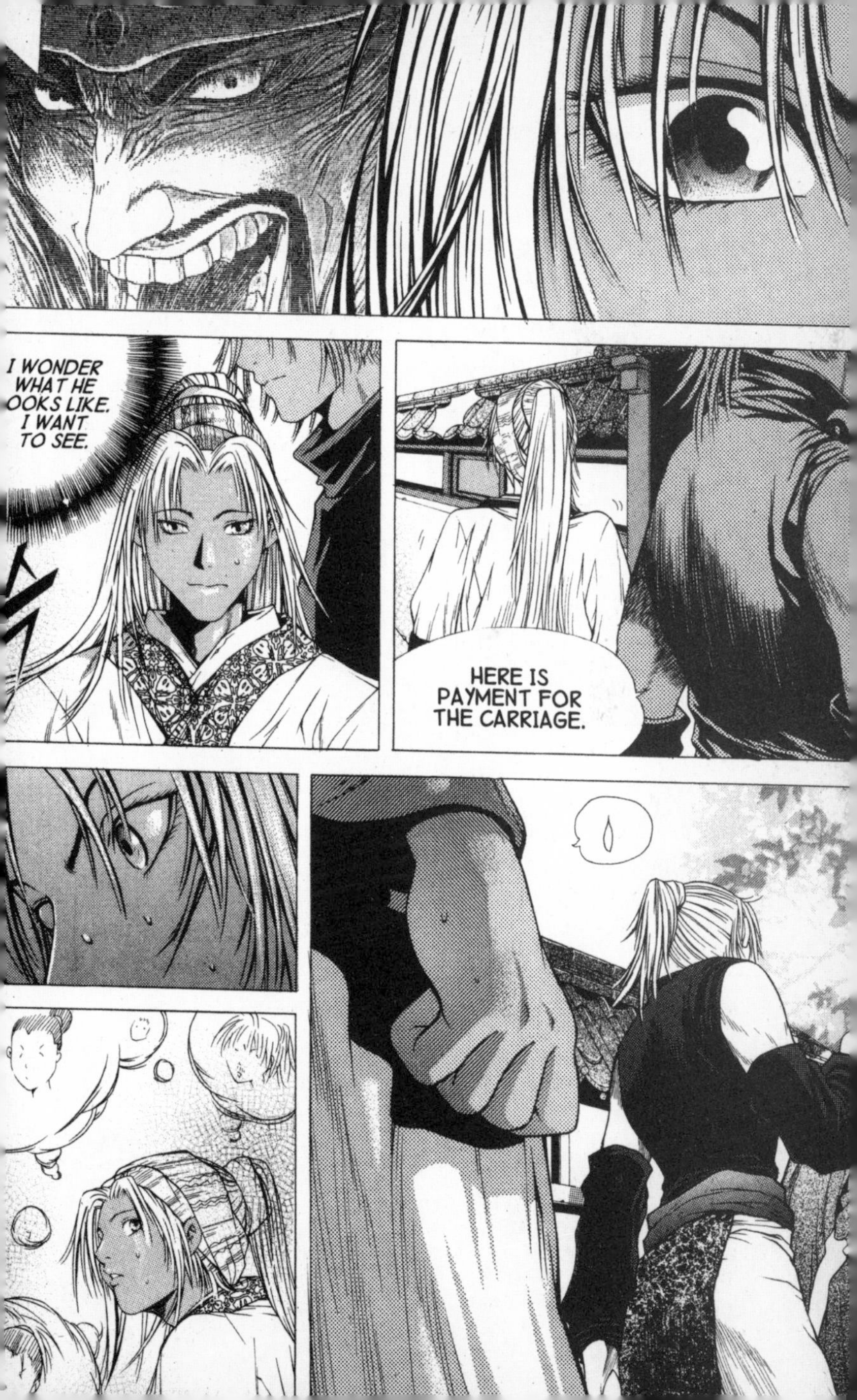
I WONDER WHAT HE OOKS LIKE. I WANT TO SEE.
HERE IS PAYMENT FOR THE CARRIAGE.

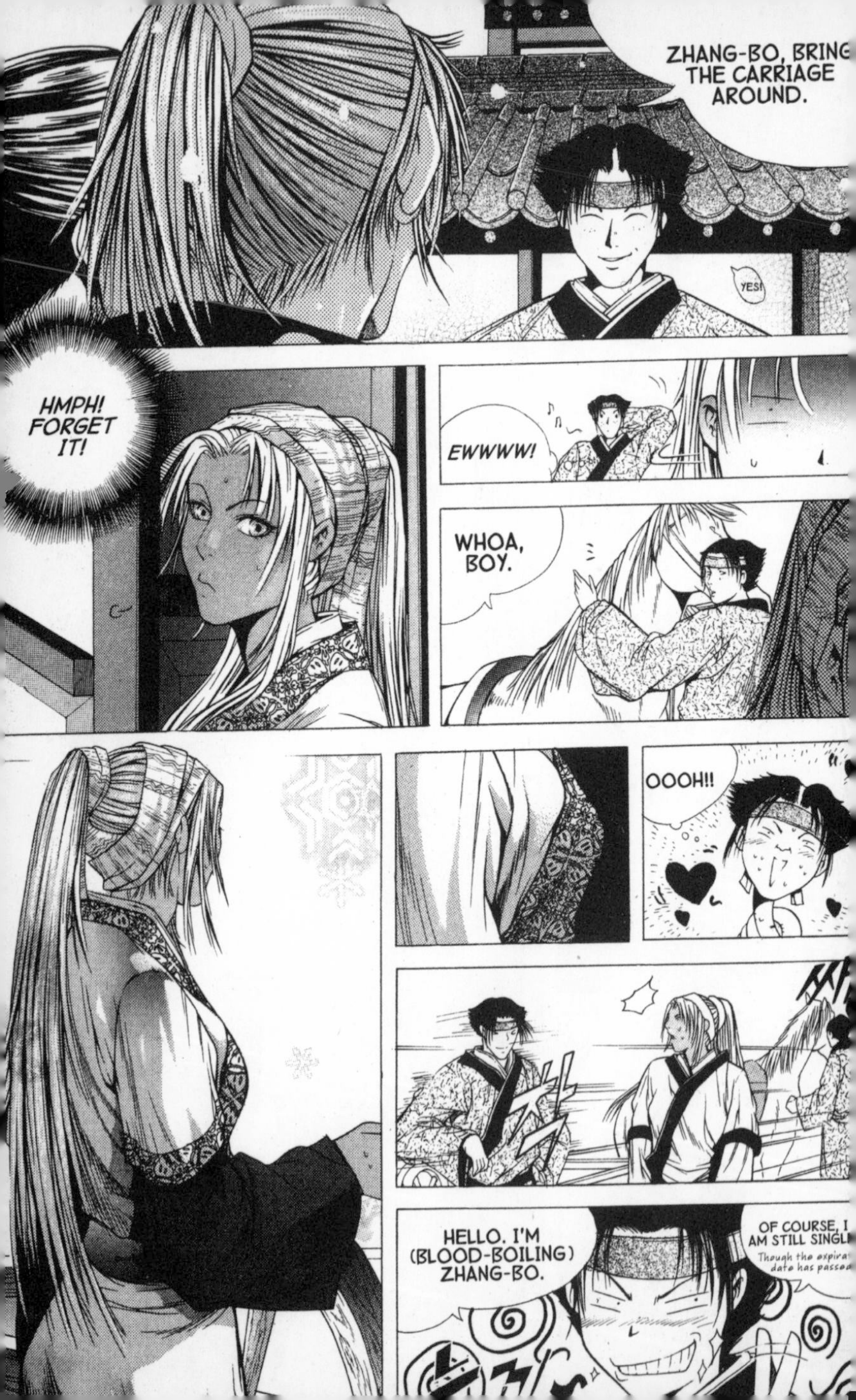

ZHANG-BO, BRING THE CARRIAGE AROUND.
YES!
HMPH! FORGET IT!
EWWWW!
WHOA, BOY.
OOOH!!
HELLO. I'M (BLOOD-BOILING) ZHANG-BO.
OF COURSE, I AM STILL SINGL
Though the expira date has passed

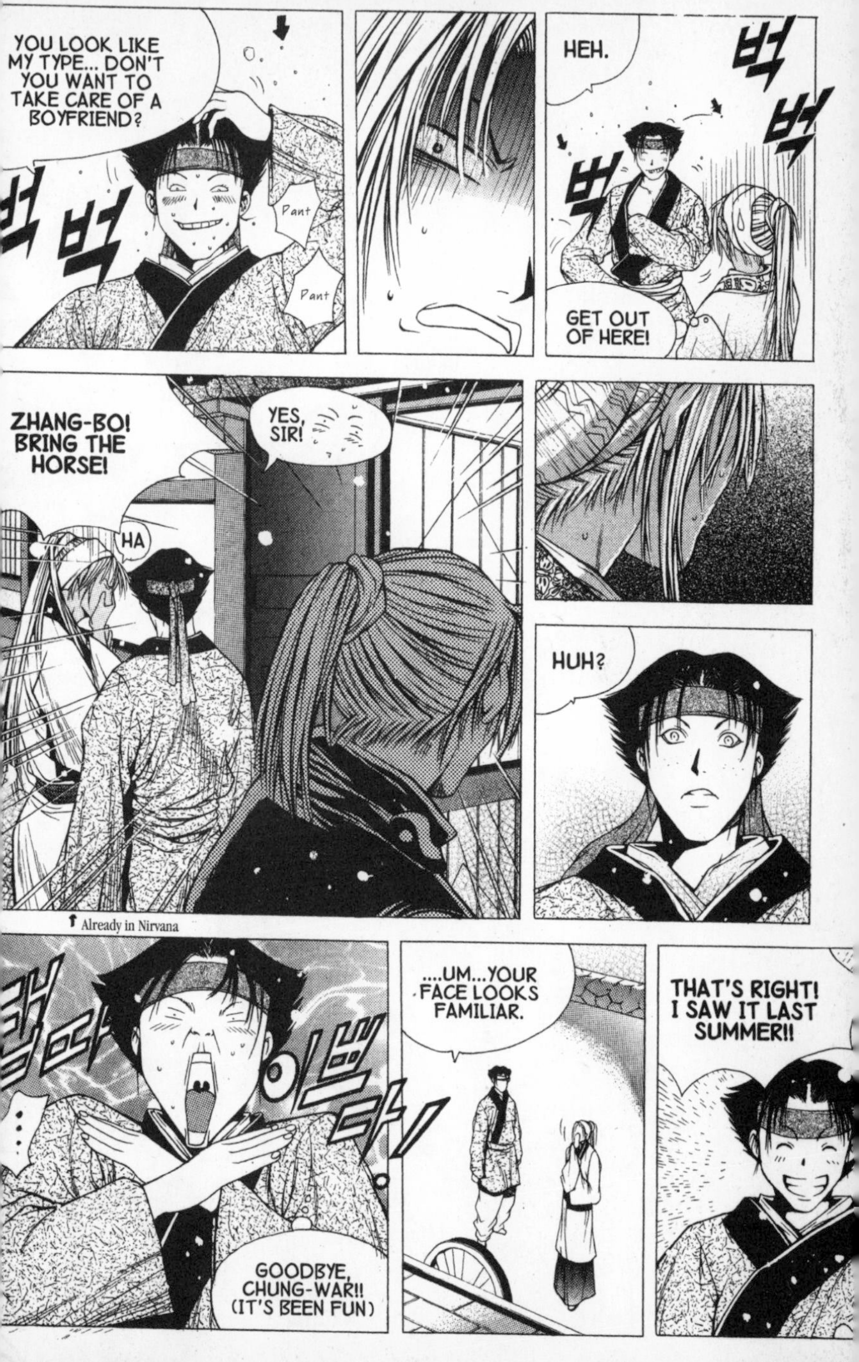
YOU LOOK LIKE MY TYPE... DON'T YOU WANT TO TAKE CARE OF A BOYFRIEND?
벅 벅
Pant
Pant
HEH.
벅 벅 벅
GET OUT OF HERE!
ZHANG-BO! BRING THE HORSE!
YES, SIR!
HA
Already in Nirvana
HUH?
GOODBYE, CHUNG-WAR!! (IT'S BEEN FUN)
....UM...YOUR FACE LOOKS FAMILIAR.
THAT'S RIGHT! I SAW IT LAST SUMMER!!

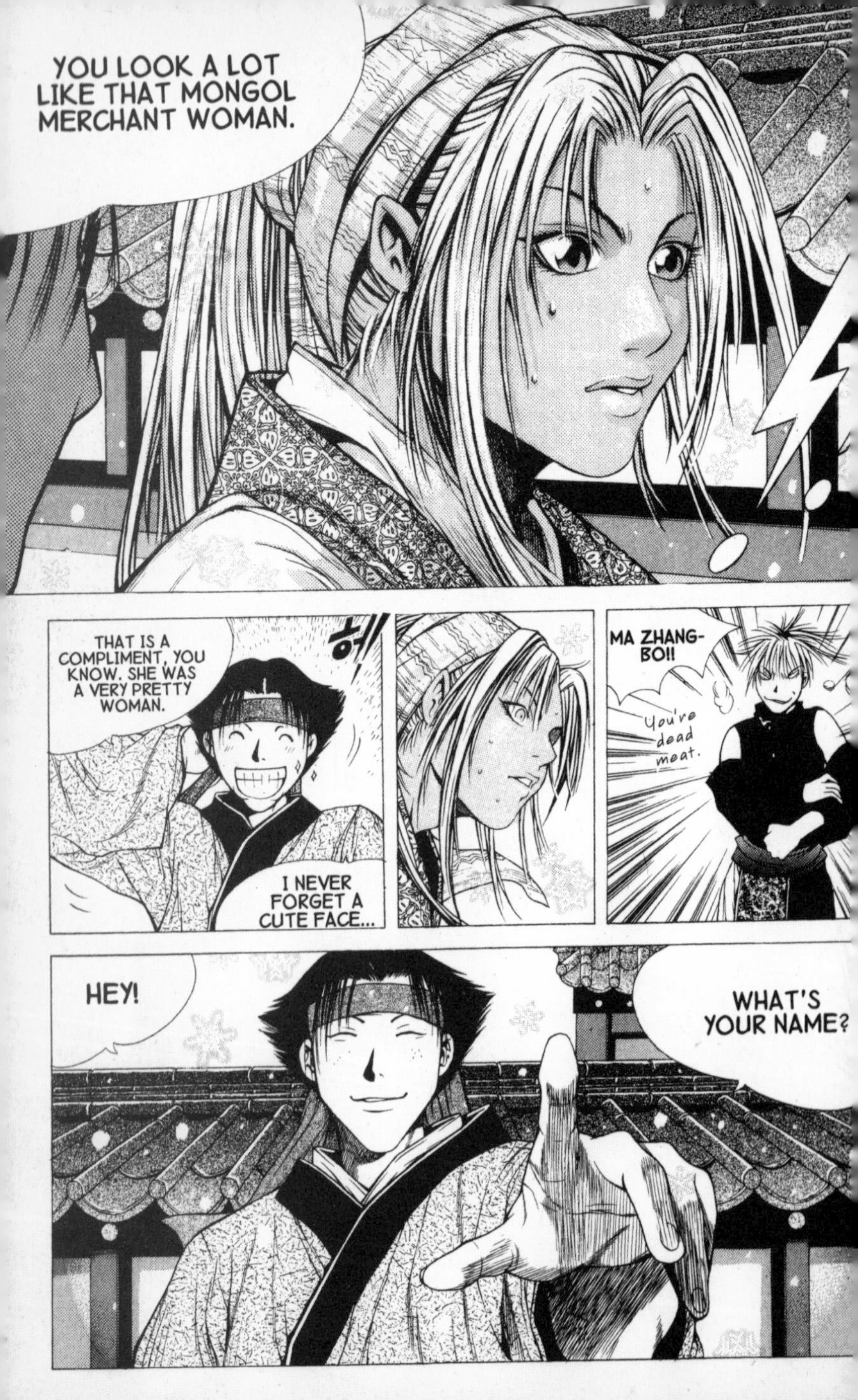
YOU LOOK A LOT LIKE THAT MONGOL MERCHANT WOMAN.
THAT IS A COMPLIMENT, YOU KNOW. SHE WAS A VERY PRETTY WOMAN.
I NEVER FORGET A CUTE FACE...
MA ZHANG-BO!!
You're dead meat.
HEY!
WHAT'S YOUR NAME?

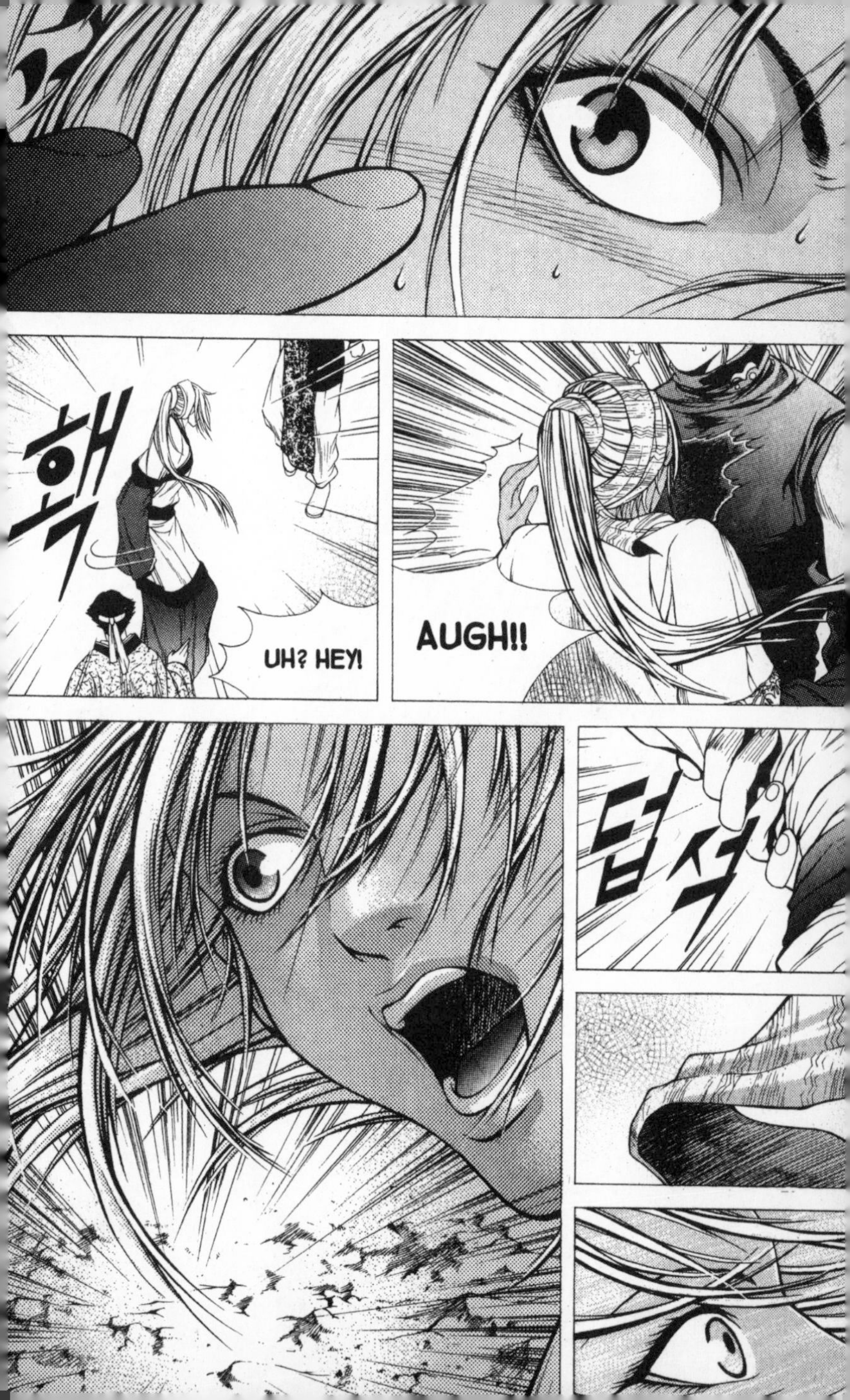

핵
UH? HEY!
AUGH!!
덥석

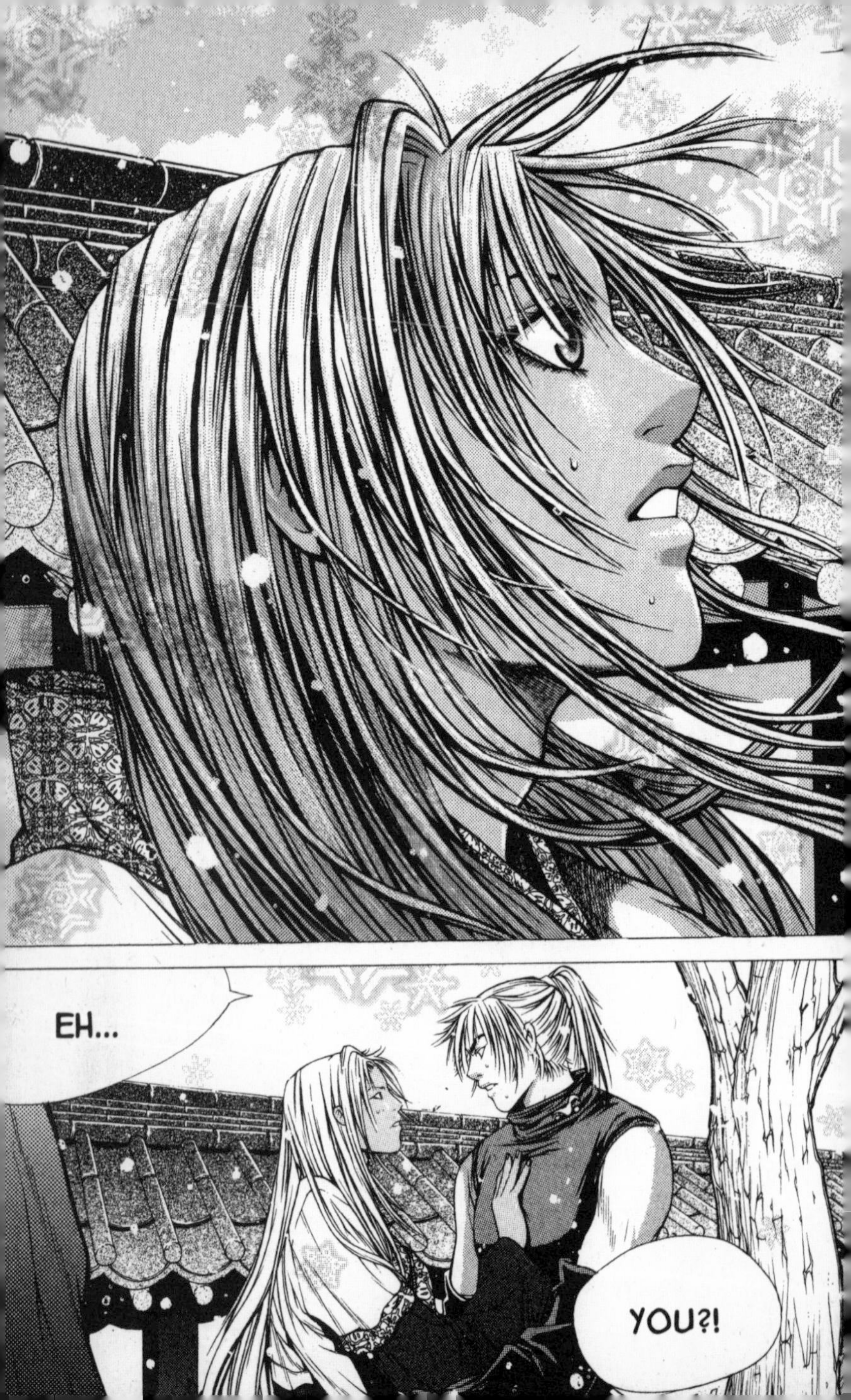
EH...
YOU?!

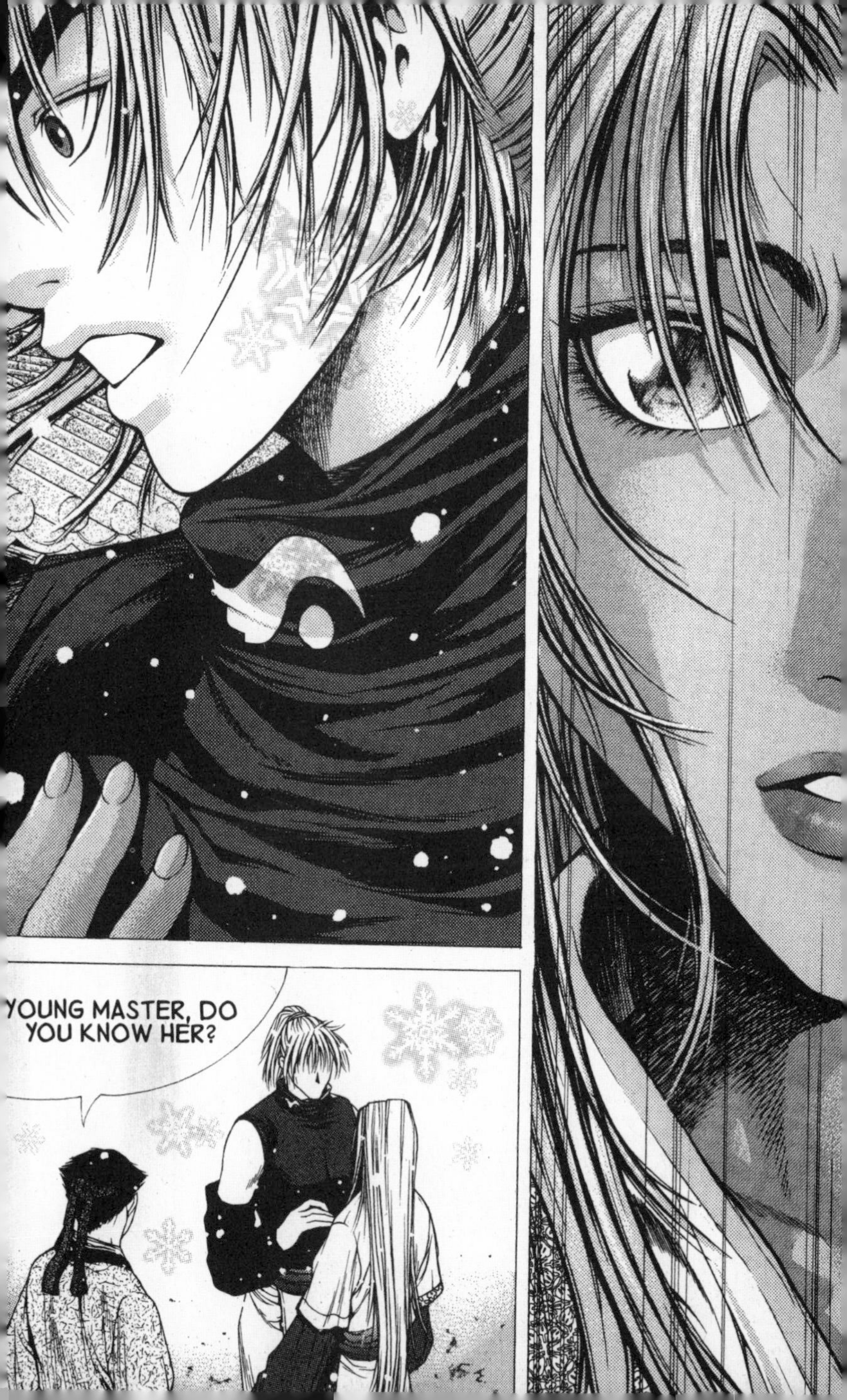
YOUNG MASTER, DO YOU KNOW HER?

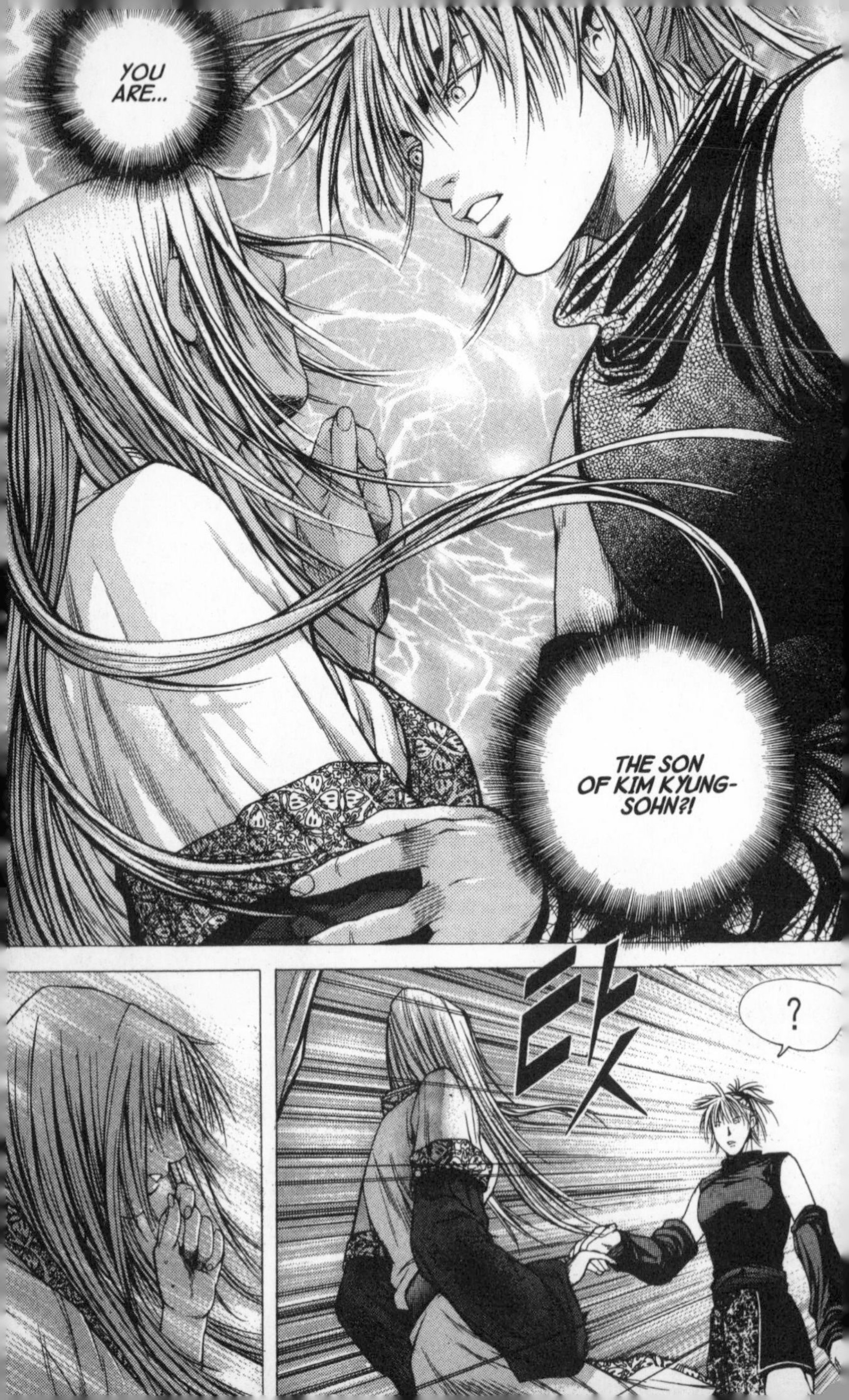
YOU ARE...
THE SON OF KIM KYUNG-SOHN?!
?

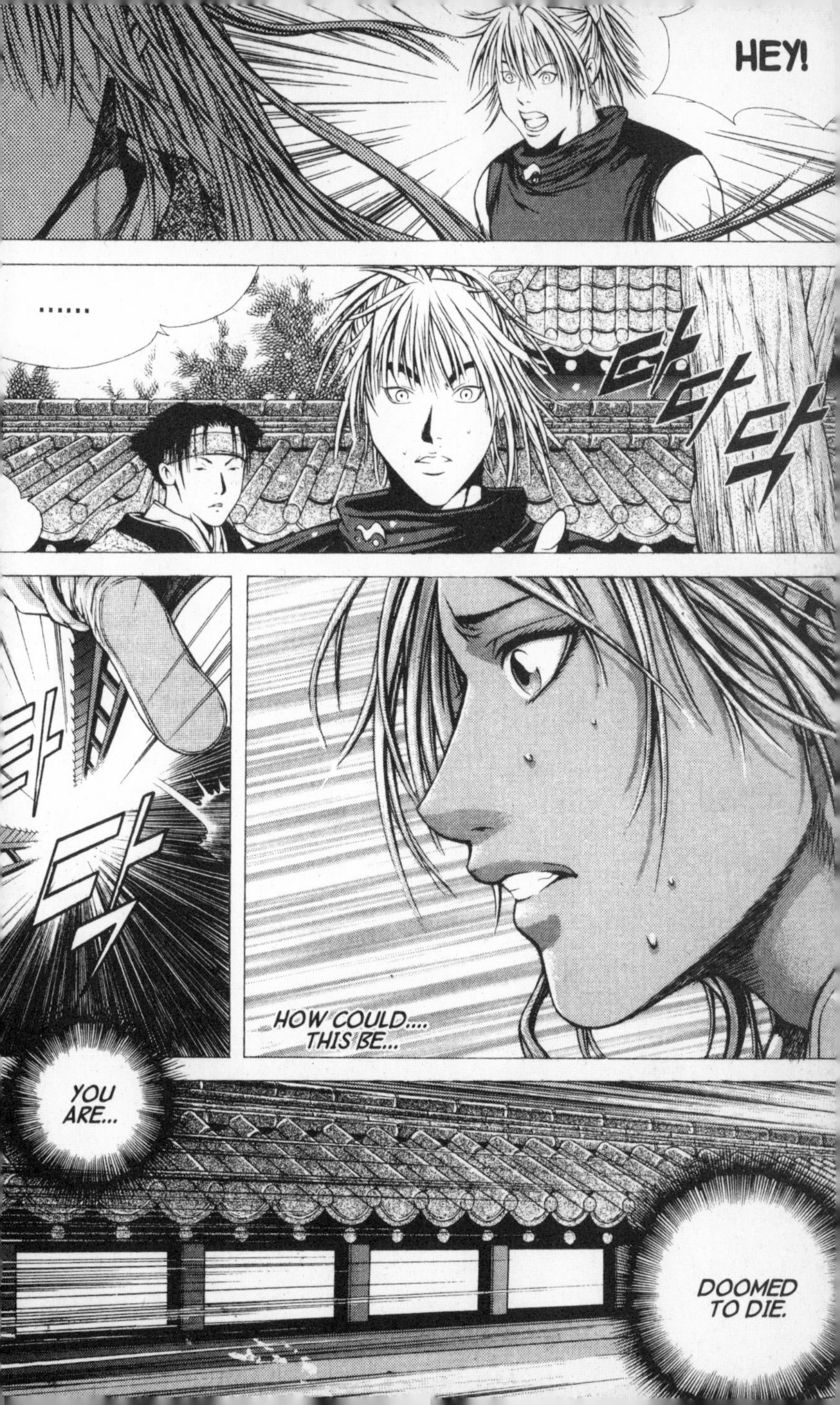
HEY!
......
다다닥
타닥
HOW COULD....
THIS BE...
YOU
ARE...
DOOMED
TO DIE.

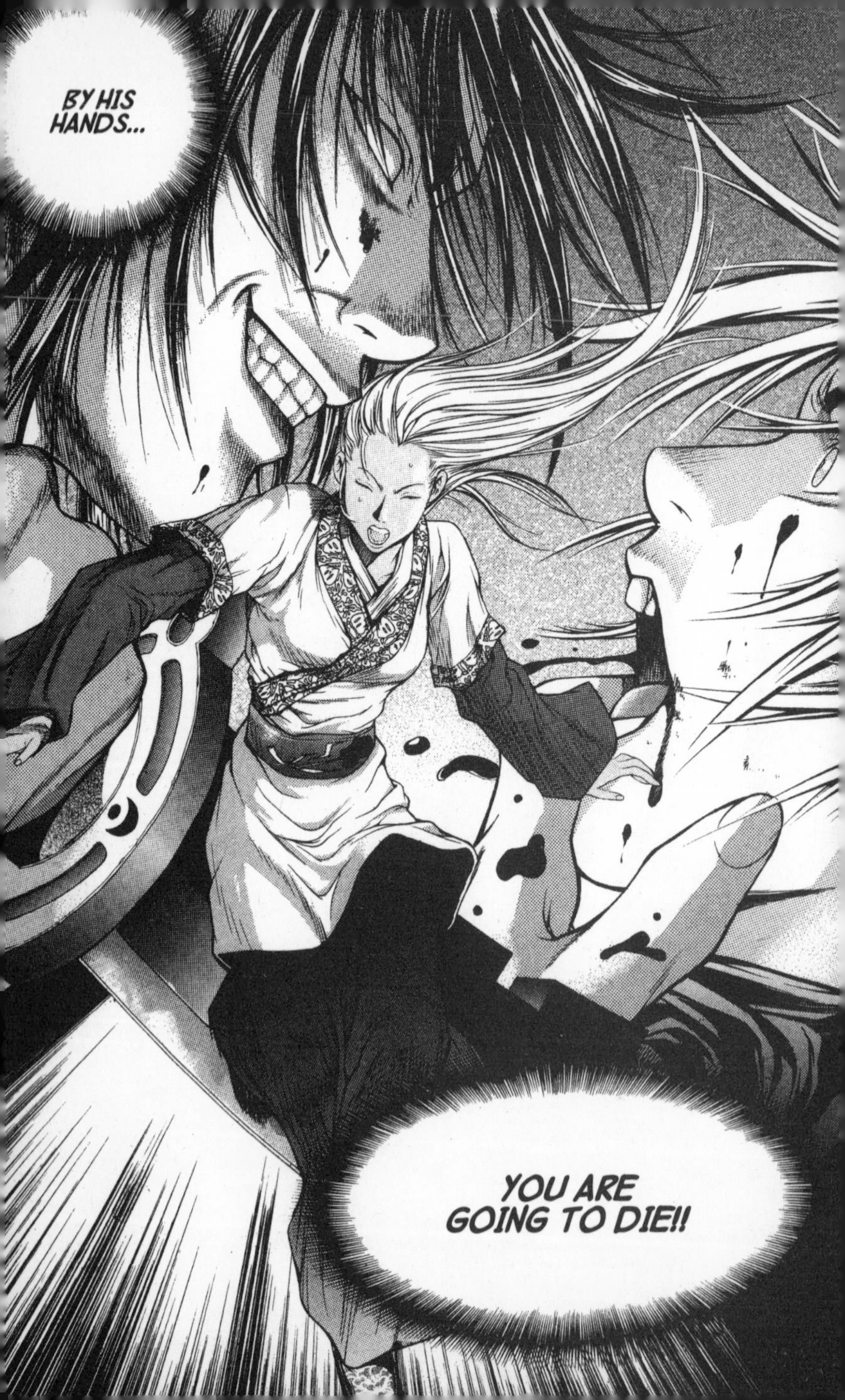
BY HIS HANDS...
YOU ARE GOING TO DIE!!

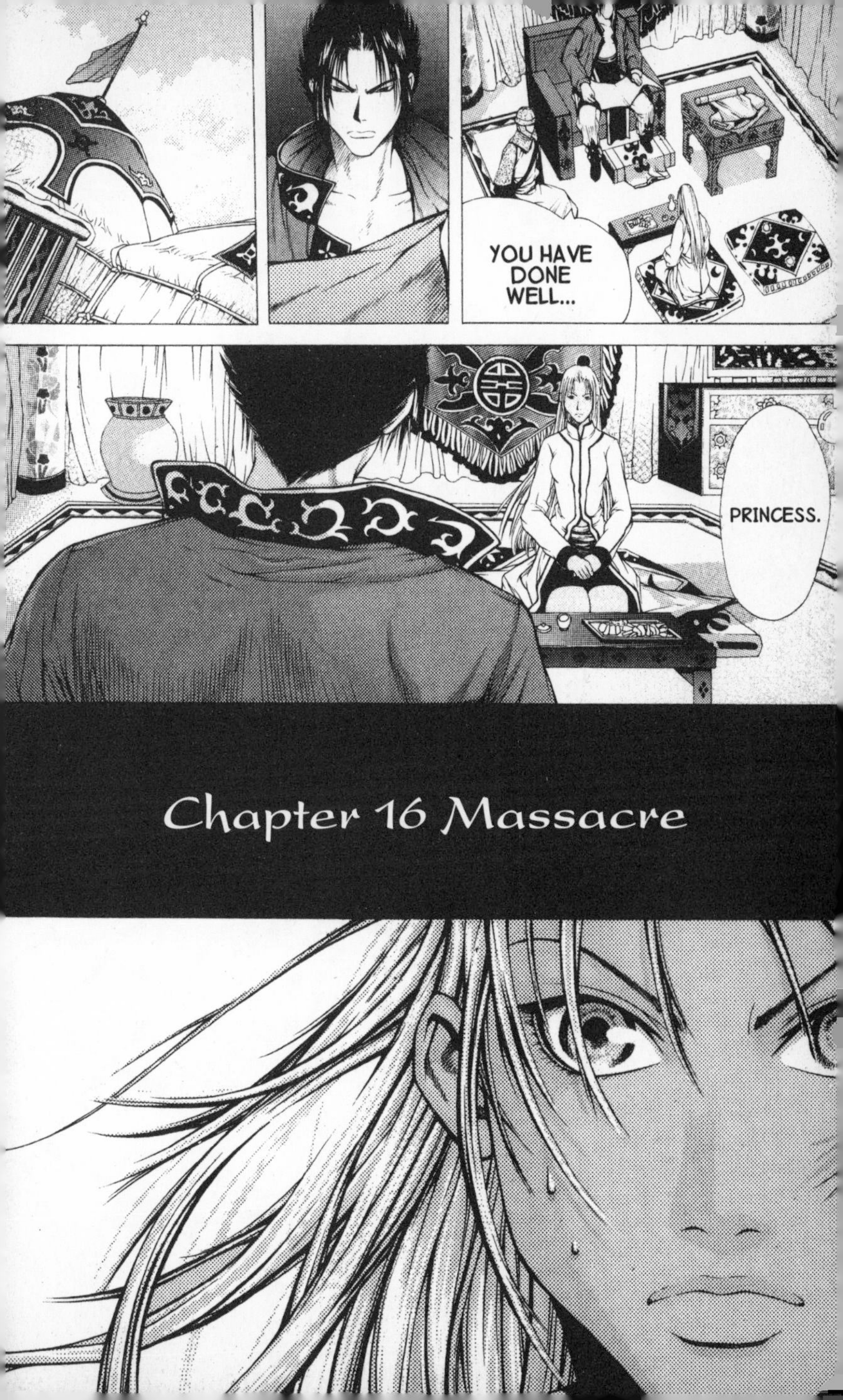
YOU HAVE DONE WELL...
PRINCESS.
Chapter 16 Massacre

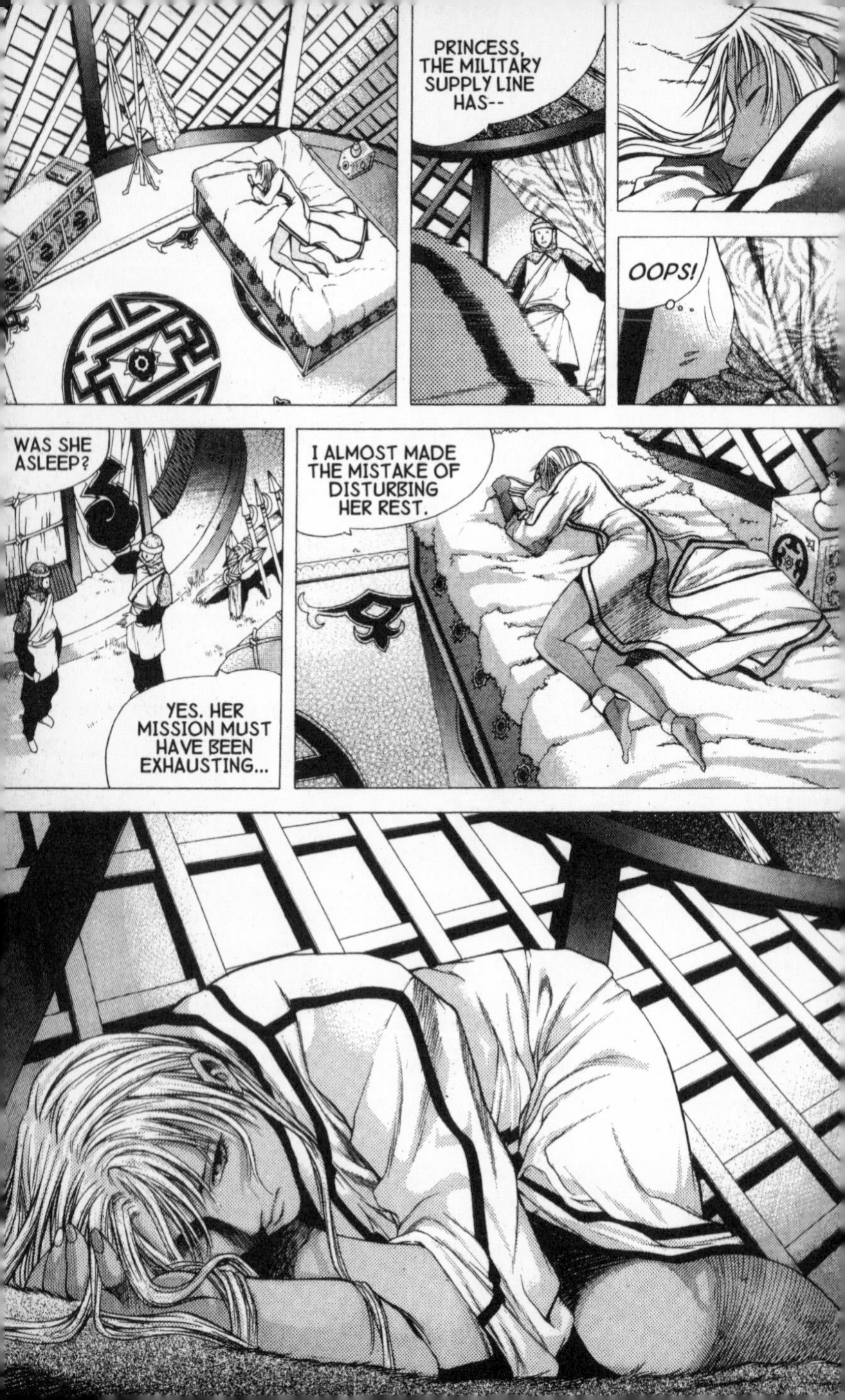
PRINCESS, THE MILITARY SUPPLY LINE HAS--
OOPS!
WAS SHE ASLEEP?
YES. HER MISSION MUST HAVE BEEN EXHAUSTING...
I ALMOST MADE THE MISTAKE OF DISTURBING HER REST.

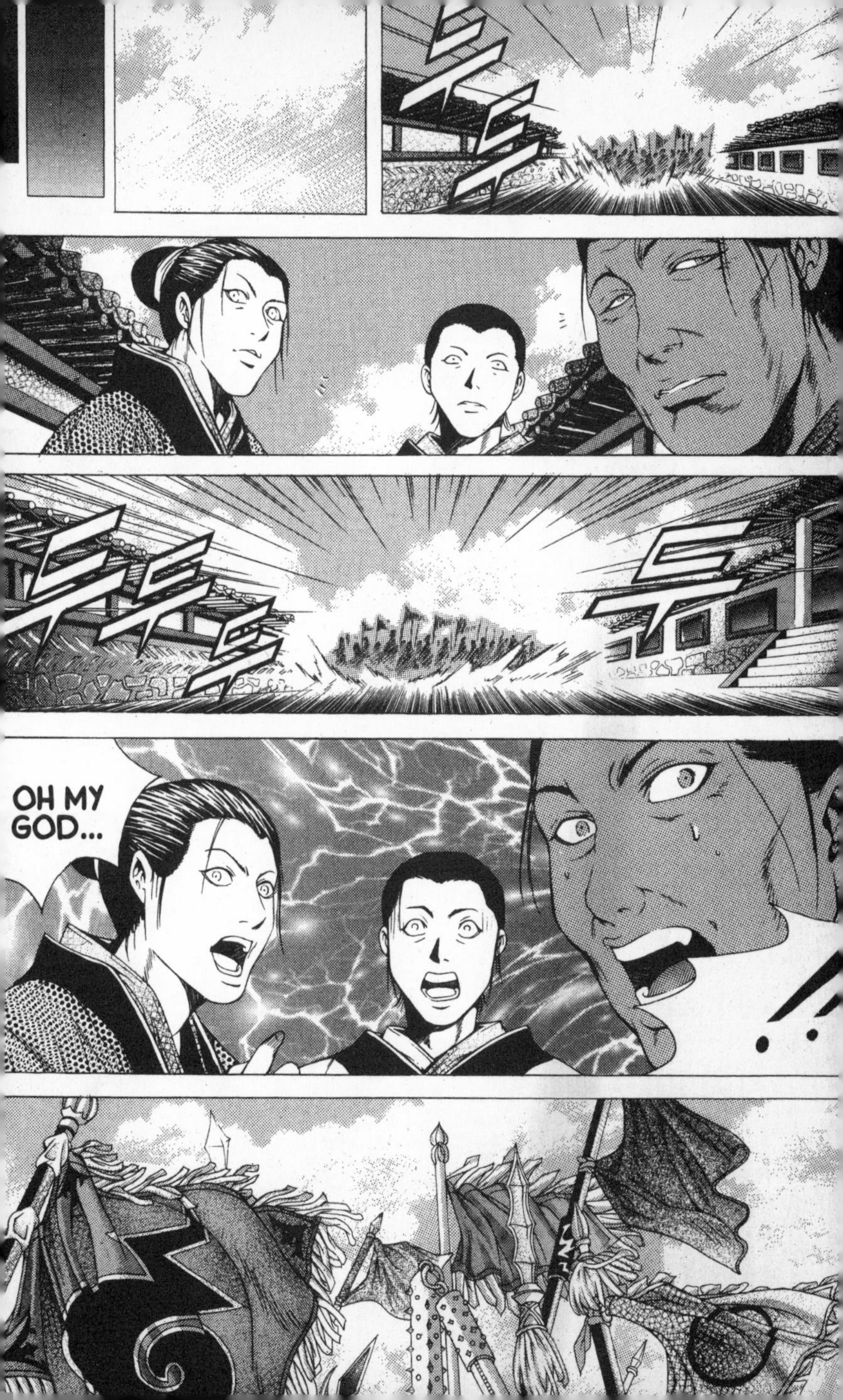
OH MY GOD...

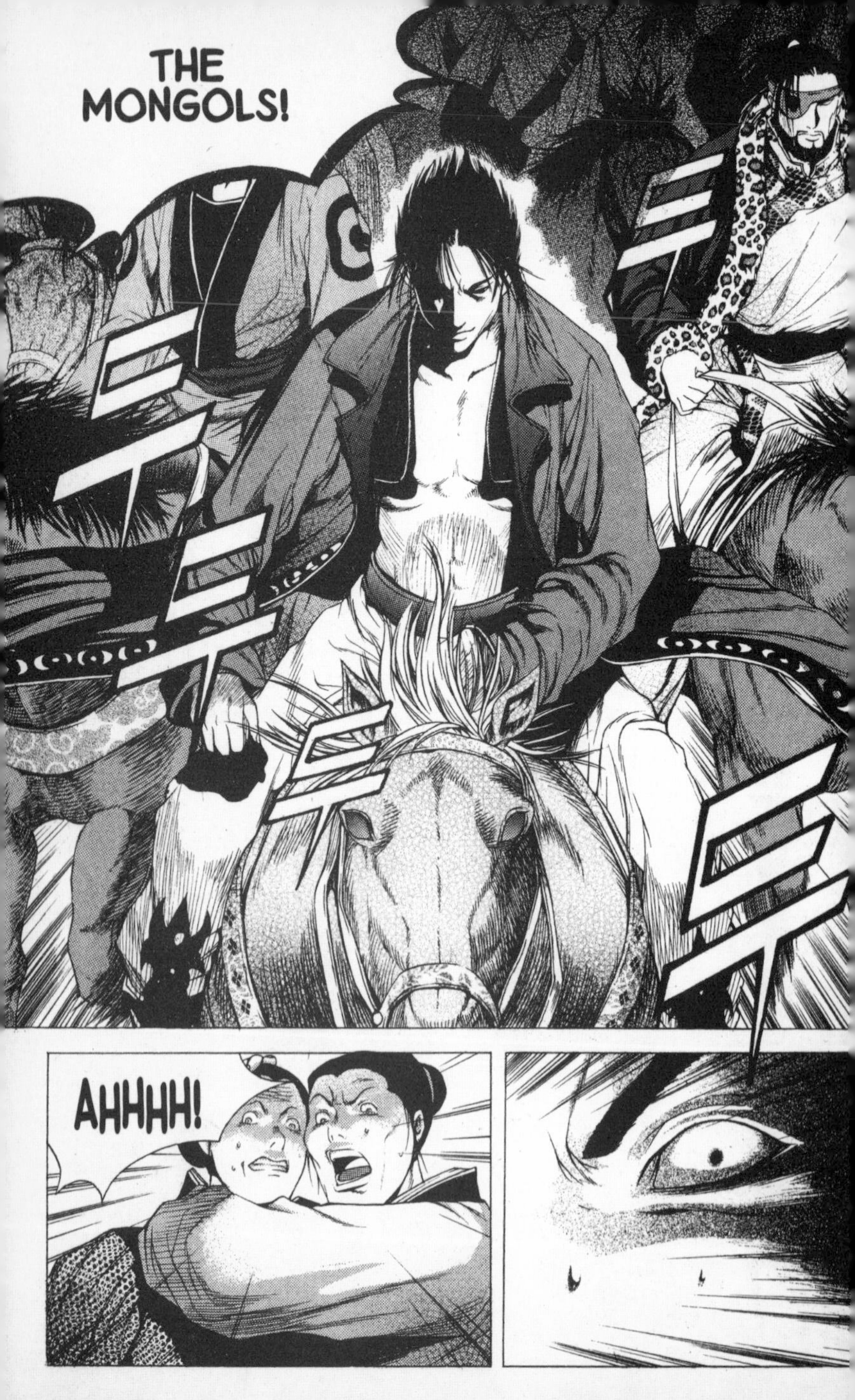
THE MONGOLS!
AHHHH!

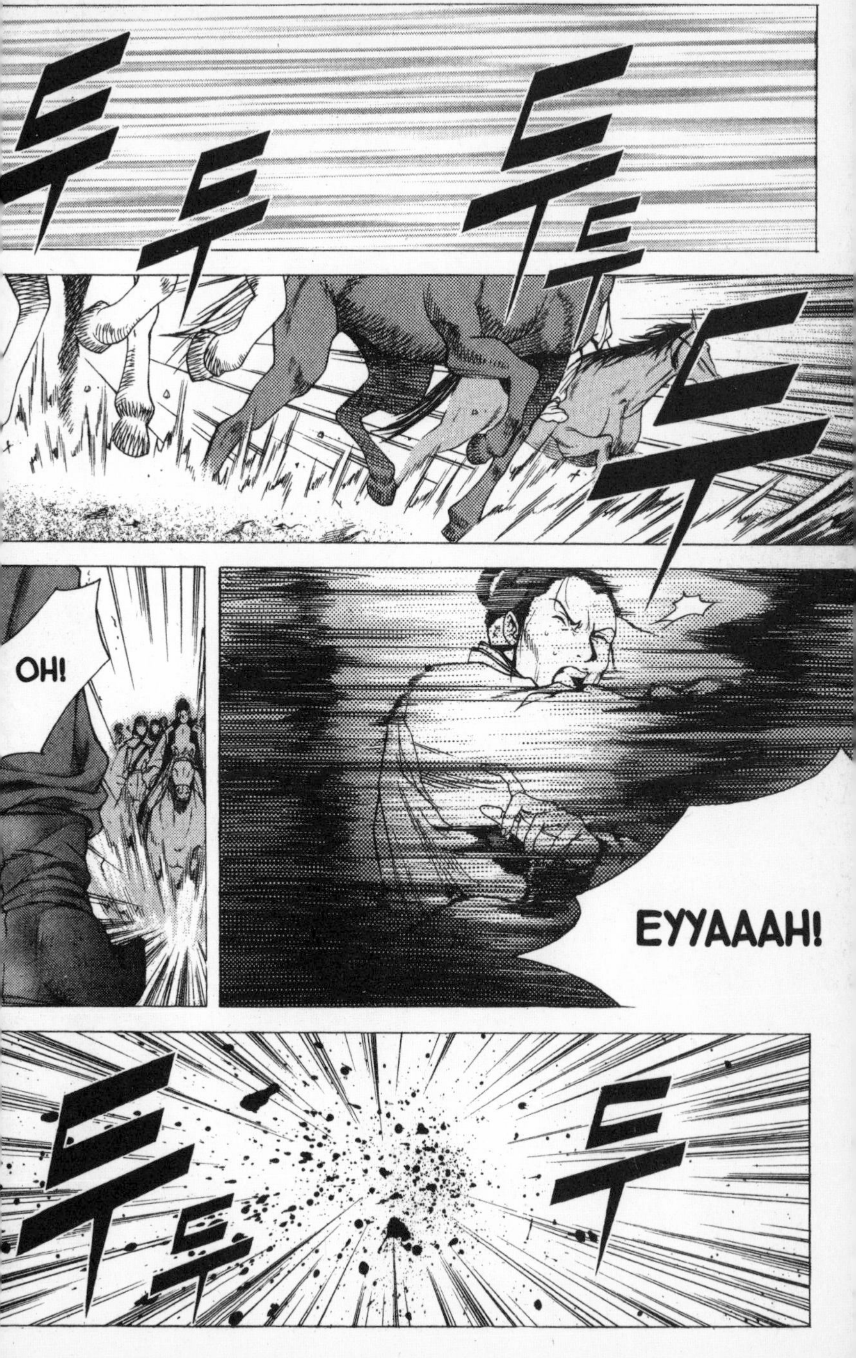
OH!
EYYAAAH!

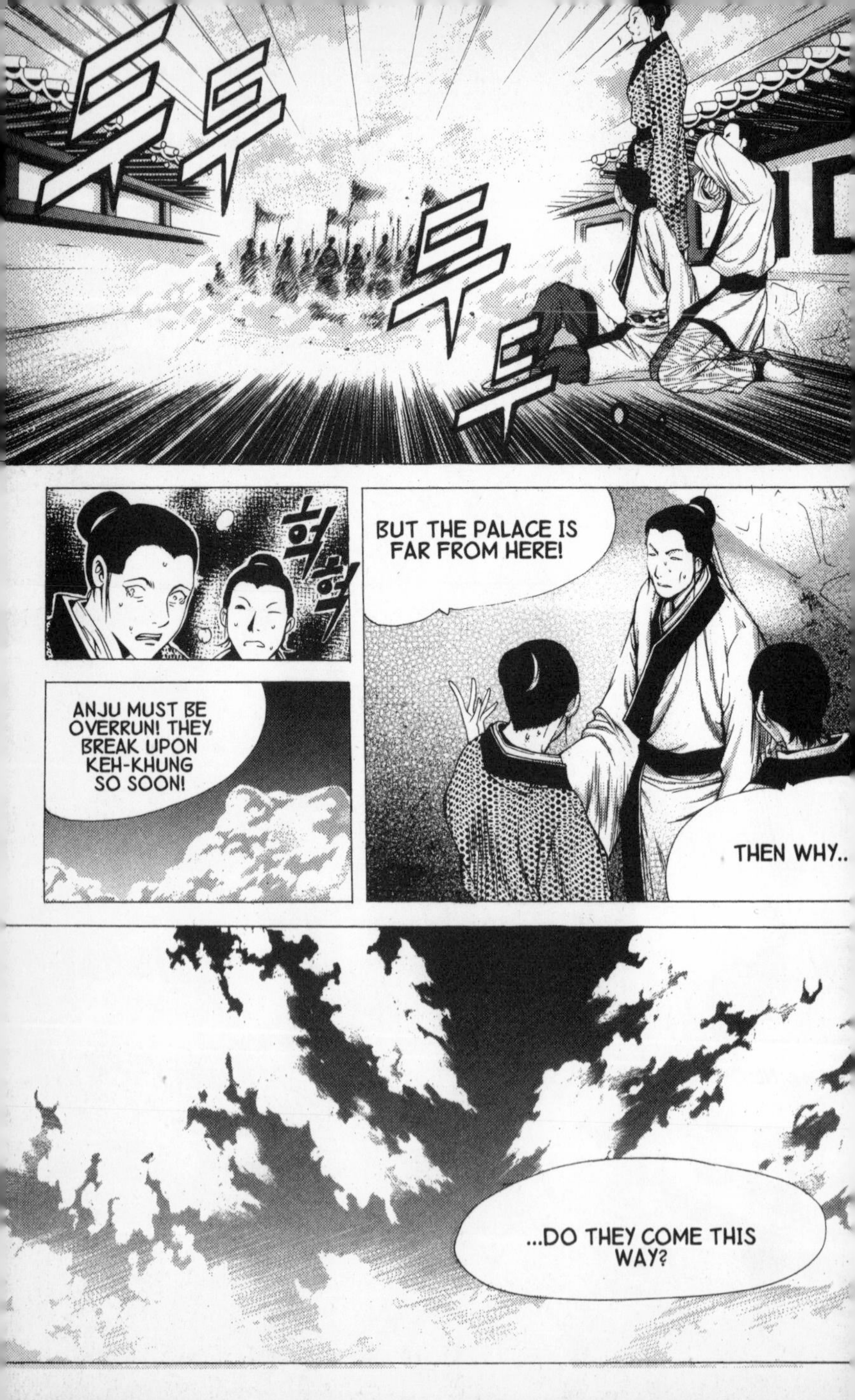
두두두두
헉헉
ANJU MUST BE OVERRUN! THEY BREAK UPON KEH-KHUNG SO SOON!
BUT THE PALACE IS FAR FROM HERE!
THEN WHY..
...DO THEY COME THIS WAY?

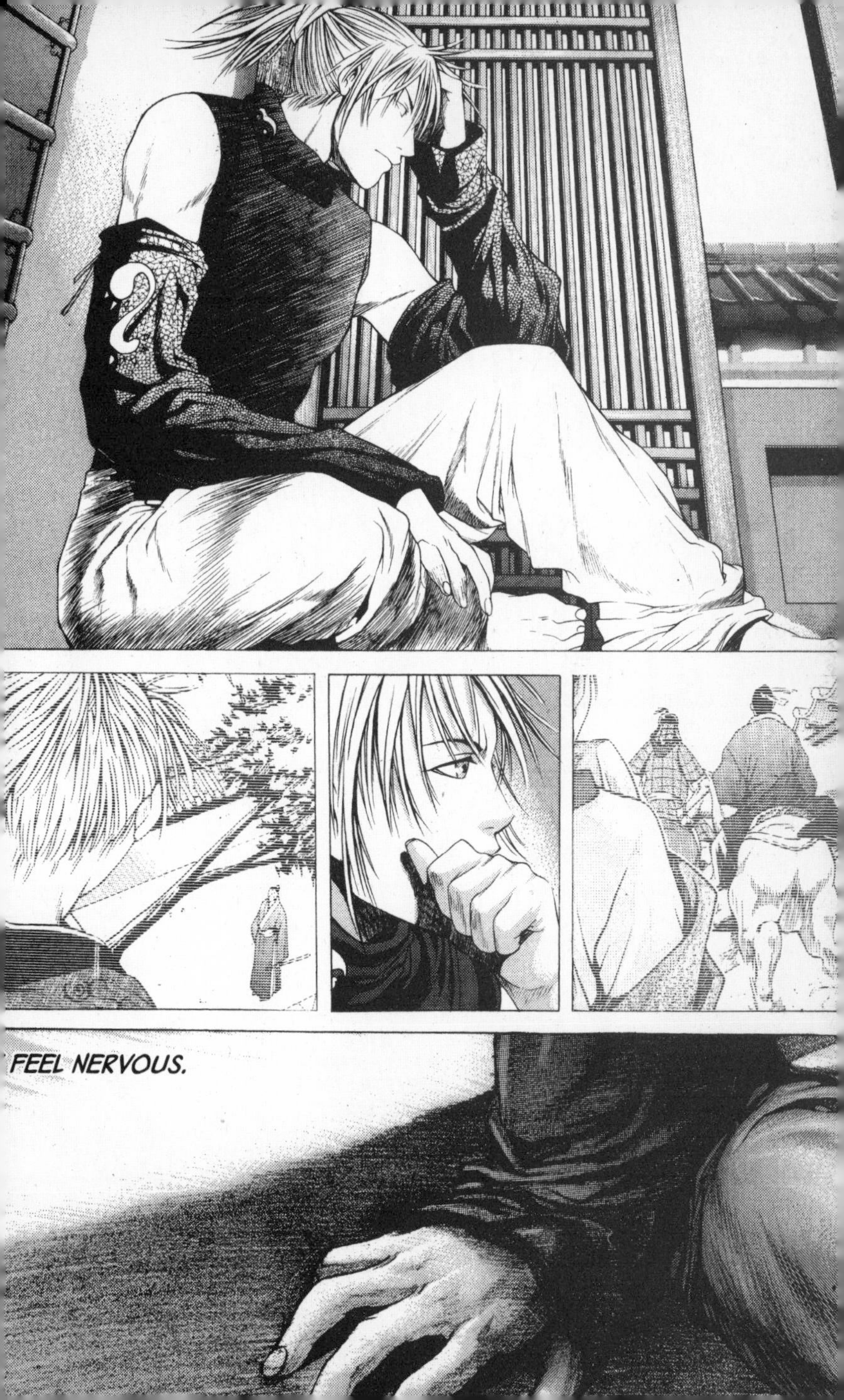
FEEL NERVOUS.

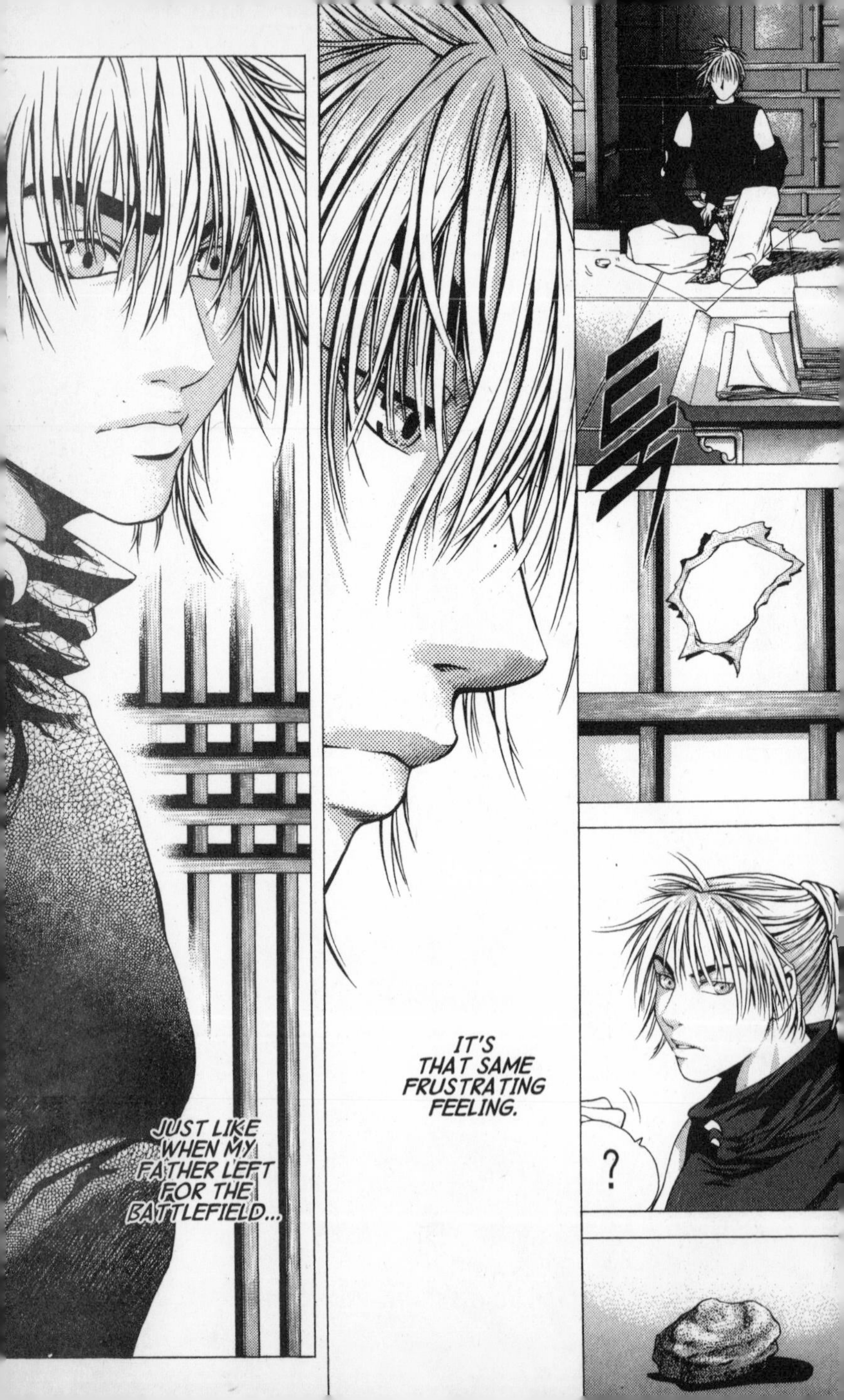
JUST LIKE WHEN MY FATHER LEFT FOR THE BATTLEFIELD...
IT'S THAT SAME FRUSTRATING FEELING.
?

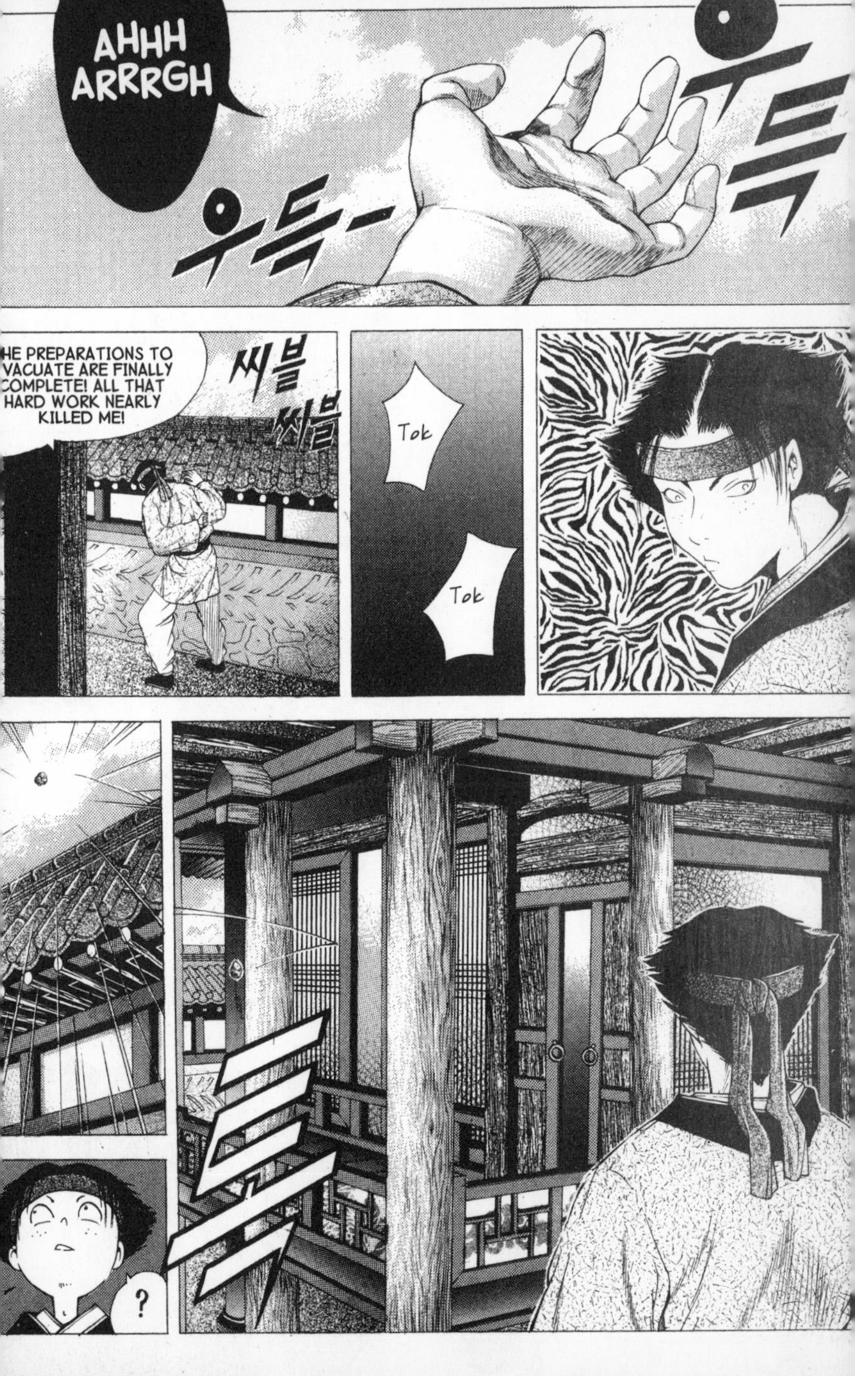

AHHH ARRRGH
HE PREPARATIONS TO VACUATE ARE FINALLY COMPLETE! ALL THAT HARD WORK NEARLY KILLED ME!
씨블
Tok
Tok
?

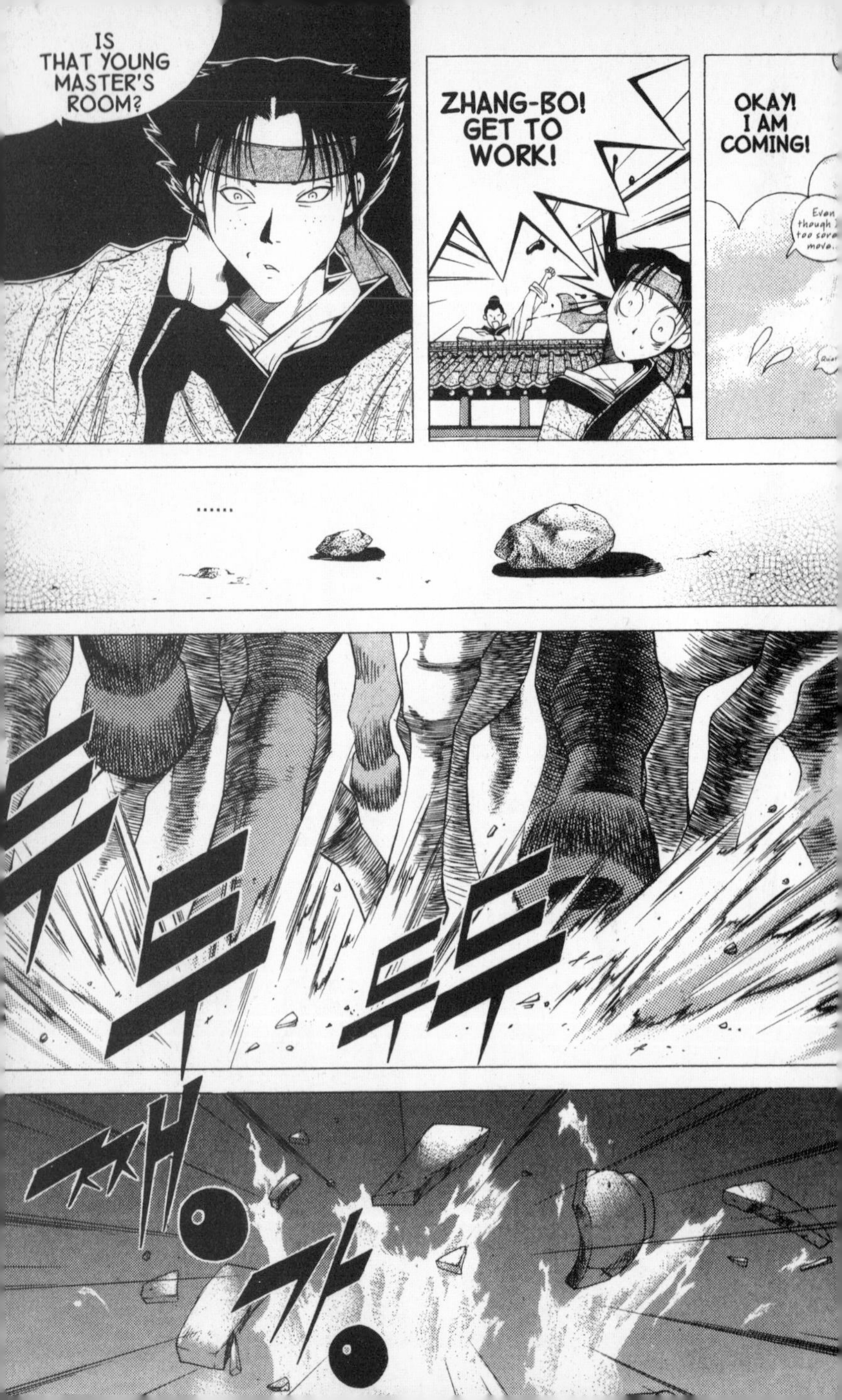
IS THAT YOUNG MASTER'S ROOM?
ZHANG-BO! GET TO WORK!
OKAY! I AM COMING!
Even though too sore move...
Quiet
......

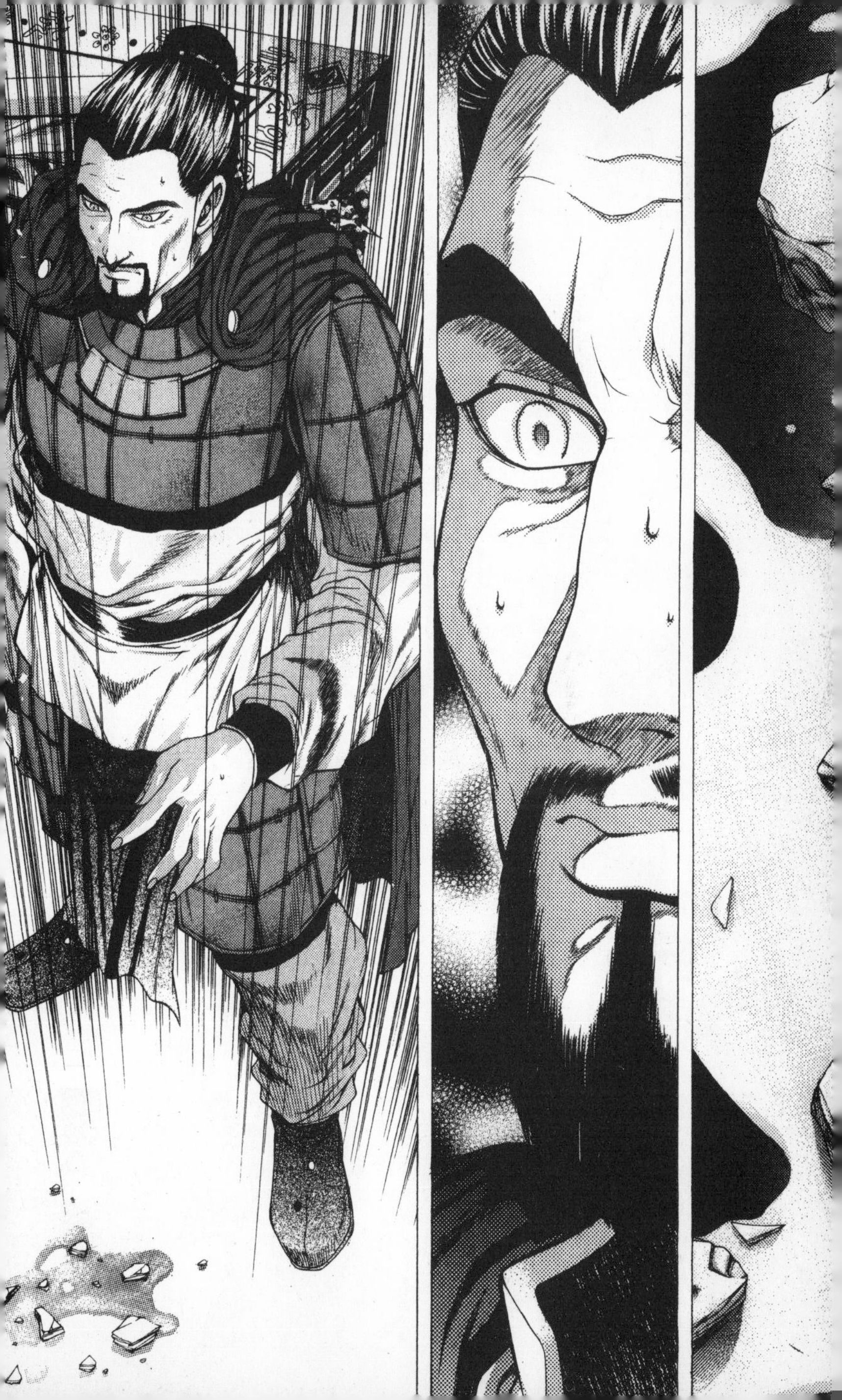

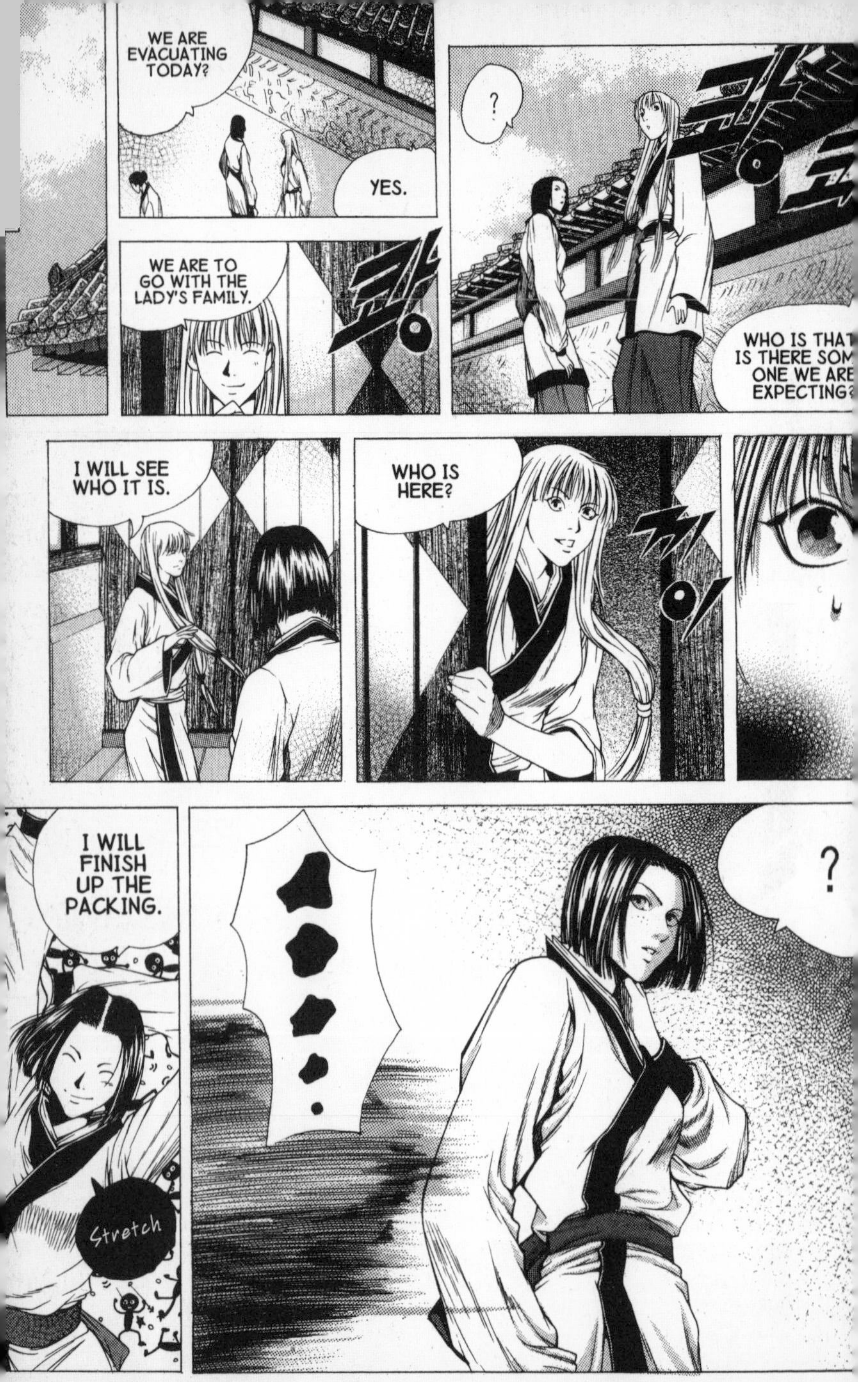
WE ARE EVACUATING TODAY?
YES.
WE ARE TO GO WITH THE LADY'S FAMILY.
?
WHO IS THAT IS THERE SOM ONE WE ARE EXPECTING?
I WILL SEE WHO IT IS.
WHO IS HERE?
I WILL FINISH UP THE PACKING.
Stretch
?

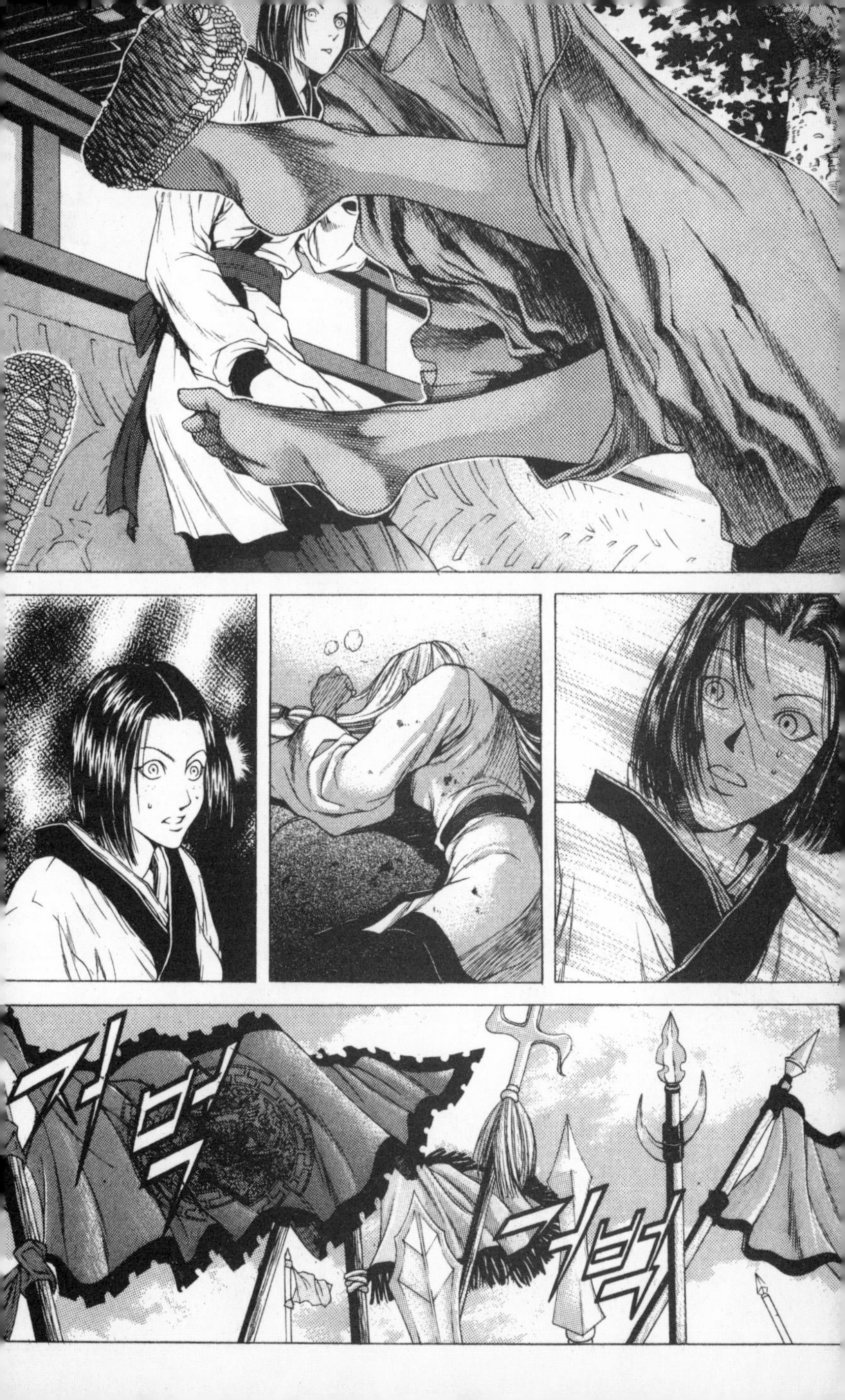

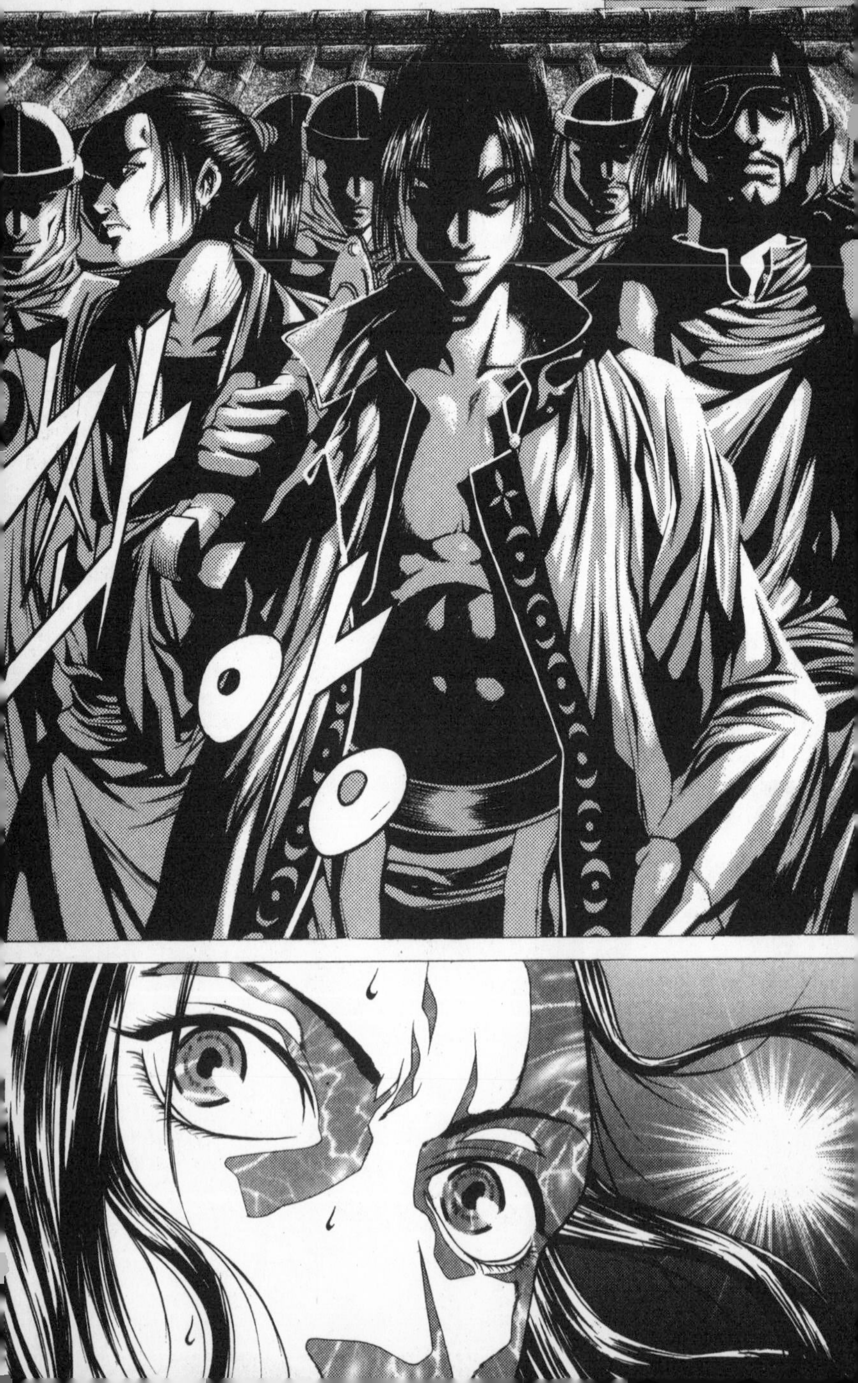

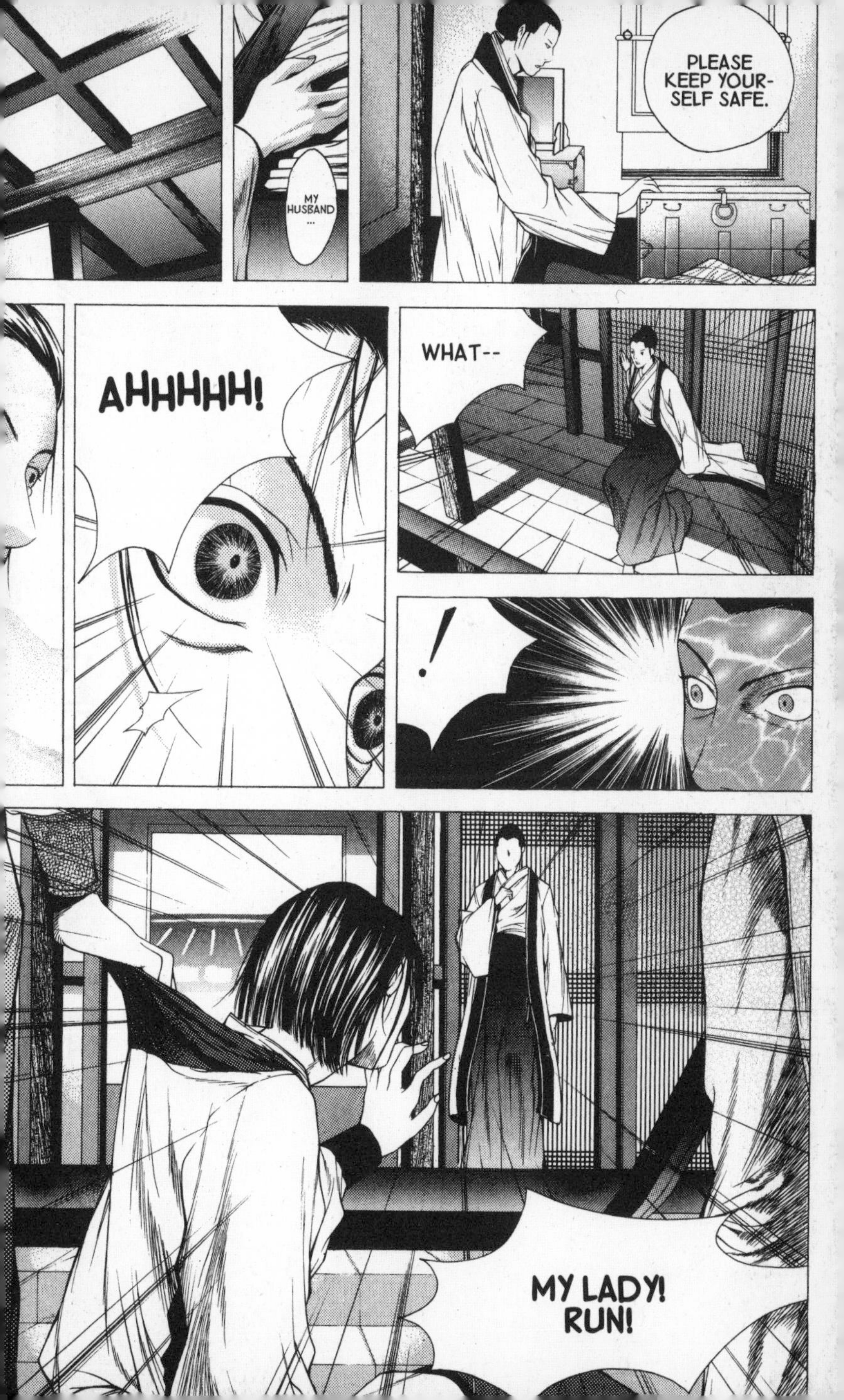
MY HUSBAND ...
PLEASE KEEP YOUR-SELF SAFE.
AHHHHH!
WHAT--
!
MY LADY! RUN!

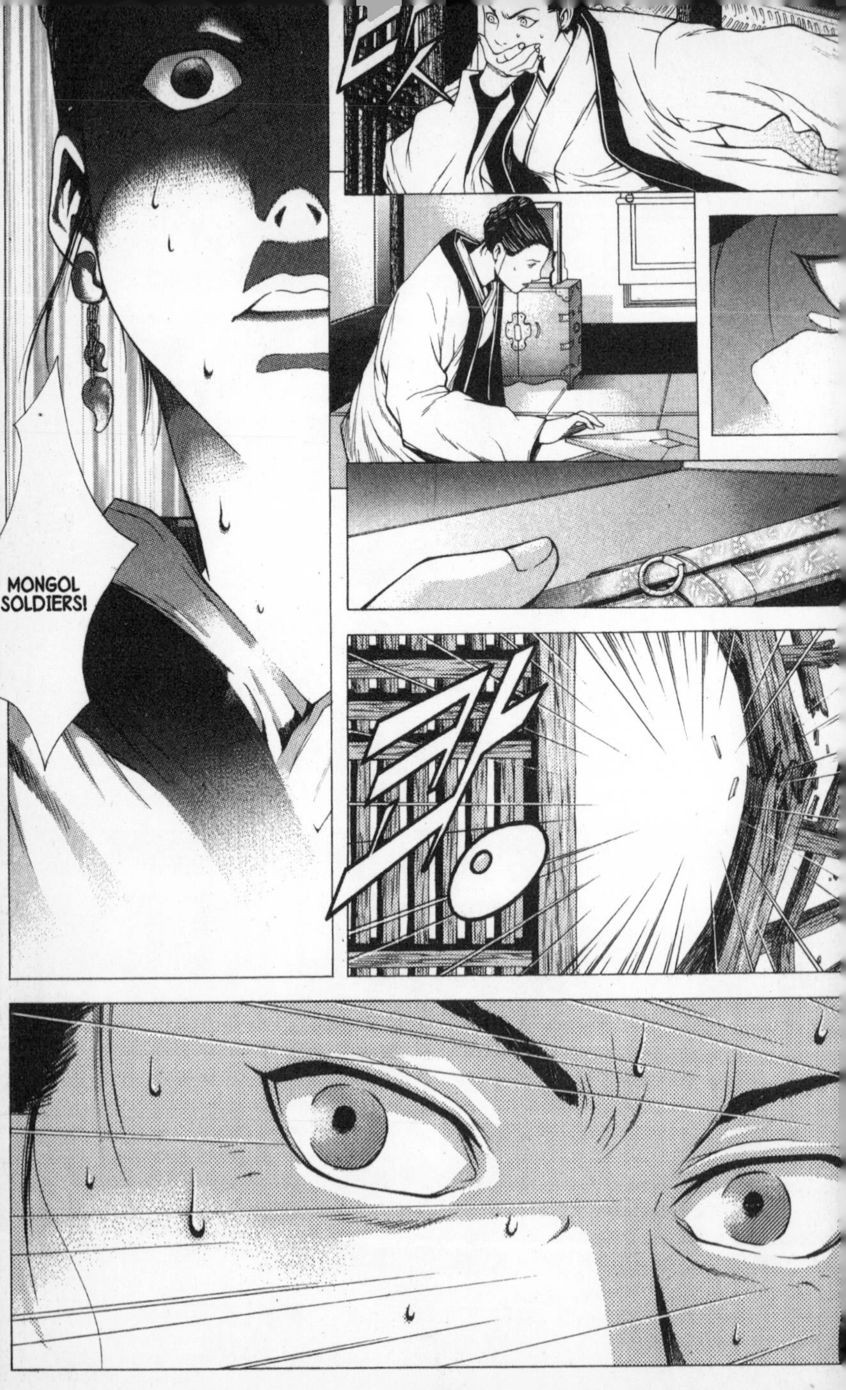
MONGOL SOLDIERS!

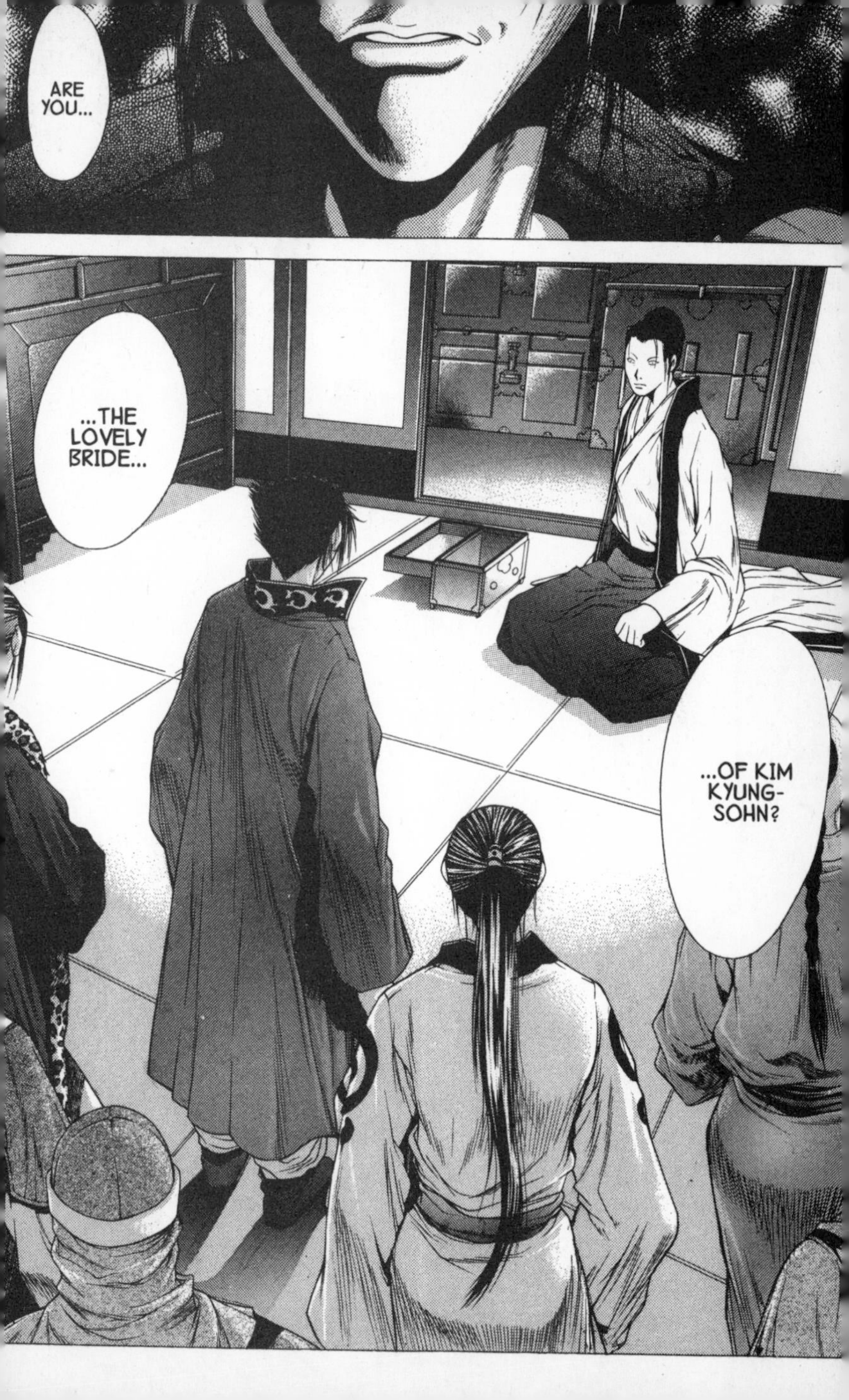
ARE YOU...
...THE LOVELY BRIDE...
...OF KIM KYUNG-SOHN?

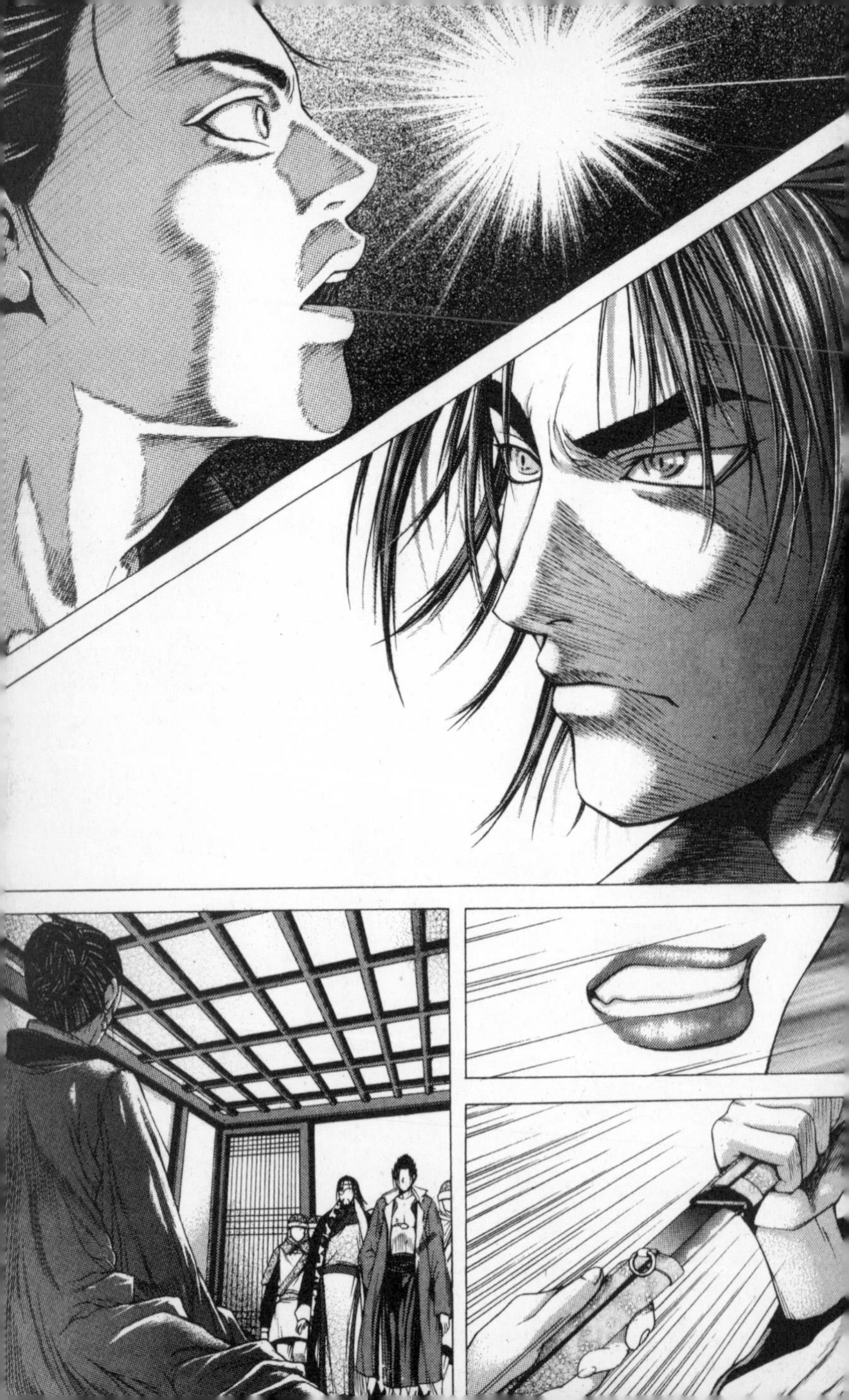

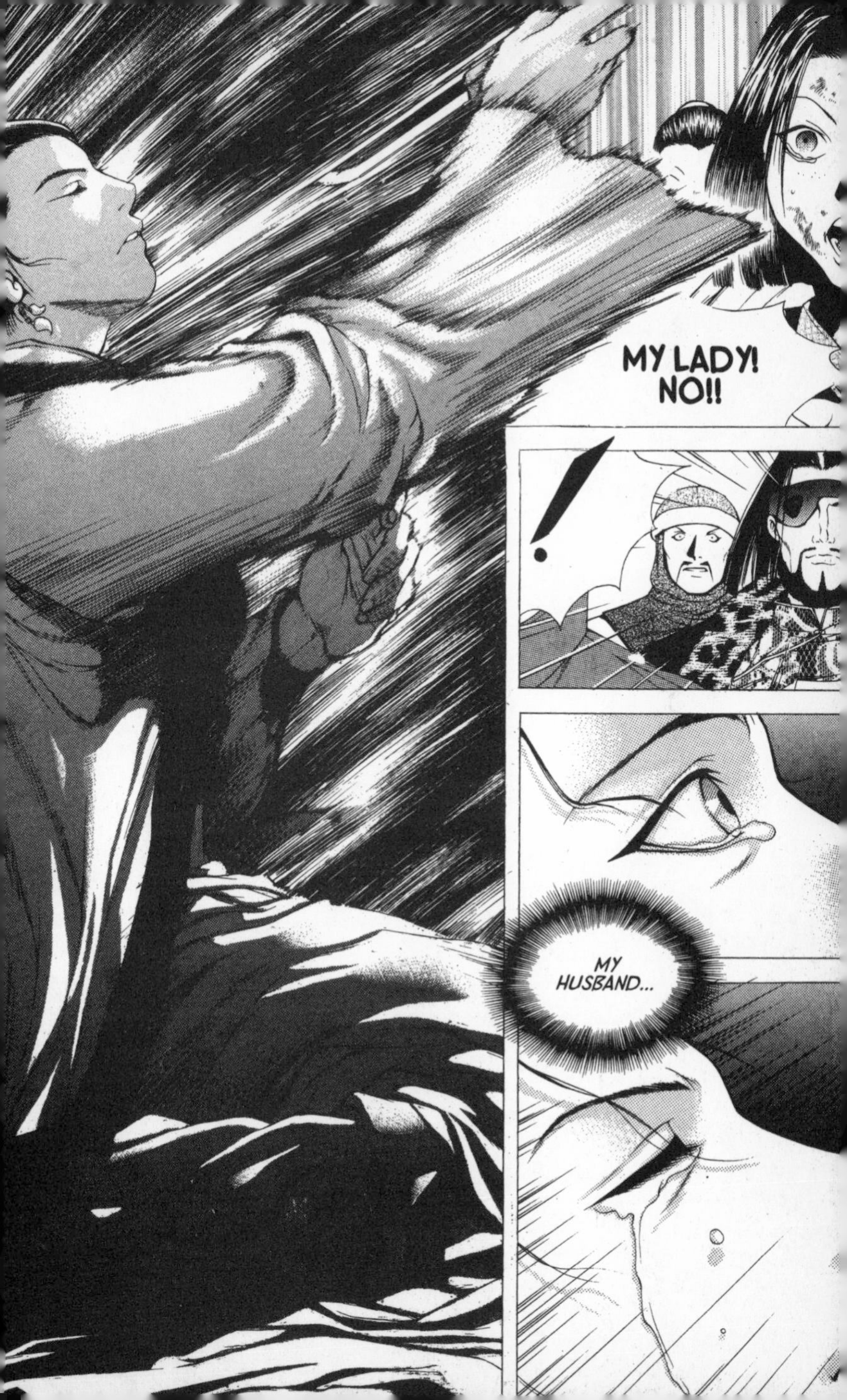
MY LADY! NO!!
!
MY HUSBAND...

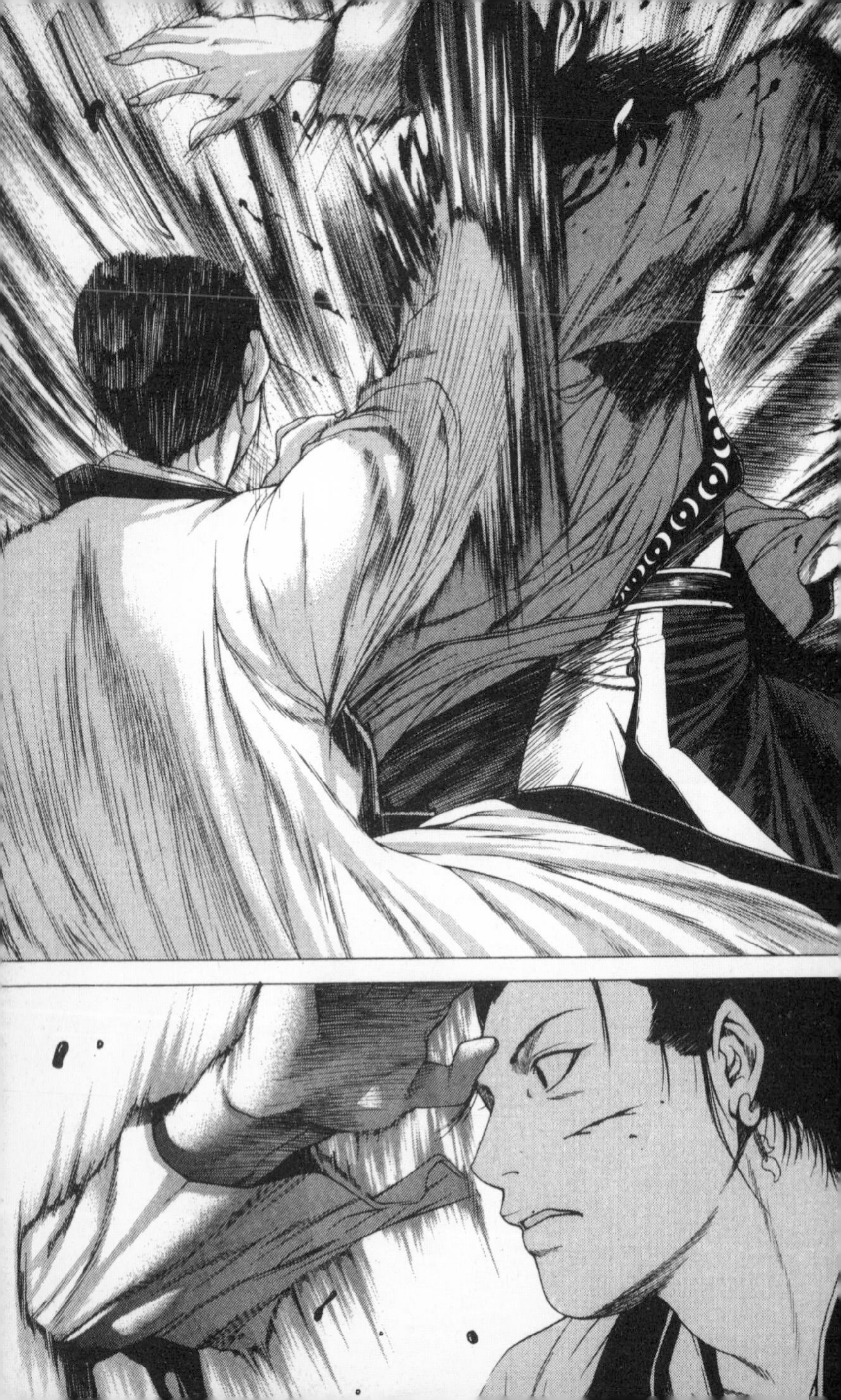

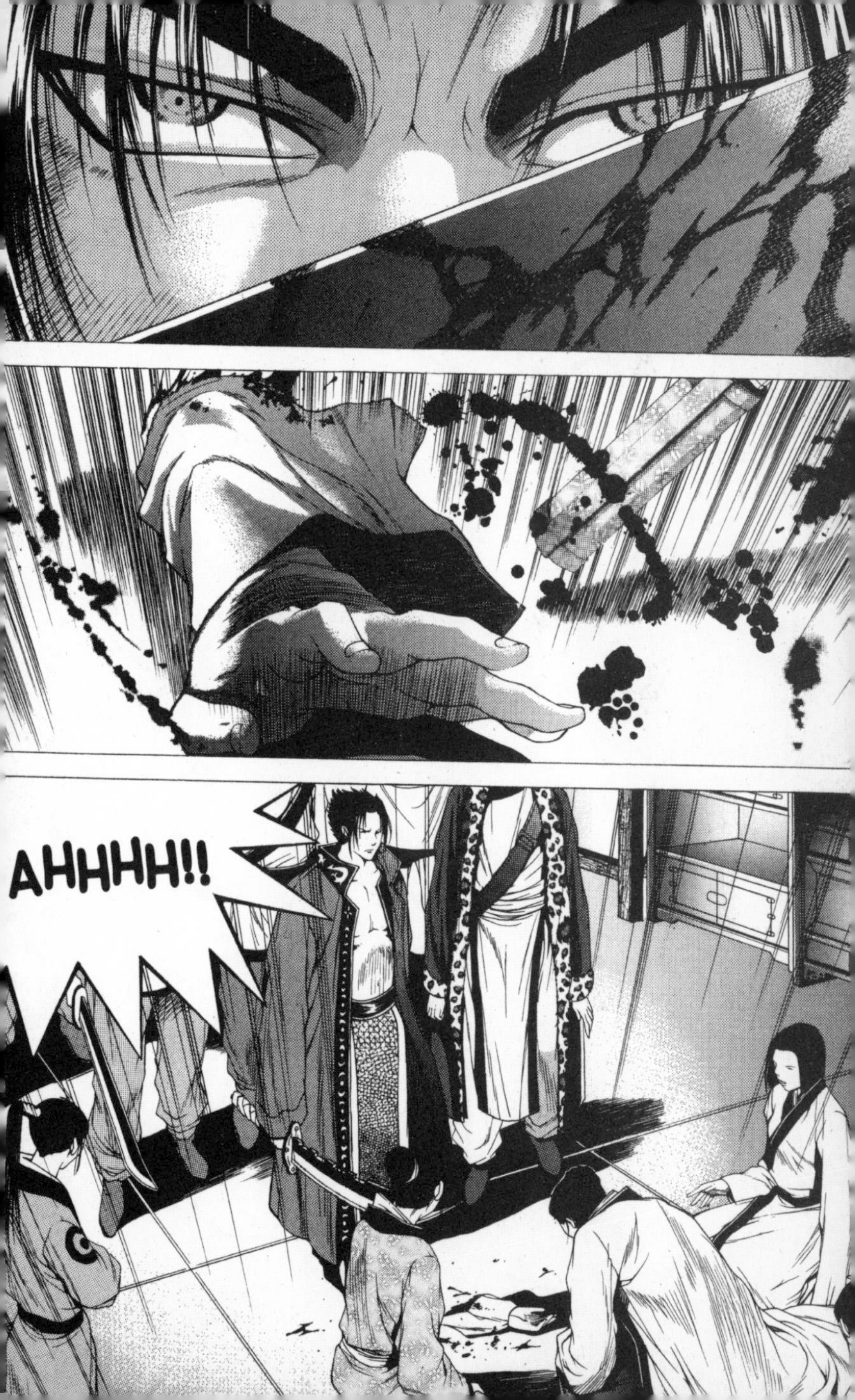
AHHHH!!

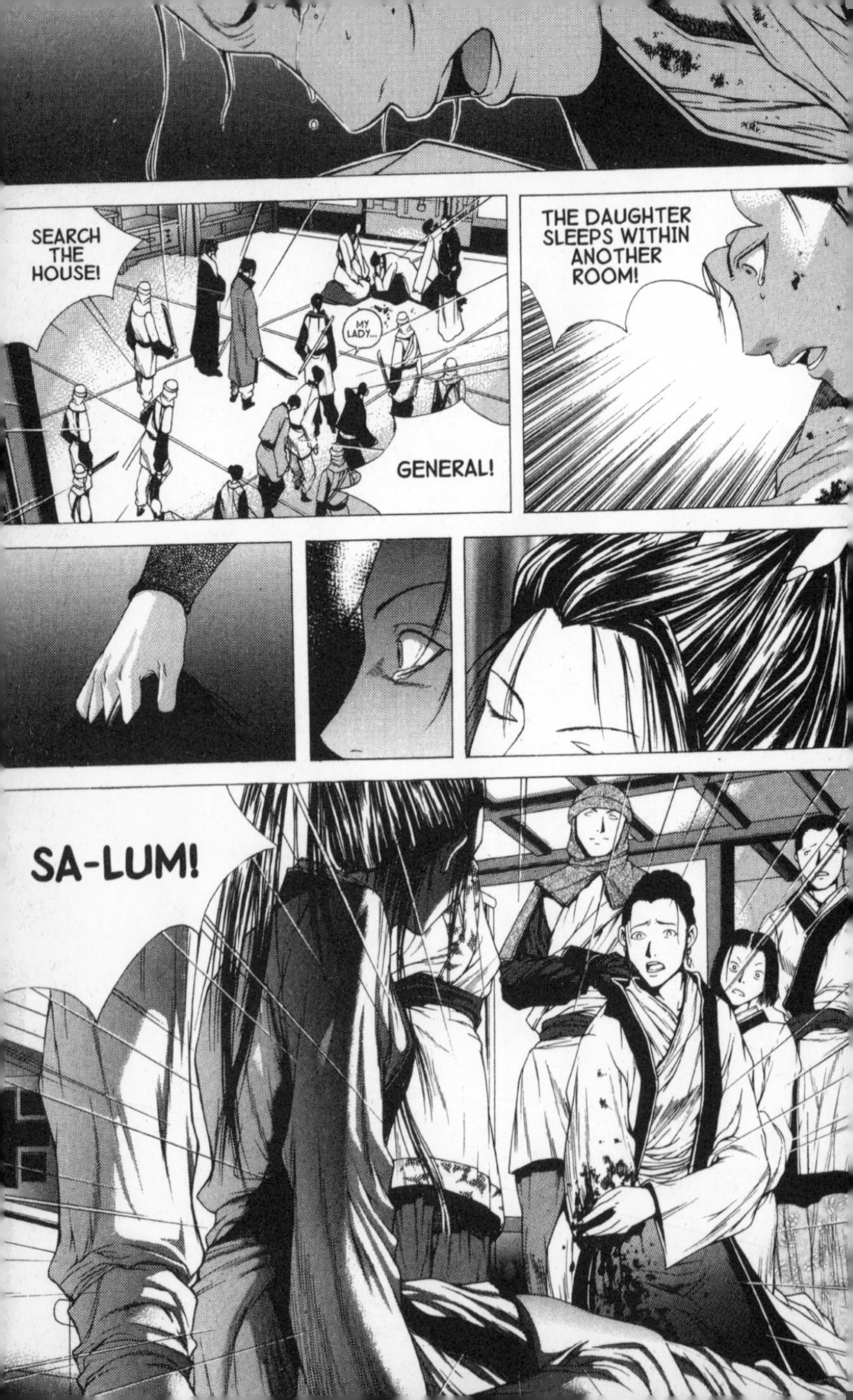
SEARCH THE HOUSE!
MY LADY...
GENERAL!
THE DAUGHTER SLEEPS WITHIN ANOTHER ROOM!
SA-LUM!

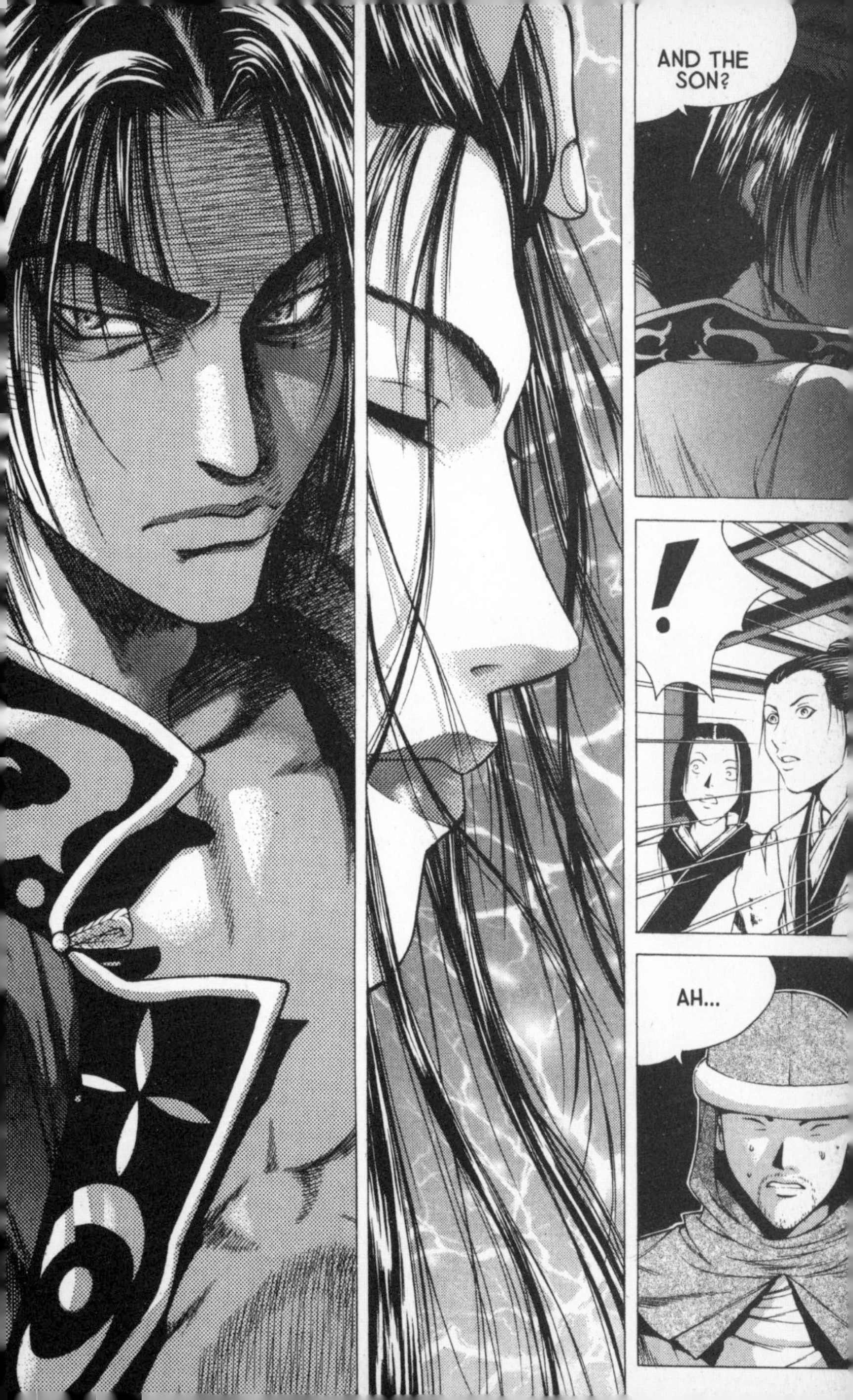
AND THE SON?
!
AH...

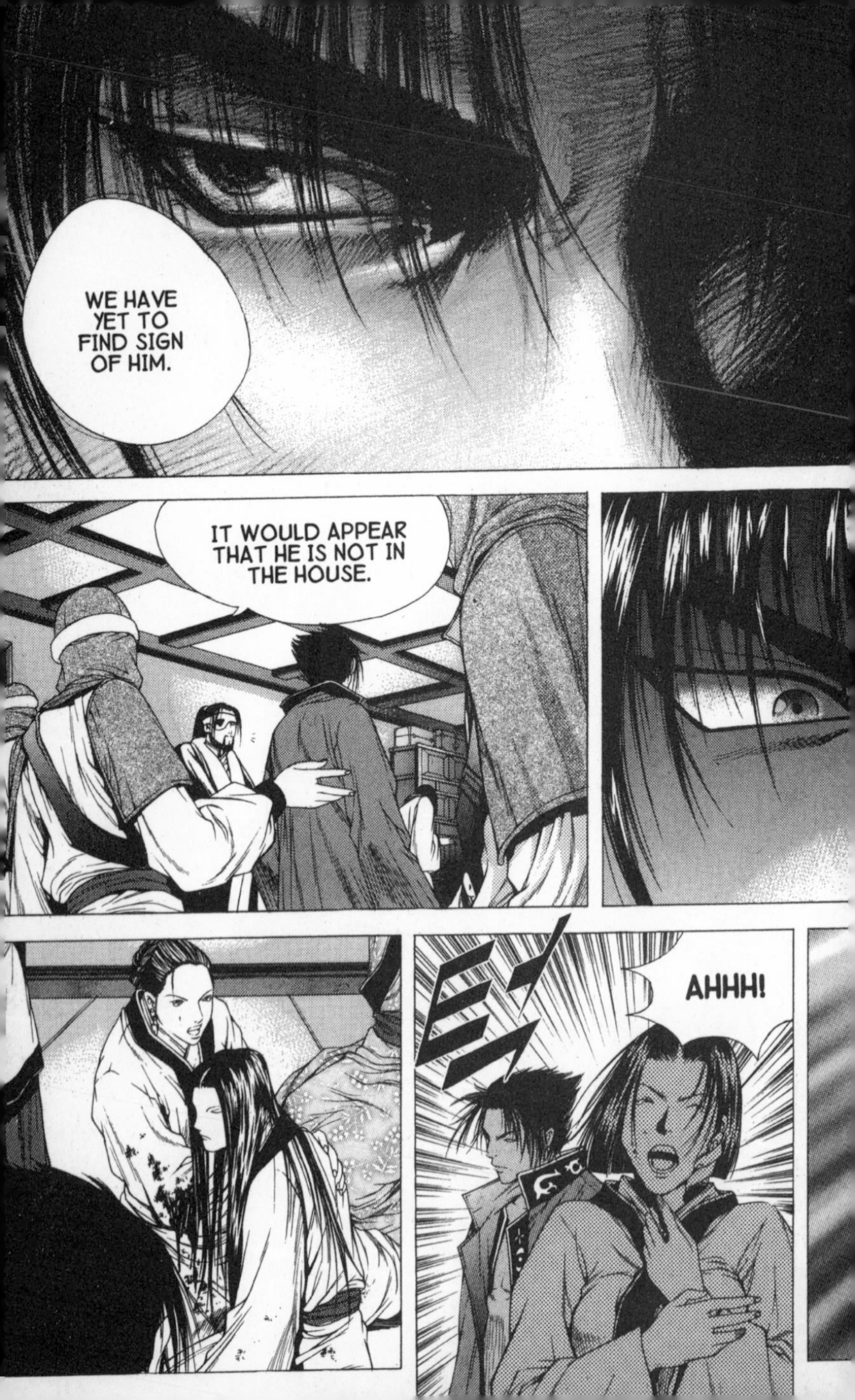
WE HAVE YET TO FIND SIGN OF HIM.
IT WOULD APPEAR THAT HE IS NOT IN THE HOUSE.
AHHH!

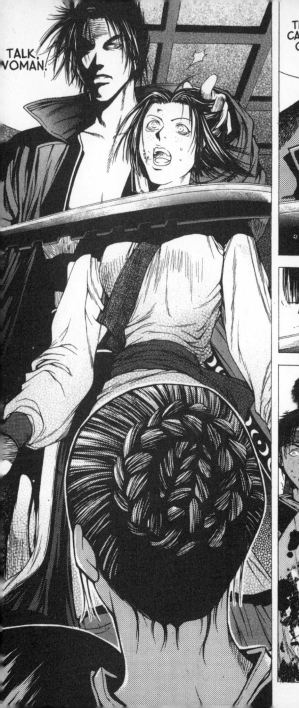

TALK,
WOMAN!

TELL ME WHERE I
CAN FIND THE SON
OF KIM KYUNG-
SOHN?

AHH.
AHH.

MY...
MY LADY
AHH
...

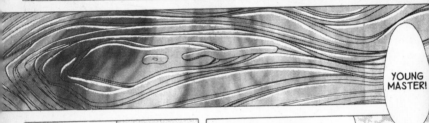

YOUNG MASTER!

WHERE ARE YOU GOING, SIR?

WE ARE TO LEAVE AT ANY MOMENT, YOU SHOULDN'T BE WANDERING!

*What if you get lost...*

IT'LL JUST BE A LITTLE WHILE.

IF...

...MOTHER LOOKS FOR ME...

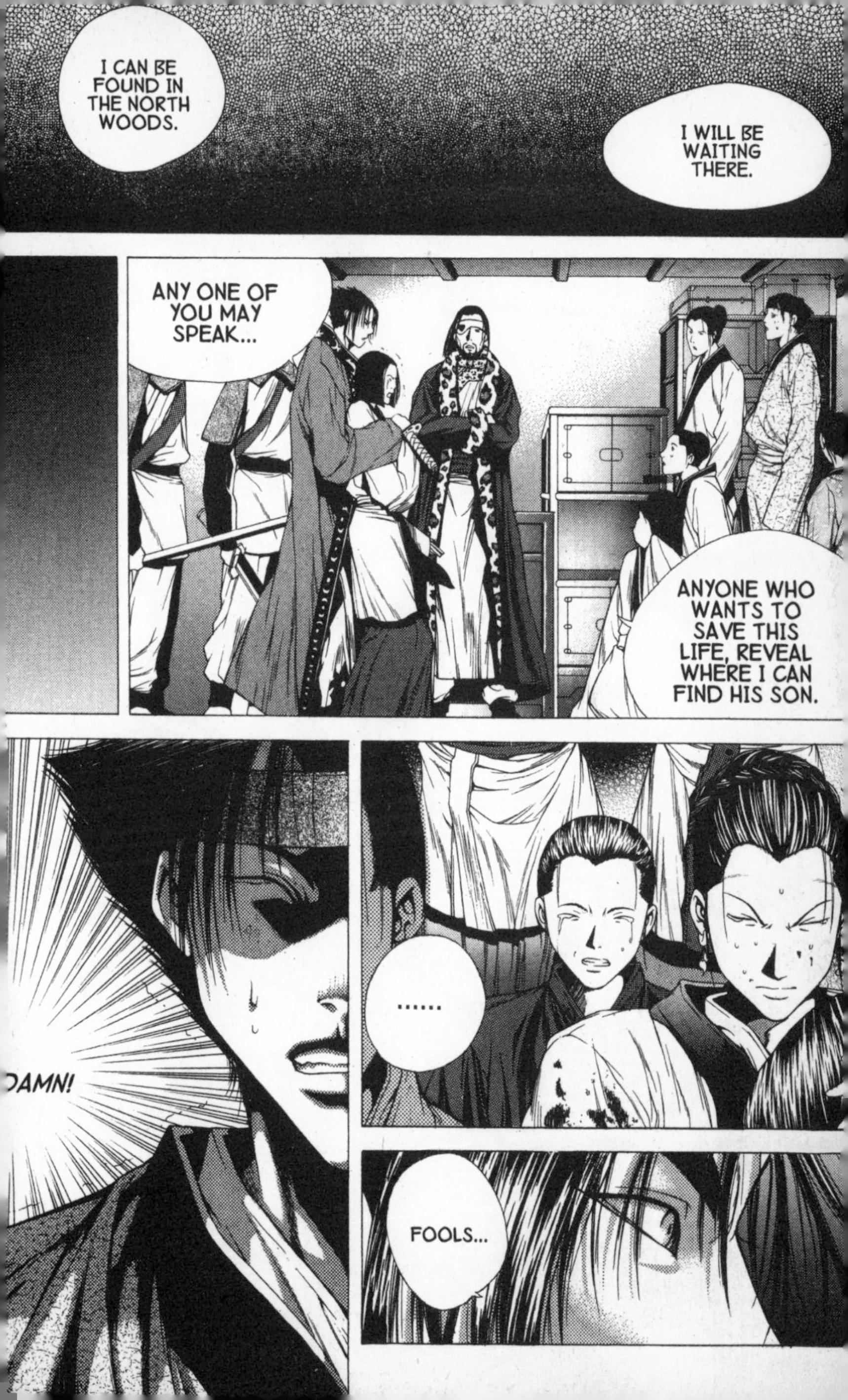

I CAN BE FOUND IN THE NORTH WOODS.
I WILL BE WAITING THERE.
ANY ONE OF YOU MAY SPEAK...
ANYONE WHO WANTS TO SAVE THIS LIFE, REVEAL WHERE I CAN FIND HIS SON.
DAMN!
......
FOOLS...

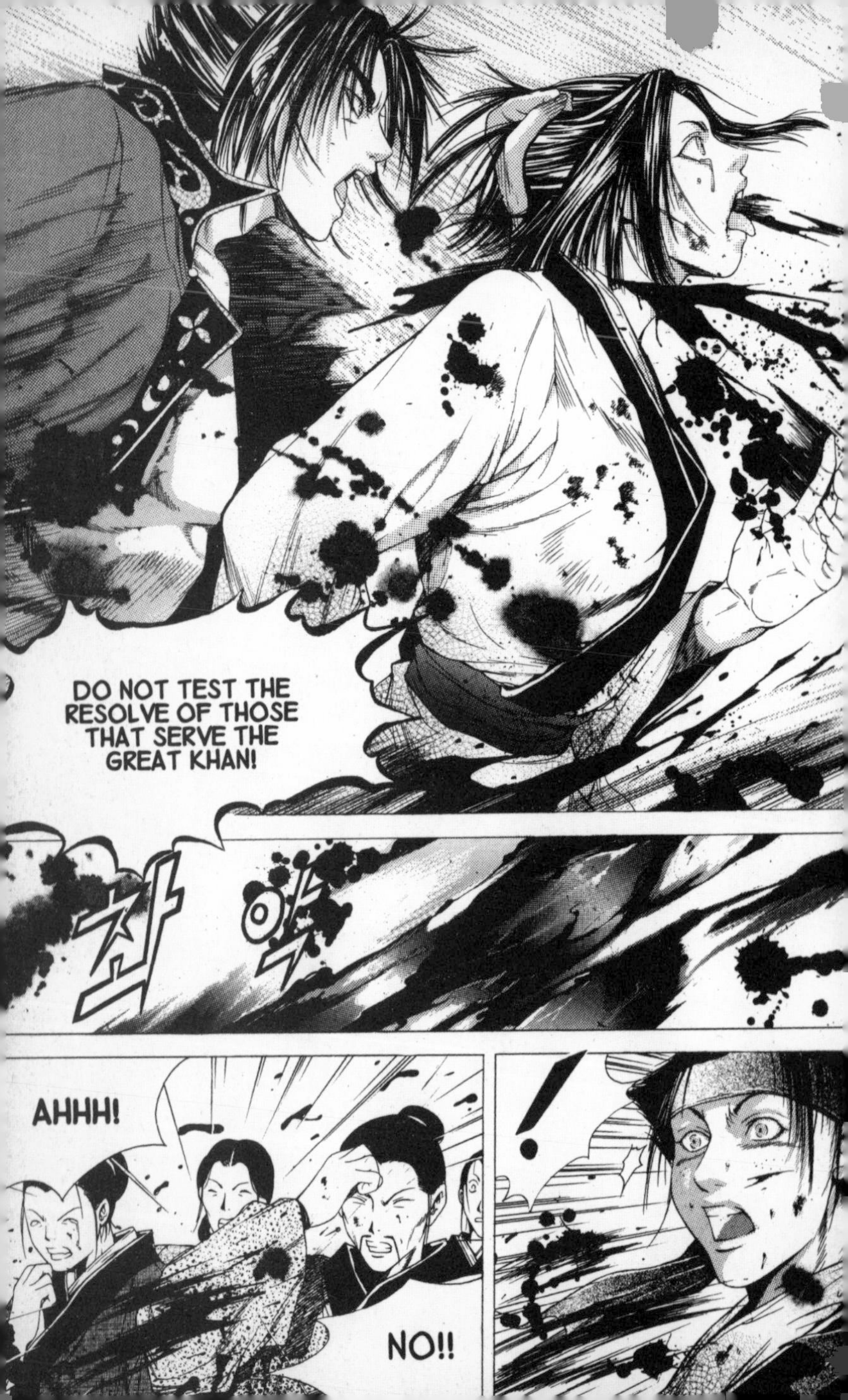
DO NOT TEST THE RESOLVE OF THOSE THAT SERVE THE GREAT KHAN!
AHHH!
NO!!
!

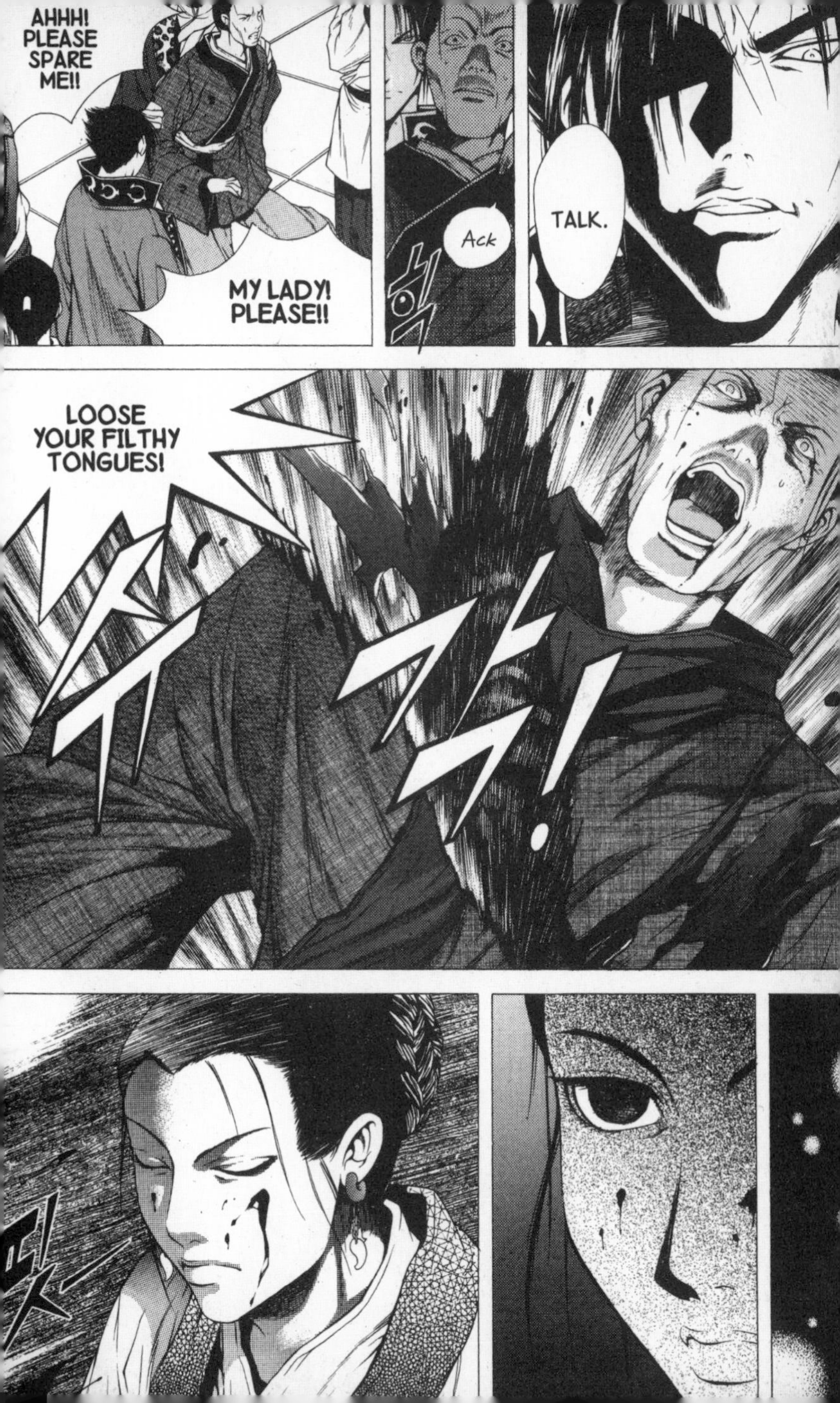
AHHH! PLEASE SPARE ME!!
MY LADY! PLEASE!!
Ack
TALK.
LOOSE YOUR FILTHY TONGUES!

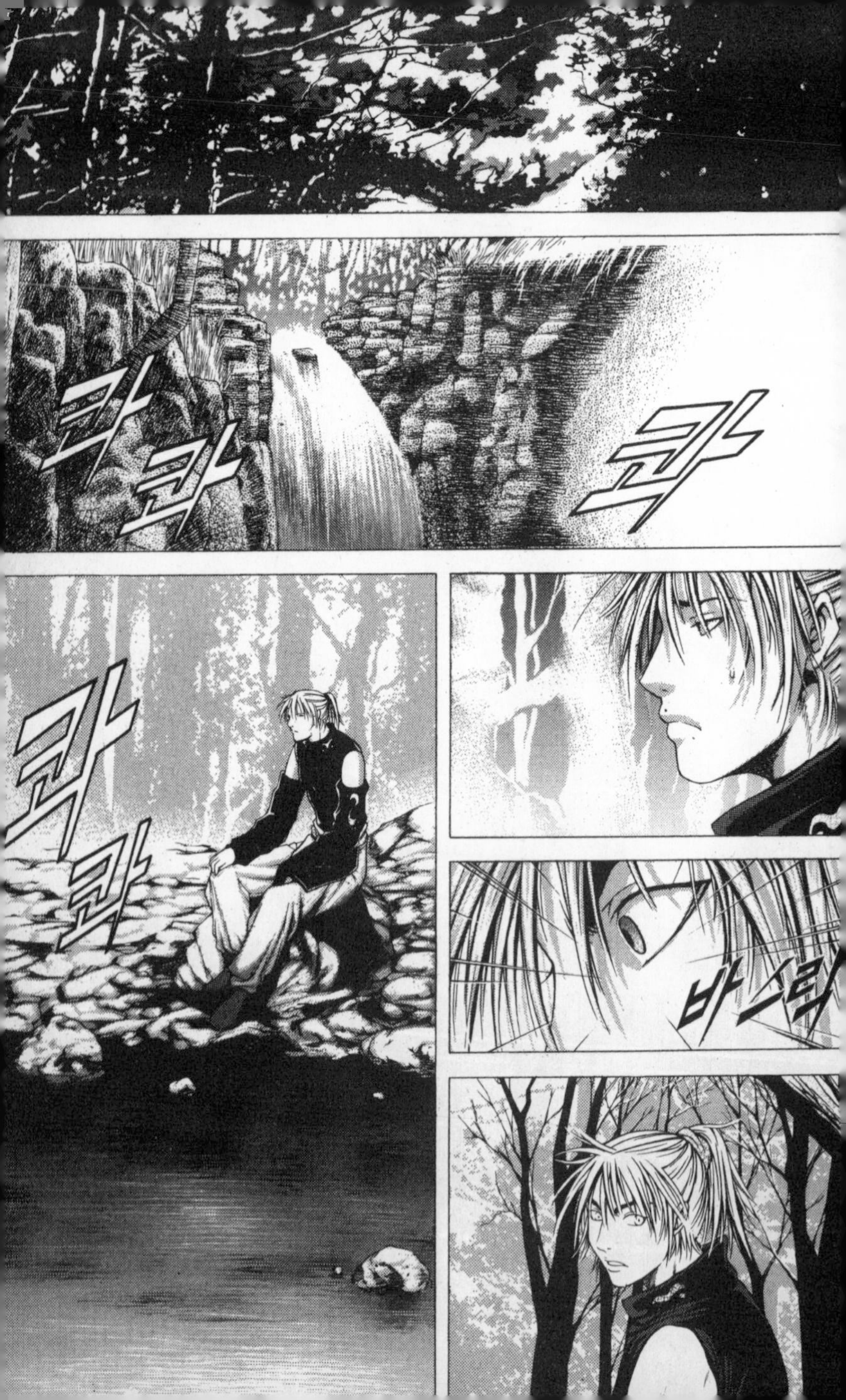

콰콰
콰
콰콰
바스락

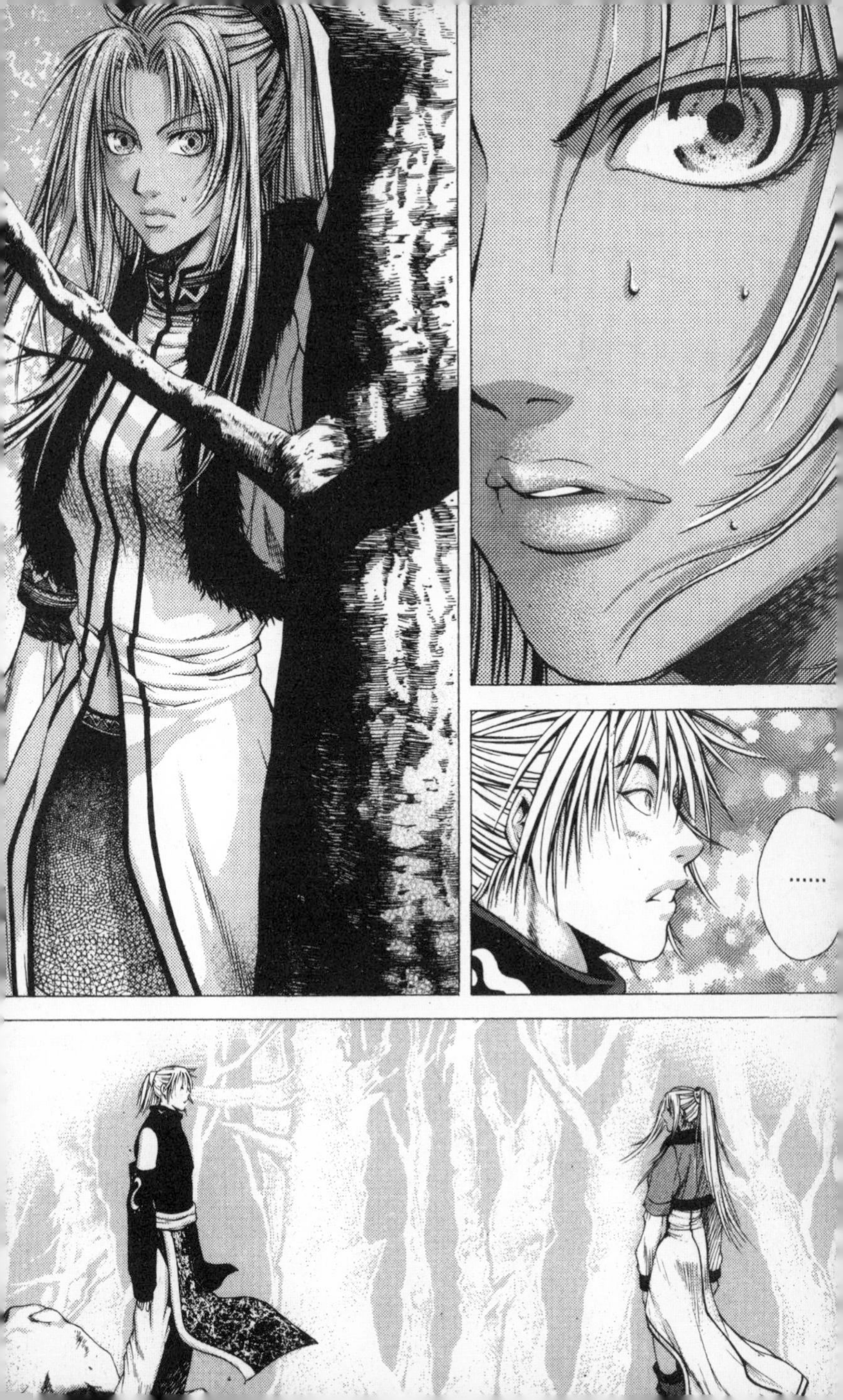
......

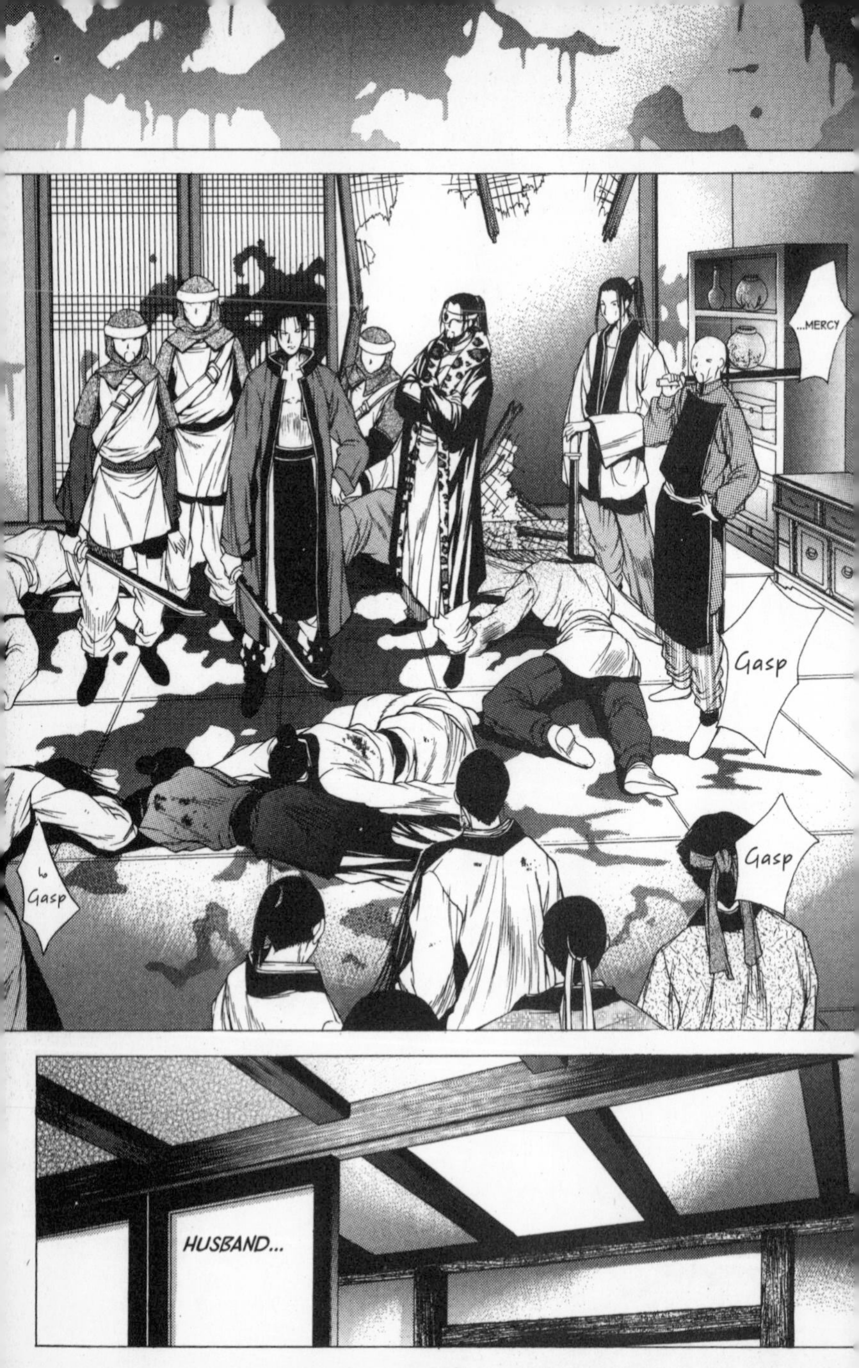
...MERCY
Gasp
Gasp
Gasp
HUSBAND...

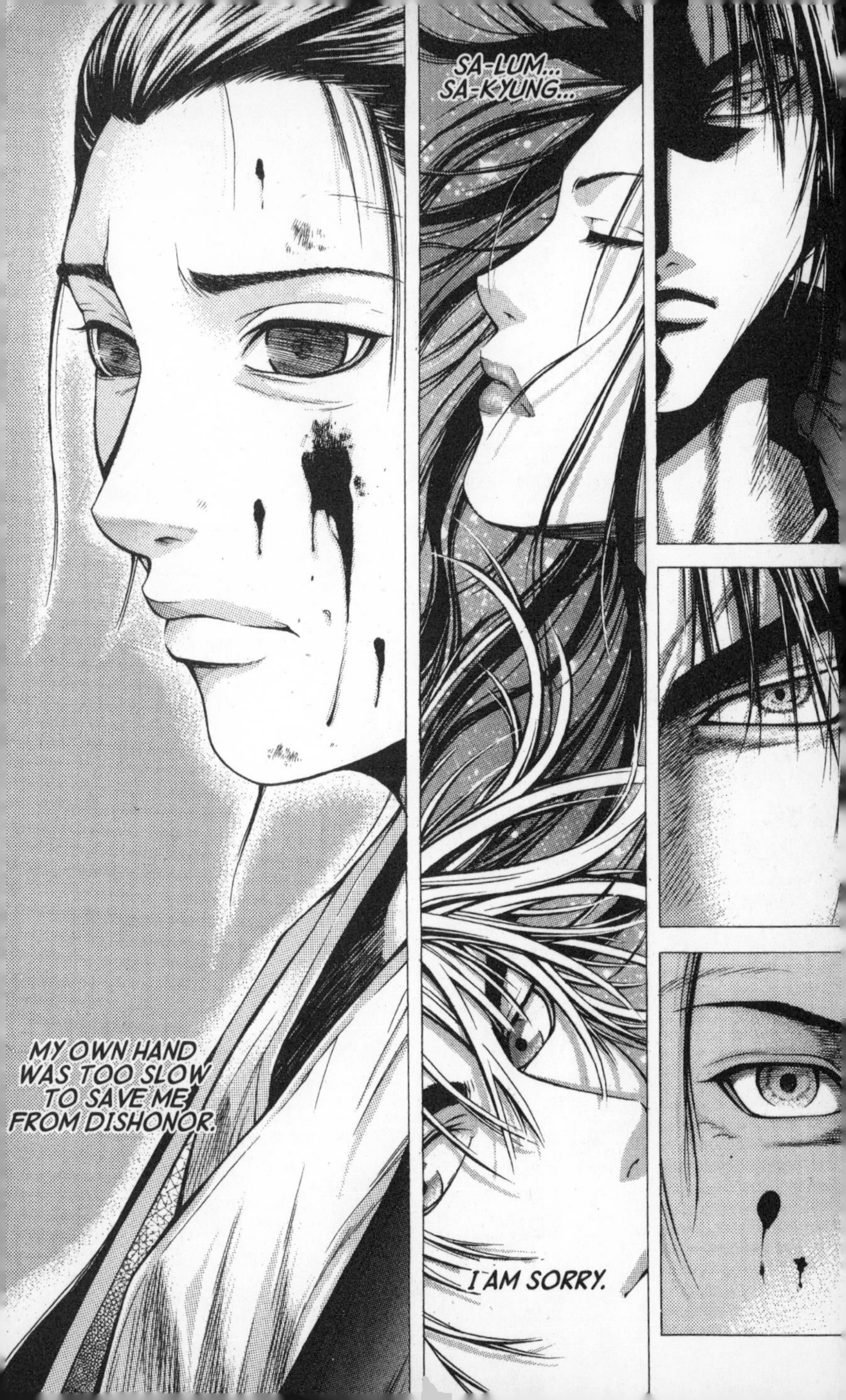
MY OWN HAND WAS TOO SLOW TO SAVE ME FROM DISHONOR.
SA-LUM... SA-KYUNG...
I AM SORRY.

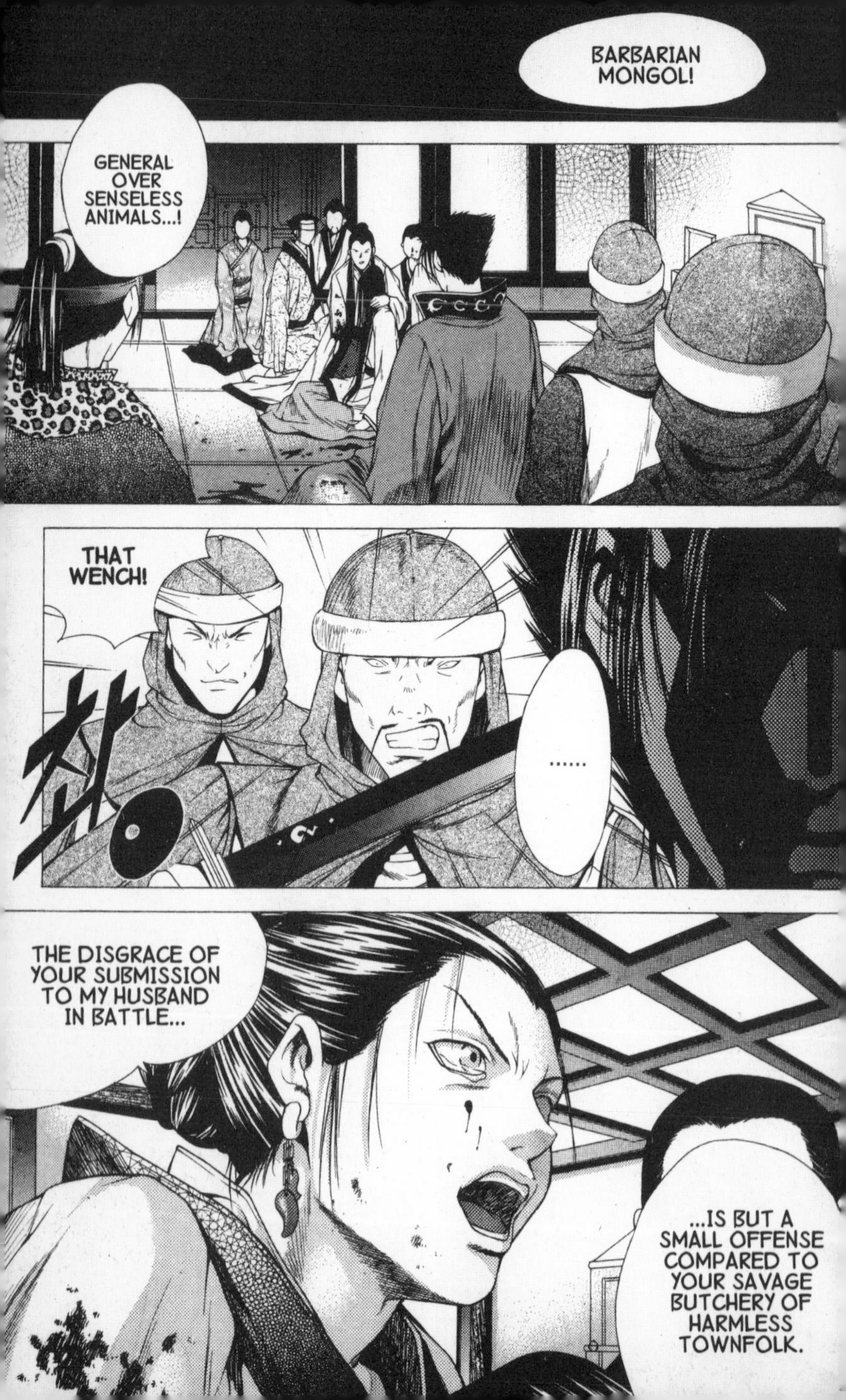
BARBARIAN MONGOL!
GENERAL OVER SENSELESS ANIMALS...!
THAT WENCH!
......
THE DISGRACE OF YOUR SUBMISSION TO MY HUSBAND IN BATTLE...
...IS BUT A SMALL OFFENSE COMPARED TO YOUR SAVAGE BUTCHERY OF HARMLESS TOWNFOLK.

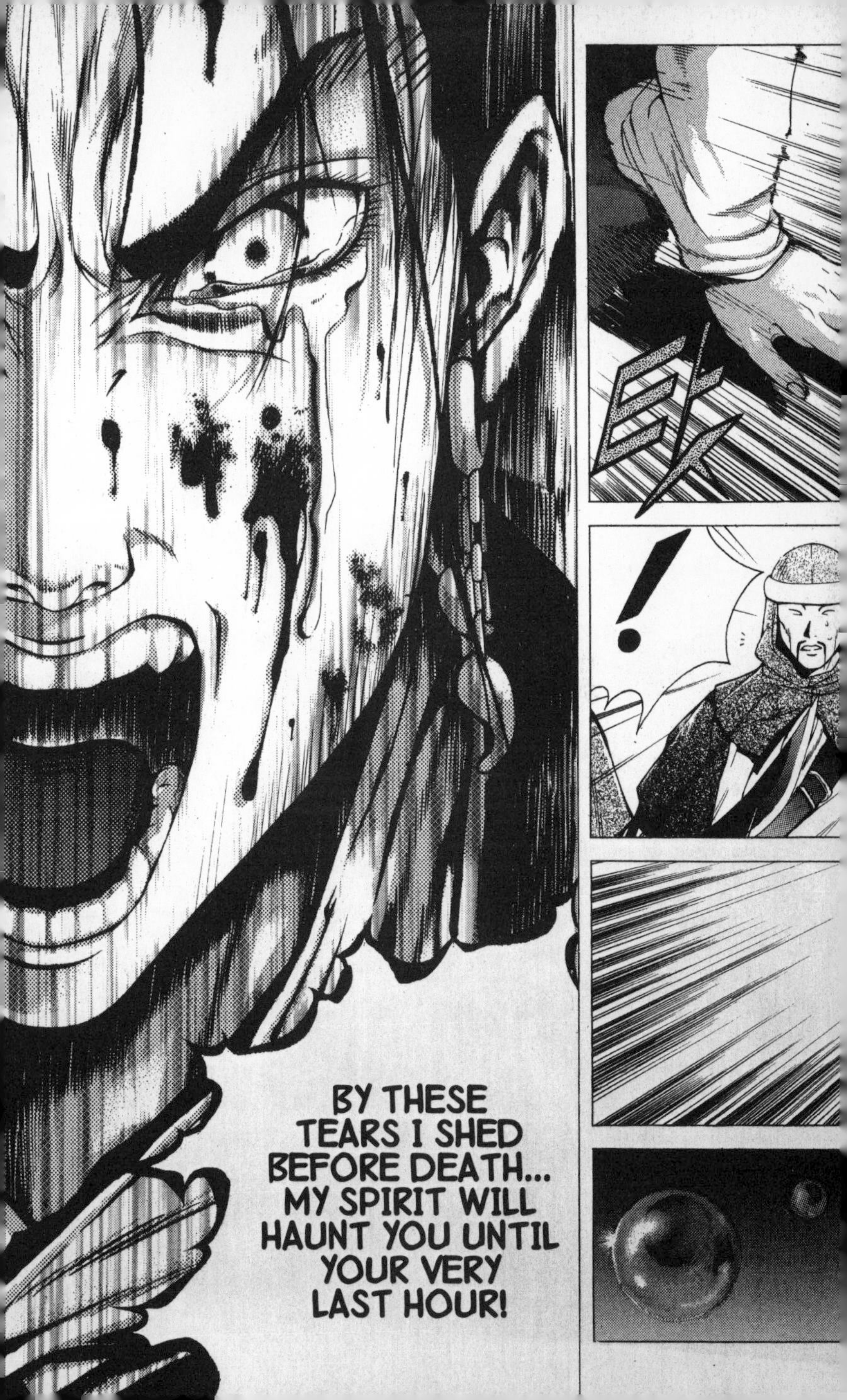
BY THESE TEARS I SHED BEFORE DEATH... MY SPIRIT WILL HAUNT YOU UNTIL YOUR VERY LAST HOUR!
!

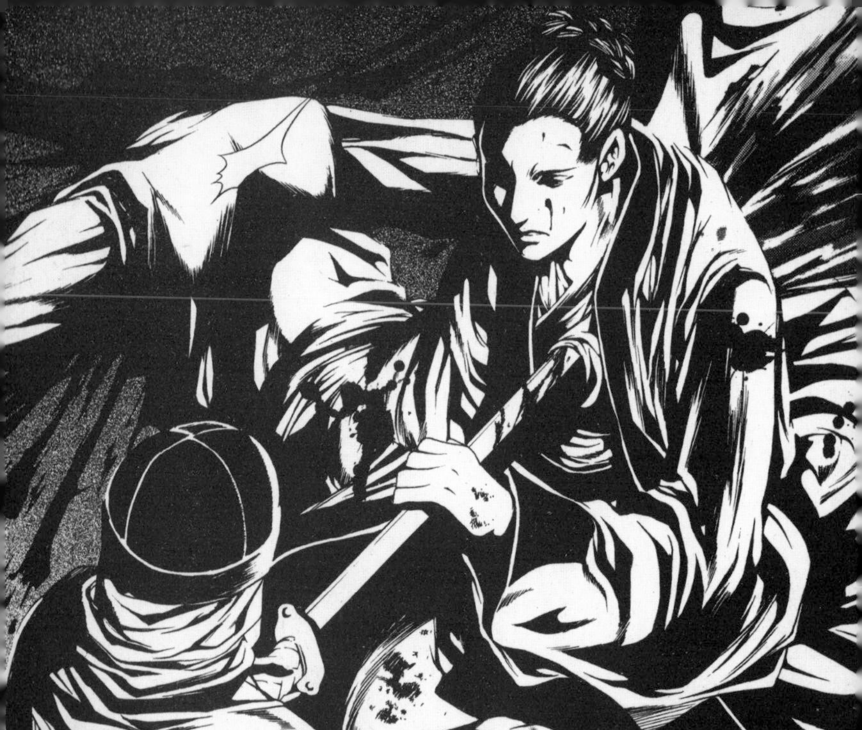

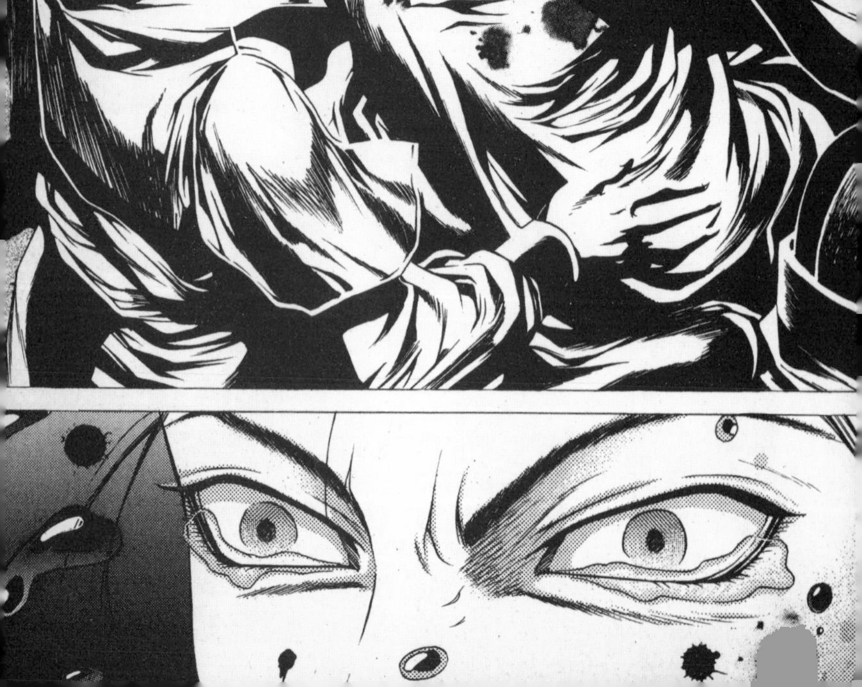

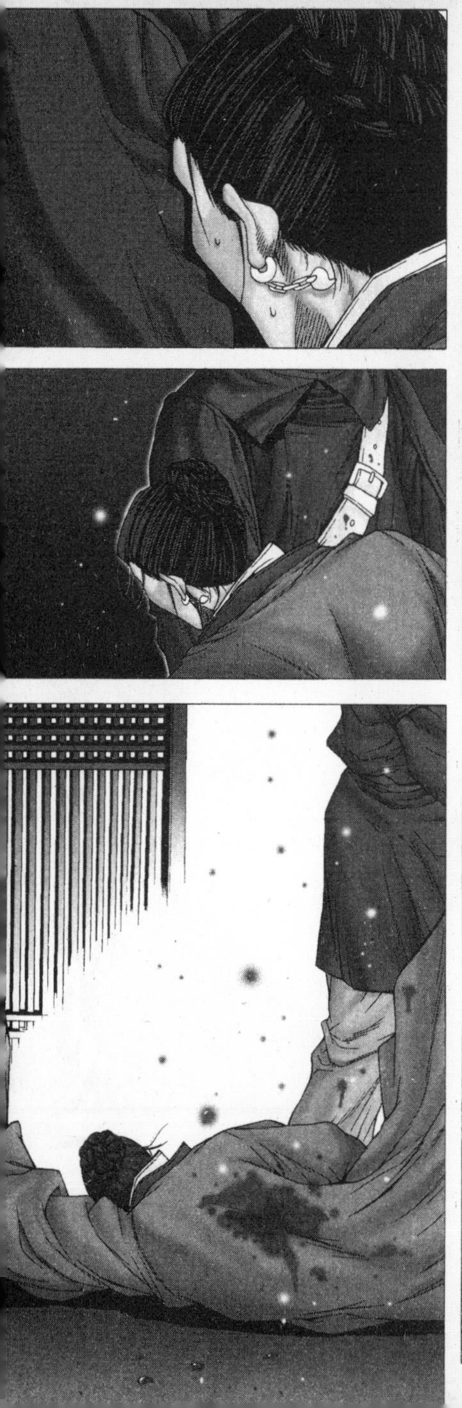

## Chapter 17
## A Swamp of Blood

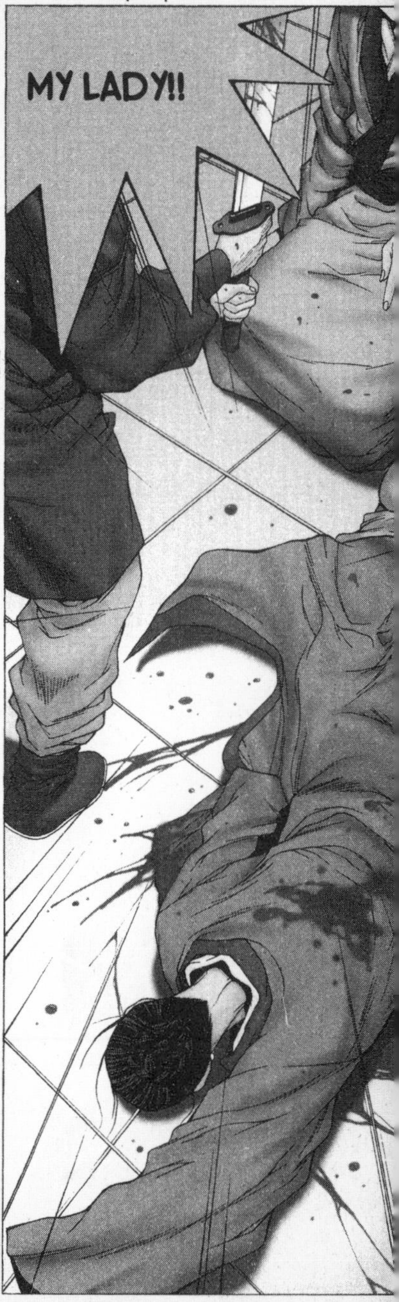
MY LADY!!

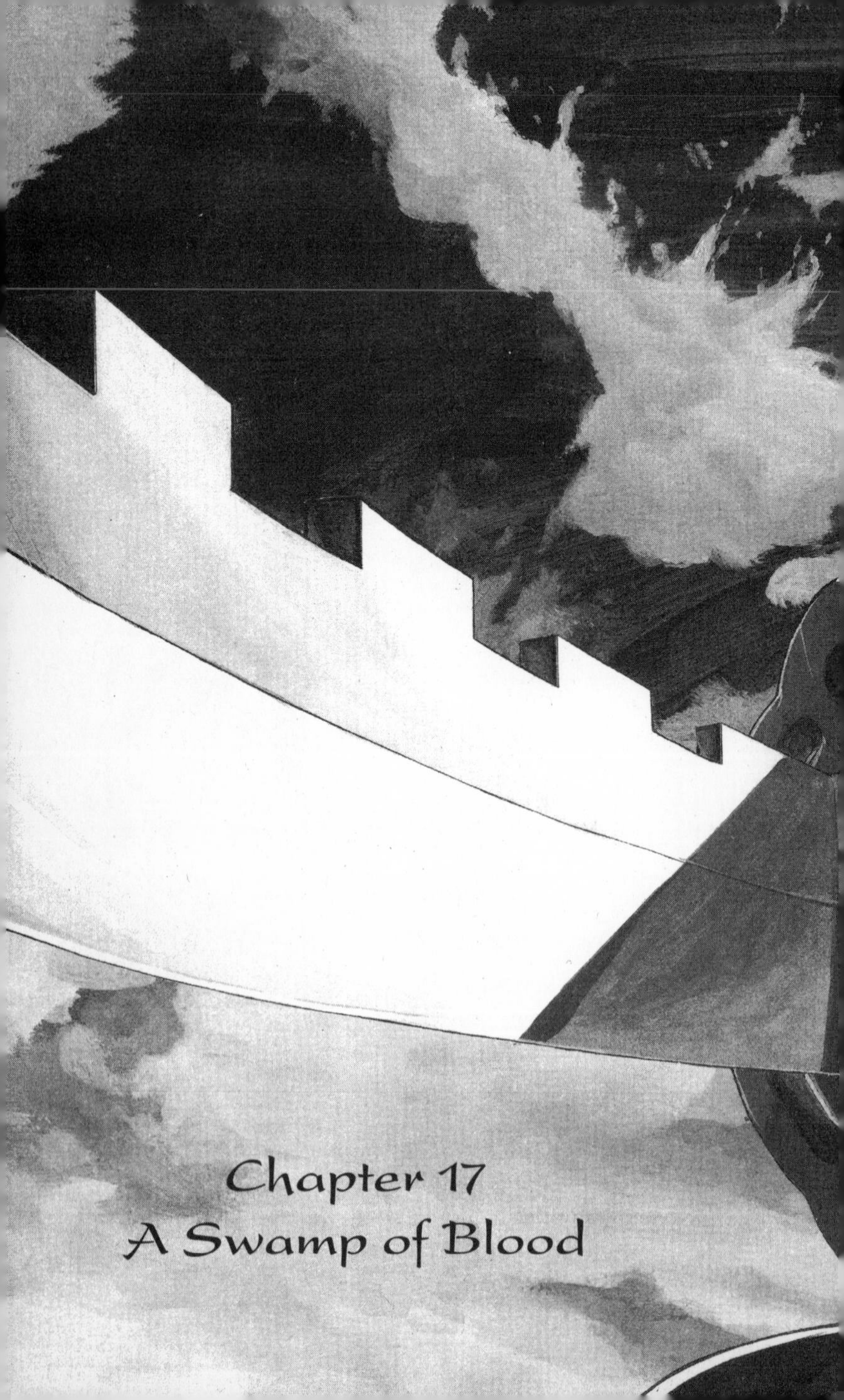
Chapter 17
A Swamp of Blood

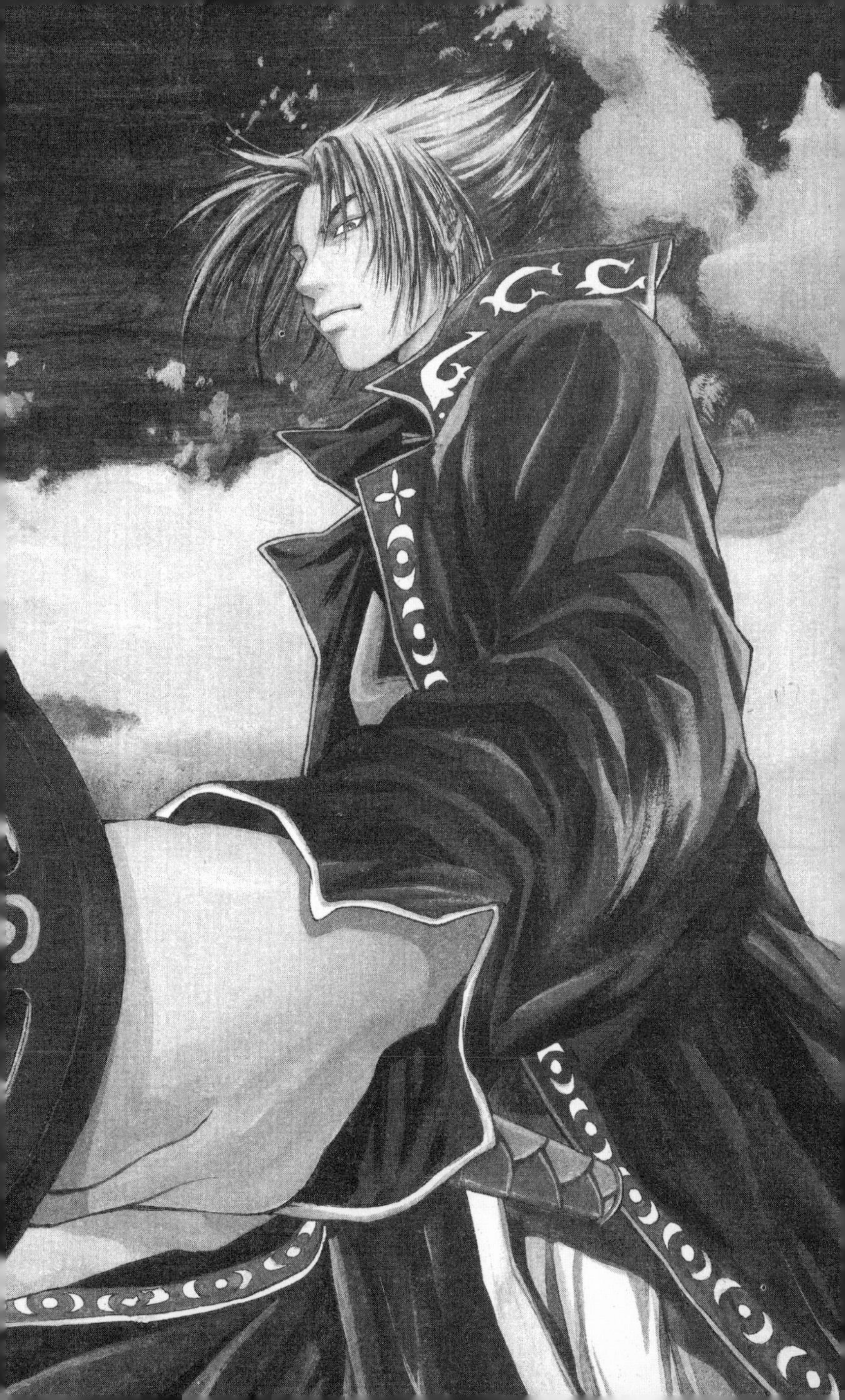

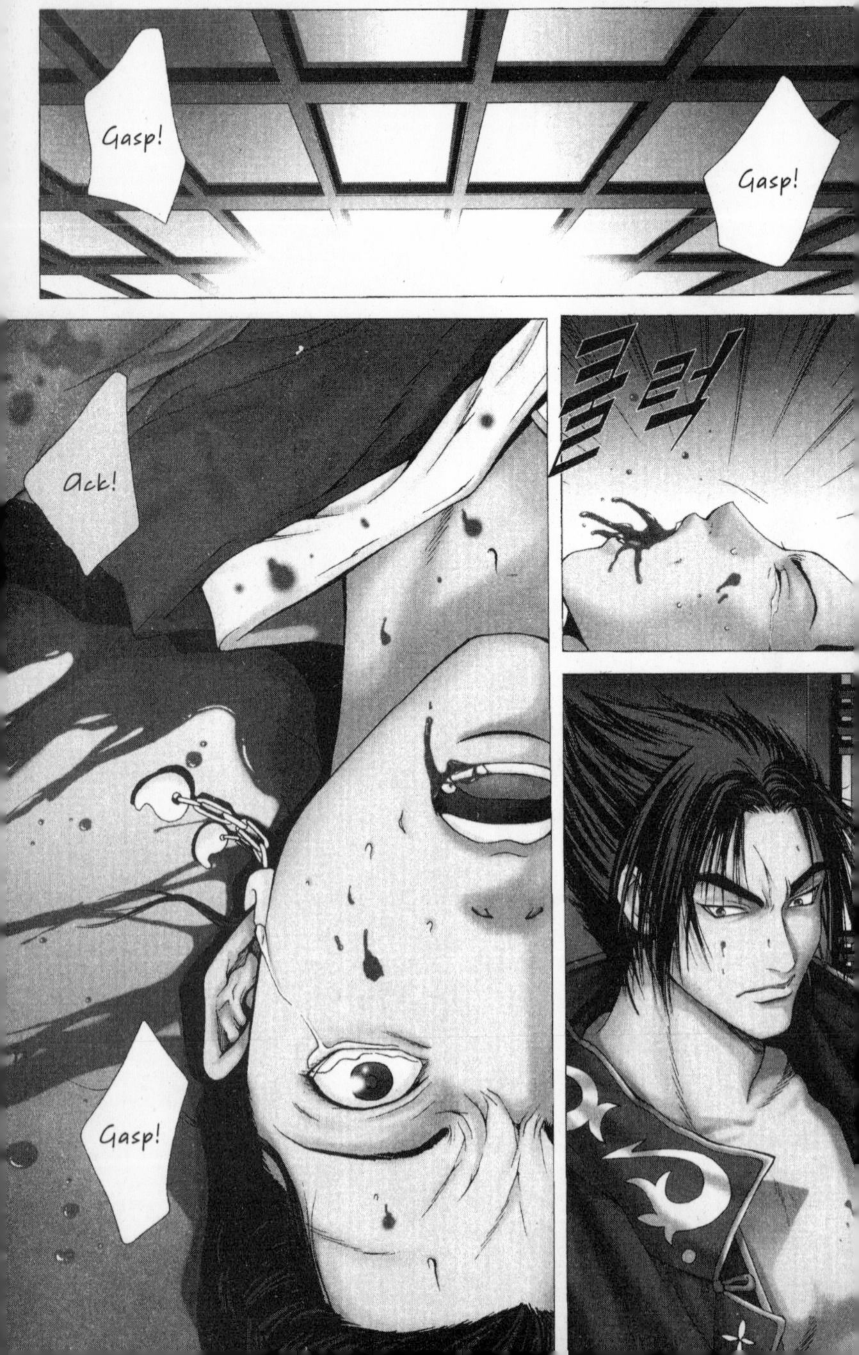
Gasp!
Gasp!
Ack!
Gasp!
쿨럭

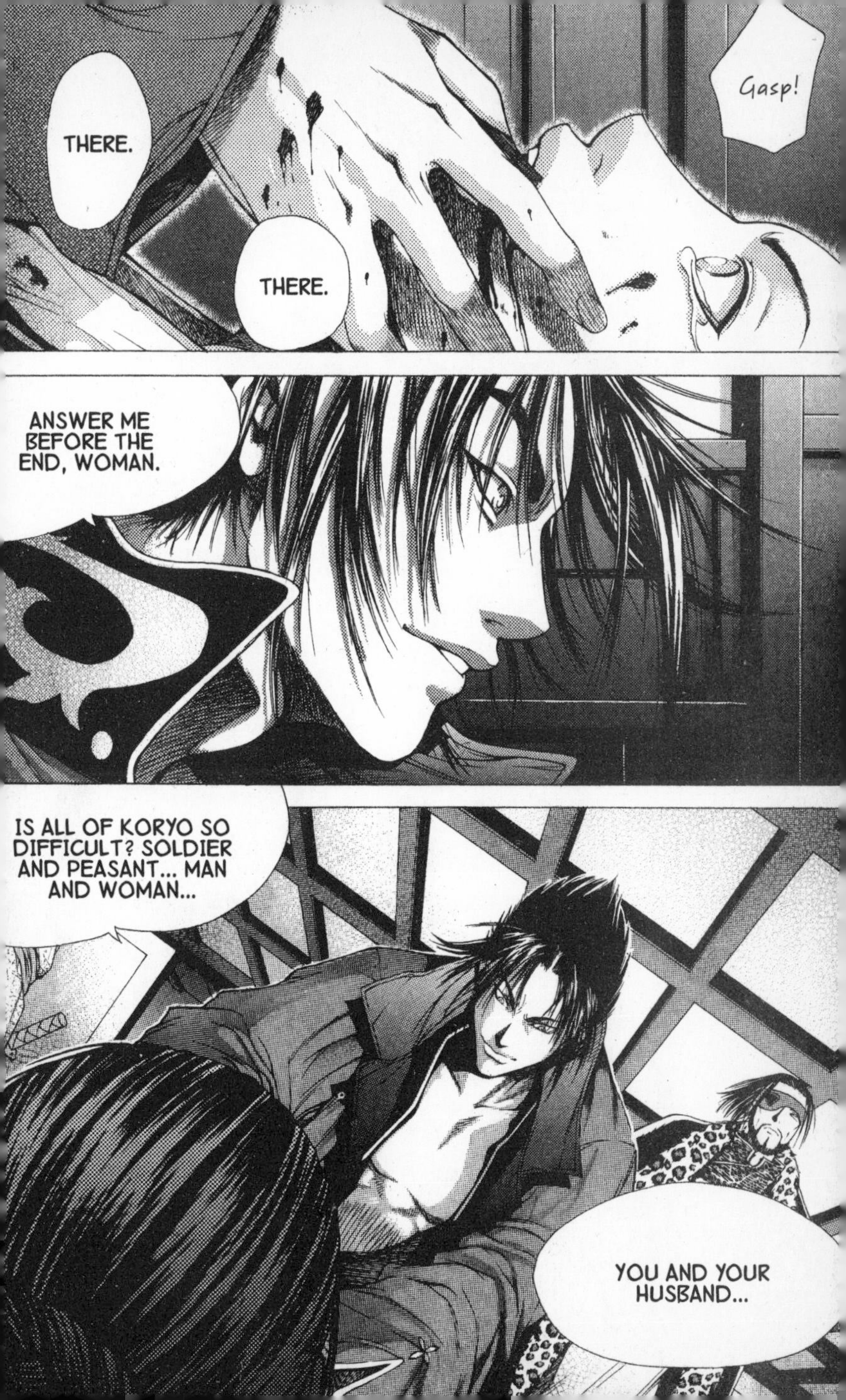
THERE.
THERE.
Gasp!
ANSWER ME BEFORE THE END, WOMAN.
IS ALL OF KORYO SO DIFFICULT? SOLDIER AND PEASANT... MAN AND WOMAN...
YOU AND YOUR HUSBAND...

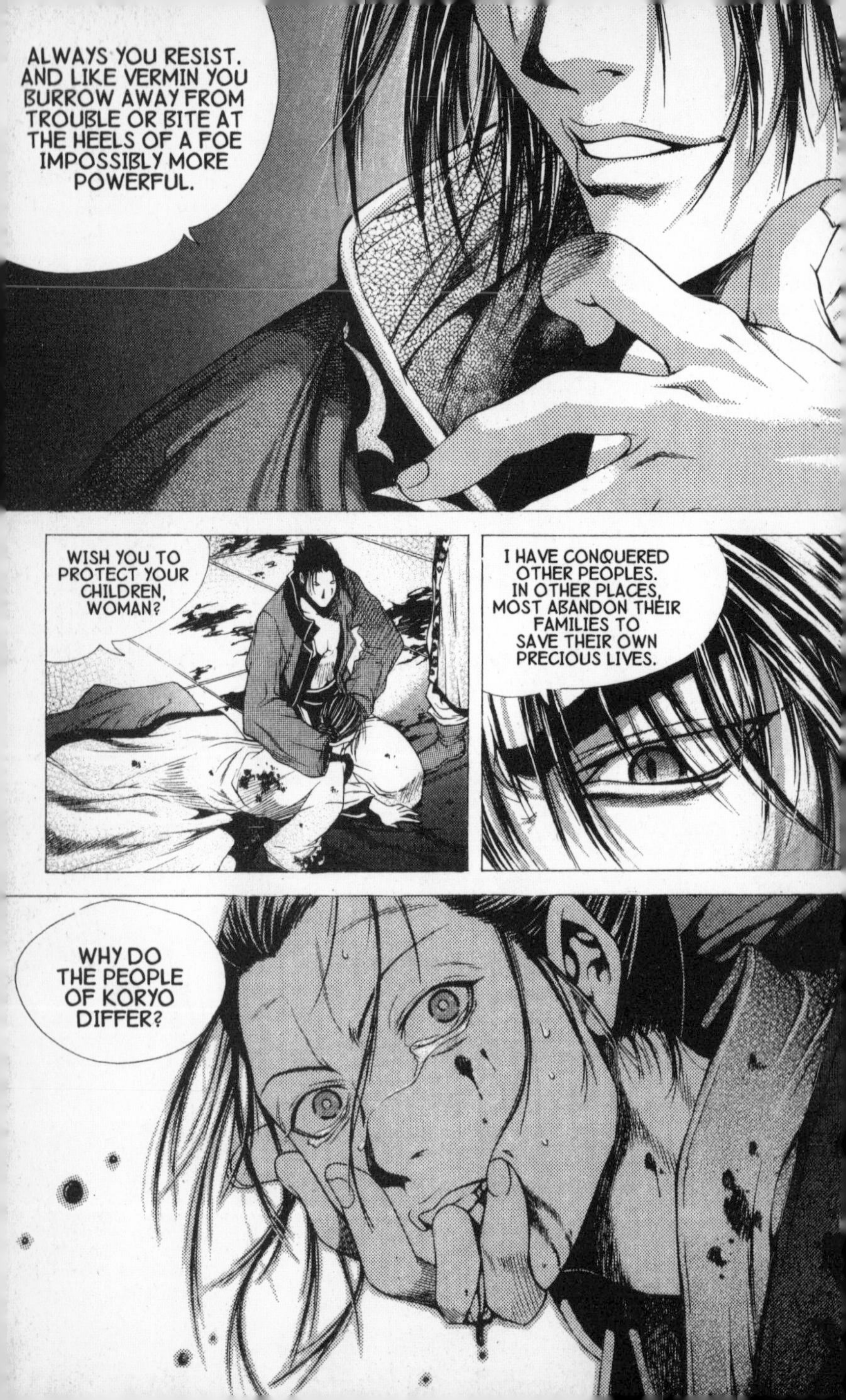
ALWAYS YOU RESIST. AND LIKE VERMIN YOU BURROW AWAY FROM TROUBLE OR BITE AT THE HEELS OF A FOE IMPOSSIBLY MORE POWERFUL.
WISH YOU TO PROTECT YOUR CHILDREN, WOMAN?
I HAVE CONQUERED OTHER PEOPLES. IN OTHER PLACES, MOST ABANDON THEIR FAMILIES TO SAVE THEIR OWN PRECIOUS LIVES.
WHY DO THE PEOPLE OF KORYO DIFFER?

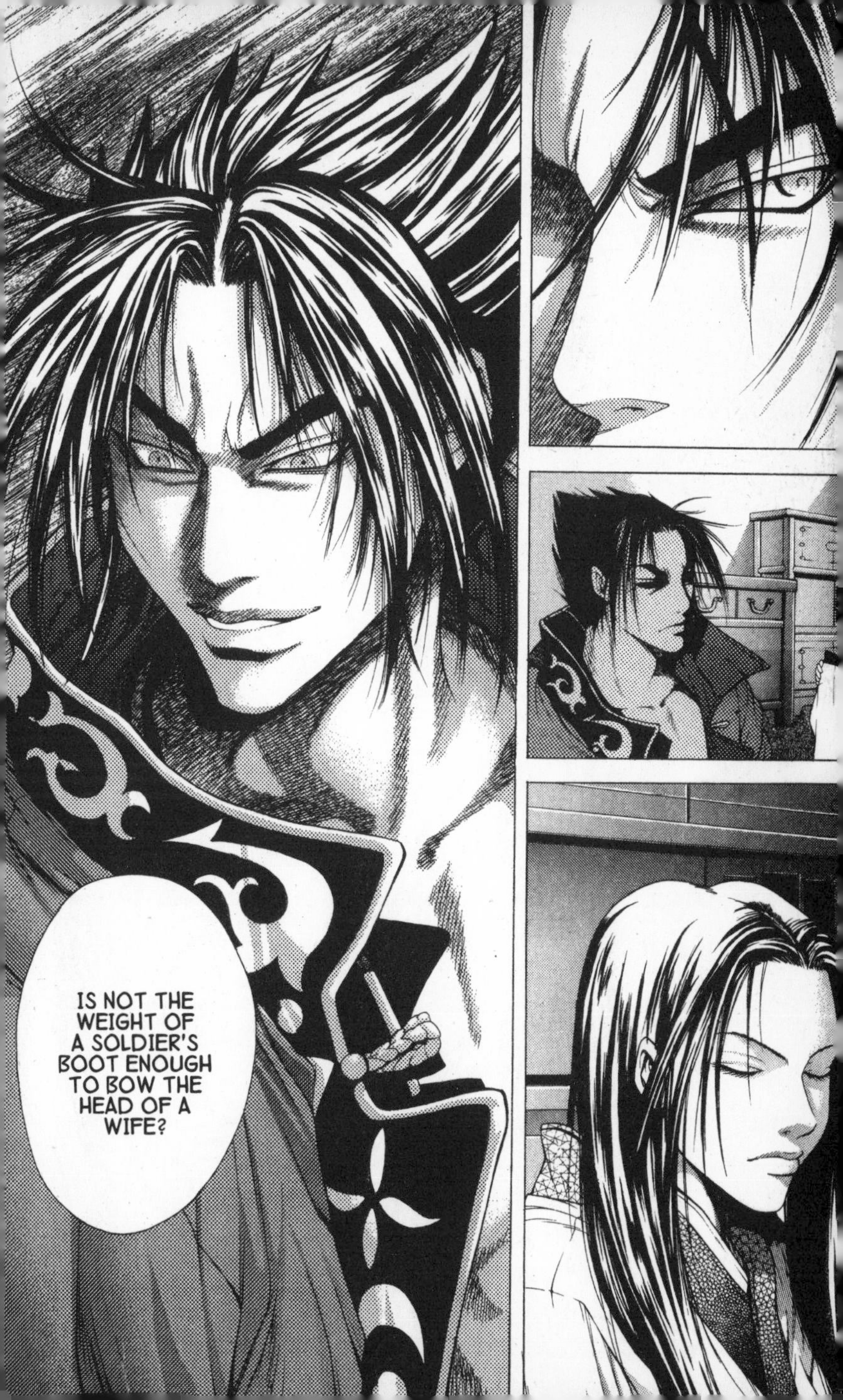
IS NOT THE WEIGHT OF A SOLDIER'S BOOT ENOUGH TO BOW THE HEAD OF A WIFE?

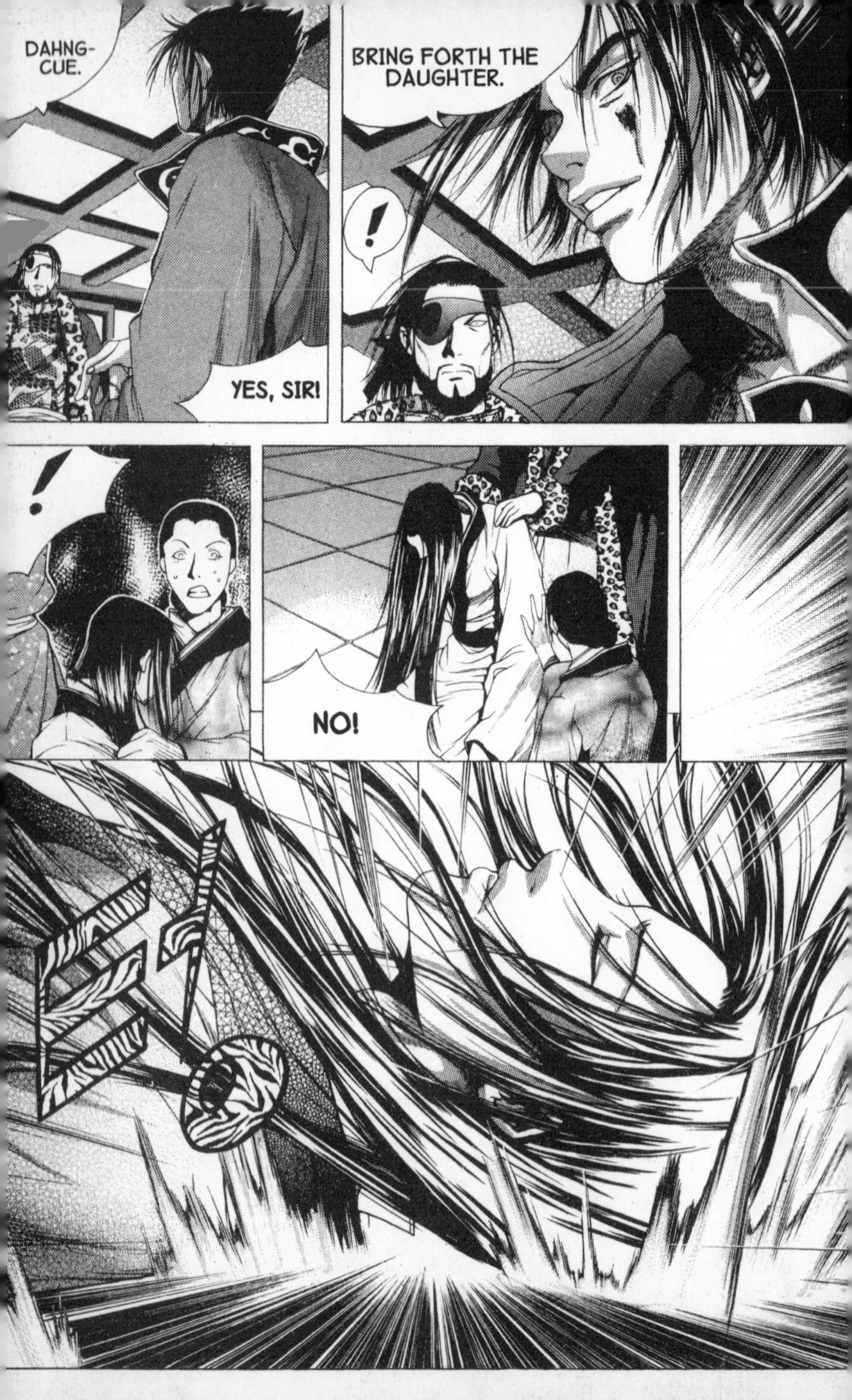
DAHNG-CUE.
YES, SIR!
BRING FORTH THE DAUGHTER.
!
!
NO!

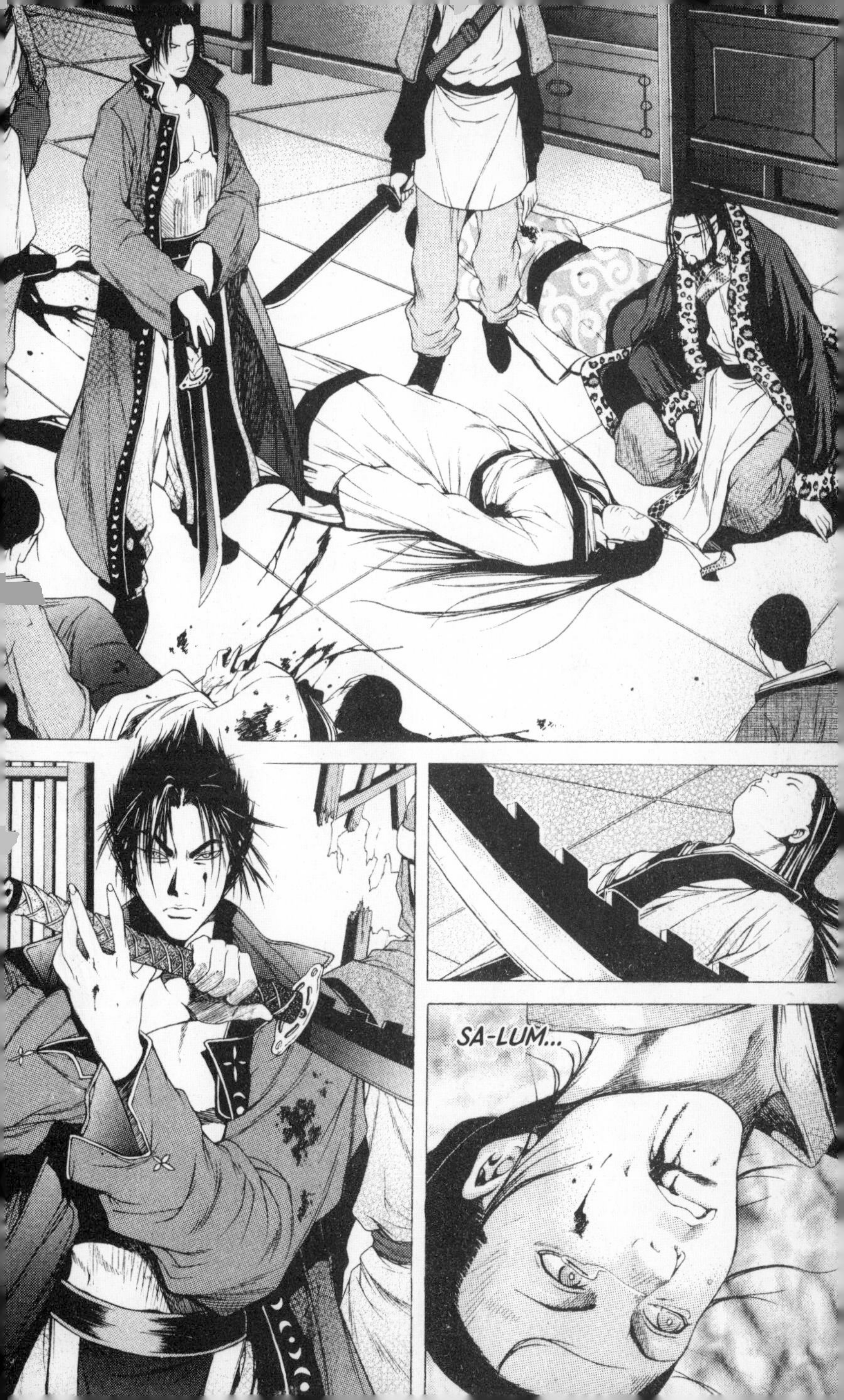
SA-LUM...

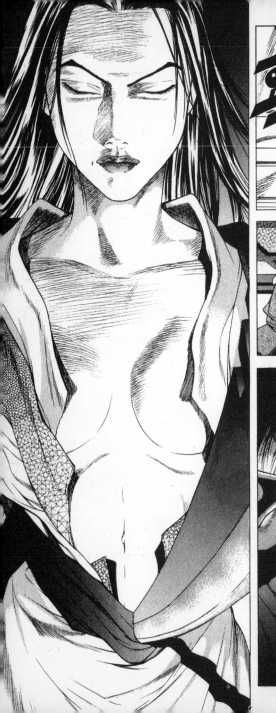

SHE IS
ALIVE
AND YET
DEAD...

BEFORE YOUR OWN LIGHT EXPIRES FOREVER, CAST YOUR EYES UPON YOUR CHILD...

MOTHER!

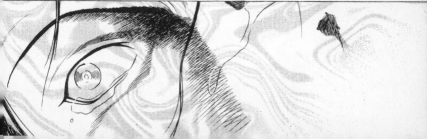

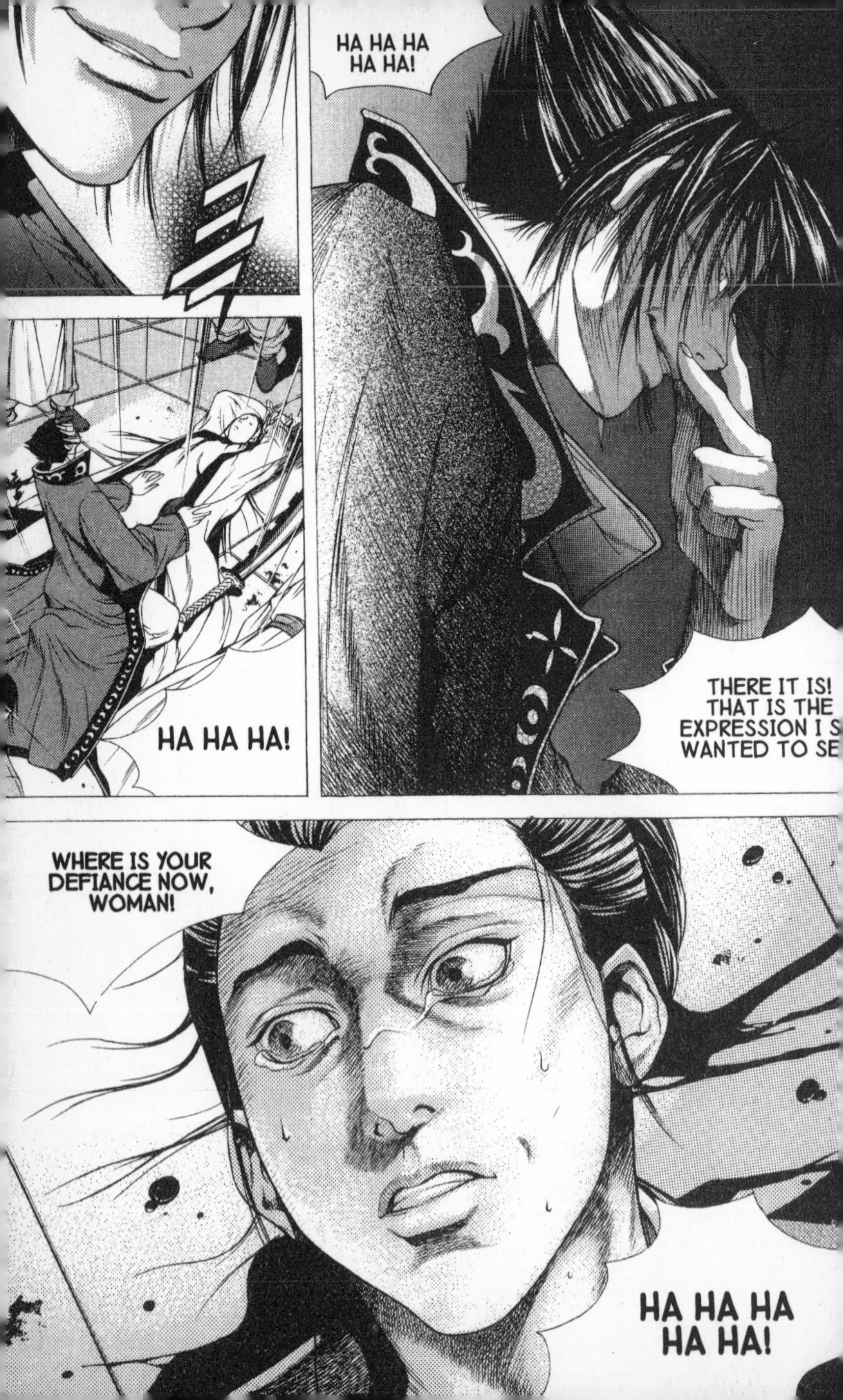
HA HA HA
HA HA!
HA HA HA!
THERE IT IS!
THAT IS THE
EXPRESSION I S
WANTED TO SE
WHERE IS YOUR
DEFIANCE NOW,
WOMAN!
HA HA HA
HA HA!

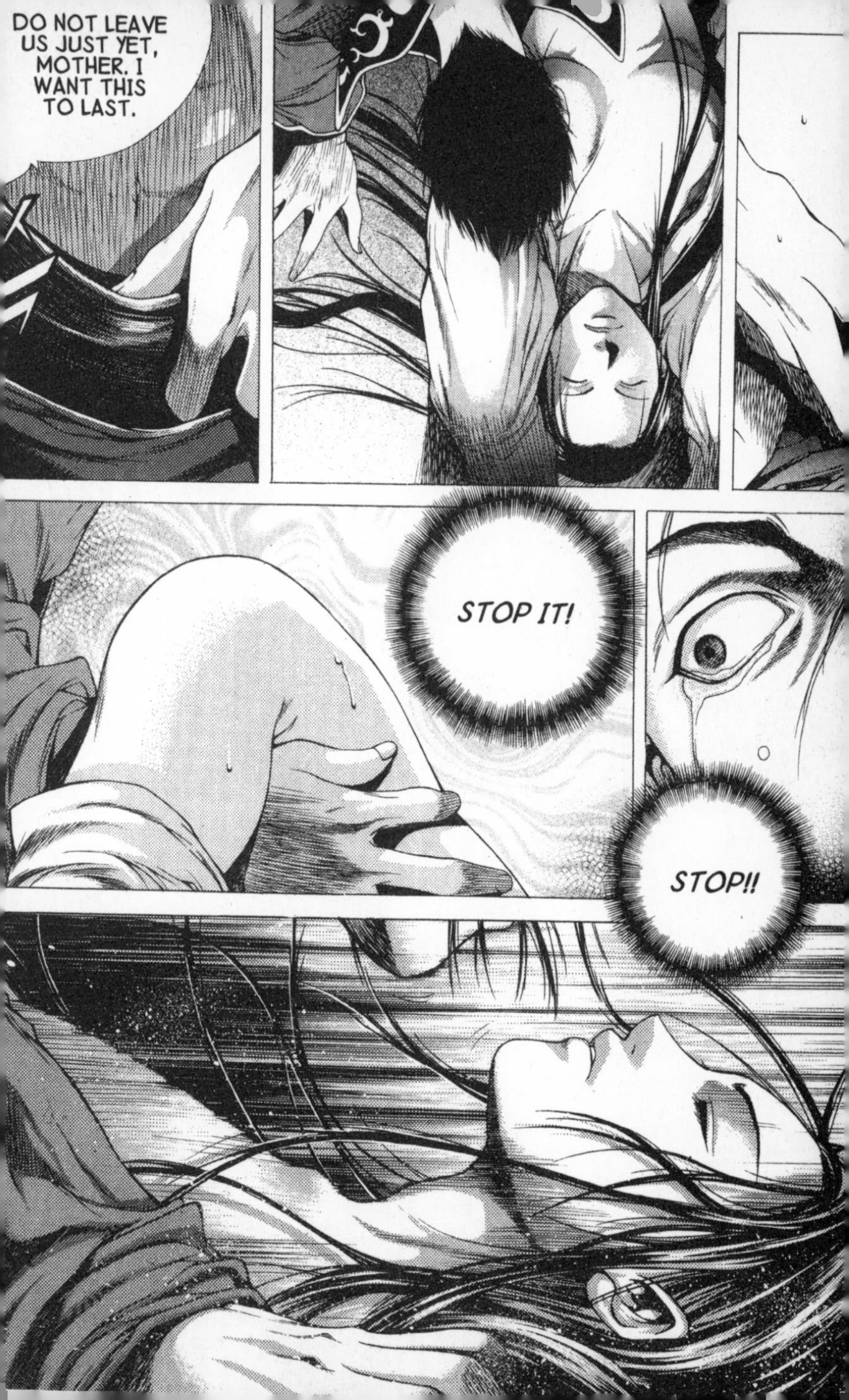
DO NOT LEAVE US JUST YET, MOTHER. I WANT THIS TO LAST.
STOP IT!
STOP!!

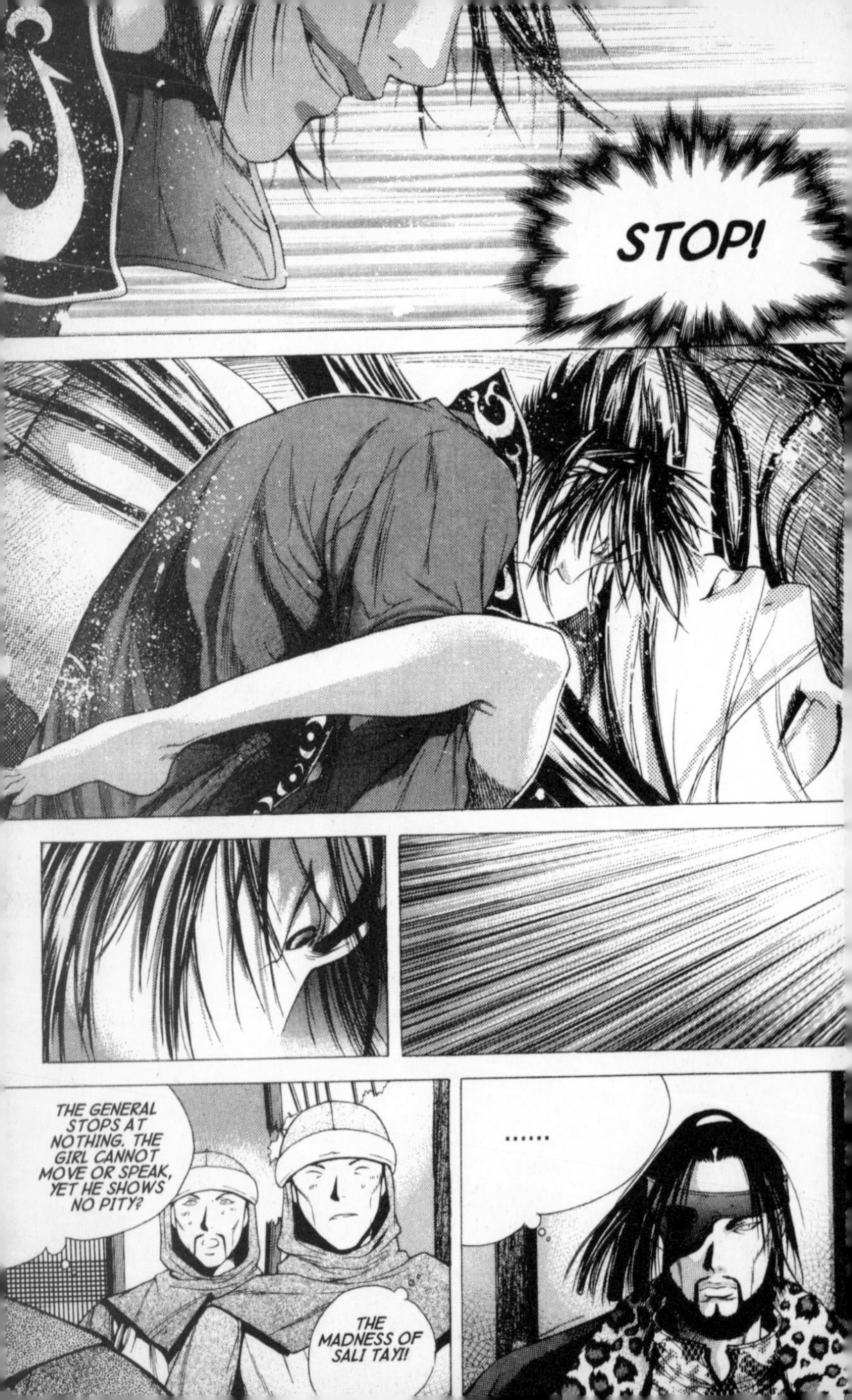
STOP!
THE GENERAL STOPS AT NOTHING. THE GIRL CANNOT MOVE OR SPEAK, YET HE SHOWS NO PITY?
THE MADNESS OF SALI TAYI!
......

SA-LUM...
SA-LUM...

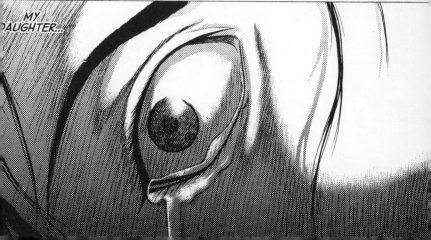

MY
DAUGHTER...

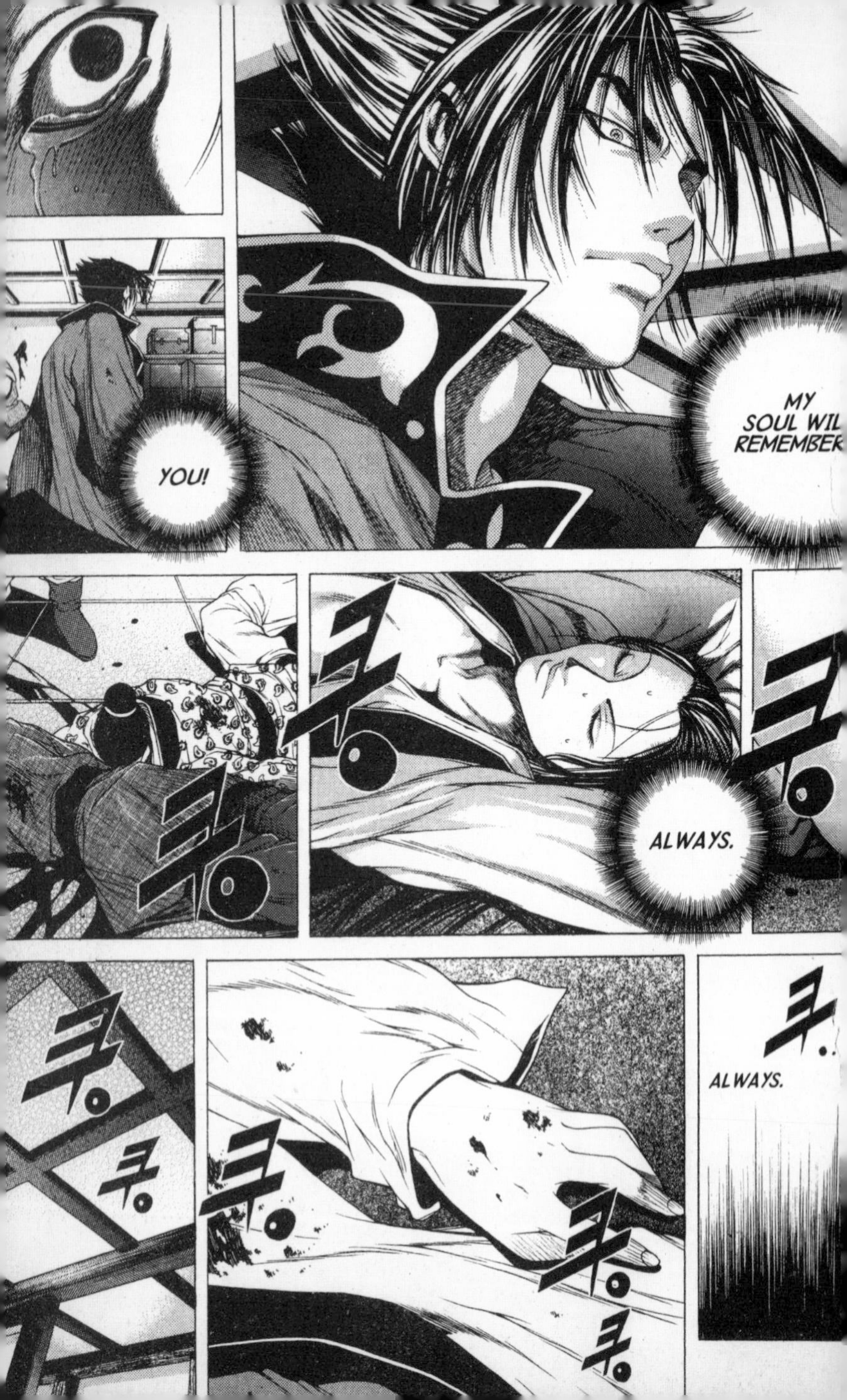
YOU!
MY SOUL WIL REMEMBER
ALWAYS.
ALWAYS.

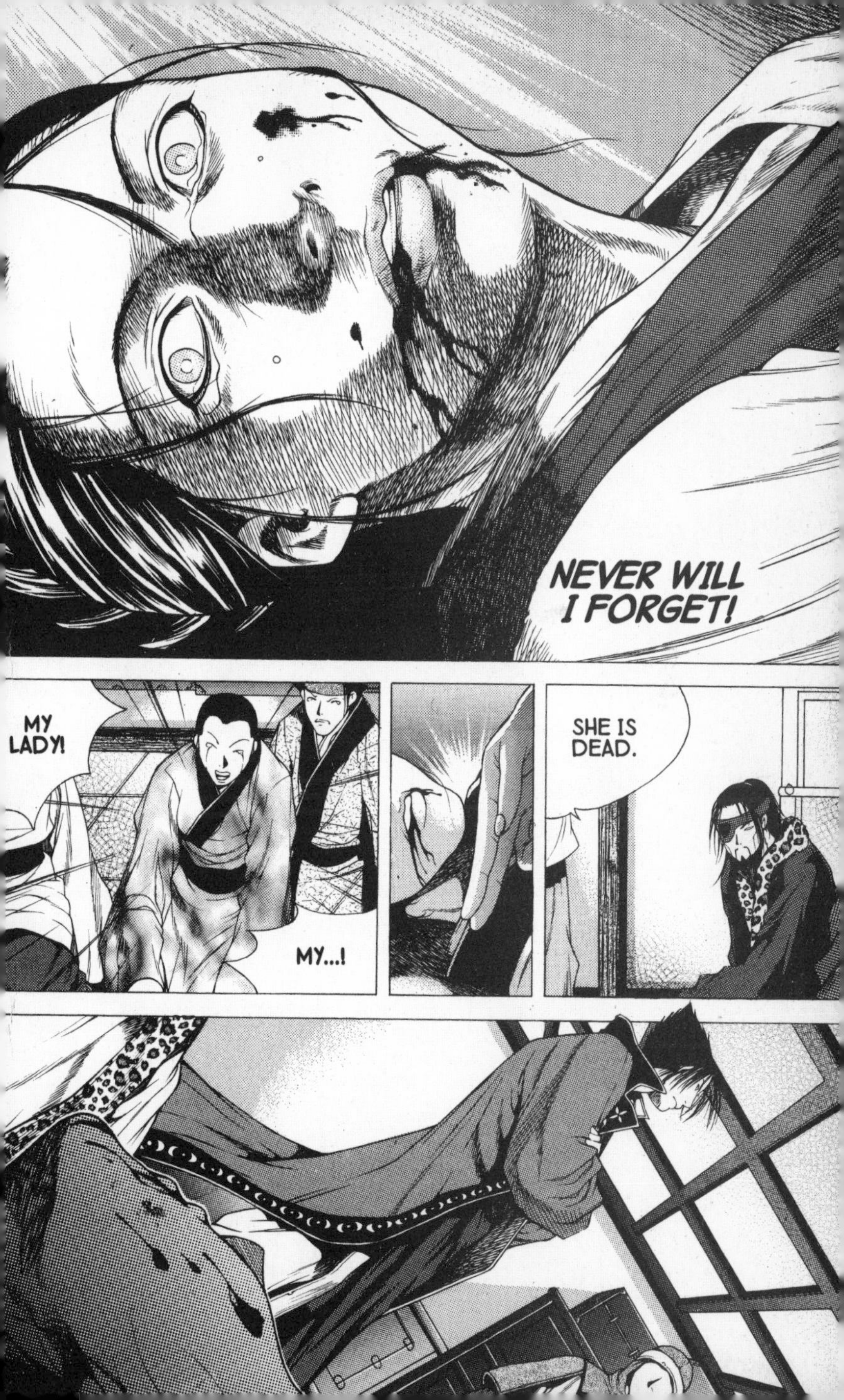
NEVER WILL I FORGET!
MY LADY!
MY...!
SHE IS DEAD.

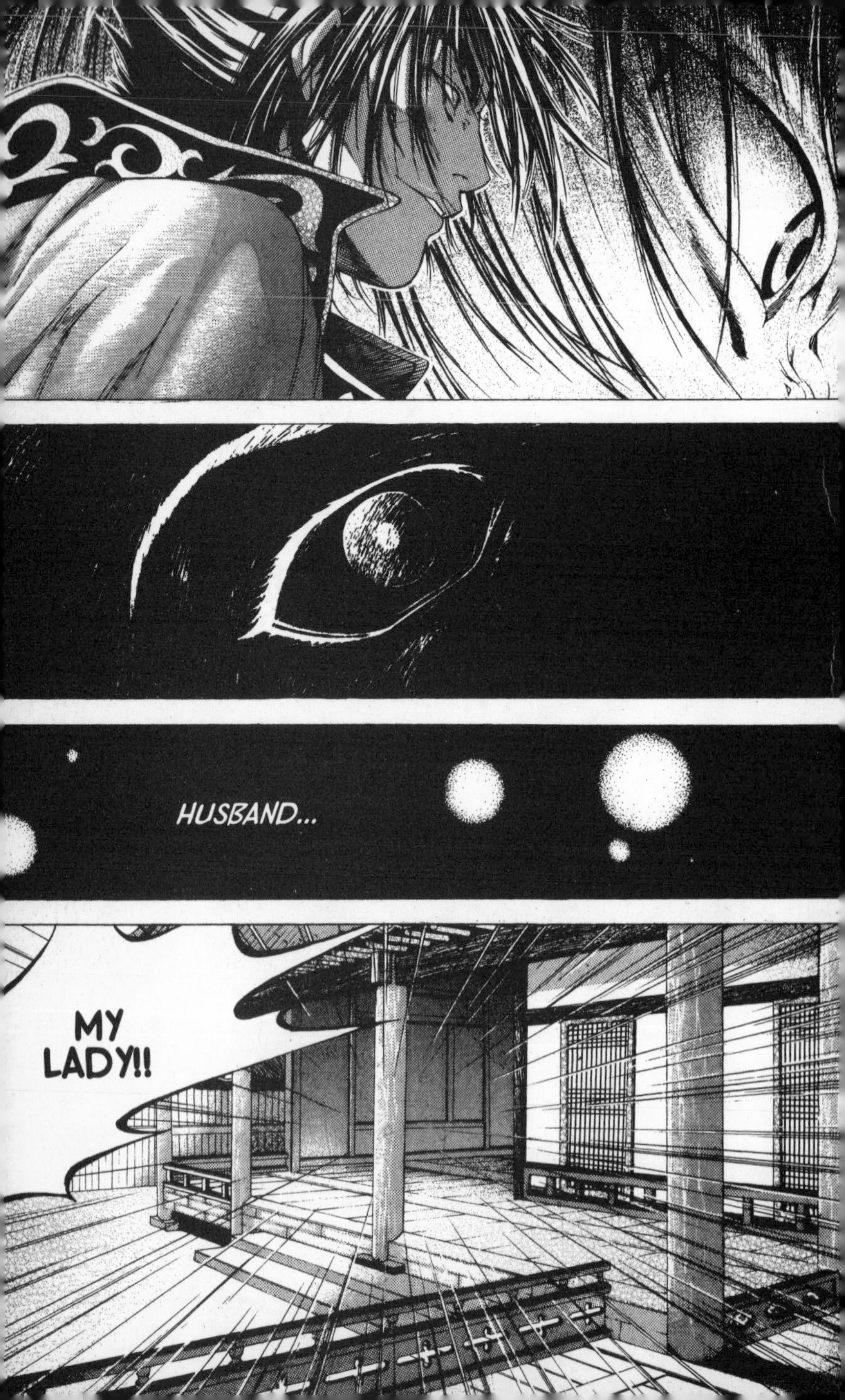
HUSBAND...
MY LADY!!

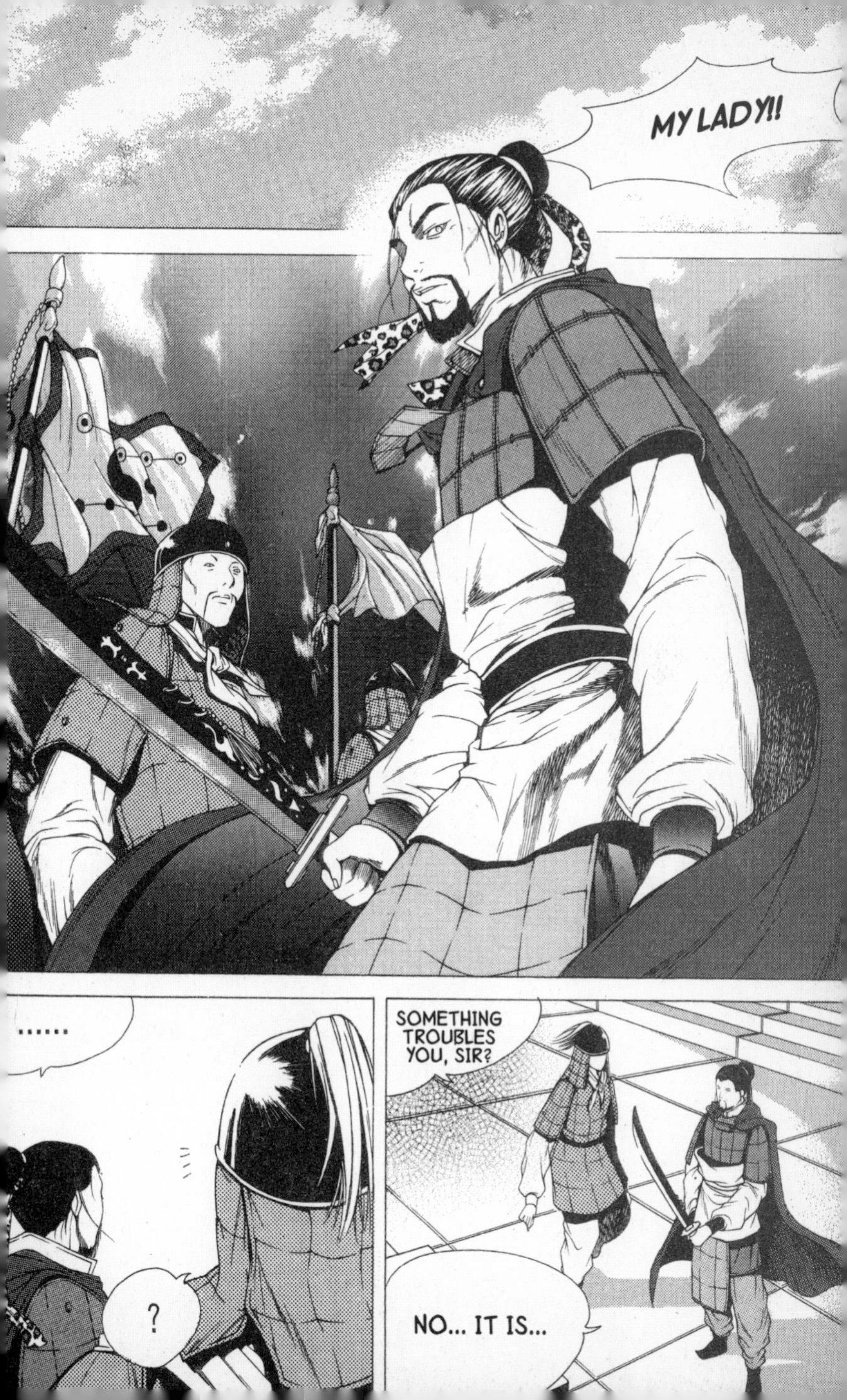
MY LADY!!
......
?
SOMETHING TROUBLES YOU, SIR?
NO... IT IS...

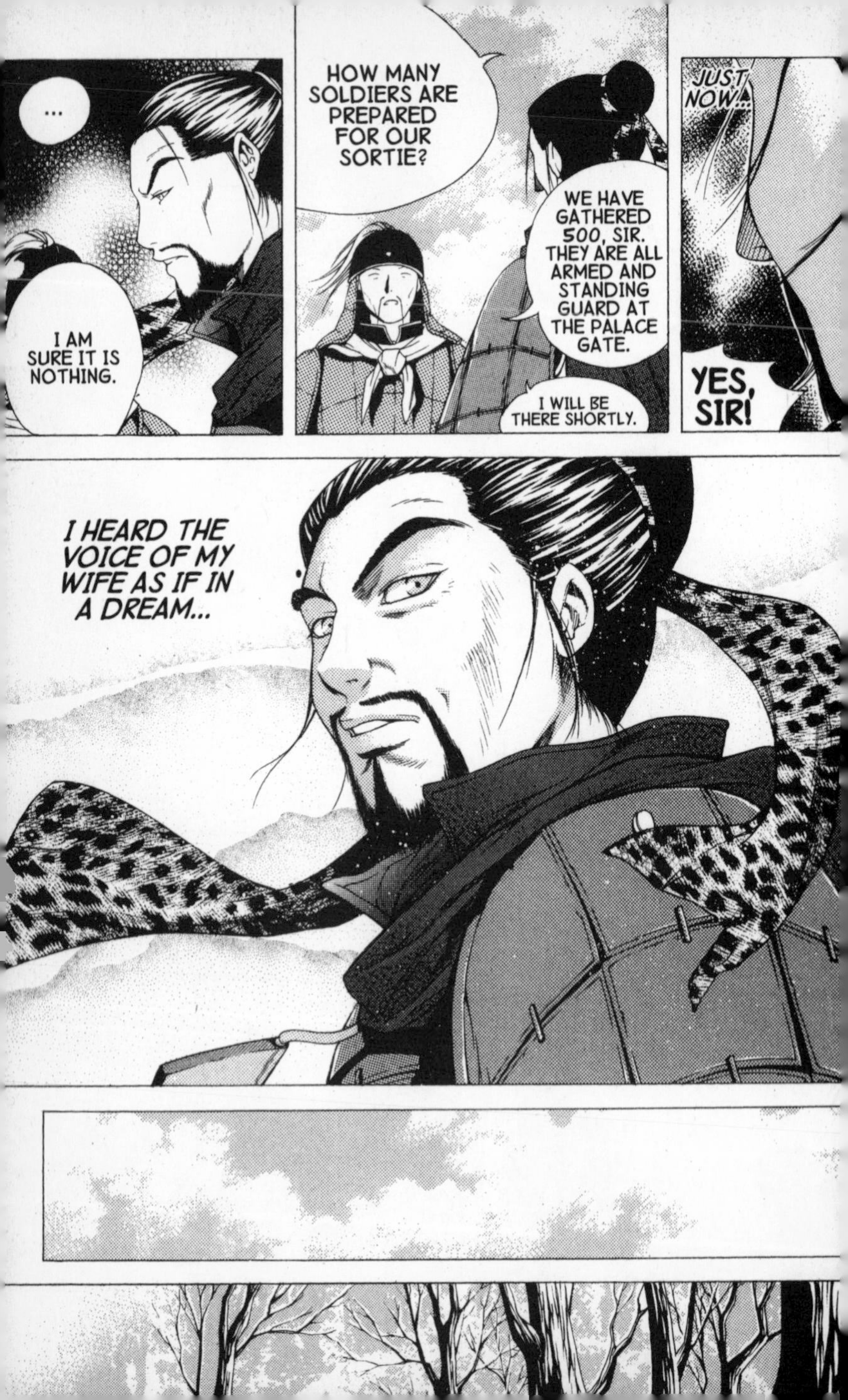
...
I AM SURE IT IS NOTHING.
HOW MANY SOLDIERS ARE PREPARED FOR OUR SORTIE?
WE HAVE GATHERED 500, SIR. THEY ARE ALL ARMED AND STANDING GUARD AT THE PALACE GATE.
I WILL BE THERE SHORTLY.
JUST NOW...
YES, SIR!
I HEARD THE VOICE OF MY WIFE AS IF IN A DREAM...

THIS...

THIS IS WHERE FIRST WE MET.

ABOUT BEFORE... I AM THANKFUL.

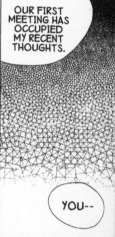

OUR FIRST MEETING HAS OCCUPIED MY RECENT THOUGHTS.

YOU--

TO SAVE A LIFE IS NO SMALL MATTER.

I HOPED FOR THE CHANCE TO REPAY YOUR KINDNESS...

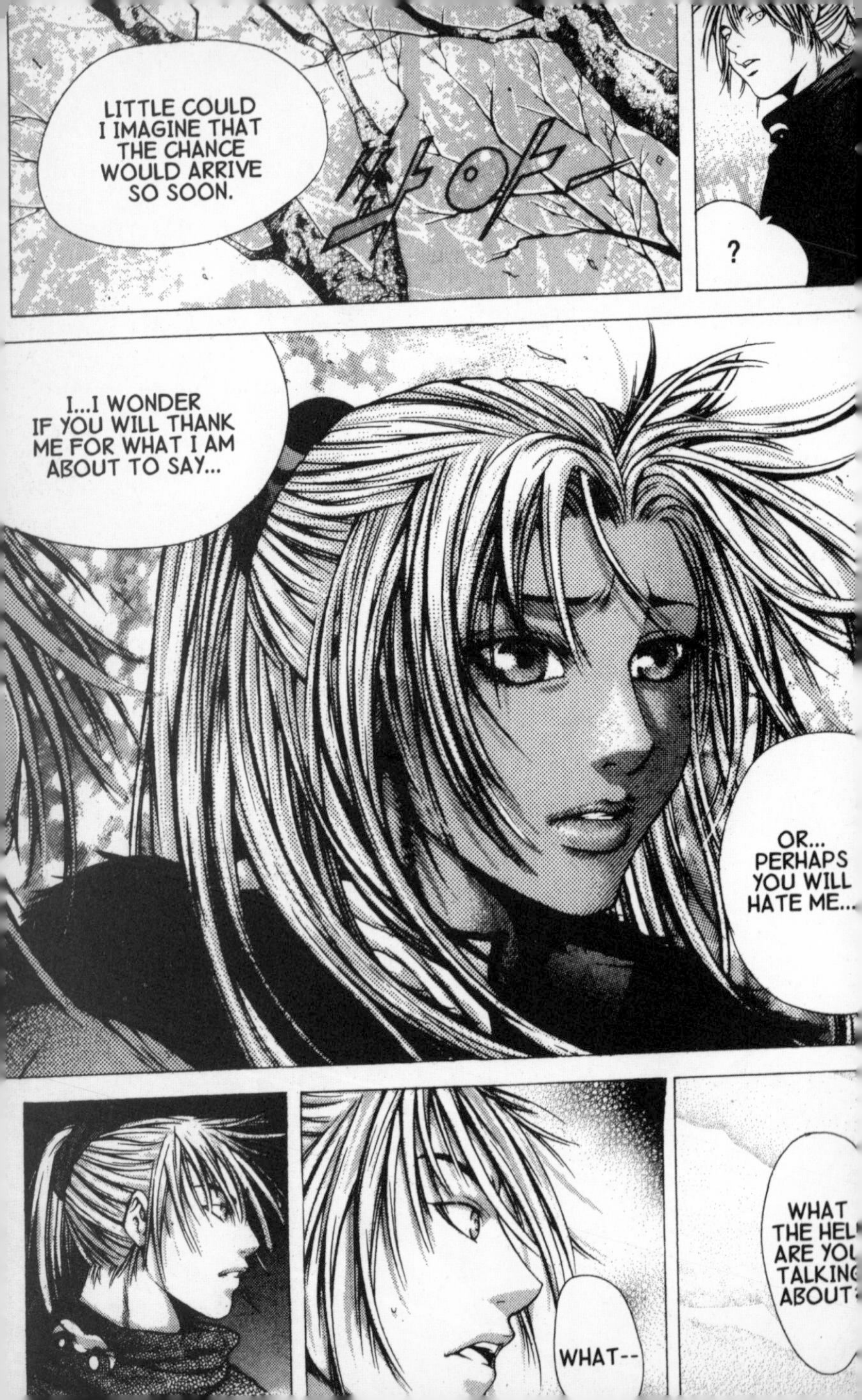

LITTLE COULD I IMAGINE THAT THE CHANCE WOULD ARRIVE SO SOON.
?
I...I WONDER IF YOU WILL THANK ME FOR WHAT I AM ABOUT TO SAY...
OR... PERHAPS YOU WILL HATE ME...
WHAT--
WHAT THE HEL ARE YOU TALKING ABOUT

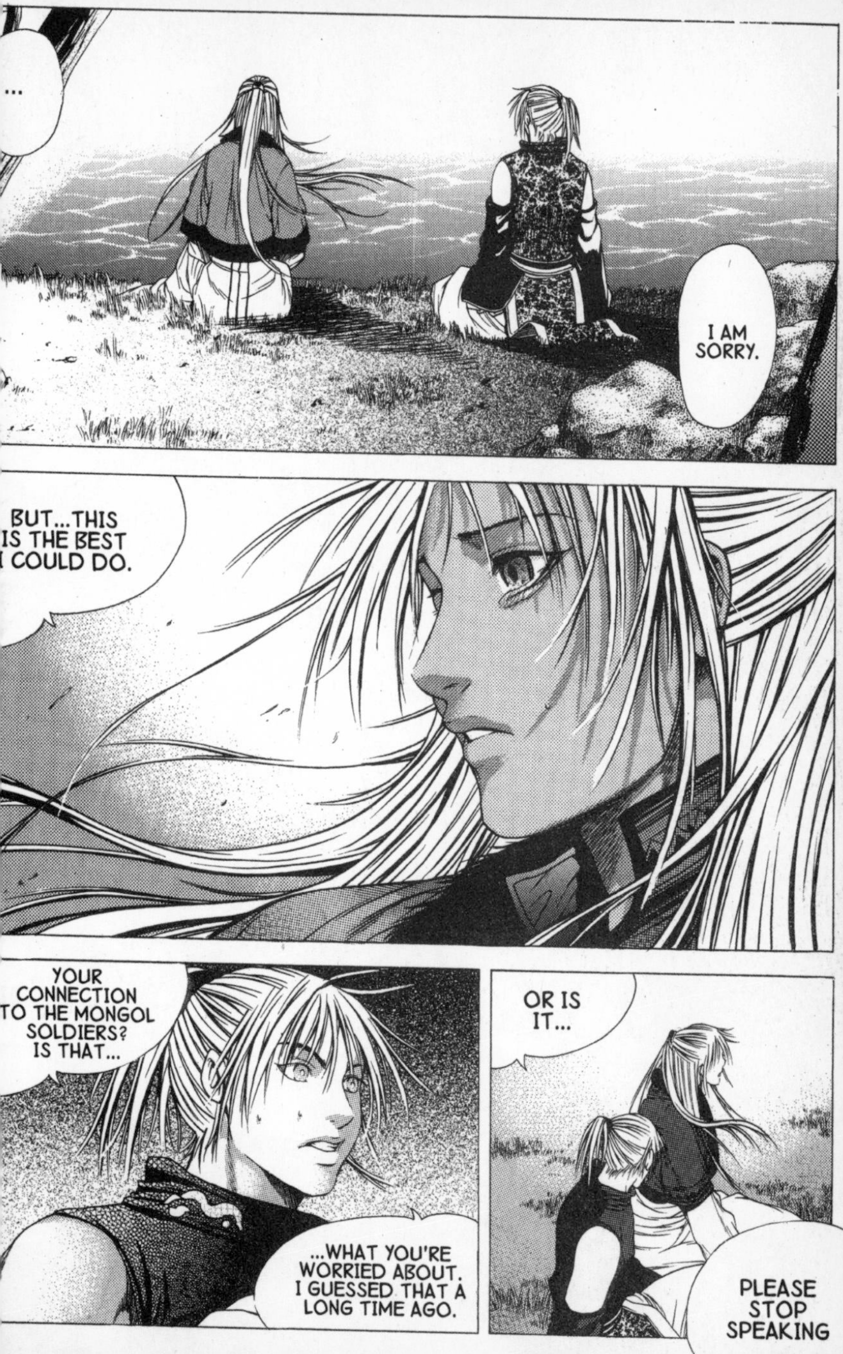
...
I AM SORRY.
BUT...THIS IS THE BEST I COULD DO.
YOUR CONNECTION TO THE MONGOL SOLDIERS? IS THAT...
...WHAT YOU'RE WORRIED ABOUT. I GUESSED THAT A LONG TIME AGO.
OR IS IT...
PLEASE STOP SPEAKING ...

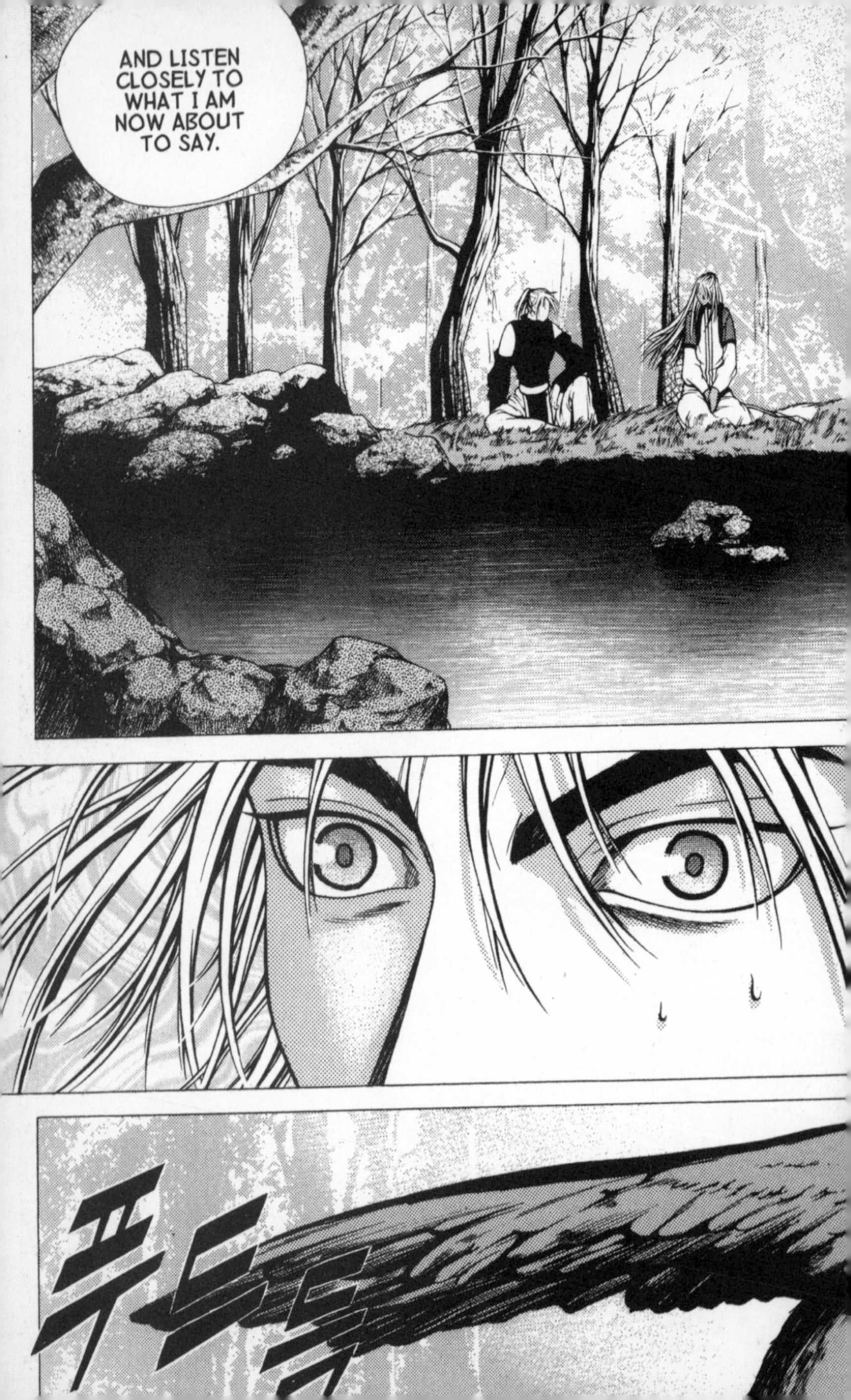
AND LISTEN CLOSELY TO WHAT I AM NOW ABOUT TO SAY.

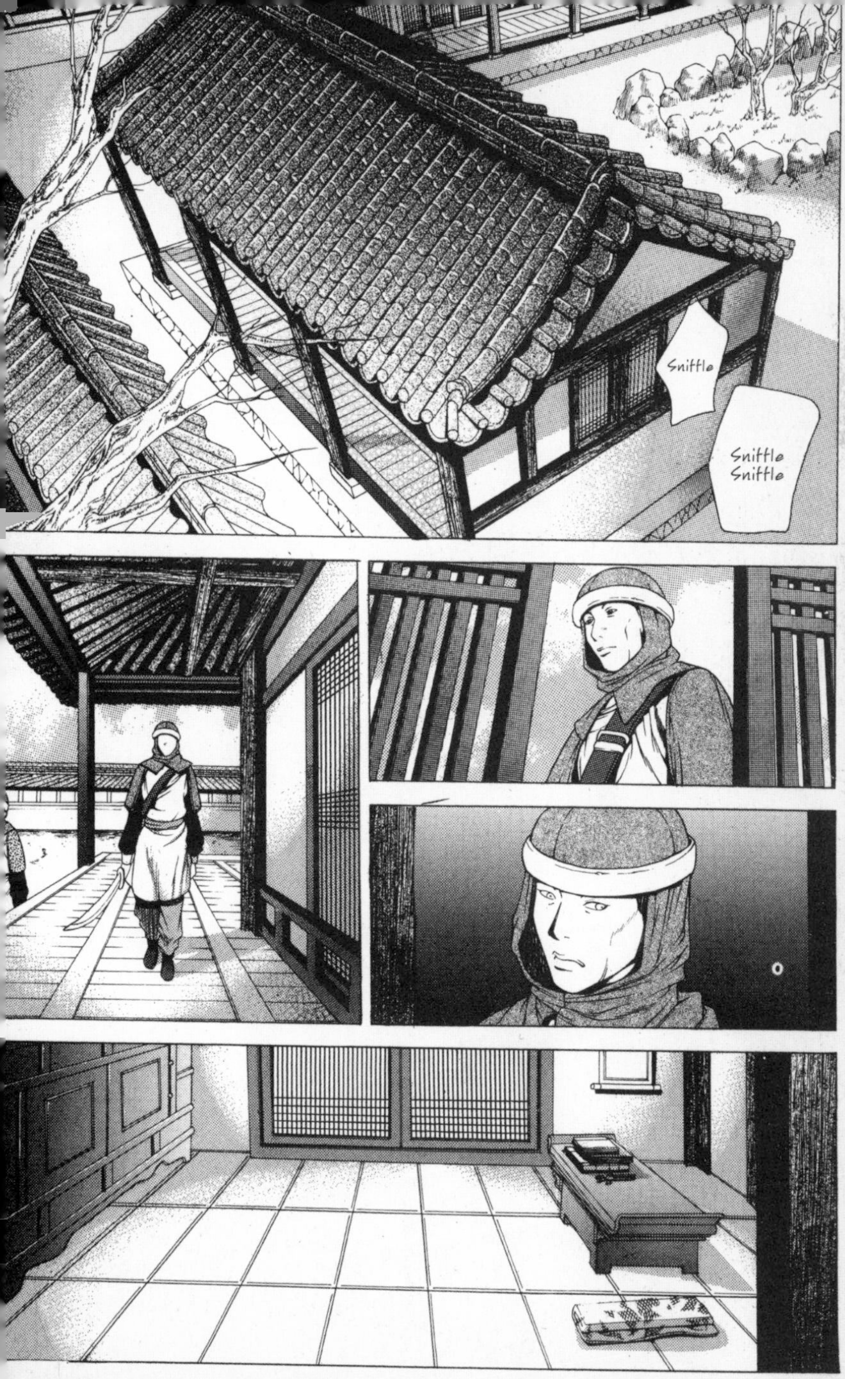
Sniffle
Sniffle
Sniffle

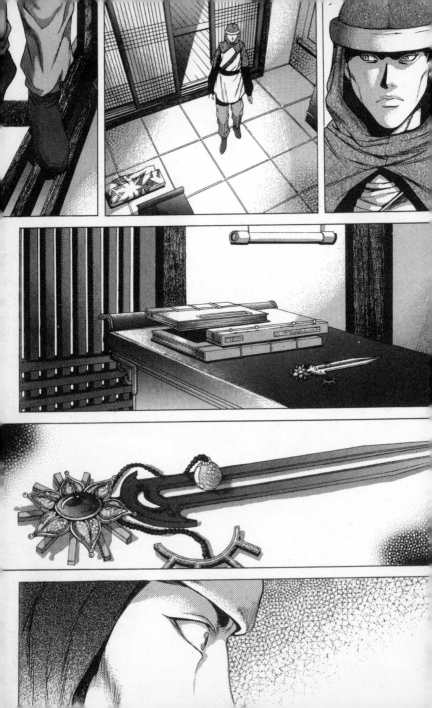

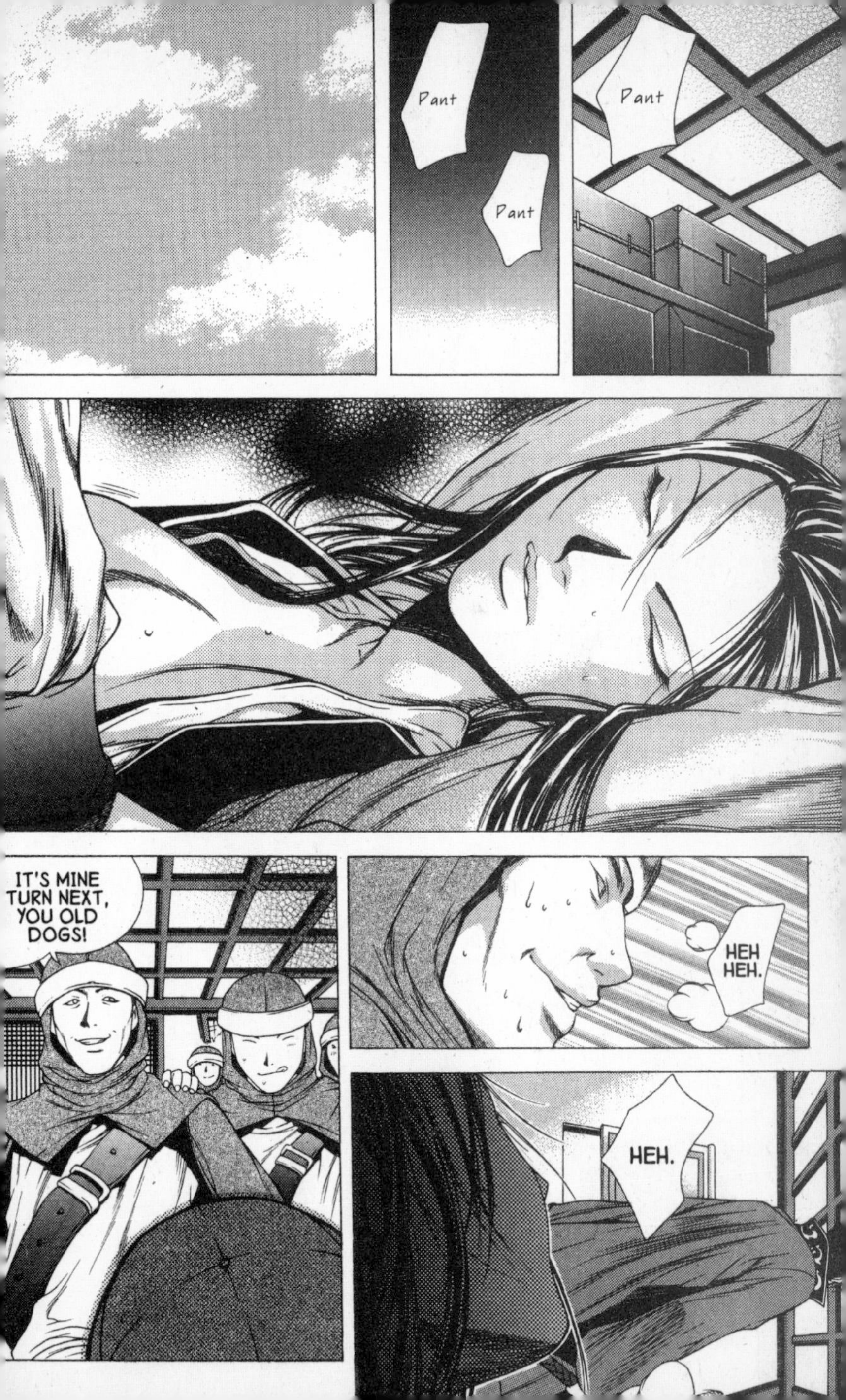
Pant
Pant
Pant
IT'S MINE TURN NEXT, YOU OLD DOGS!
HEH HEH.
HEH.

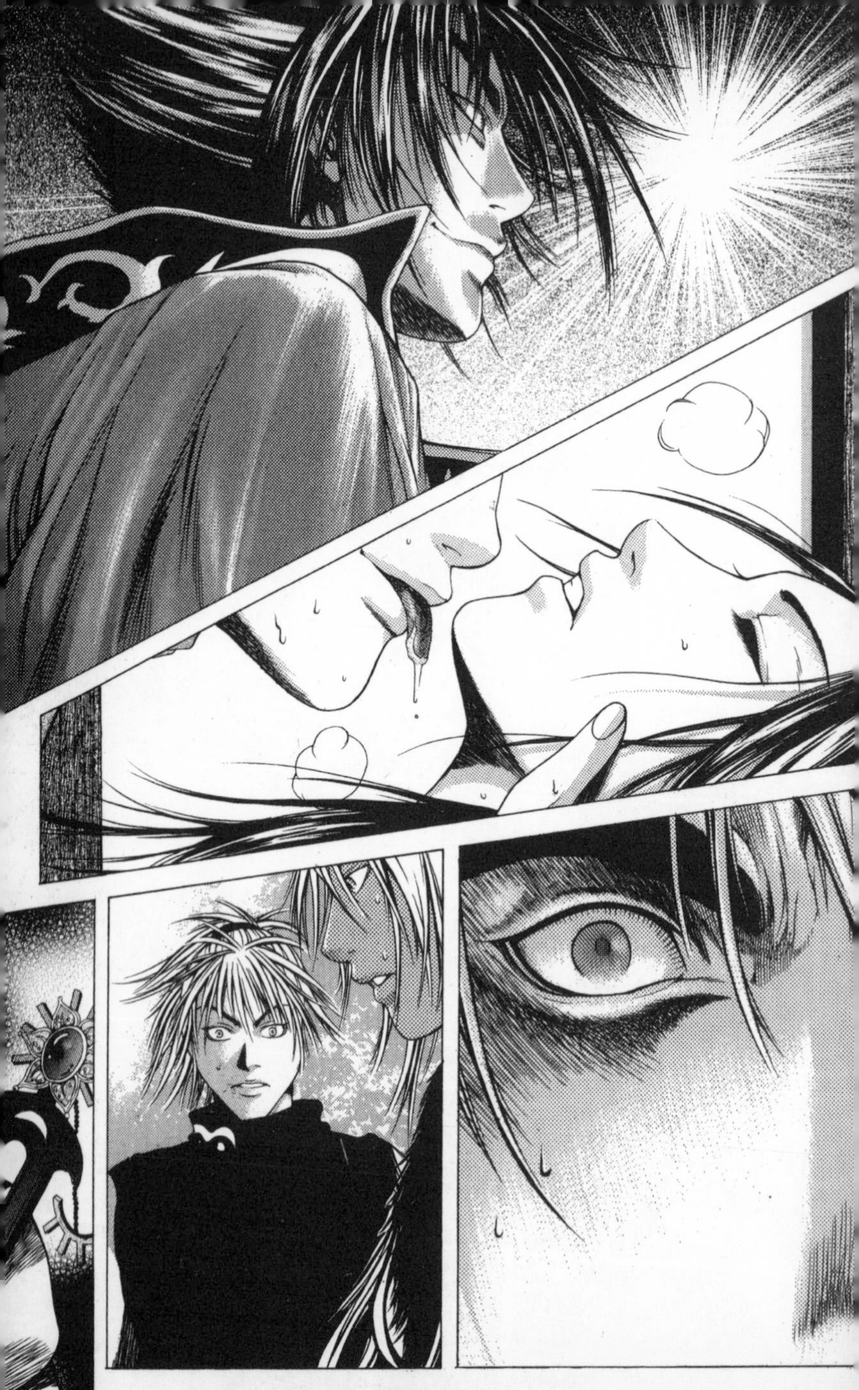

# Chapter 18
# A Scream

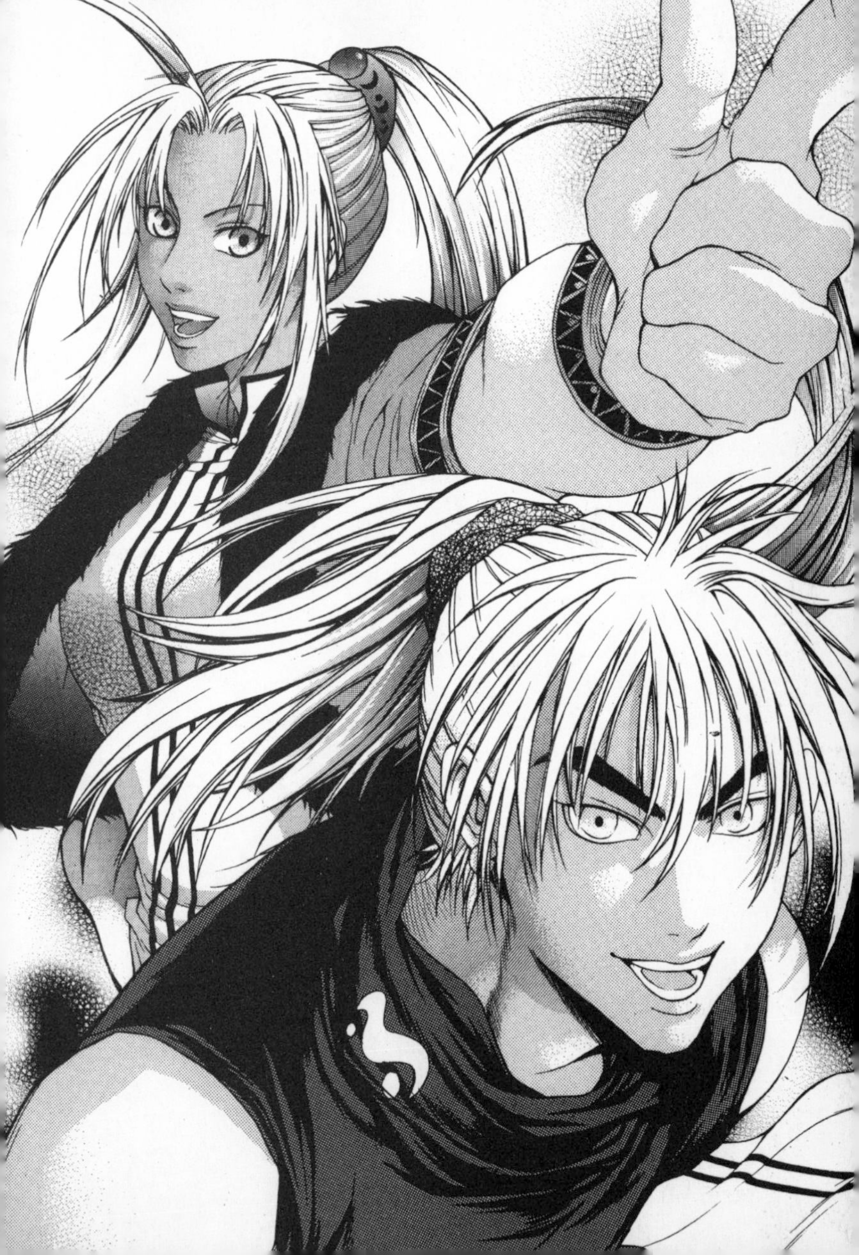

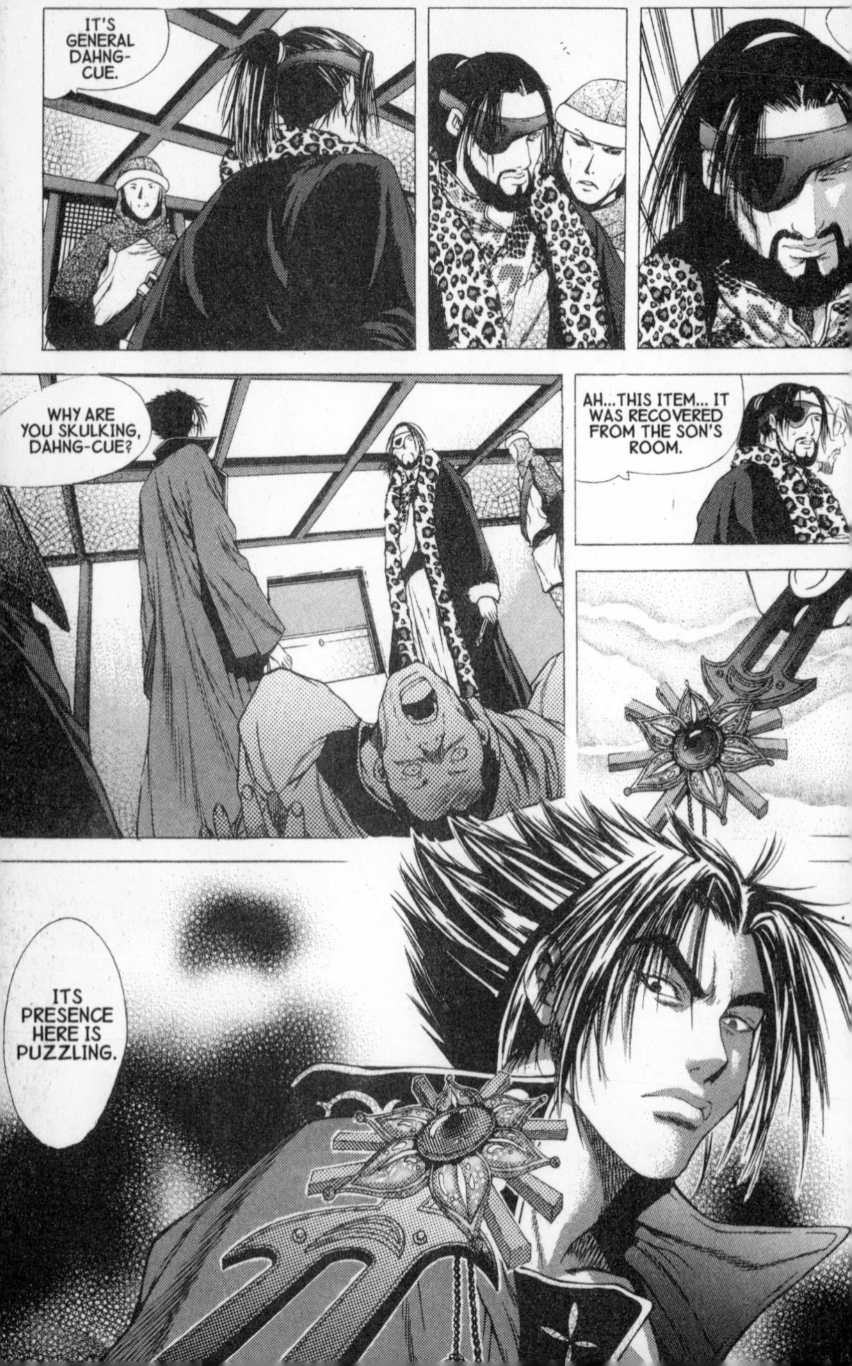
IT'S GENERAL DAHNG-CUE.
WHY ARE YOU SKULKING, DAHNG-CUE?
AH...THIS ITEM... IT WAS RECOVERED FROM THE SON'S ROOM.
ITS PRESENCE HERE IS PUZZLING.

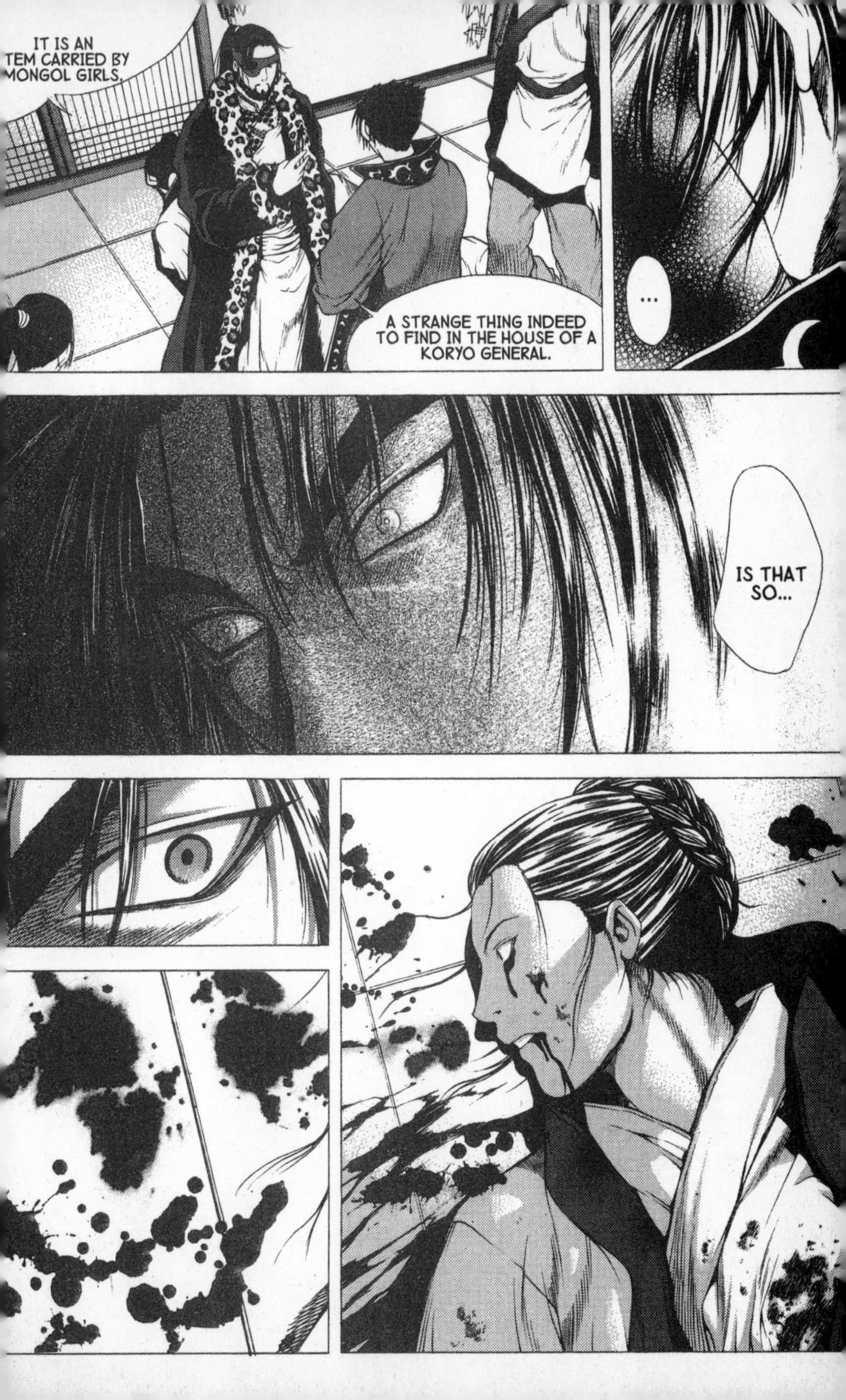
IT IS AN
TEM CARRIED BY
MONGOL GIRLS.
A STRANGE THING INDEED TO FIND IN THE HOUSE OF A KORYO GENERAL.
...
IS THAT SO...

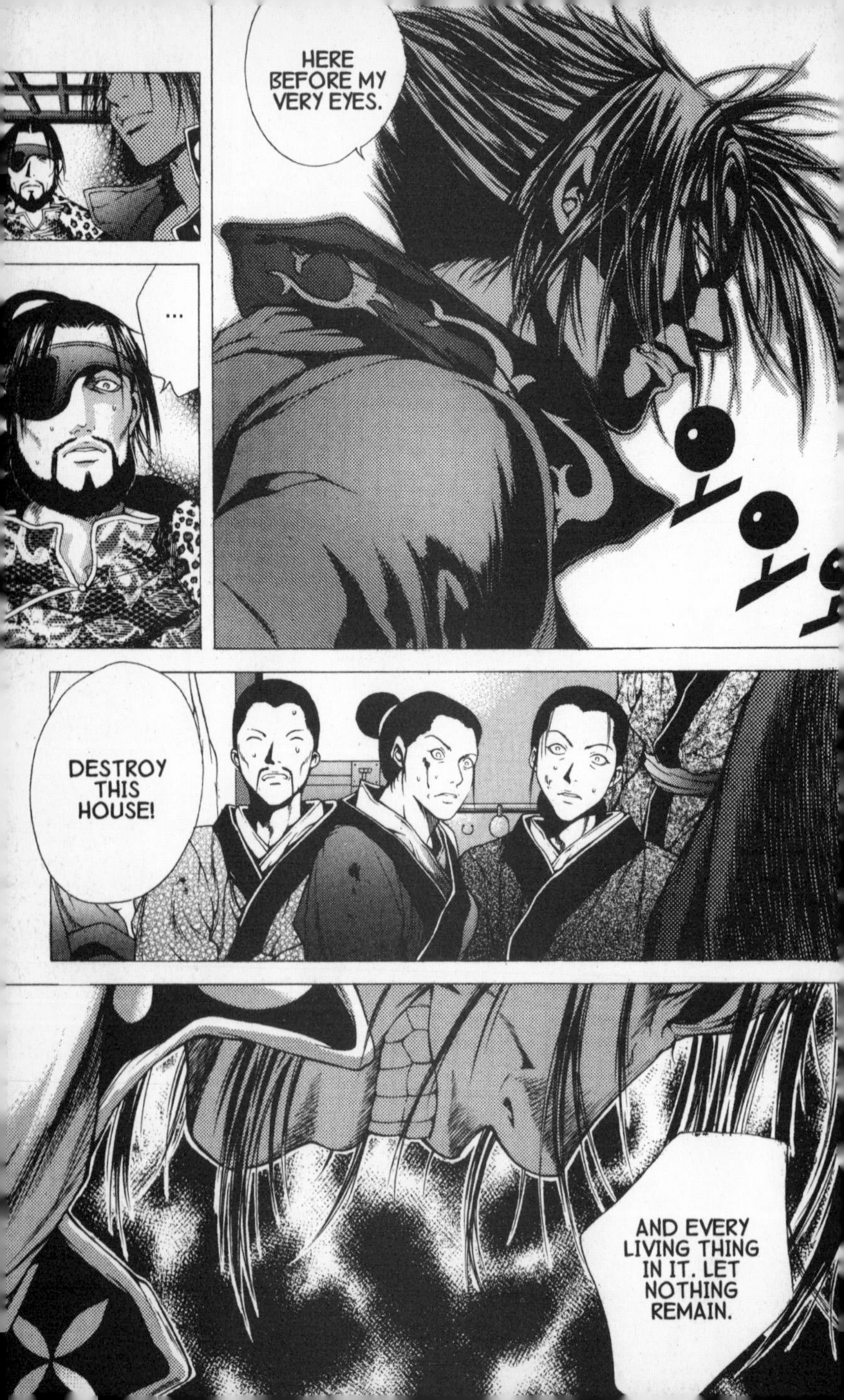
...
HERE BEFORE MY VERY EYES.
DESTROY THIS HOUSE!
AND EVERY LIVING THING IN IT. LET NOTHING REMAIN.

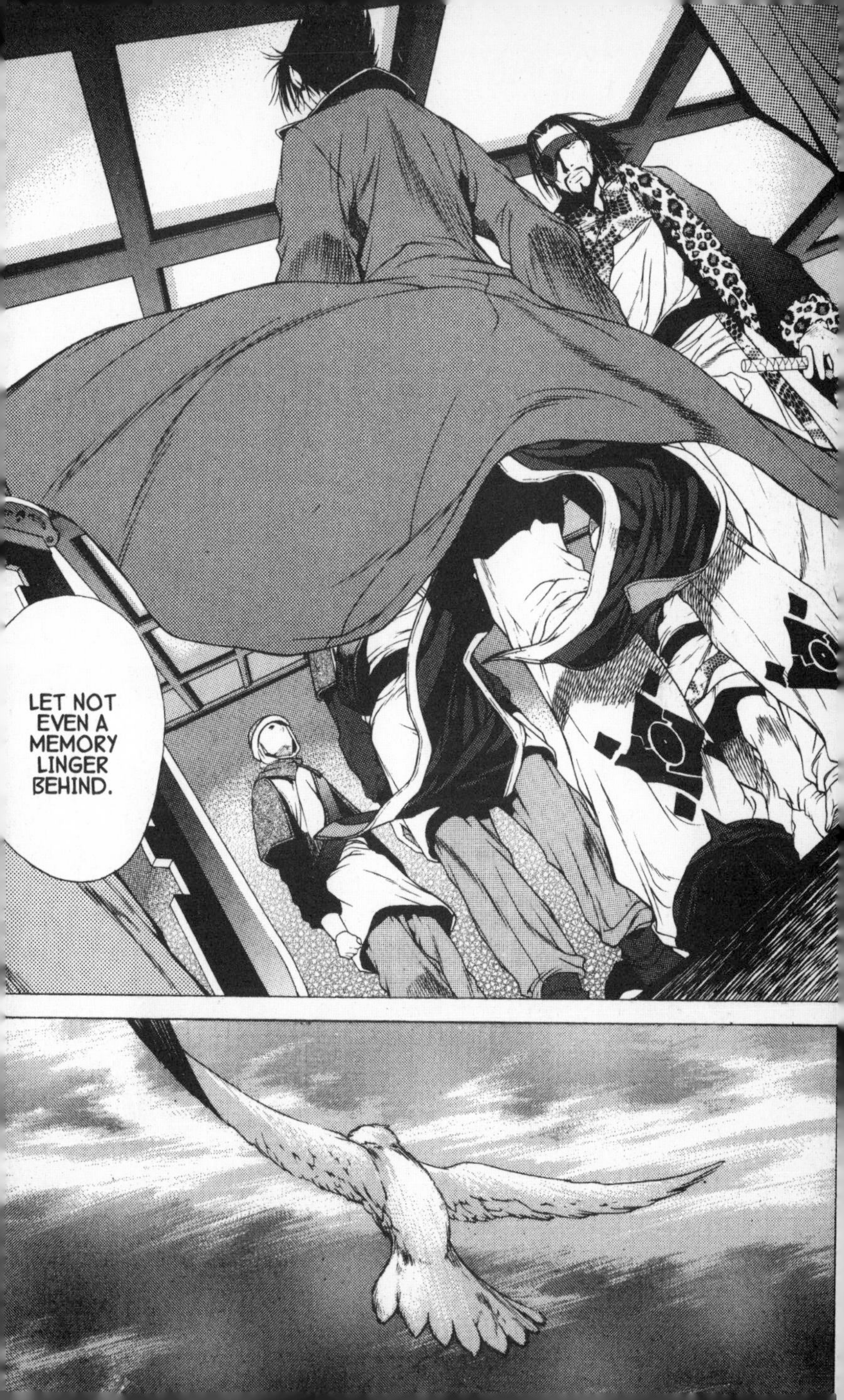
LET NOT EVEN A MEMORY LINGER BEHIND.

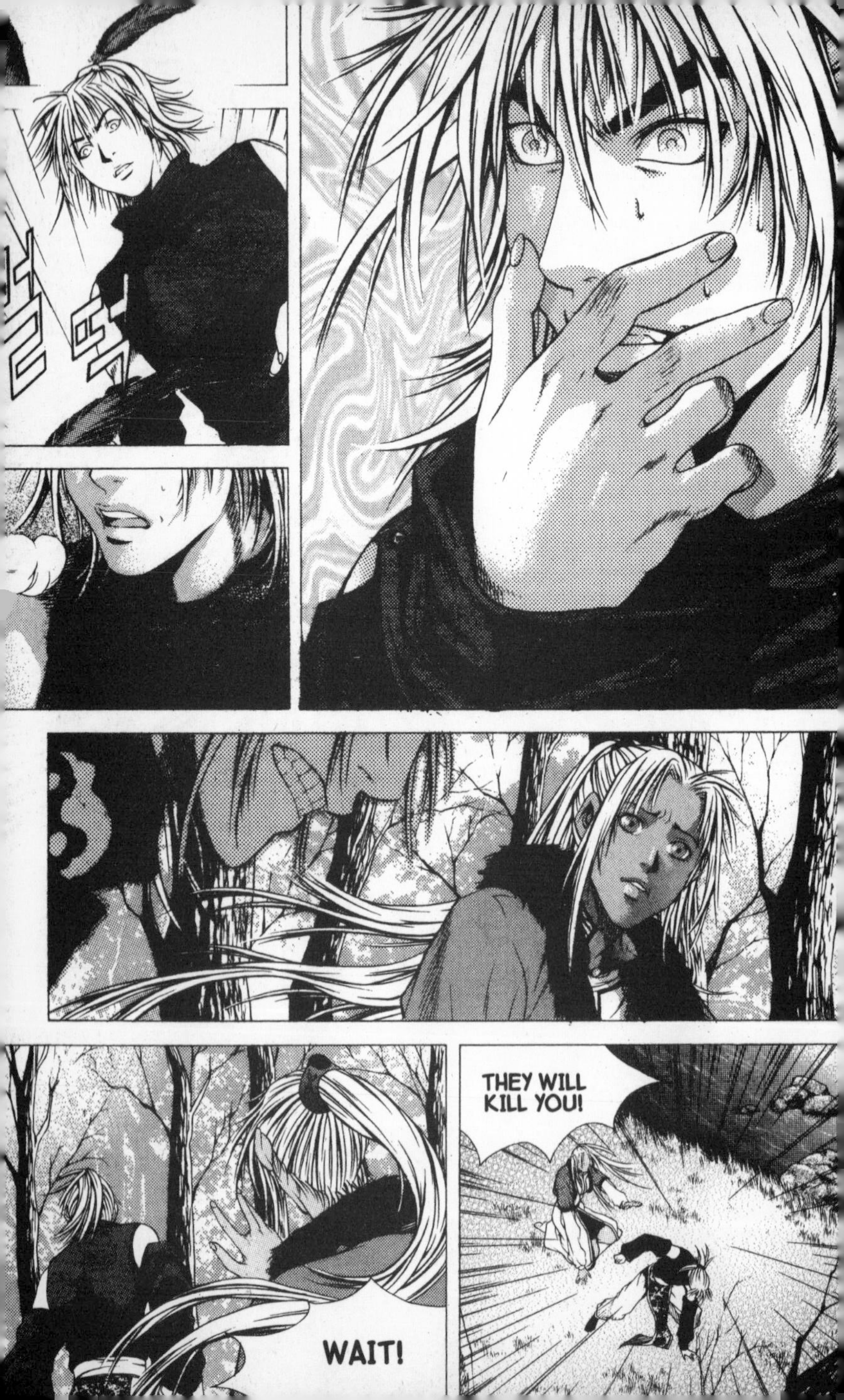
WAIT!
THEY WILL
KILL YOU!

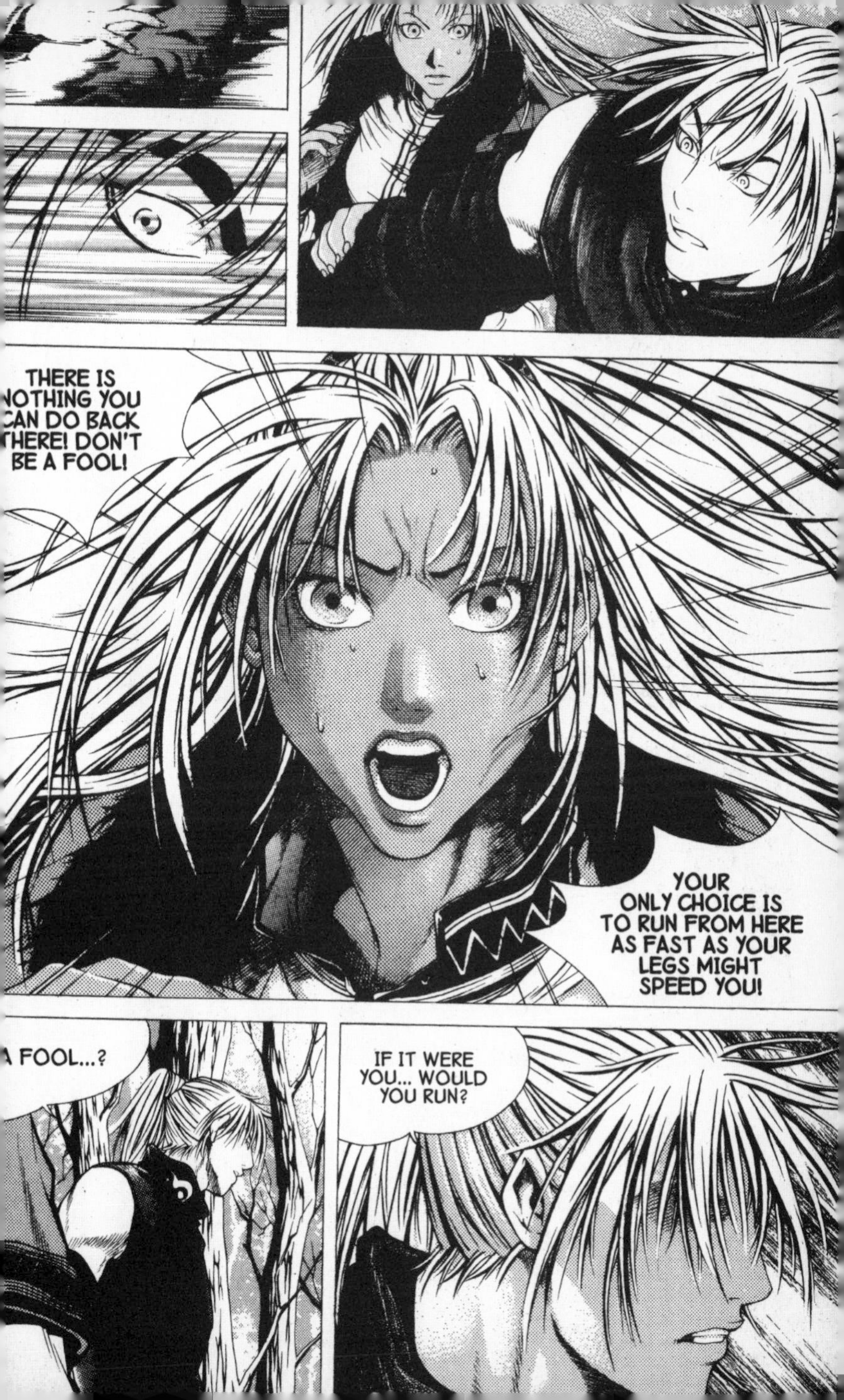
THERE IS NOTHING YOU CAN DO BACK THERE! DON'T BE A FOOL!
YOUR ONLY CHOICE IS TO RUN FROM HERE AS FAST AS YOUR LEGS MIGHT SPEED YOU!
A FOOL...?
IF IT WERE YOU... WOULD YOU RUN?

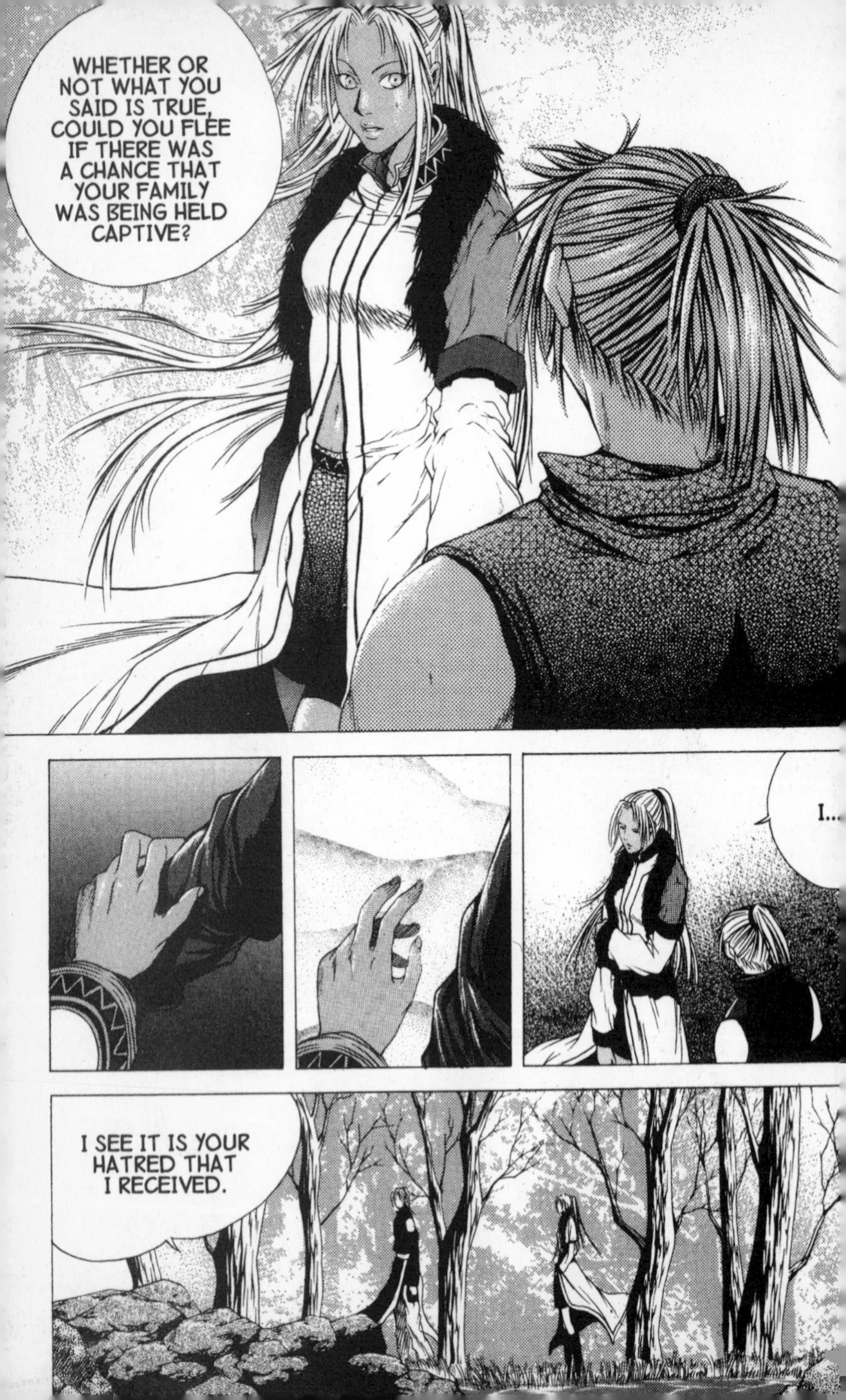
WHETHER OR NOT WHAT YOU SAID IS TRUE, COULD YOU FLEE IF THERE WAS A CHANCE THAT YOUR FAMILY WAS BEING HELD CAPTIVE?
I...
I SEE IT IS YOUR HATRED THAT I RECEIVED.

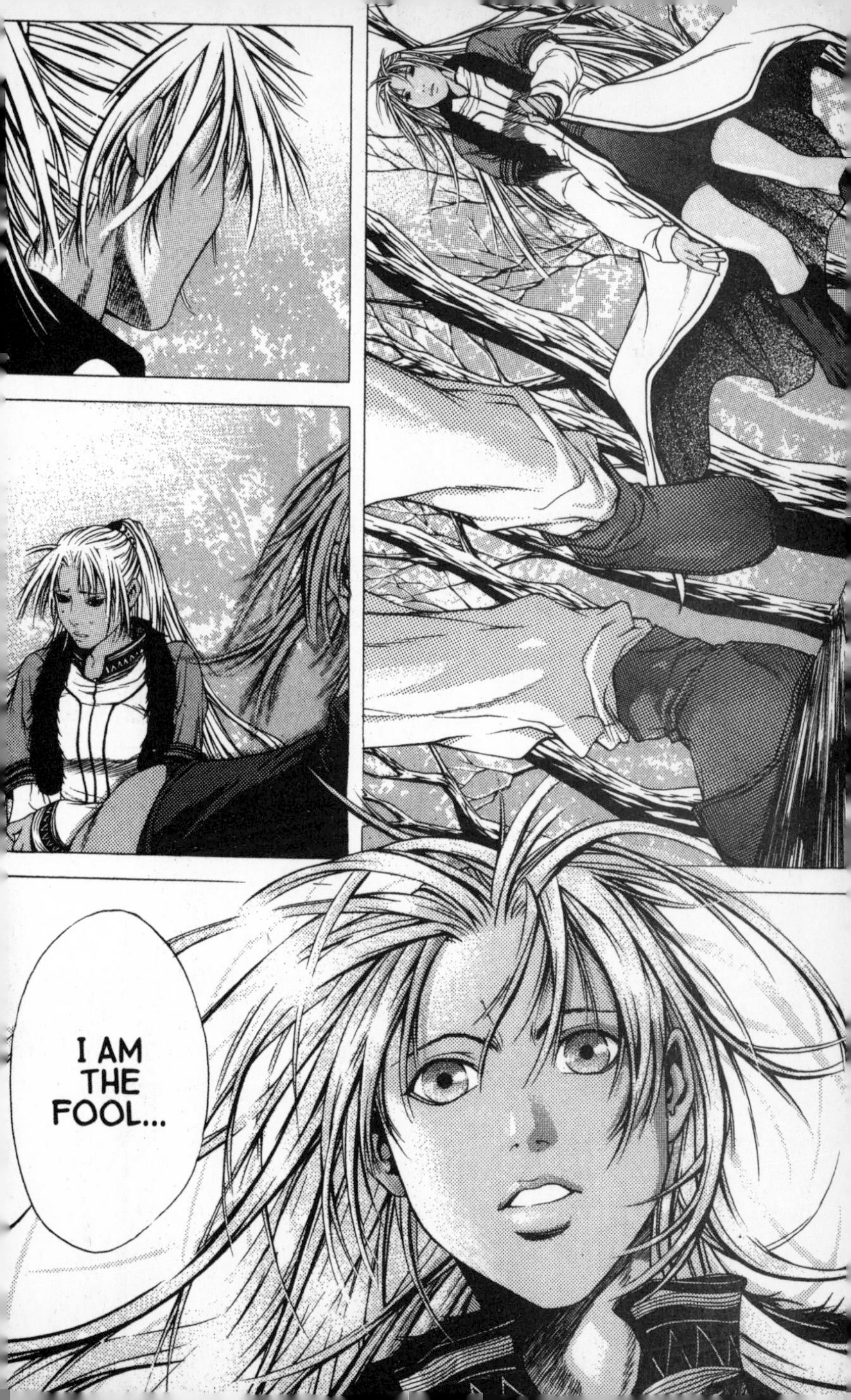
I AM THE FOOL...

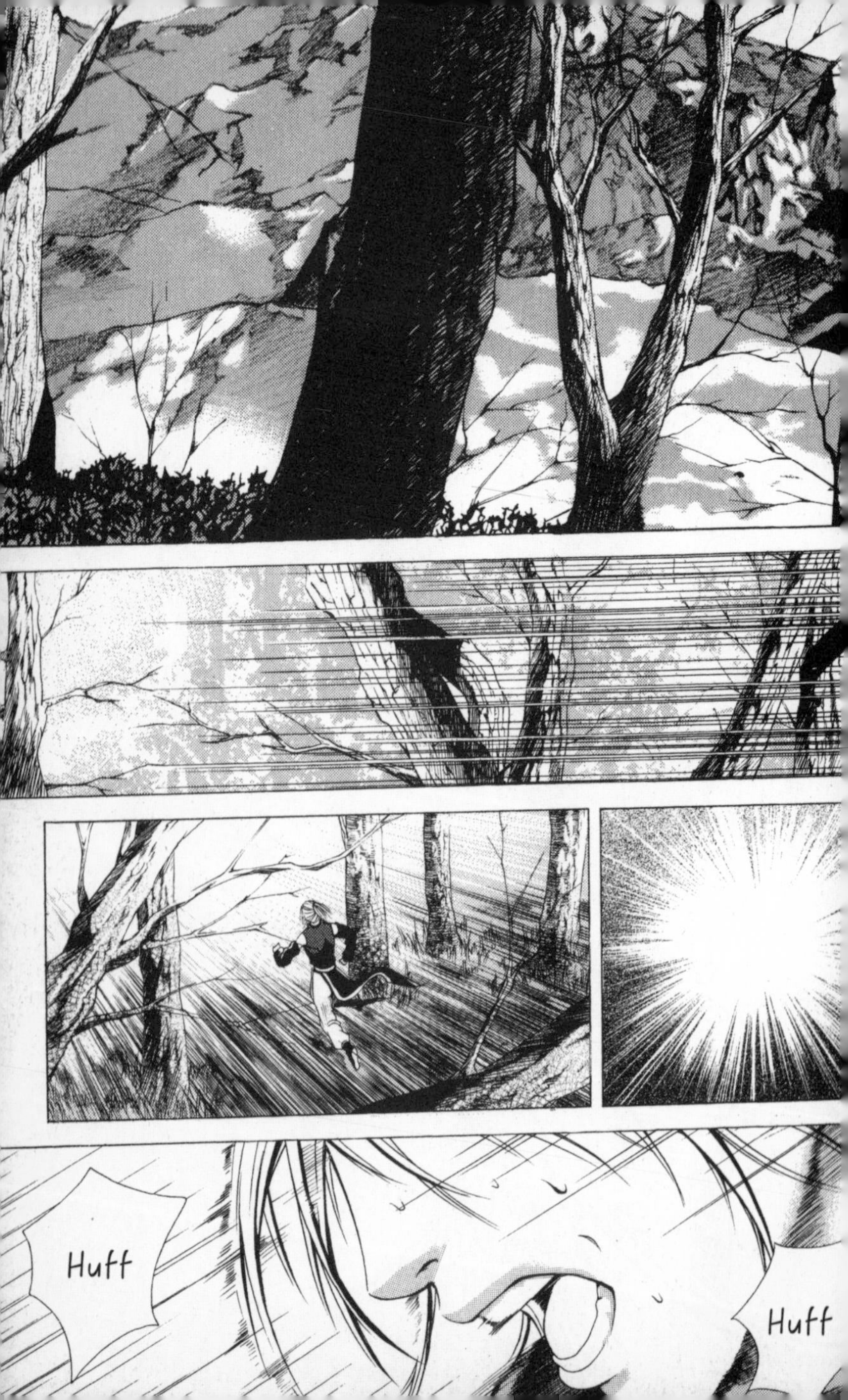
Huff
Huff

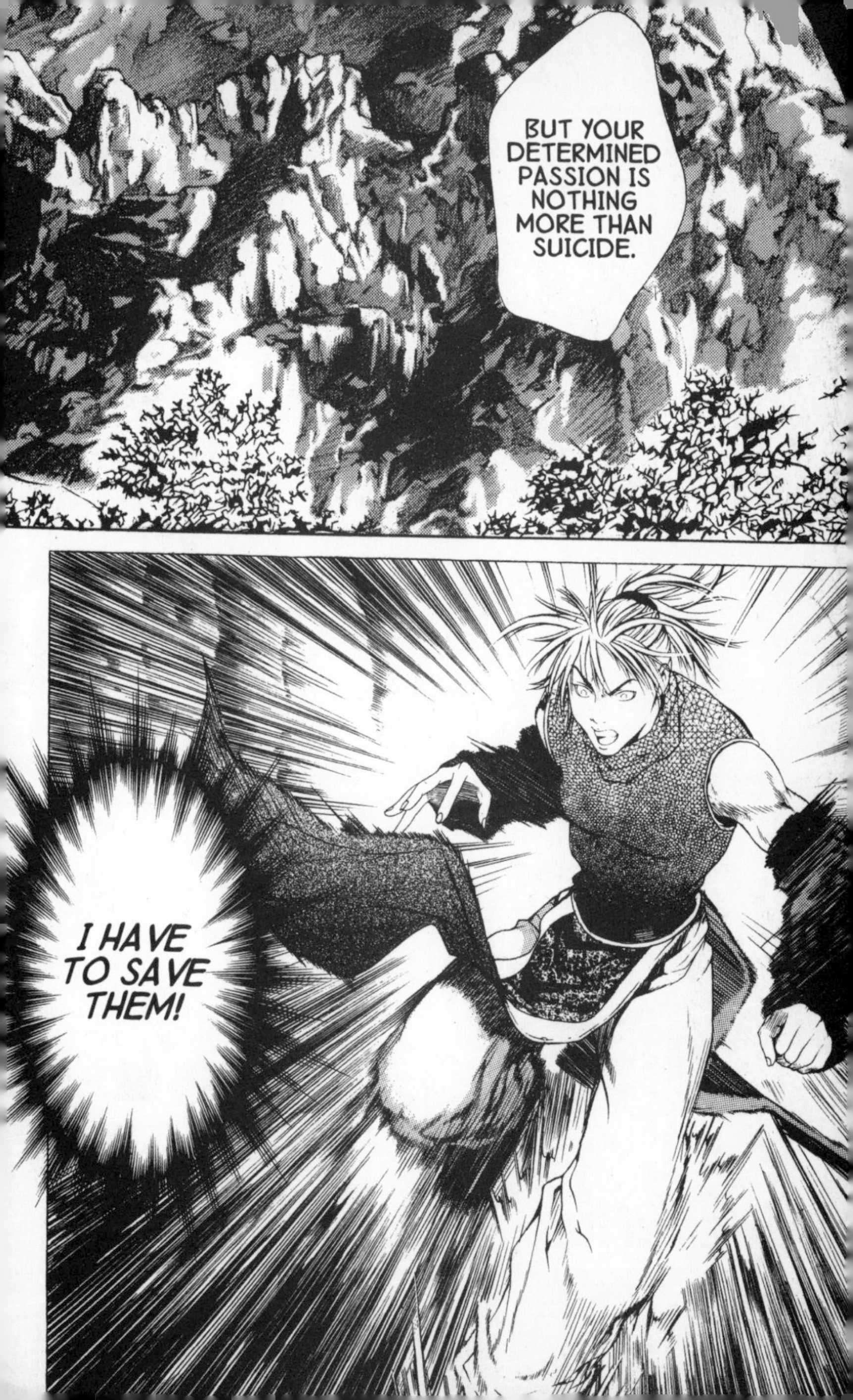
BUT YOUR DETERMINED PASSION IS NOTHING MORE THAN SUICIDE.
I HAVE TO SAVE THEM!

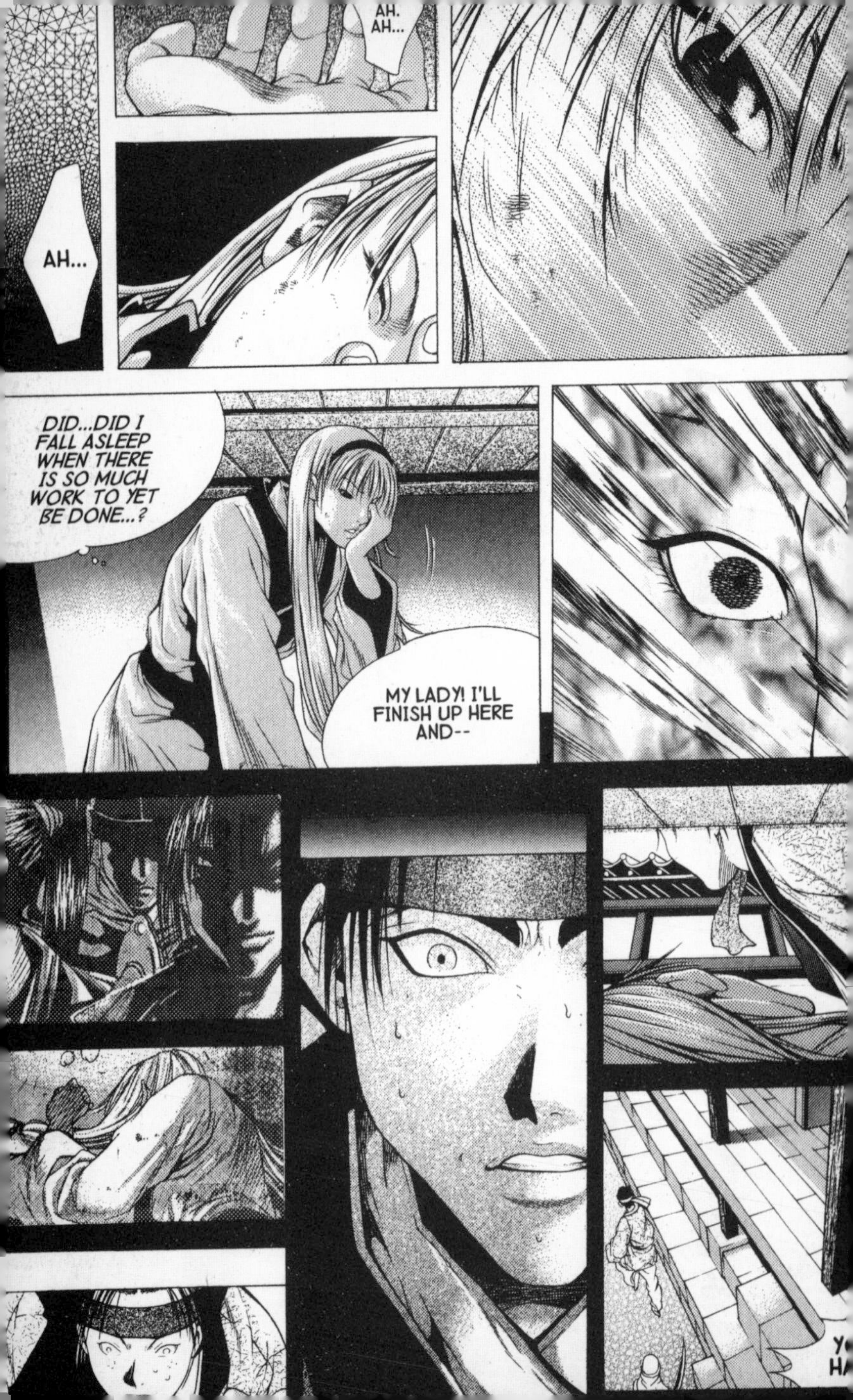
AH...
AH. AH...
DID...DID I FALL ASLEEP WHEN THERE IS SO MUCH WORK TO YET BE DONE...?
MY LADY! I'LL FINISH UP HERE AND--

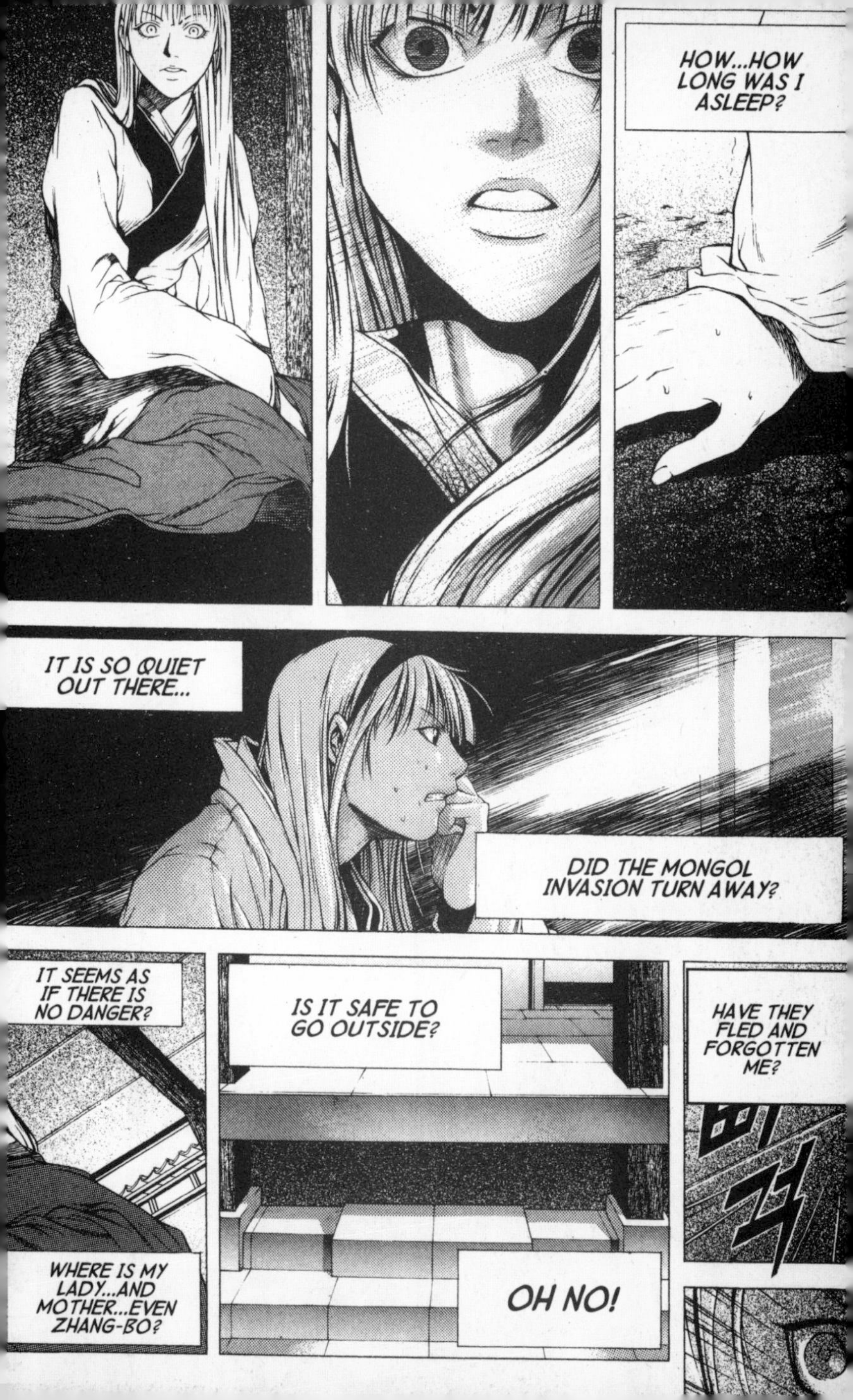
HOW...HOW LONG WAS I ASLEEP?
IT IS SO QUIET OUT THERE...
DID THE MONGOL INVASION TURN AWAY?
IT SEEMS AS IF THERE IS NO DANGER?
WHERE IS MY LADY...AND MOTHER...EVEN ZHANG-BO?
IS IT SAFE TO GO OUTSIDE?
OH NO!
HAVE THEY FLED AND FORGOTTEN ME?

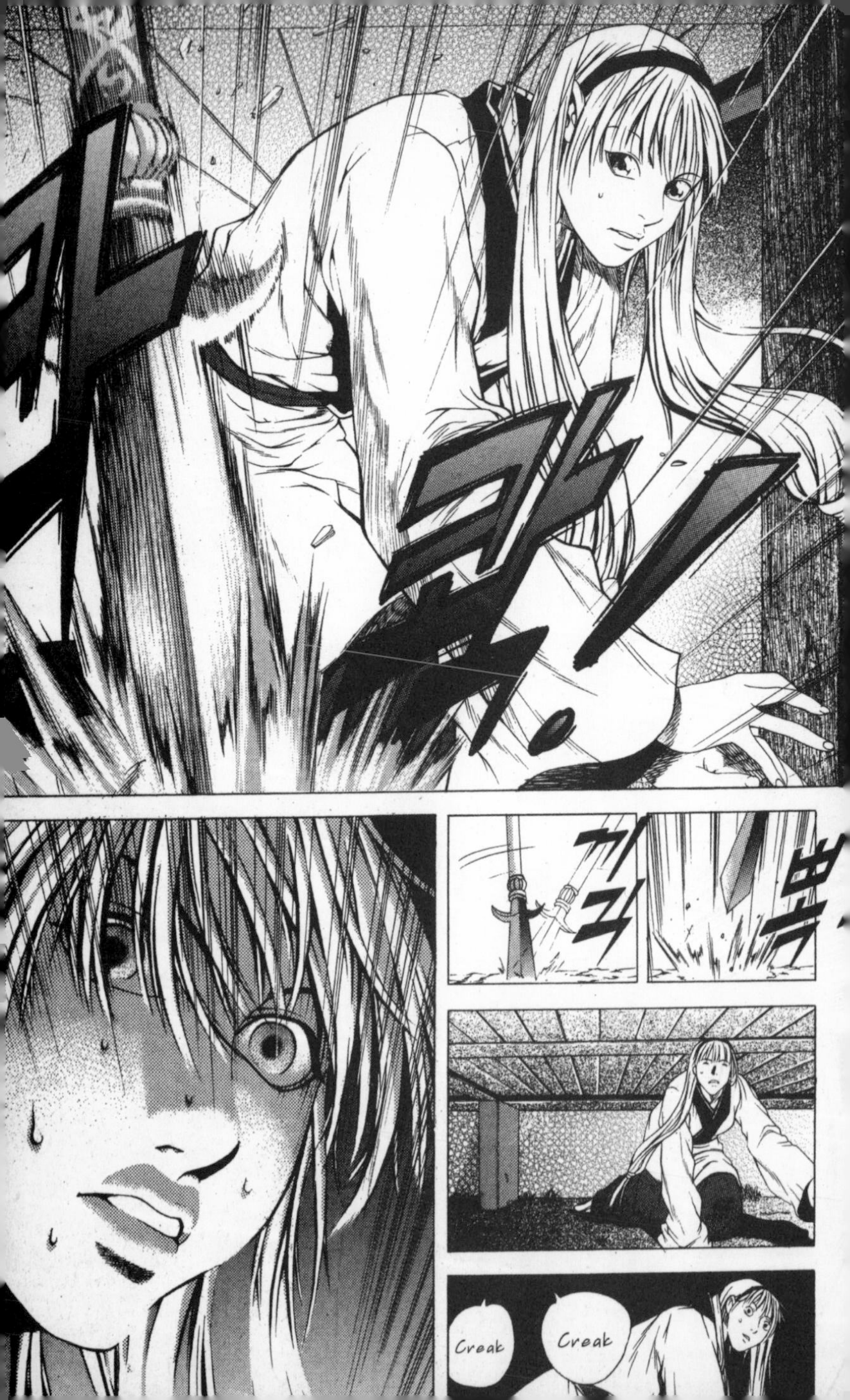
Creak
Creak

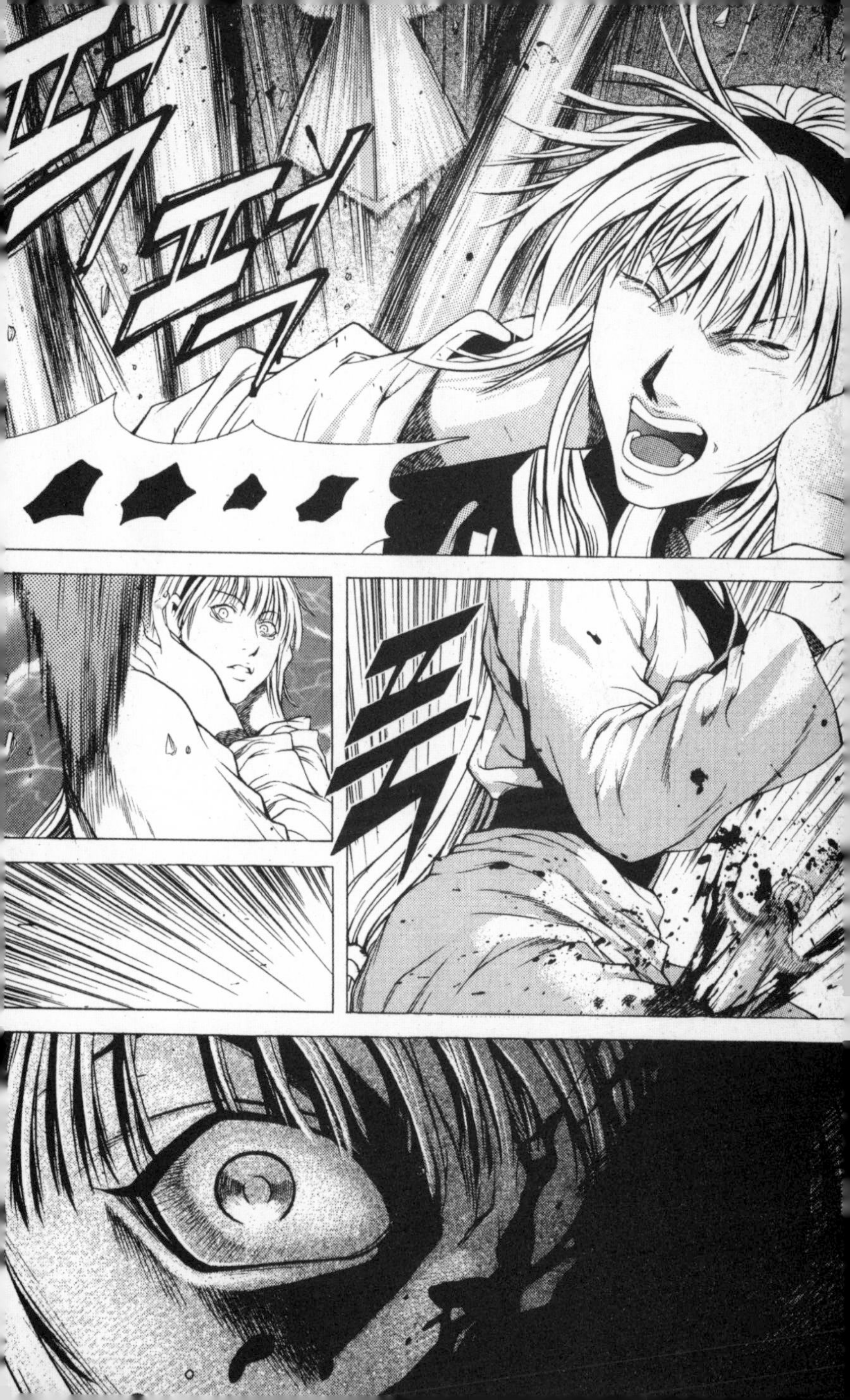

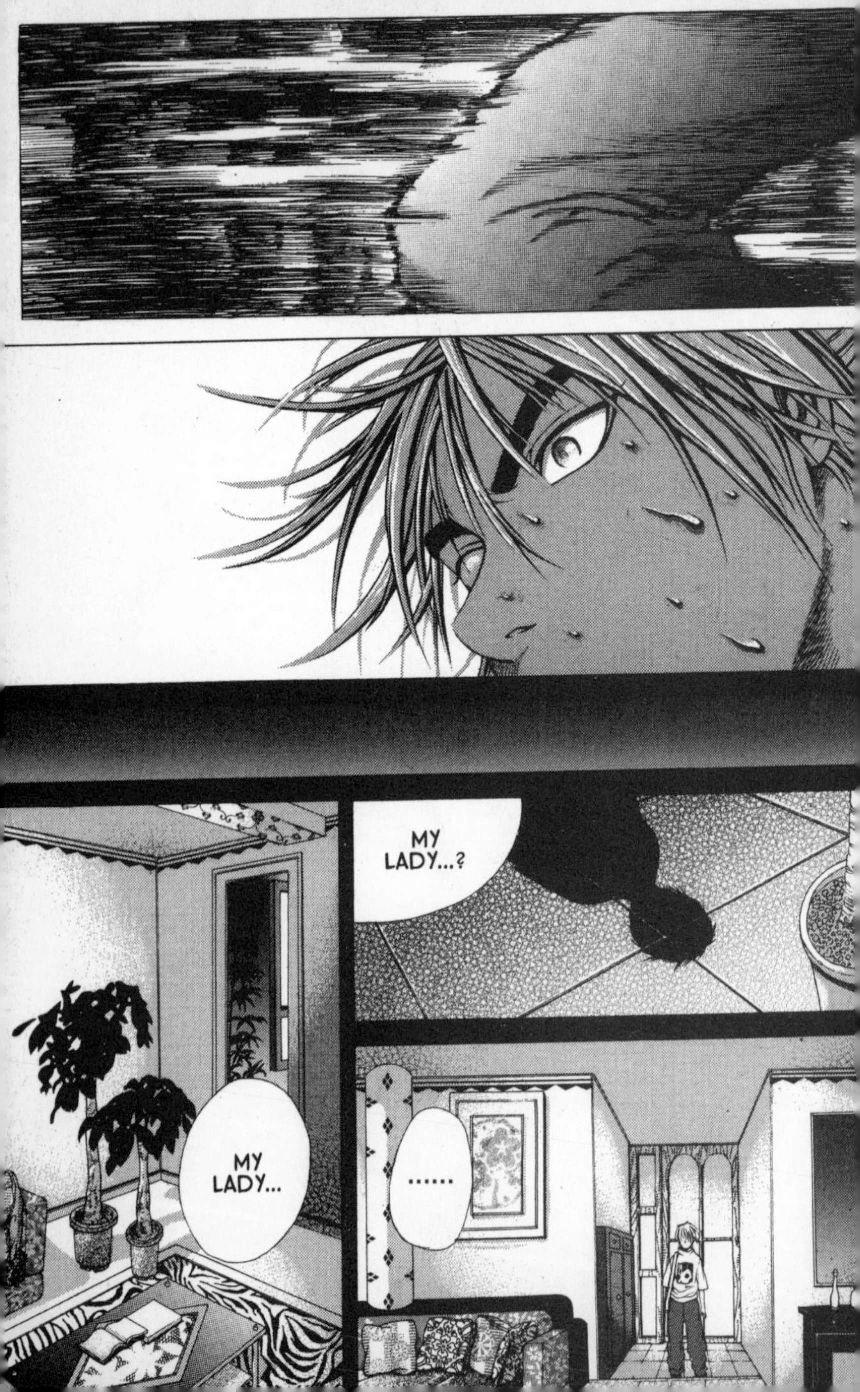
MY LADY...
MY LADY...?
......

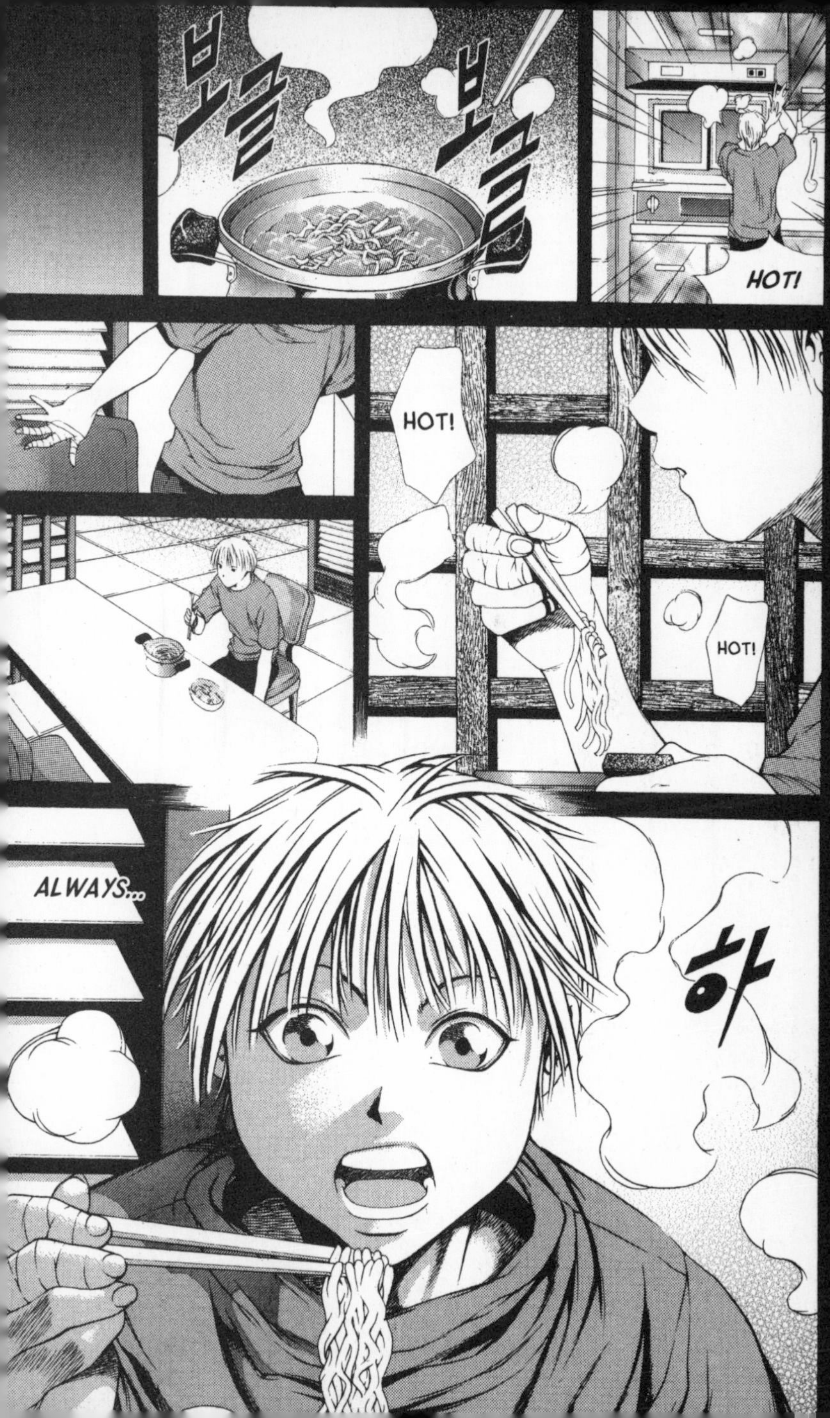
보글
보글
HOT!
HOT!
HOT!
ALWAYS...
하

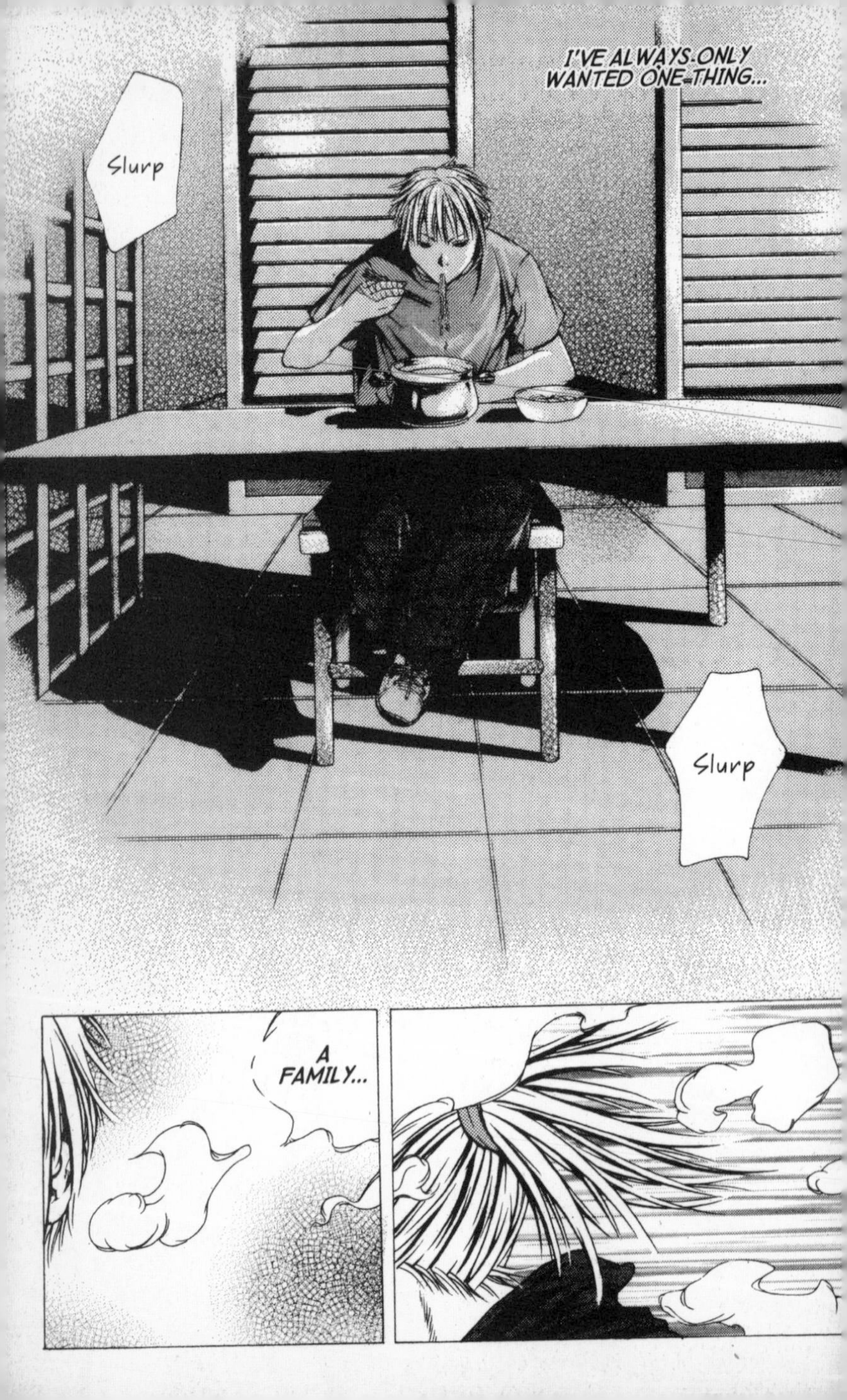
I'VE ALWAYS ONLY WANTED ONE THING...
Slurp
Slurp
A FAMILY...

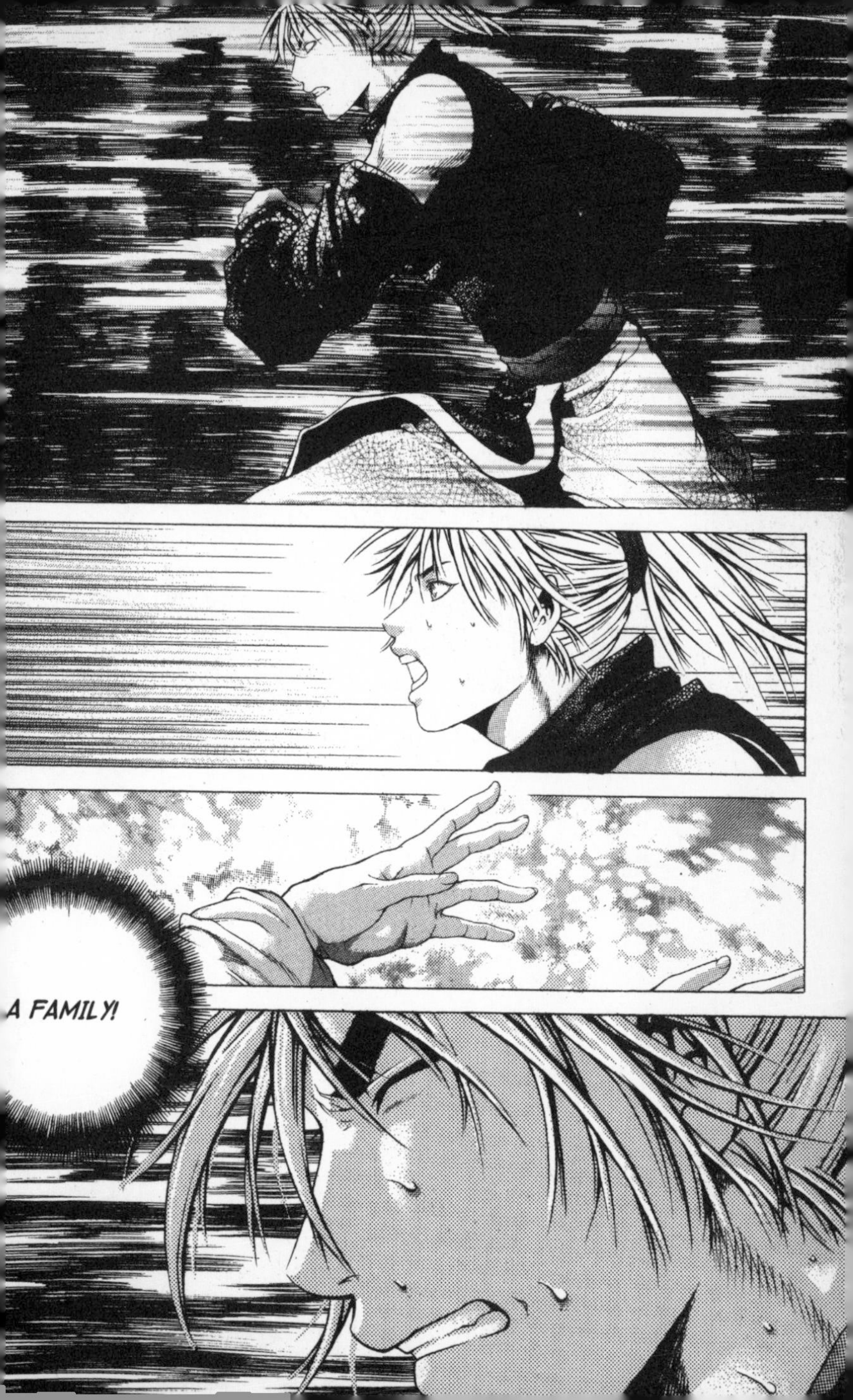
A FAMILY!

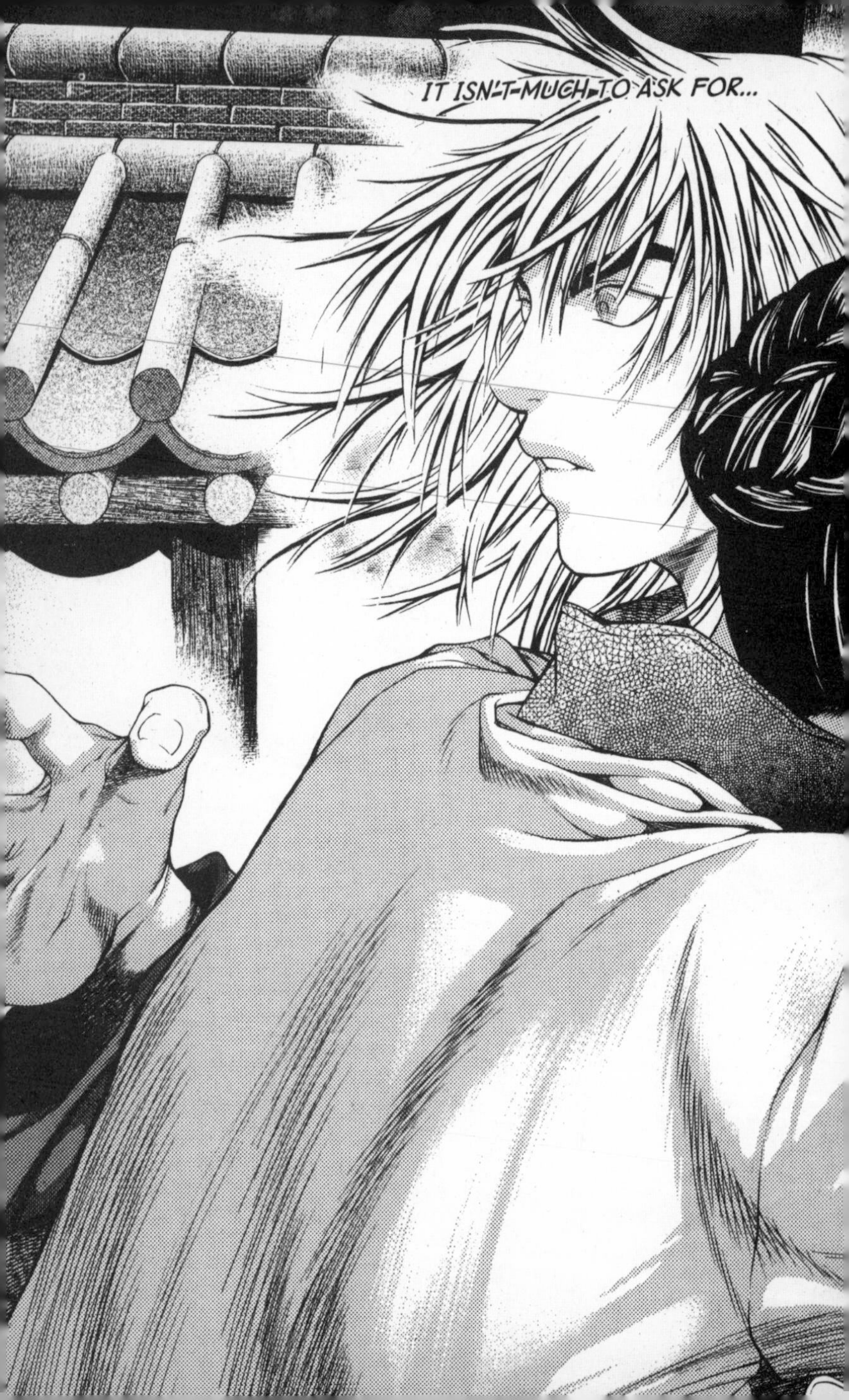
IT ISN'T MUCH TO ASK FOR...

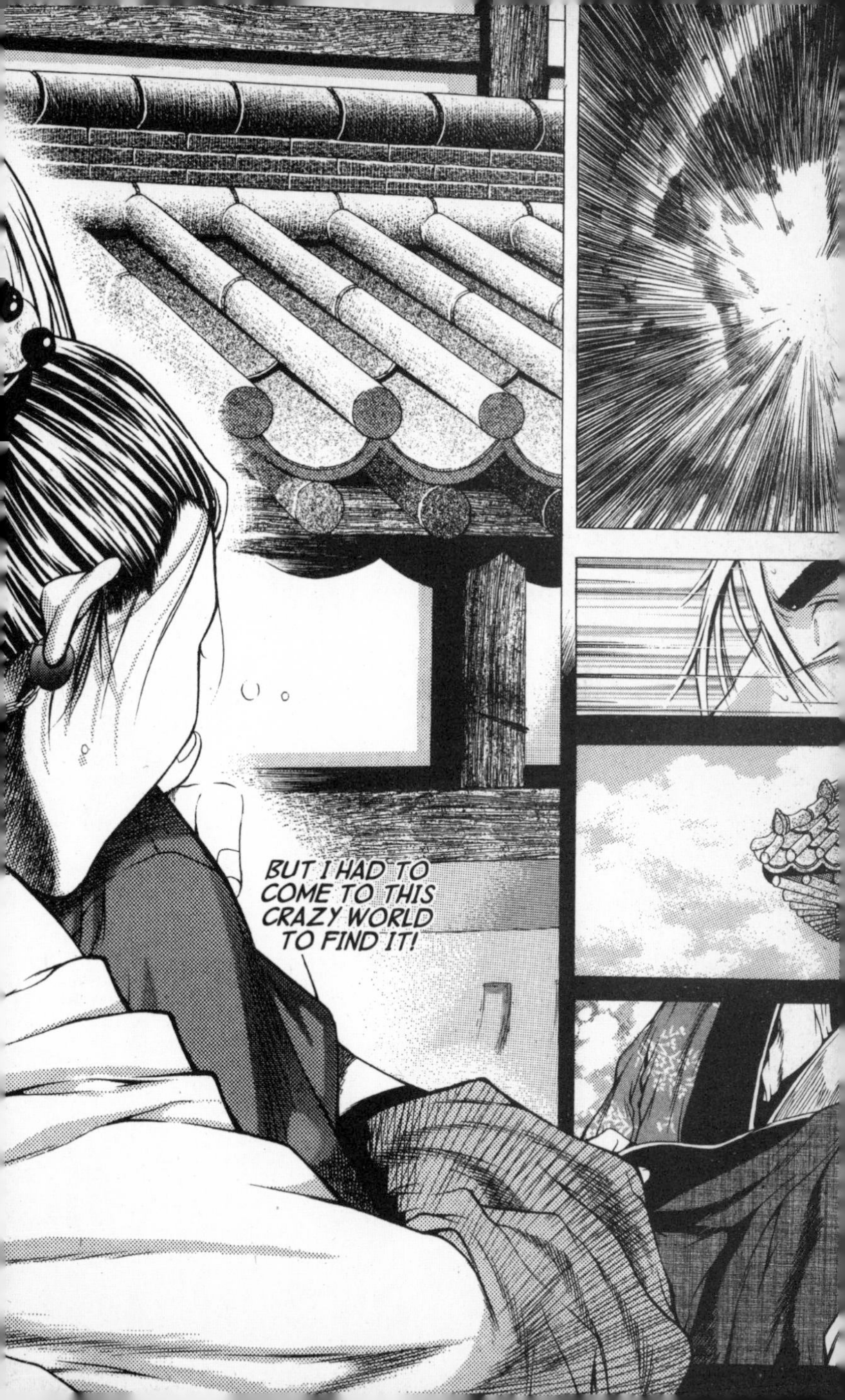
BUT I HAD TO COME TO THIS CRAZY WORLD TO FIND IT!

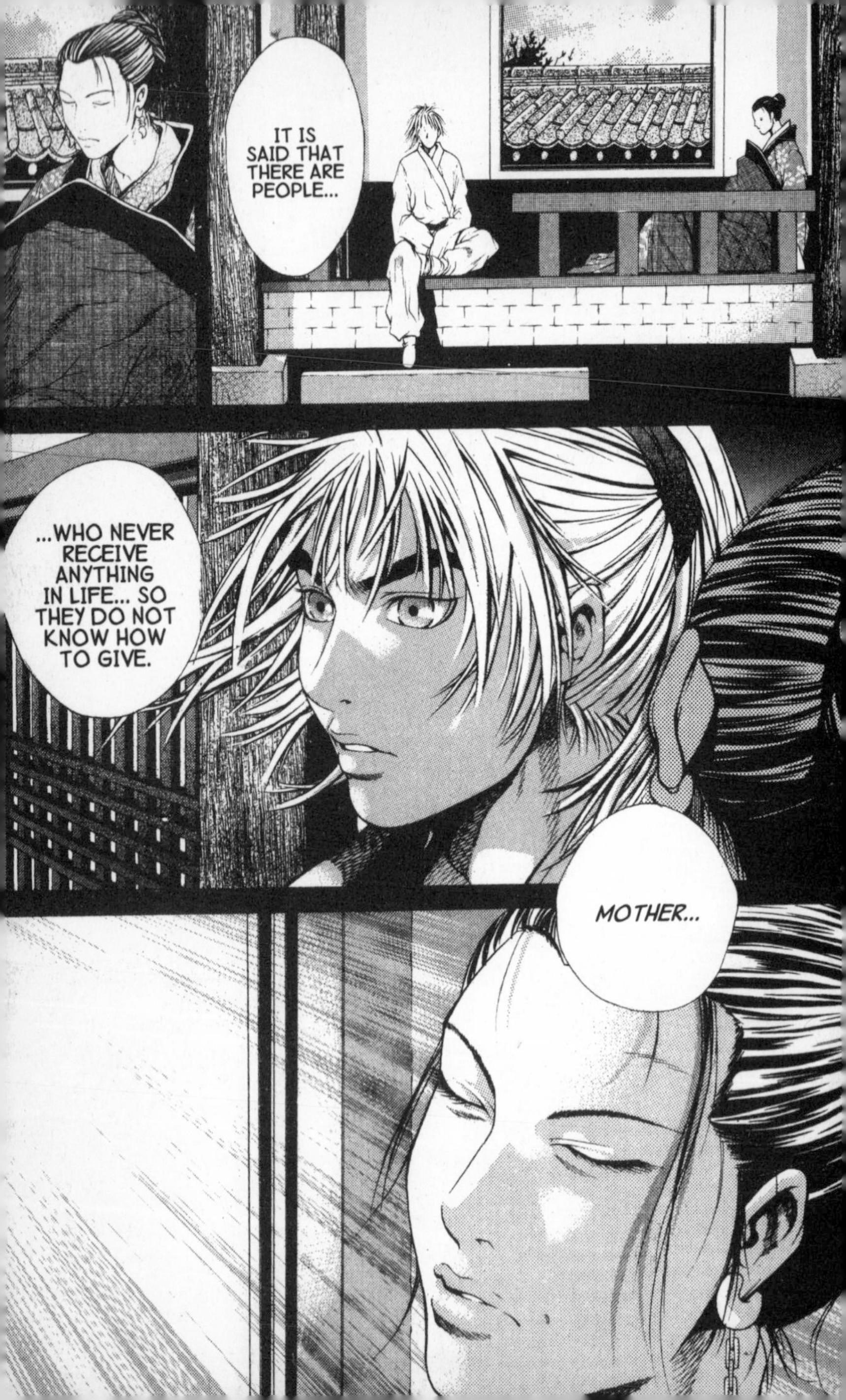
IT IS SAID THAT THERE ARE PEOPLE...
...WHO NEVER RECEIVE ANYTHING IN LIFE... SO THEY DO NOT KNOW HOW TO GIVE.
MOTHER...

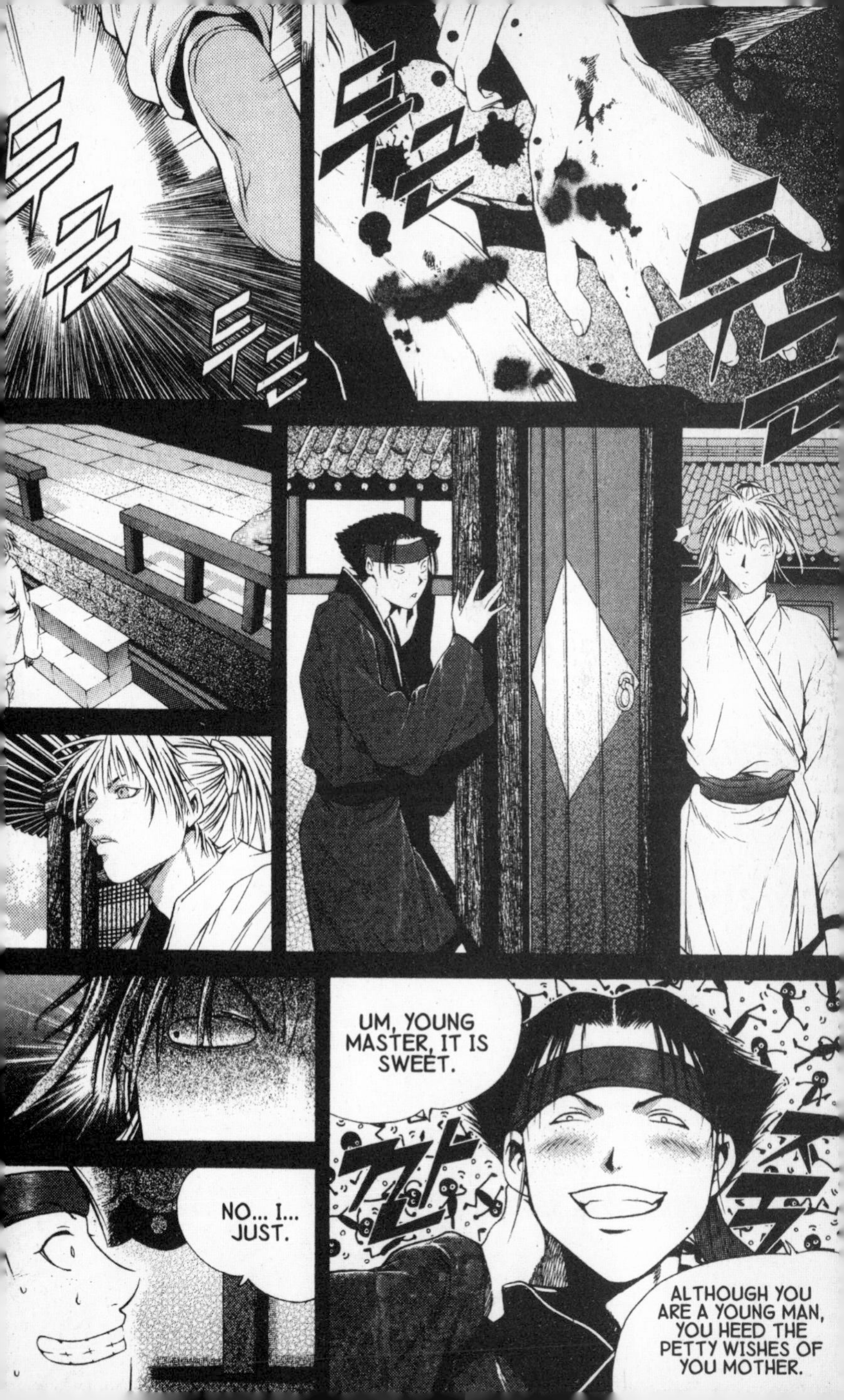
NO... I... JUST.
UM, YOUNG MASTER, IT IS SWEET.
ALTHOUGH YOU ARE A YOUNG MAN, YOU HEED THE PETTY WISHES OF YOU MOTHER.

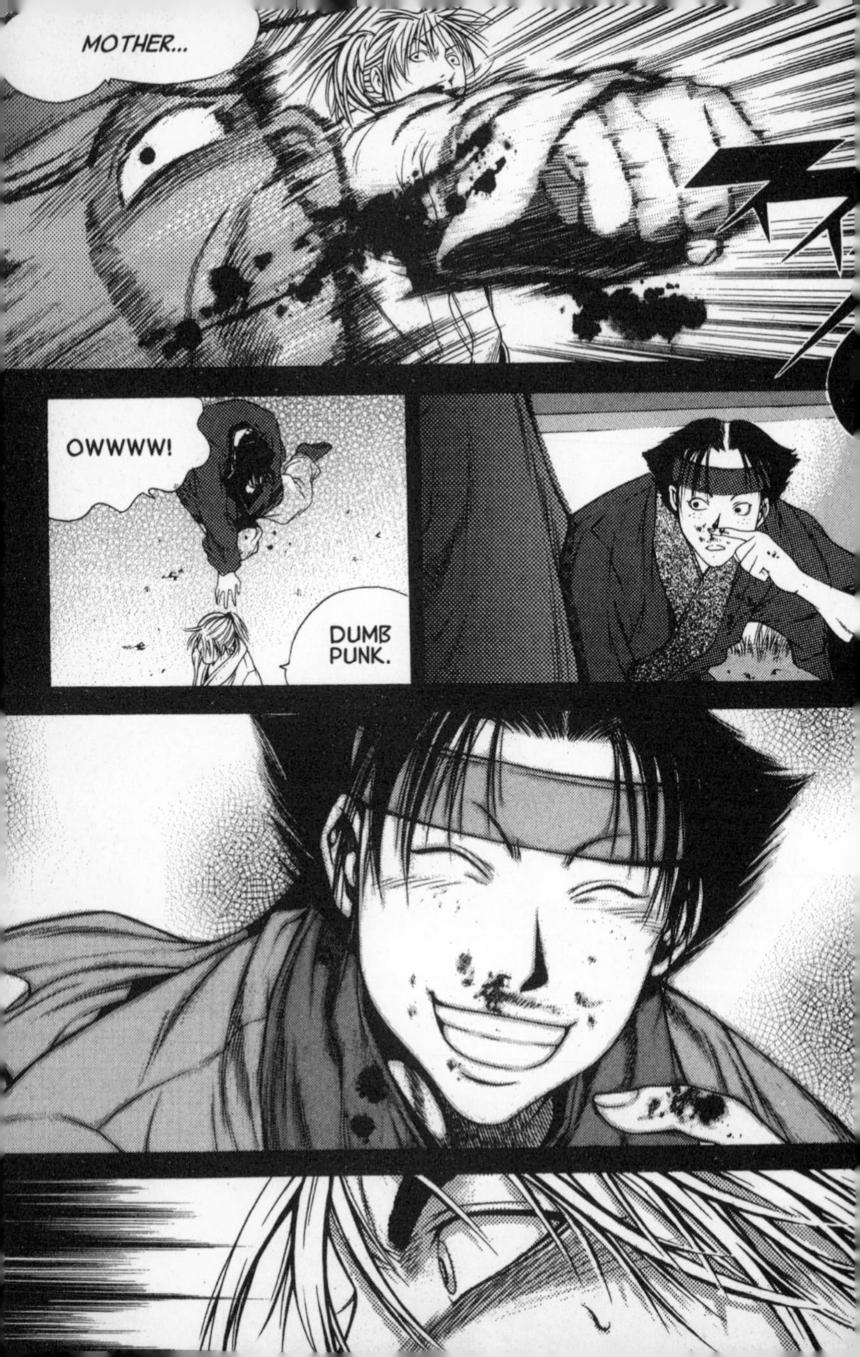
MOTHER...
OWWWW!
DUMB PUNK.

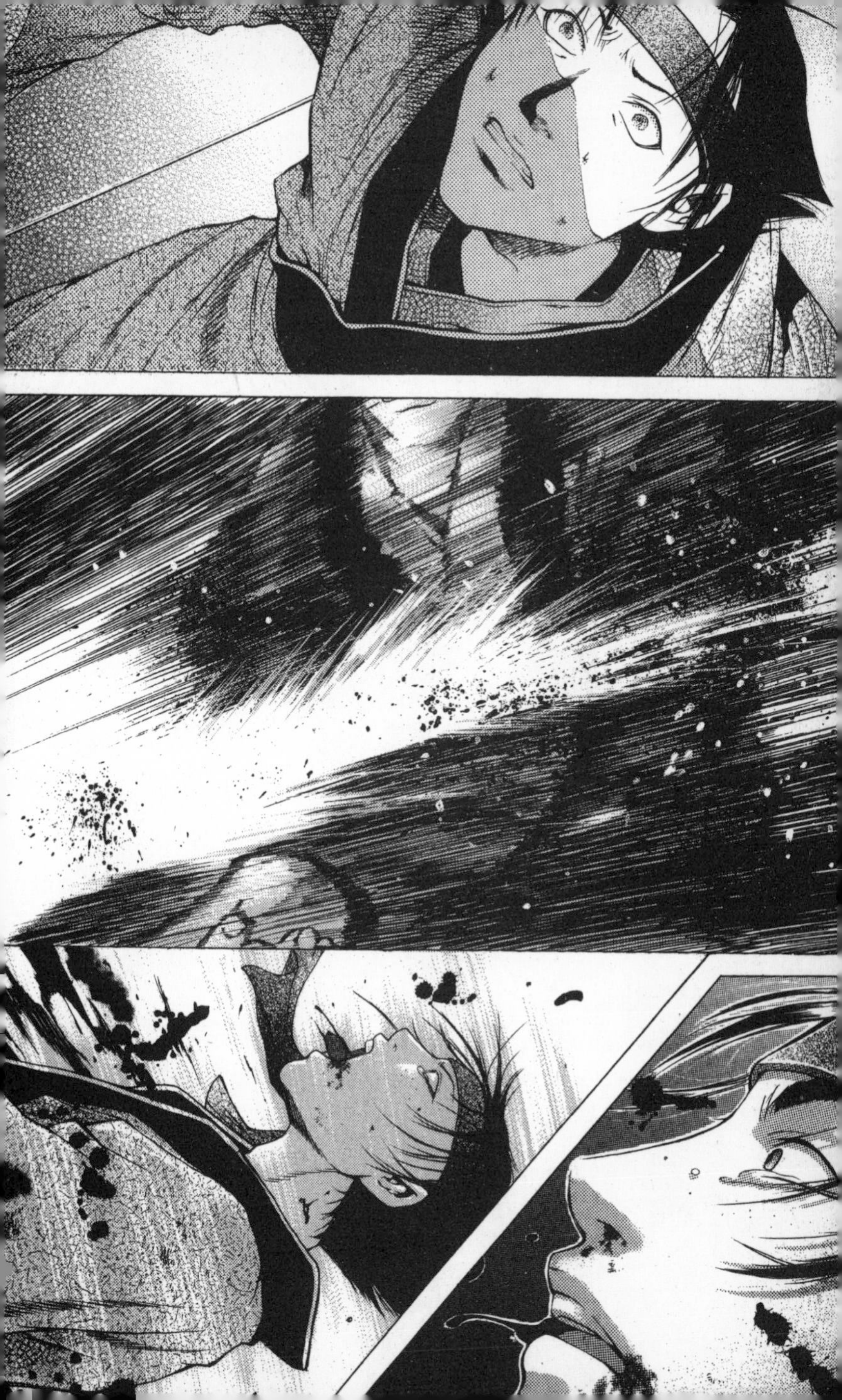

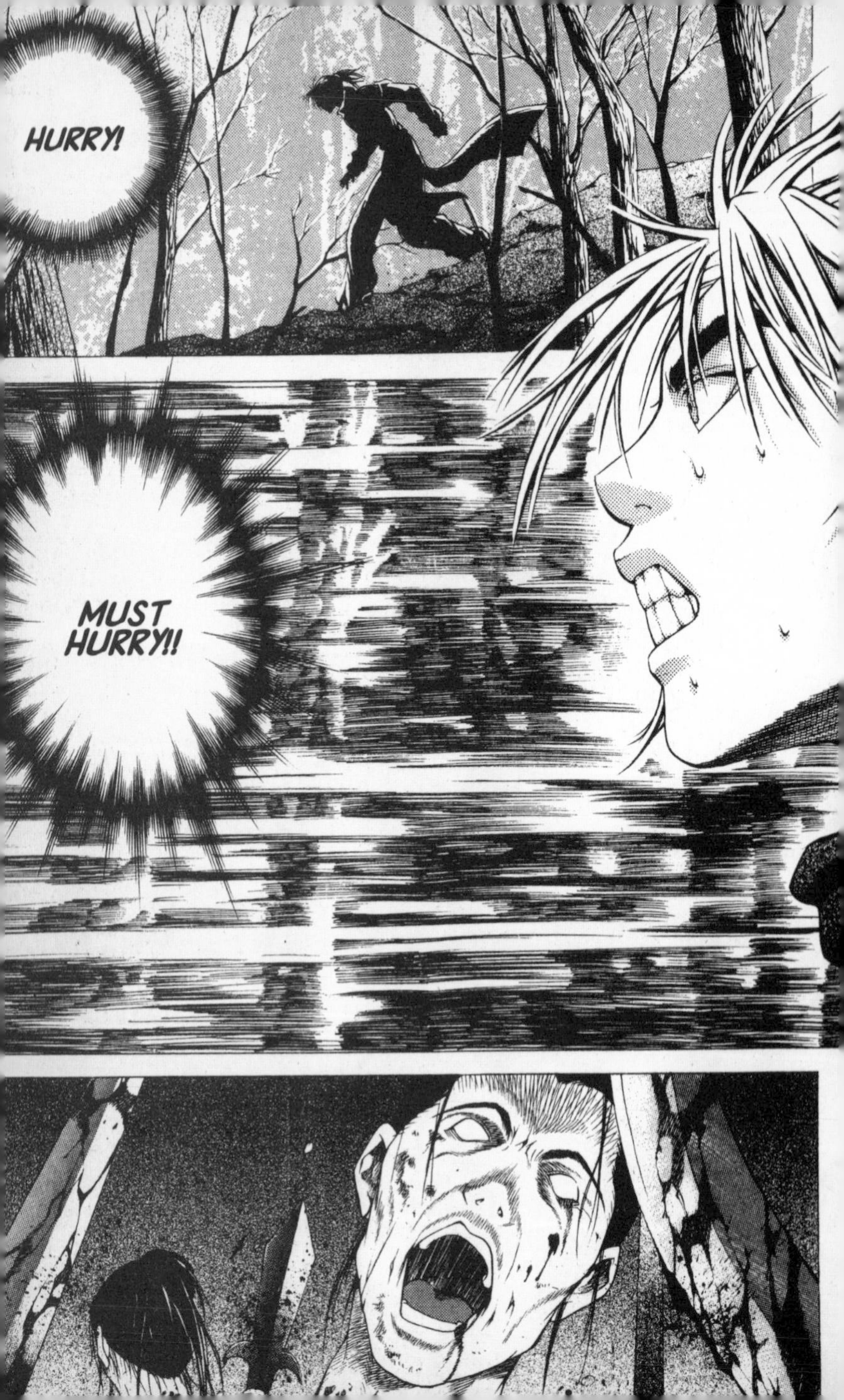
HURRY!
MUST HURRY!!

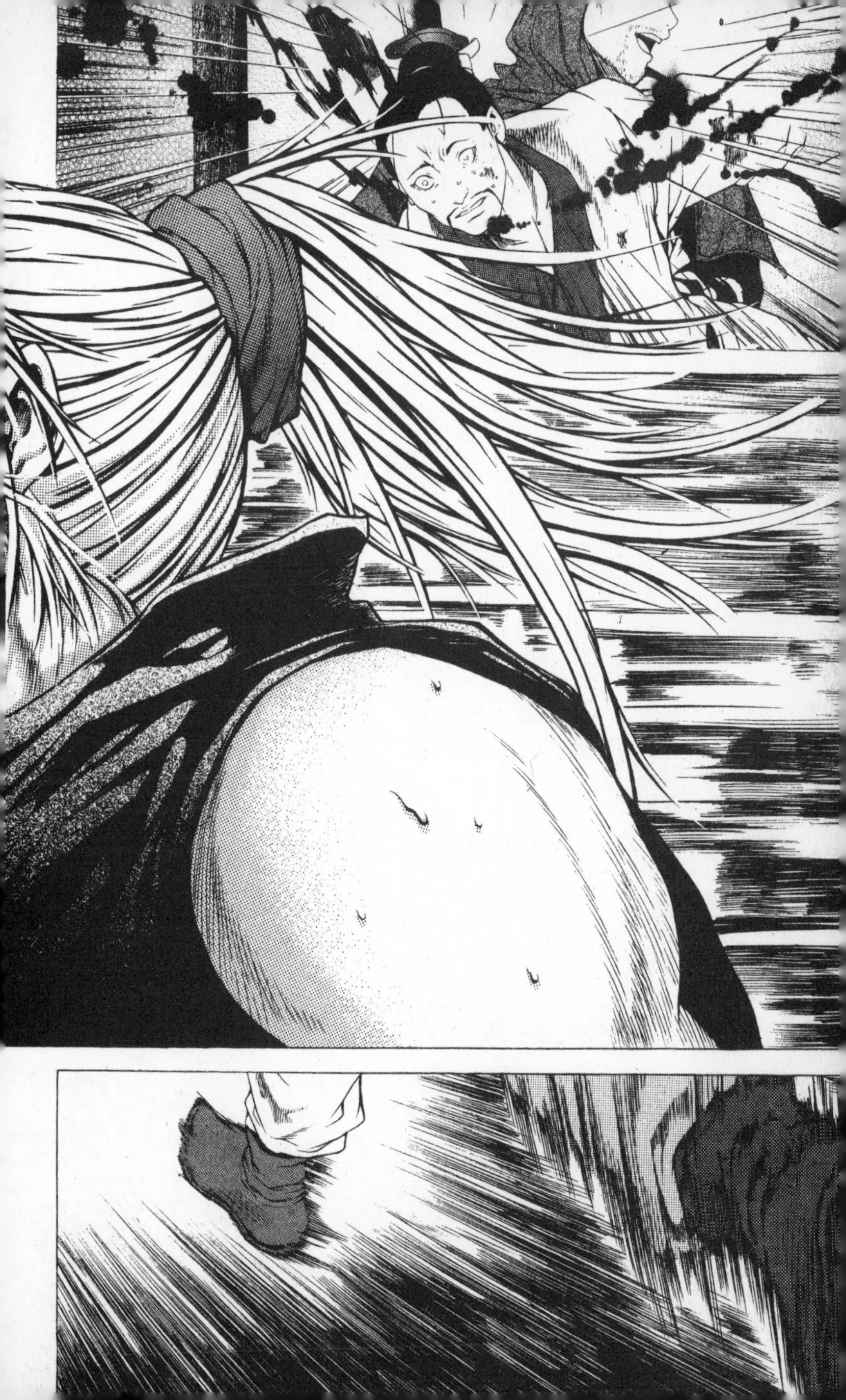

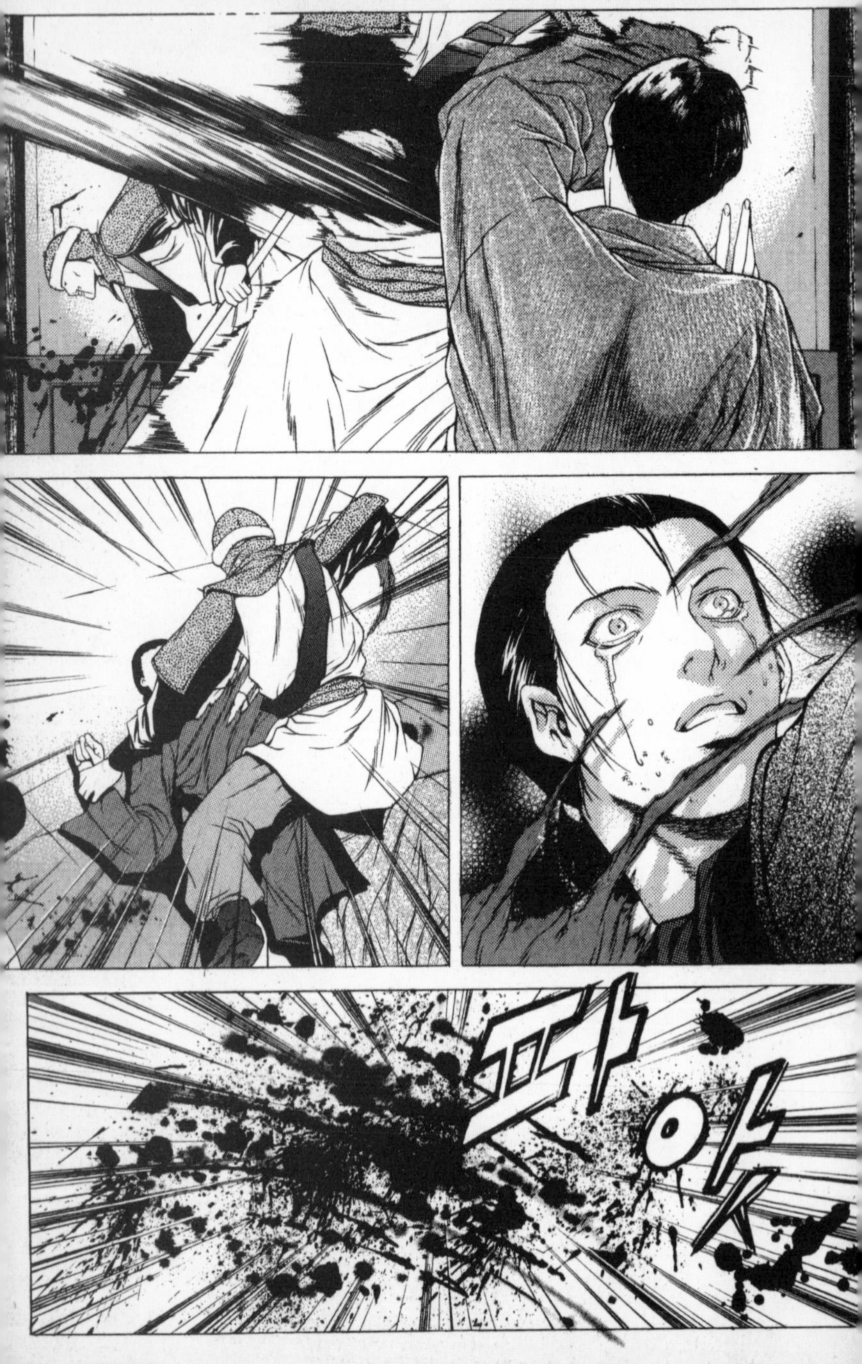

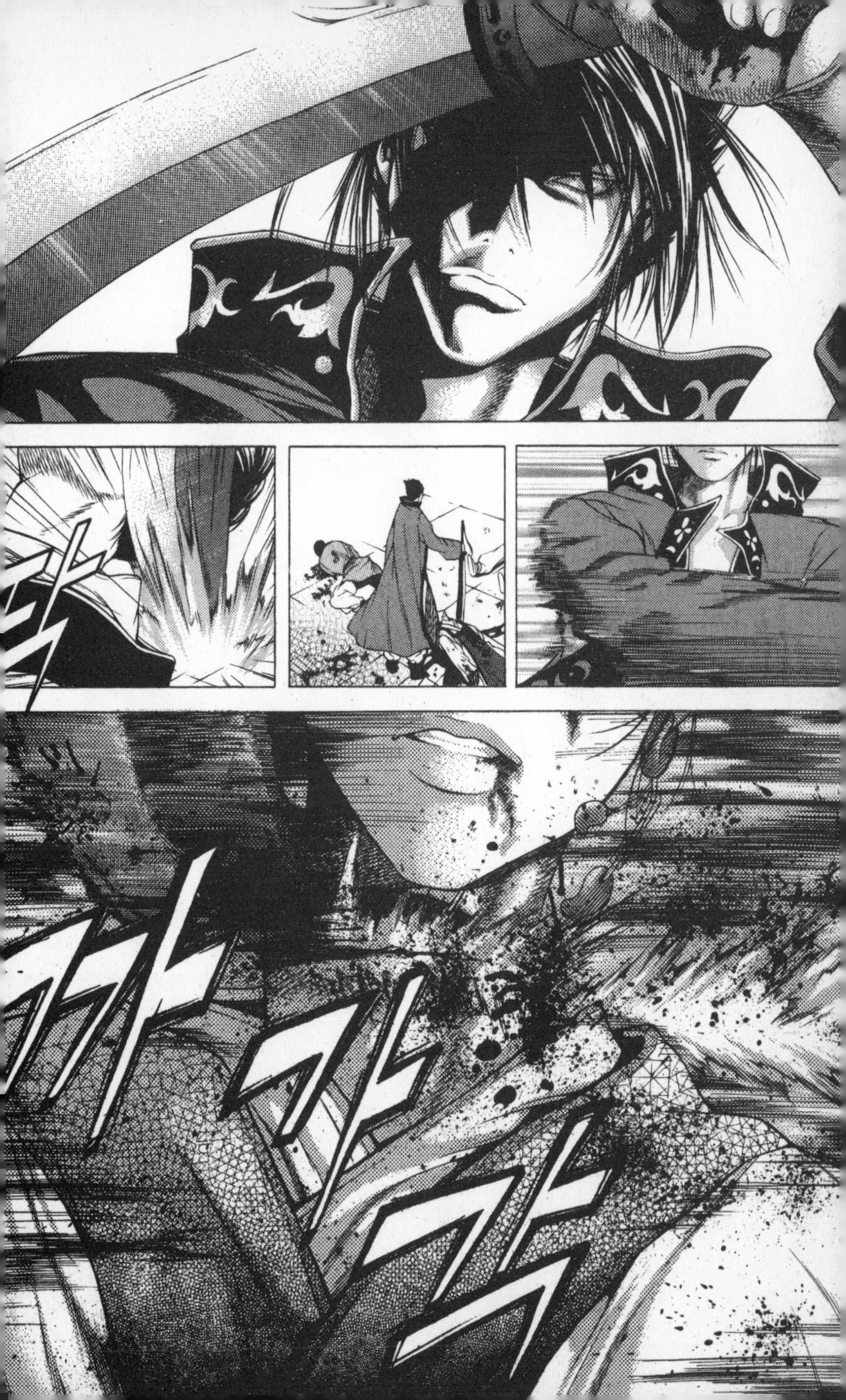

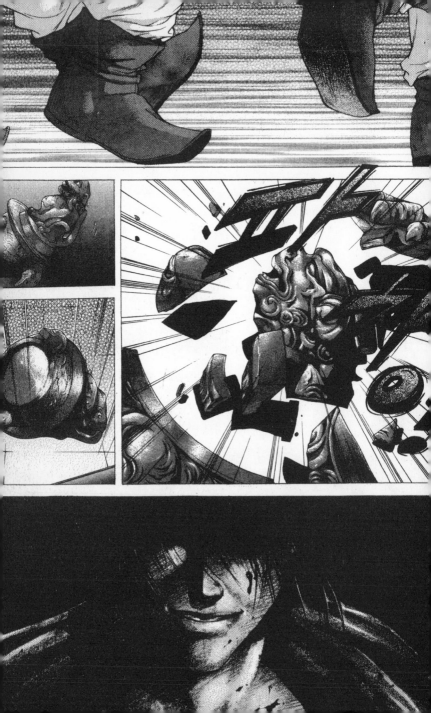

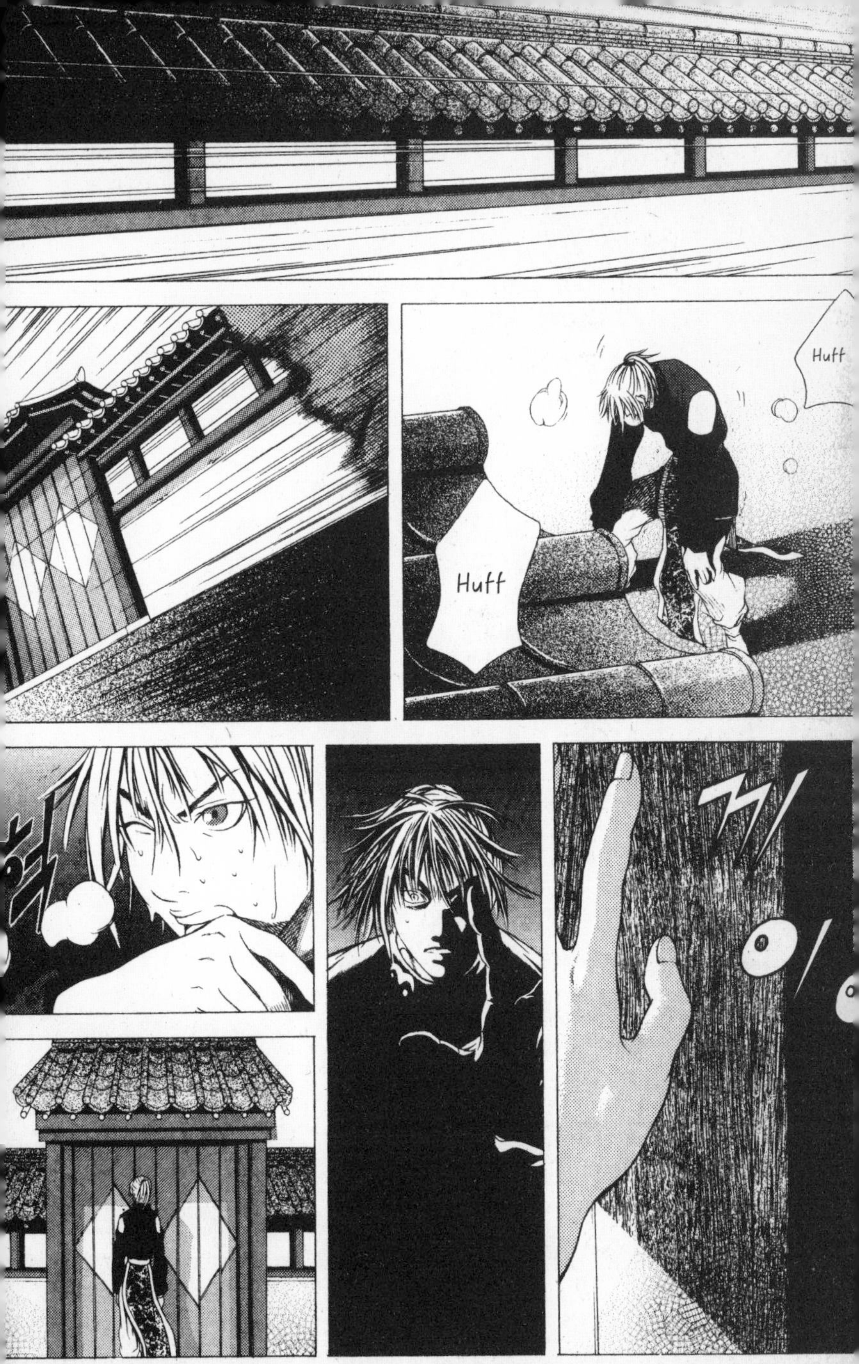
Huff
Huff

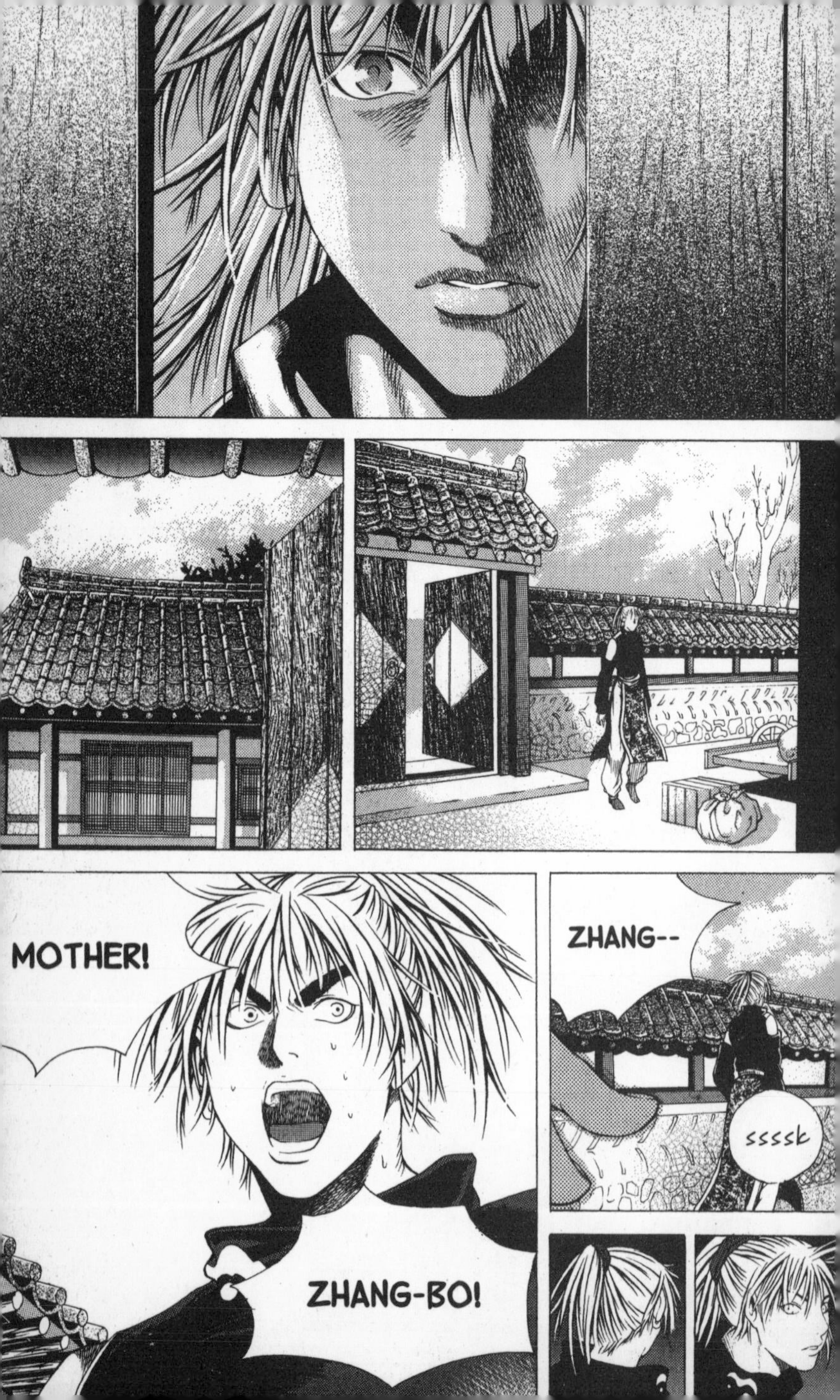
MOTHER!
ZHANG-BO!
ZHANG--
sssk

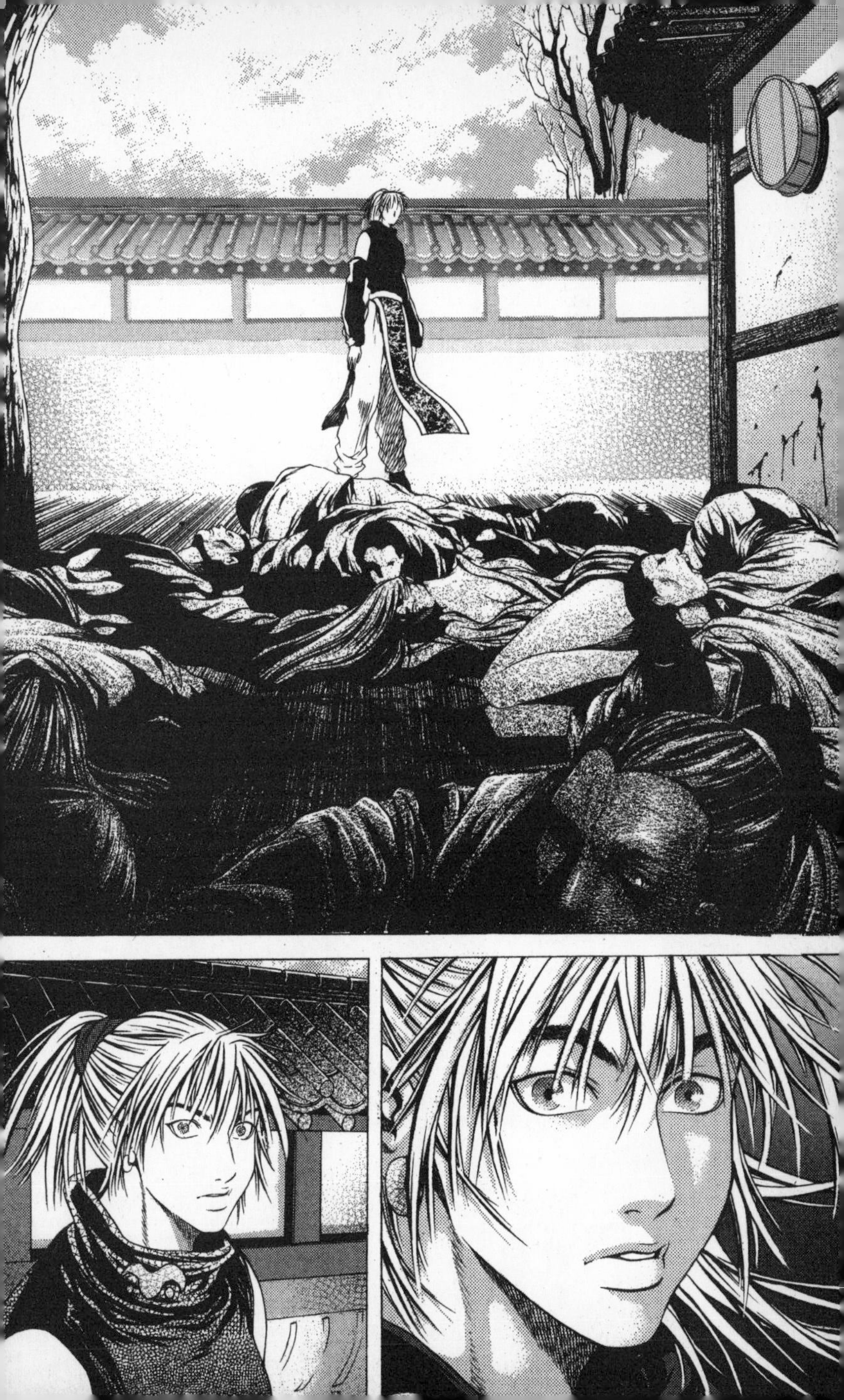

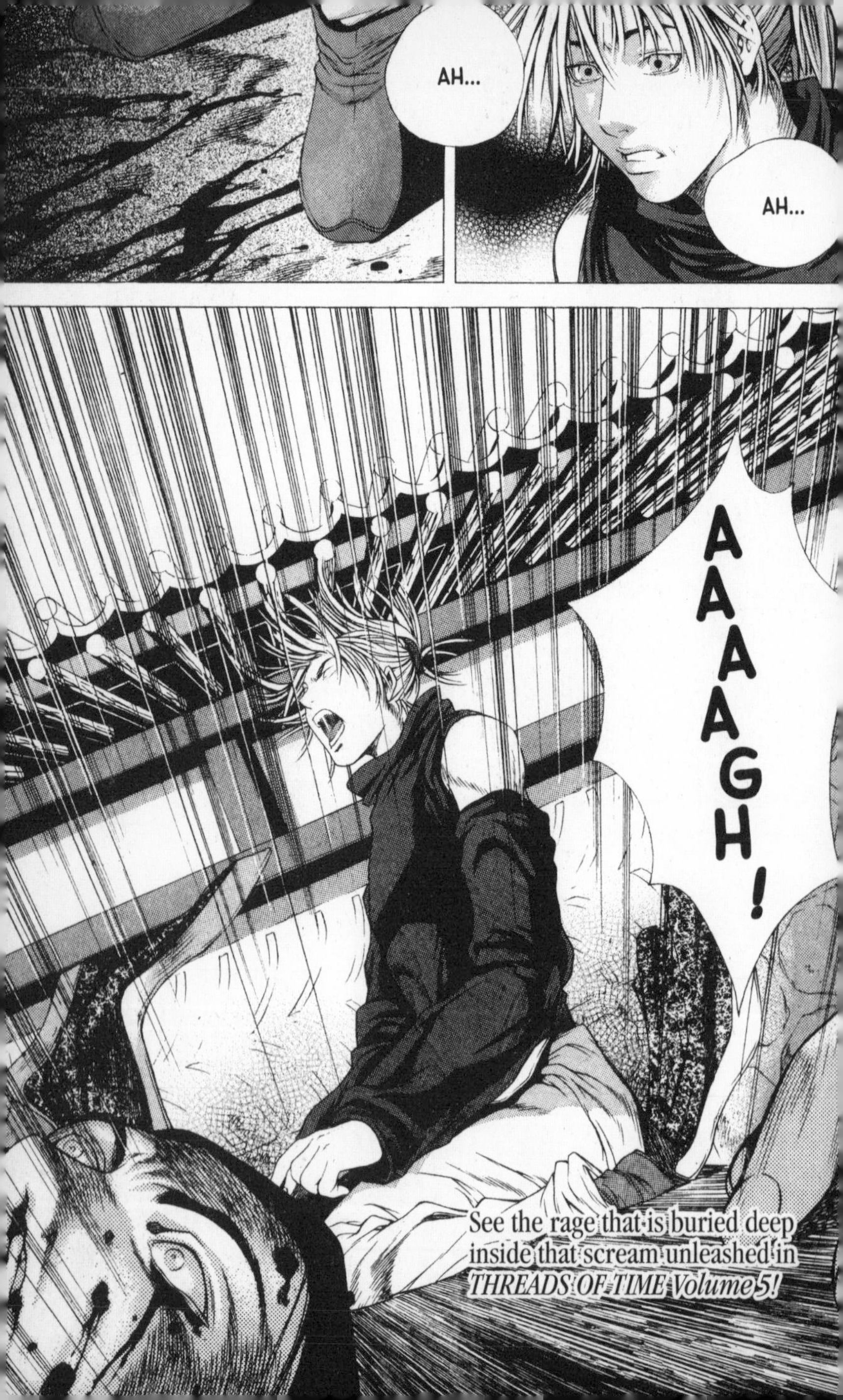
AH...
AH...
AAAAGH!
See the rage that is buried deep inside that scream unleashed in *THREADS OF TIME Volume 5!*

# Threads of Time ™

撥神塔

## In Volume 5

After the rape, pillage and massacre at Keh Kung, Moon Bin begins to doubt his own sanity. He grieves the loss of his 13th Century mother and the brutalities of war but at the same time is confused as to what is his true reality. He curses the fate that keeps him trapped in the past, and tries to unravel the mystery of his temporal displacement. At the same time, he is tormented by the ghost of his 13th Century sister calling for revenge. Even if he decides to join his father at Ghu-Zhu Palace, getting there will be no easy task, as every Mongol warrior in the land is after the head of Kim Kyung-Sohn's son. Will Moon Bin survive the manhunt? And what role will the conflicted Mongol princess Atan Hadas have to play?

TOKYOPOP presents a special and continuing supplement to Threads of Time...

# The Chronicles of Koryo

## The Legend of Yoo Gaeshae

Art by Jeong Mo, Yang
Written by Brandon Montclare

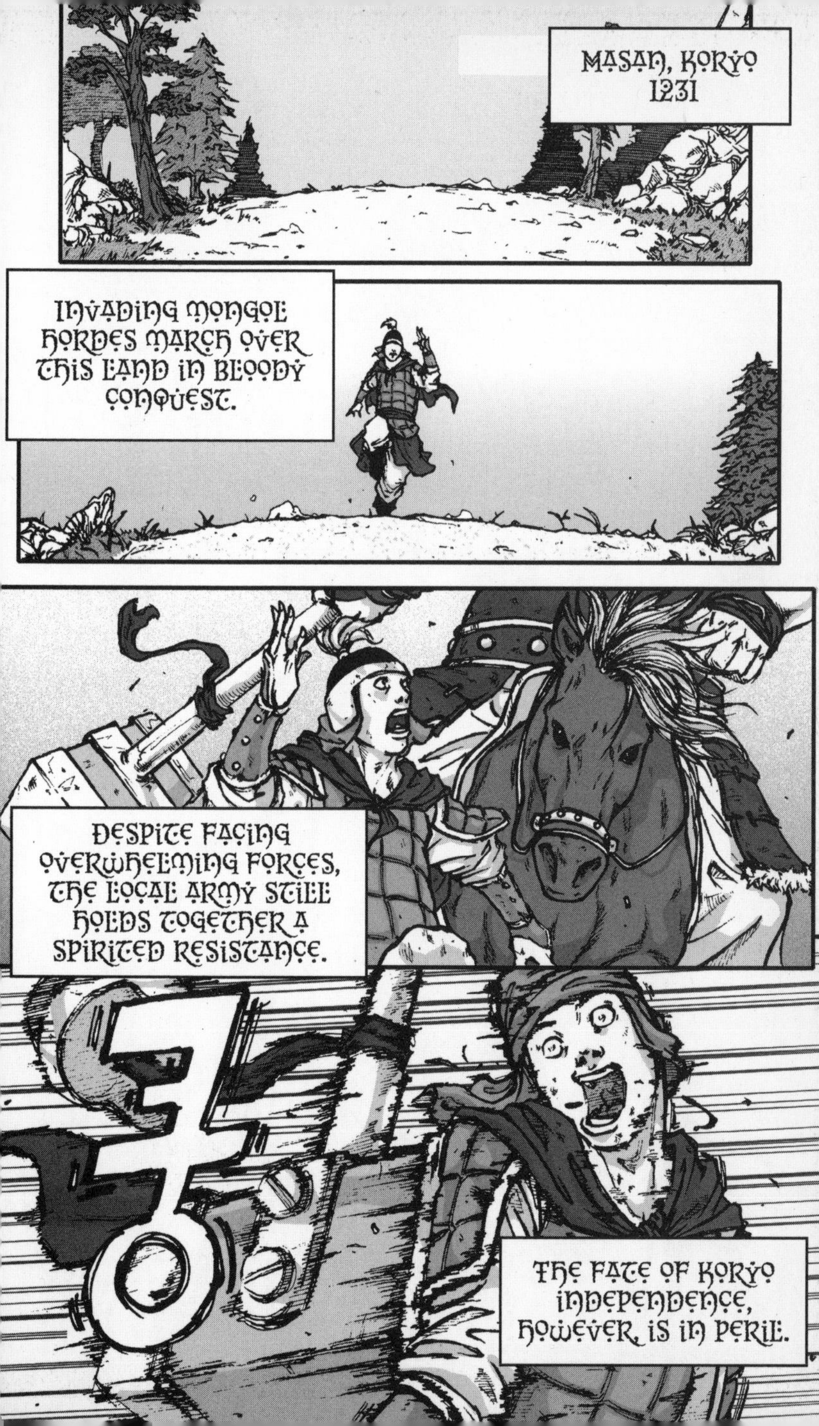
MASAN, KORYO
1231
INVADING MONGOL HORDES MARCH OVER THIS LAND IN BLOODY CONQUEST.
DESPITE FACING OVERWHELMING FORCES, THE LOCAL ARMY STILL HOLDS TOGETHER A SPIRITED RESISTANCE.
THE FATE OF KORYO INDEPENDENCE, HOWEVER, IS IN PERIL.

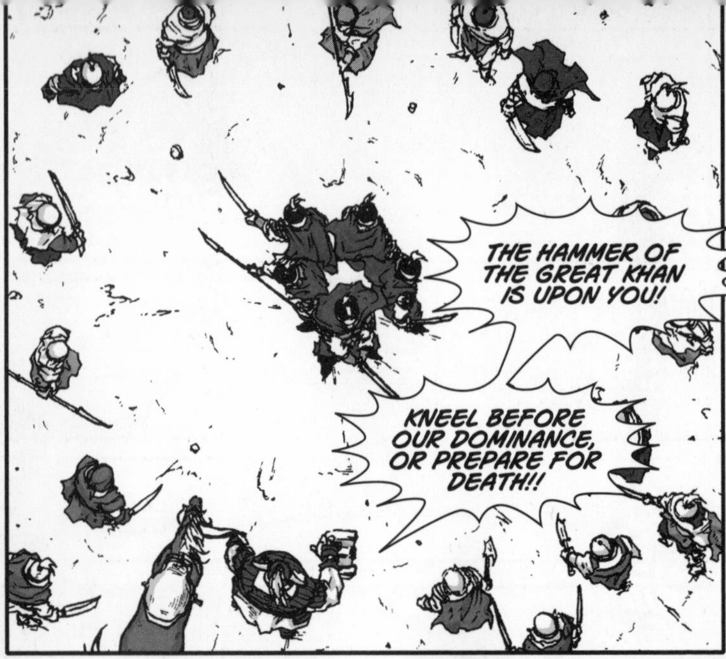
THE HAMMER OF THE GREAT KHAN IS UPON YOU!
KNEEL BEFORE OUR DOMINANCE, OR PREPARE FOR DEATH!!
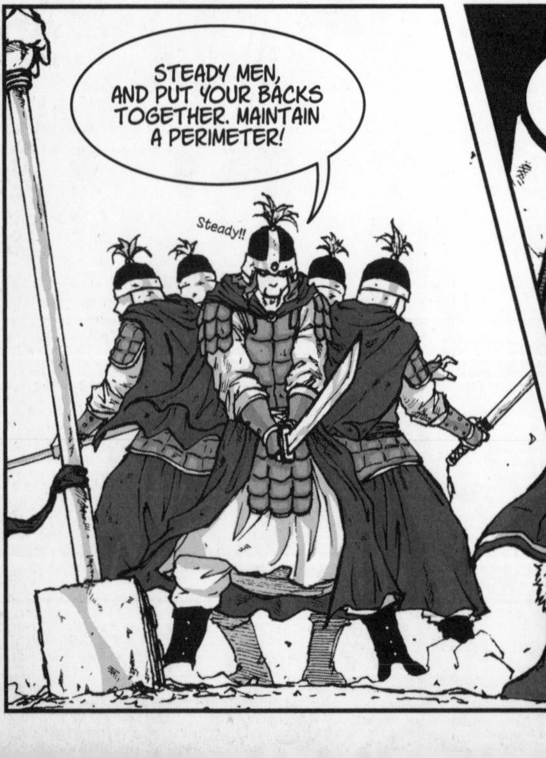
STEADY MEN, AND PUT YOUR BACKS TOGETHER. MAINTAIN A PERIMETER!
Steady!!
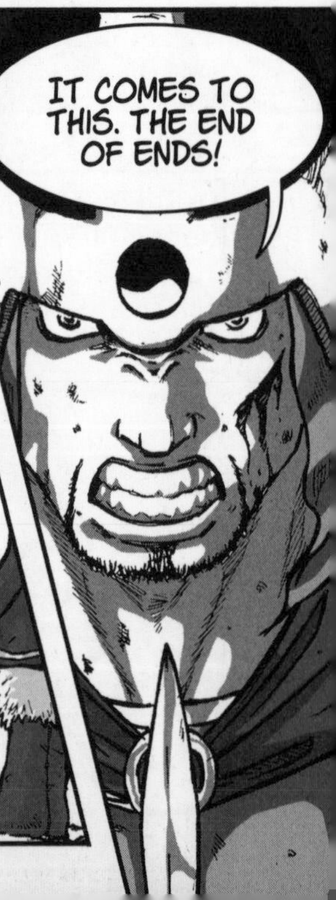
IT COMES TO THIS. THE END OF ENDS!

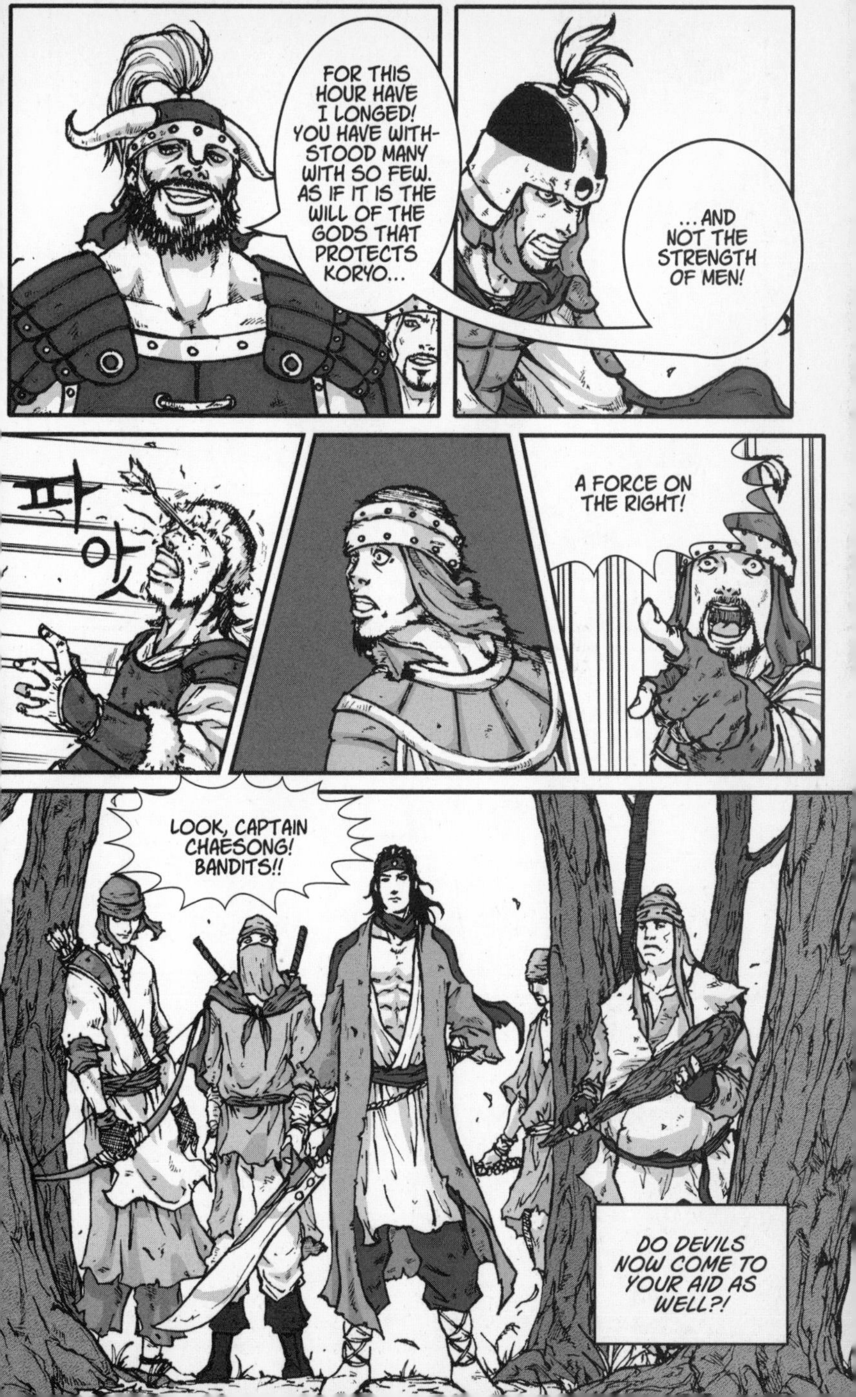
FOR THIS HOUR HAVE I LONGED! YOU HAVE WITH-STOOD MANY WITH SO FEW. AS IF IT IS THE WILL OF THE GODS THAT PROTECTS KORYO...
...AND NOT THE STRENGTH OF MEN!
파앗
A FORCE ON THE RIGHT!
LOOK, CAPTAIN CHAESONG! BANDITS!!
DO DEVILS NOW COME TO YOUR AID AS WELL?!

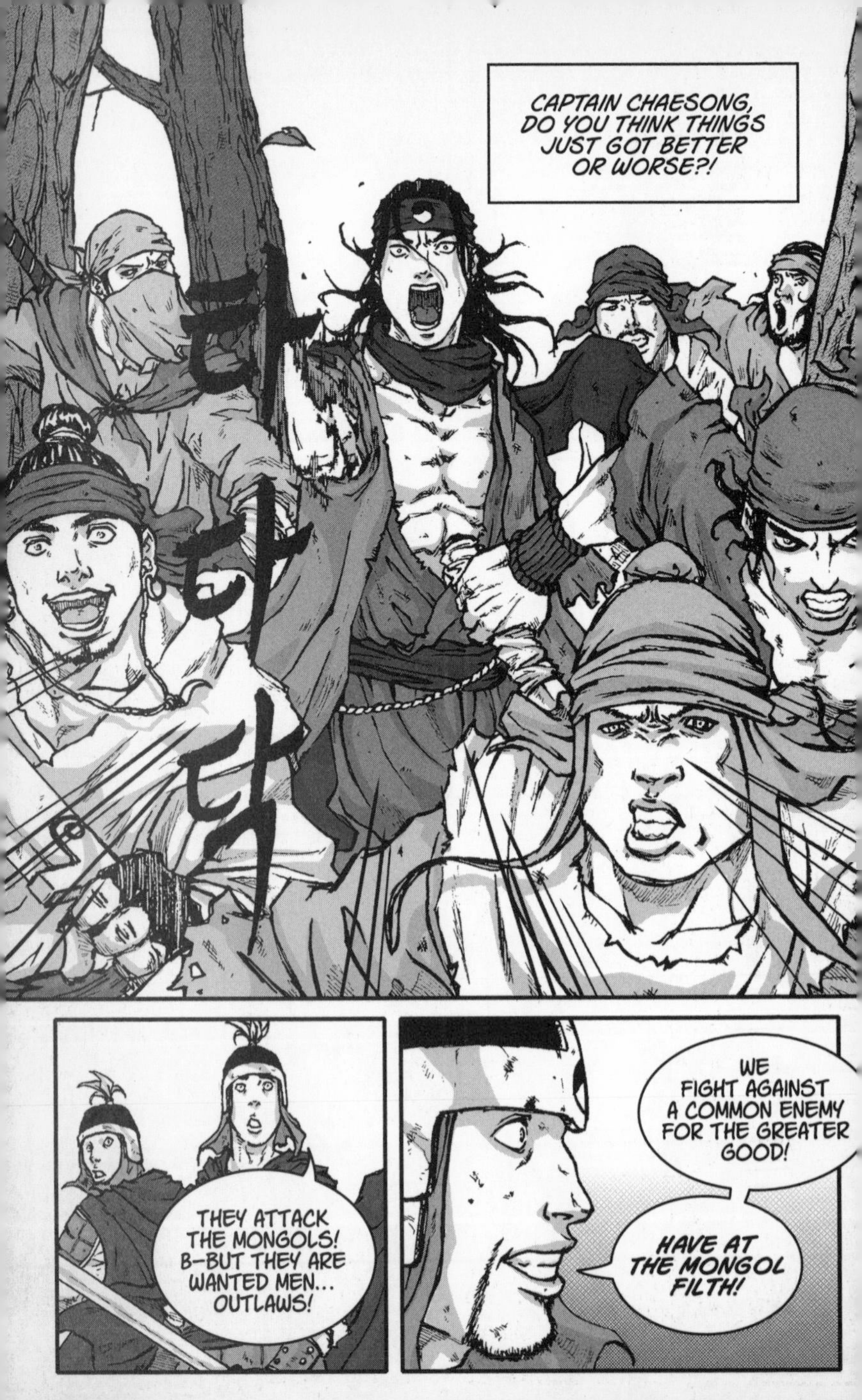
CAPTAIN CHAESONG, DO YOU THINK THINGS JUST GOT BETTER OR WORSE?!
THEY ATTACK THE MONGOLS! B-BUT THEY ARE WANTED MEN... OUTLAWS!
WE FIGHT AGAINST A COMMON ENEMY FOR THE GREATER GOOD!
HAVE AT THE MONGOL FILTH!

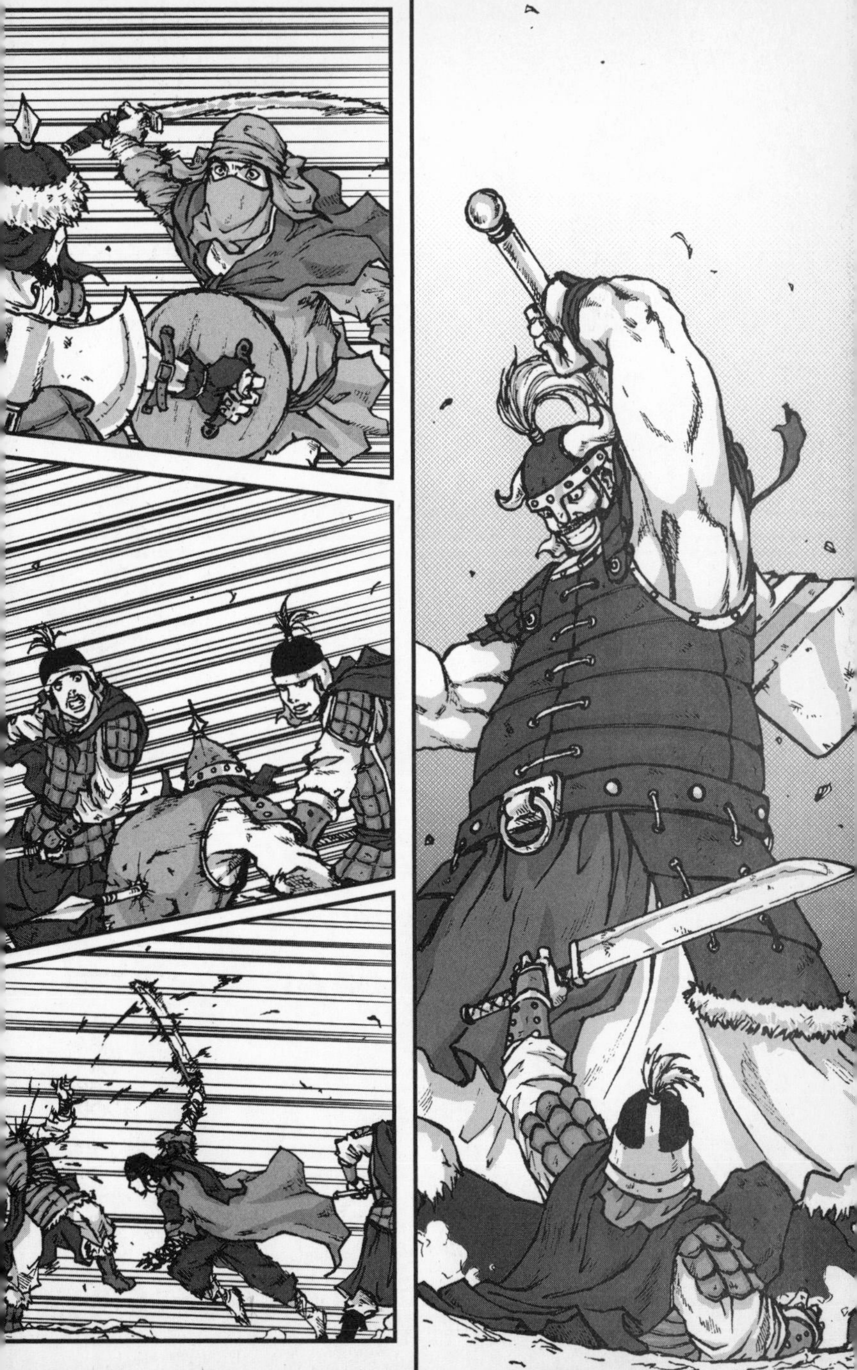

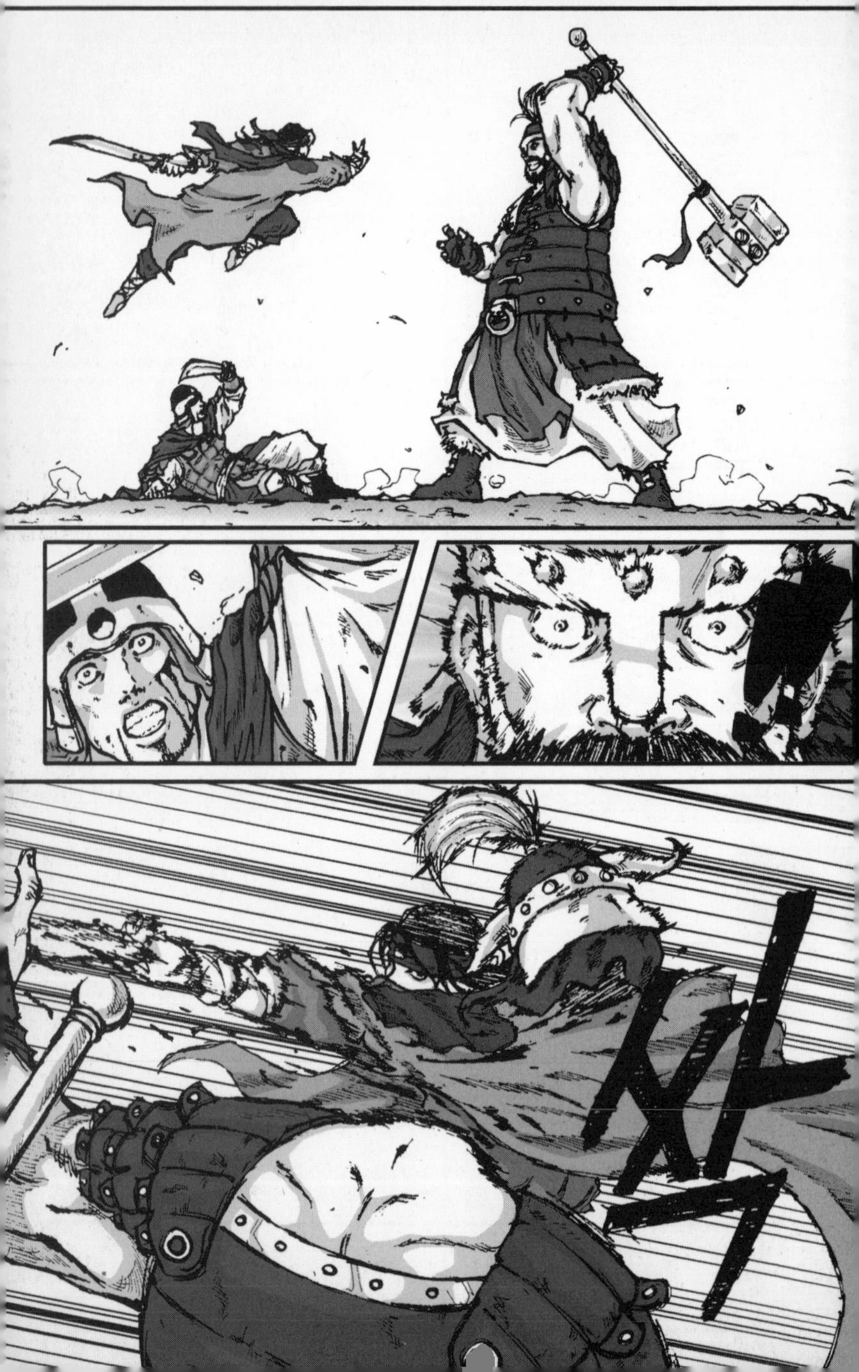

WITHOUT THEIR HULKING CHIEFTAN, THE MONGOLS FLEE!

LET THEIR COWARDLY FEET CARRY THEM ALL THE WAY BACK TO THE HIGH STEPPE!

CAPTAIN CHAESONG... TH—THE BANDIT PRINCE AND HIS MEN... WE—WE'RE SUPPOSED TO DETAIN THEM. THEY ARE CRIMINALS!

NO! IN THEIR EFFORTS AGAINST THE MONGOL FIENDS, THESE FIERCE AND DESPERATE OUTLAWS ARE NOW A BOON TO THE PEOPLE THEY ONCE TORMENTED.

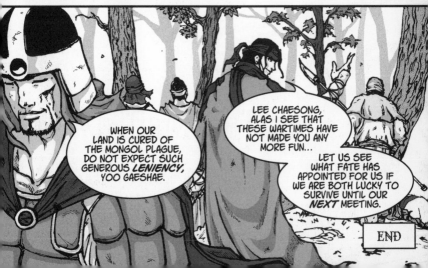

WHEN OUR LAND IS CURED OF THE MONGOL PLAGUE, DO NOT EXPECT SUCH GENEROUS *LENIENCY*, YOO GAESHAE.

LEE CHAESONG, ALAS I SEE THAT THESE WARTIMES HAVE NOT MADE YOU ANY MORE FUN...

LET US SEE WHAT FATE HAS APPOINTED FOR US IF WE ARE BOTH LUCKY TO SURVIVE UNTIL OUR *NEXT* MEETING.

END

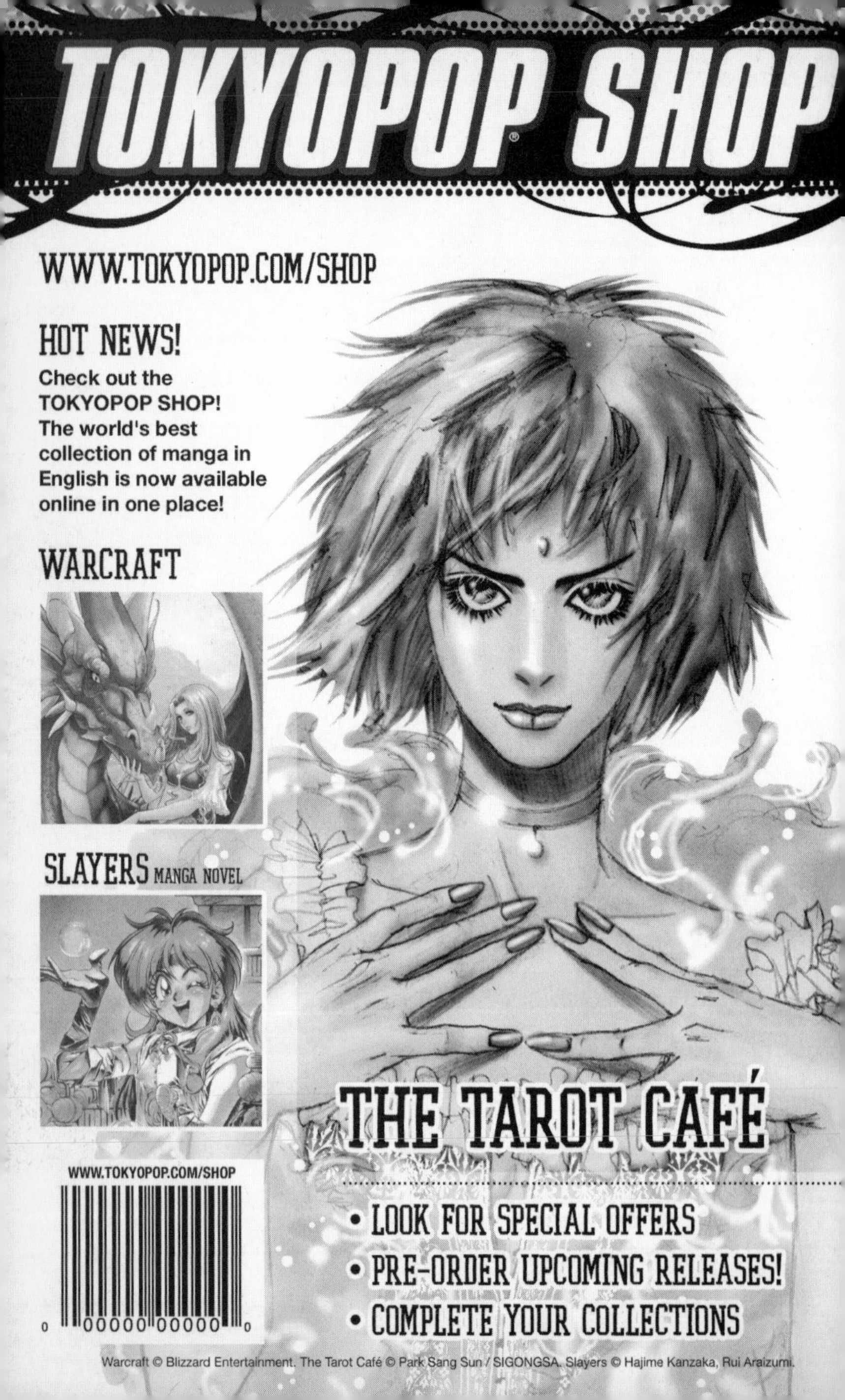
TOKYOPOP® SHOP
WWW.TOKYOPOP.COM/SHOP
HOT NEWS!
Check out the TOKYOPOP SHOP! The world's best collection of manga in English is now available online in one place!
WARCRAFT
SLAYERS MANGA NOVEL
THE TAROT CAFÉ
WWW.TOKYOPOP.COM/SHOP
0 00000 00000 0
• LOOK FOR SPECIAL OFFERS
• PRE-ORDER UPCOMING RELEASES!
• COMPLETE YOUR COLLECTIONS
Warcraft © Blizzard Entertainment. The Tarot Café © Park Sang Sun / SIGONGSA. Slayers © Hajime Kanzaka, Rui Araizumi.

The savior of a world without hope faces her greatest challenge: Cleavage!

# SOKORA REFUGEES™

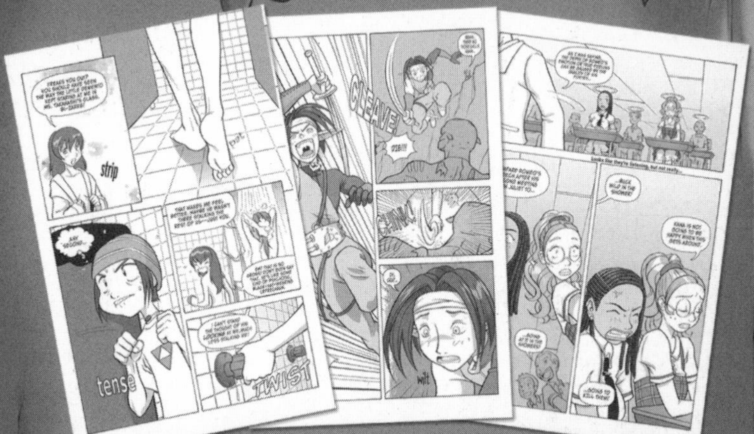
strip
tense
TWIST
CLEAVE!

Kana thought life couldn't get any worse—behind on her schoolwork and out of luck with boys, she is also the only one of her friends who hasn't "blossomed." When she falls through a magical portal in the girls' shower, she's transported to the enchanted world of Sokora—wearing nothing but a small robe! Now, on top of landing in this mysterious setting, she finds that her body is beginning to go through some tremendous changes.

**Preview the manga at:**
**www.TOKYOPOP.com/sokora**

T
TEEN
AGE 13+

## TOKYO TRIBES

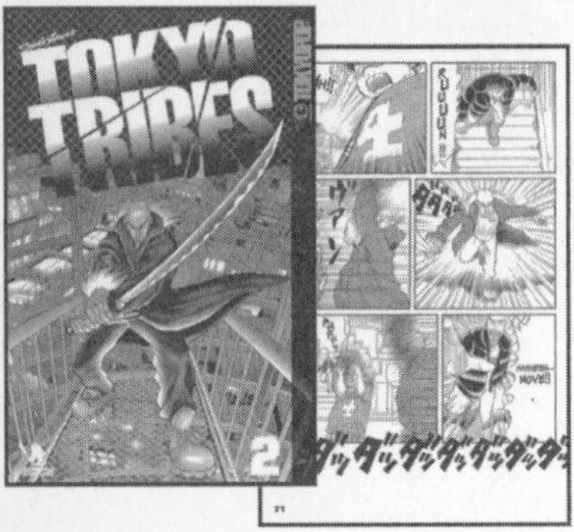
TOKYO TRIBES
2

BY SANTA INOUE

*Tokyo Tribes* first hit Japanese audiences in the sleek pages of the ultra-hip skater fashion magazine *Boon*. Santa Inoue's hard-hitting tale of Tokyo street gangs battling it out in the concrete sprawl of Japan's capital raises the manga storytelling bar. Ornate with hip-hop trappings and packed with gangland grit, *Tokyo Tribes* paints a vivid, somewhat surreal vision of urban youth: rival gangs from various Tokyo barrios clash over turf, and when the heat between two of the tribes gets personal, a bitter rivalry explodes into all-out warfare.

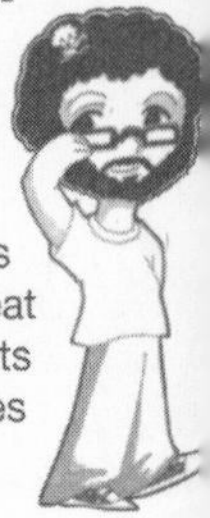

~Luis Reyes, Editor

## LEGAL DRUG

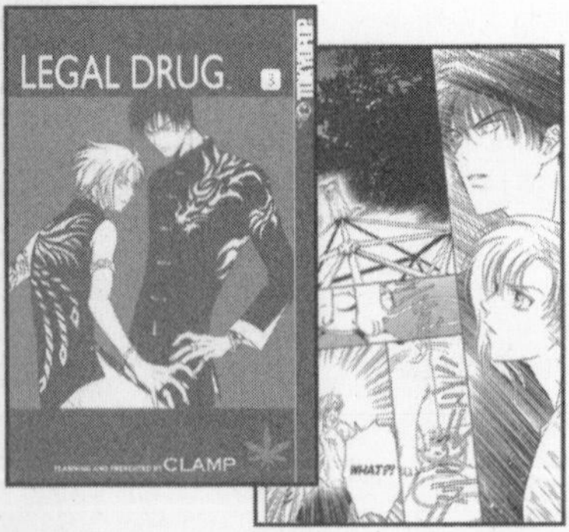
LEGAL DRUG
3
CLAMP
WHAT?!

BY CLAMP

CLAMP is the four-woman studio famous for creating much of the world's most popular manga. For the past 15 years they have produced such hits as the adorable *Cardcaptor Sakura,* the dark and brooding *Tokyo Babylon,* and the sci-fi romantic comedy *Chobits.* In *Legal Drug,* we meet Kazahaya and Rikuou, two ordinary pharmacists who moonlight as amateur sleuths for a mysterious boss. *Legal Drug* is a perfect dose of mystery, psychic powers and the kind of homoerotic tension for which CLAMP is renowned.

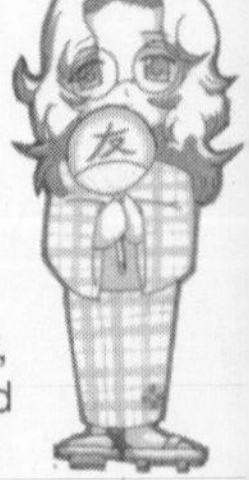

~Lillian Diaz-Przybyl, Jr. Editor